Iran, Israel, and the United States

An American Foreign Policy Background Study

HENRY PAOLUCCI

Iran, Israel, and the United States

[From the Founding of "Post-Biblical Judaism"
Under Artaxerxes and Nehemiah in 445 B.C. to the Shiite
Republic of the Ayatollah Khomeini and the Tehran
Hostage and "Arms-Transfer" Crises
of 1979-1989 A.D.]

ISBN 0-918680-44-1
Copyright © 1991 by Henry Paolucci

Published for The Bagehot Council by
GRIFFON HOUSE PUBLICATIONS
P.O. Box 81, Whitestone, New York 11357

Distribution in Europe & the Middle East
PRESS MARKETING SERVICES
Via Manzoni 122
Naples, Italy 80123

Library of Congress Cataloging-in-Publication Data

Paolucci, Henry
    Iran, Israel, and the United States: an American foreign policy background
study/Henry Paolucci. Includes index.
        pp. xxii + 404
    "A Medusa's head book."
    "From the founding of 'post-biblical Judaism' under Artaxerxes and Ne-
hemiah in 445 B.C. to the Shiite republic of the Ayatollah Khomeini and the
Tehran hostage and 'arms-transfer' crises of 1979-1989 A.D."
    ISBN 0-918680-44-1
    1.United States—Foreign relations—Iran. 2. Iran—Foreign relations—
United States. 3. Iran—Foreign relations—Israel. 4. Israel—Foreign relations—
Iran. 5. Israel—Foreign relations—United States. 6. United States—Foreign
relations—Israel.
I. Title
E183.8.17P36 1991
327.73055—dc20

89-71452
CIP

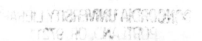

A MEDUSA'S HEAD BOOK

Thus saith Cyrus the king: 'Since God Almighty hath appointed me to be king of the inhabitable earth, I believe that he is the God whom the nation of the Israelites worship; for indeed he foretold my name by the prophets; and that I should build him a house at Jerulsalem. . . . I have given permission to as many of the Jews in my country as please to return to their own country, and to rebuild their city, and to build the temple of God. . .; and the same order extends to the altar whereon they offer sacrifices. . .according to the laws of Moses in Jerusalem: and when they offer them, they shall pray to God for the preservation of the king, and of his family; that the kingdom of Persia may continue. . . .'

Now Alexander, when he had taken Gaza, made haste to go up to Jerusalem. . . . And when he went up into the temple, he offered sacrifice to God, according to the high-priest's direction. . . . And when the book of Daniel was shown to him, wherein Daniel declared that one of the Greeks should destroy the empire of the Persians, he supposed that himself was the person intended. And he was then glad. . . .

Josephus, *Antiquities of the Jews*, XI. i, viii

CONTENTS

FOREWORD

What Barbara Tuchman's *Bible and Sword* did to place in historical perspective British policy toward the Holy Land, Henry Paolucci does, with equal understanding, to place in contrapuntal perspective the evolution of the political realities between Iran, Israel, and the United States.

This remarkable study contains all the intrigue of a le Carré novel, the solid research of a good investigative reporter, and the sound analysis of a brilliant historian. The end result, especially the latter chapters on the hostage crisis, provides the political junkie with much food for thought regarding the complexities of man and his politics, of private ego versus public interest, as applied in the Middle East. Dr. Paolucci's book is a highly informative, credible, and delightfully readable insight into a crucial corner of American Foreign Policy, an insight based on solid research of extensive sources, an insight worth pondering over.

Edmund Alexander Bator

PREFACE

Iran and Israel exist in an area of the world described in the Bible as the center or navel of the earth (*Ezekiel* 38: 10-12). This is not so much a geographical distinction as it is an identification of the area which, just before the latter days and Armageddon, will become the leading cultural, religious, and economic center of the inhabited world, and then the site of the last and greatest war of all times. Today, Iran and Israel exist as independent nations, enemies yet collaborators, each strong in the conviction that they are "God's chosen people," theocracies that walk like states.

Since the end of World War II, historians and political theorists of the western world have trembled at the forecast of a thermonuclear holocaust brought about by such antagonistic nation-states turning, as a last resort, to their superpower protectors and their nuclear arsenals. A wave of nationalism is now sweeping through eastern Europe and cries and anthems long smothered by the shroud of Soviet imperialism are being heard for the first time in over forty years. It is not so much a failure of Communism as an overdue splintering of the Russian Empire itself.

This rebirth of nation-states in the east, challenging the Russo-Communist imperial peace from within, is in contrast with the continued efforts in western Europe to bring to birth a supranational political "Community" capable of enforcing peace among its national members as effectively as the American national union has done among its sub-national members since the Civil War. The so-called European Community of our day grew from six to twelve members between 1973 and 1986 by confining itself to strictly economic collaboration. Yet many of its current managers in Brussels, Luxembourg, and Strasbourg still apparantly hope that member states will voluntarily surrender their established right to nullify majority decisions by exercising an "absolute veto" regardless of the size of the majority.

It may fairly be said that nationalism politically organized as nationhood is no longer perceived as a major threat to global peace

— or at least certainly not as a threat powerful enough to justify imposition of a supranational enforceable peace, whether of the Soviet, American, or European Community varieties. But what about the fervor of religions whose kingdoms are of this world, and whose zealots long for a religious reign of universal peace under "God's laws"? How will the challenge of such longings for religious earthly kingdoms affect our future well-being in our separate and equal station among the powers of this earth? This is a question that, until recently, American policy makers have not had to face. Since its creation in 1948, little Israel, through the daring statecraft of its politicians and diplomats and the influence of its faithful supporters and friends within the power structure of the United States, has shown repeatedly how, with its appeal to religious imperatives, it can effectively contribute to the formation of our foreign policy. And in recent decades Islamic Iran has proved it too can bring a superpower to its knees by threatening bodily harm and even death to innocent hostages.

This book is not about Armageddon; nor does it deal in depth with nationalism vs. imperialism. It is a book about the politics of religion as a factor in the conduct of American international relations. It is a critically important book.

John H. Ryan Jr.

AUTHOR'S INTRODUCTION

The public law of the federal republic of the United States has made clear from the beginning that religion is to be accorded every conceivable liberty for practice and propagation, short of establishment as the faith of a ruling majority. In putting aside hereditary kingship and aristocracy, the American founders had indeed authorized an ever broadening of the franchise in the direction of republican majority rule. But, as *The Federalist* papers made clear, any tyranny of the majority that might surface as a consequence was to be checked and balanced. That was the primary burden of the mixed constitutions of the several states as also of the government of their federal union.

A "zeal for different opinions concerning religion" is, of course, listed among the "latent causes of factions" in James Madison's famous *Federalist* paper 10. And Madison returns to the subject in papers 51 and 52 where he discusses remedies against the evil of a tyrannical majority rule. In our federal republic, Madison observes, the society taken as a whole will fortunately be broken up into many parts, with a large diversity of interests flourishing in the secular order and a comparable number of sects in the religious order. If that diversity is respected and encouraged, if it is protected and fostered by law, education, and custom, then we can remain confident that, in the long run, the "rights of individuals, or of the minority, will be in little danger from interested combinations of majorities."

Madison acknowledges that in theory it is possible for hereditary kings or independently-appointed magistrates (like our new federal special prosecutors) to serve as guardians of individual and minority rights in a mixed constitution. But that, he insists, is at best a "precarious security; because a power independent of the society may as well espouse the unjust views of the major as the rightful interests of the minor party, and may possibly be turned against both parties." Just as, in the world at large, it is a severalty of states (all more or less middle-sized) that most securely guarantees the liberty of the least members of that severalty, so within states it is the severalty of interest groups and religious sects that guarantees the flourishing of all citizens — individuals, minorities, and majorities alike. What public law must seek to prevent in a mixed constitution is the formation of a majority party dominated by unified secular or religious-sectarian interests. Madison is mindful of the fact that, as the British Commons moved toward partisan majority rule after 1688, the religion of the reigning party became ever more securely established in public law. To guard against a parallel development in our lower legislative house, it was necessary, according to Madison, to keep accession to it ever "open to merit of every description, whether native or adoptive, whether young or old, and without regard to poverty or wealth, or any particular profession of religious faith."

Despite his overriding concern to provide the new nation with an independent executive empowered to check and balance an otherwise omnipotent legislature, Alexander Hamilton also stresses the importance of excluding religion as a factor in ultimate governmental decision making. His detailed comparison and contrast between our chief executive, as head of our presidential government, and the hereditary king who heads England's parliamentary government, is deservedly famous. It is worth noting, moreover, that it reaches a rhetorical climax in *Federalist* paper 69, where Hamilton writes: "The one has no particle of spiritual jurisdiction; the other is the supreme head and governor of the national church!"

But what about foreign entanglements that can tempt us into permanent alliances or permanent enmities with theocratic governments — like those of the State of Israel and the Islamic Republic of Iran today? Until fairly recently, the entire world seemed to be steadily moving in an increasingly secular direction. What Italy had become in political consciousness by the time of Machiavelli and what western Europe in general had become by the time of the French Revolution, old Russia itself finally became in 1917, with its supranational Communist revolution. Paired as allies in World War II, a secularized United States and an atheist Union of Soviet Socialist Republics have indeed come to divide the entire world between them, as Alexis de Tocqueville had prophesied in the 1830s. The dominance of two such superpowers in the post-war period convinced many that, if not the state in general, surely the politics of religion which had once dominated states would soon be put where it belonged in the Marxist vision: beside the spinning wheel and the bronze axe, in the Museum of Antiquities.

The new State of Israel established in 1948 claimed indeed to be a theocracy; and that claim scandalized many western secularist thinkers, like Arnold Toynbee. Still, the Jews in general were too well known in the western world as champions of religious tolerance to be taken seriously as potential religious fanatics in international relations. Certainly decision makers in Washington remained persuaded until it was almost too late that their government could continue to pursue a pro-Israeli course indefinitely on purely secular grounds. Israel, it seemed, would become in short order the catalyst for general modernization and secularization in the Middle East. But then came the Muslim religious political reanimation of the 1970s and 1980s. In 1979, the last dynasty of Iranian Shahs, a dynasty that gloried in its pre-Islamic name, fell before the spiritual might of unarmed Shiite masses. In 1981, Anwar Sadat, President of a nominally Islamic Egypt which was induced to look back to the times of King Tut for greater pre-Islamic glories, was assassinated by fanatically faithful Muslims among his own military guards.

Suddenly the politics of religion in international affairs became a new kind of burden for American decision makers. The American notion of internal checks and external balances of power, to secure our individual freedom at home and our sovereignly separate station among the powers of this planet, has ancient roots dating back at least as far as the wisest speculations of the ancient Greeks and Romans on the subject. But the politics of religion in international relations is still apparently something new and strange for most Americans interested in foreign affairs. We all have much to learn; and we can perhaps go about learning it most advantageously by reviewing Iranian-Israel relations in their present and historical perspectives, before focusing on the American involvement with both these ancient peoples since the early years of World War II.

Henry Paolucci
January 22, 1991

PART I

Present Perspectives

CHAPTER ONE

Dealing with "God's People" in International Relations

Overtly or covertly, through good times and bad, Iranians and Israelis have been doing business together for over 2,500 years. Through all those centuries of what has been called an "uninterrupted and continuous association between Iran and Israel," it has always been rather hard for "third parties" to deal directly with Israelis without also having to deal at least indirectly with Iranians as well, and vice versa.

The American experience as a "third party" is this regard has, of course, been relatively brief: With an independent national existence that dates back little more than two centuries, the United States has only recently gained even a modicum of experience in dealing with Iranians and Israelis simultaneously. And, needless to say, the fact that American diplomats and political decision-makers involved in such dealings still have a lot to learn has been amply proven by events of the last years.

The phrase "uninterrupted and continuous association between Iran and Israel" (meant to characterize a relationship dating back to the 6th century B.C.) is quoted from Walter J. Fischel's "Israel in Iran," an authoritative article written in 1948, on the eve of modern Israel's declaration of independence as a sovereign state. Intended for inclusion in Louis Finkelstein's monumental four-volume work, *The Jews: Their History, Culture, and Religion* (Philadelphia, The Jewish Publication Society of America, 5710-1949), the article begins by noting that, on the Iranian side of the long association with Israel, we have a "history covering twenty-five centuries" —

from Cyrus the Great to Mohammed Reza Pahlavi — "equally divided by the Arab conquest of the year 642 into a pre-Islamic and an Islamic period." But the point to be stressed, Professor Fischel continued, is that, despite the fundamental break in Iranian history marked by the Islamic conquest, there has never been any real break in Iranian/Israeli relations. Fischel, who ranked in 1948 as "*the* authority on Jewish culture in Iran," then sums it all up:

> Israel has been living on Iran's soil from the dawn of the first Persian Empire, as an inseparable part of Iran's national destiny and development. Jews were the eyewitnesses of all the historical events in Persia under every dynasty — the Achamenids, Parthians and Sassanids, the Omayyads and the Abbassids, the Seljuks, Mongols, Safavids and Kajars, under every ruler, Caliph, Sultan, Ilkhan, Emir, or Shah. Jews were the contemporaries of all the manifold religious movements and sects that were born on Persian soil, such as Zoroastrianism, Manicheism, Shi'a, Sufism, Bahaism; they were companions of the great classical poets, of a Firdusi, Hafiz, Sa'adi, Jami, and of all other great Persian masters of art, literature and philosophy who made their everlasting contributions to world culture.

One should add here that many historians of the ancient Near East like to credit Imperial Iran with a large share of the transformation of Israel that made it capable of surviving as a nation in exile, after the destruction of Jerusalem and the Second Temple by the Romans in 70 A.D. The claim is that, together with the last great figures of Biblical Judaism, namely Nehemiah and Ezra, the early Iranian Emperors, especially Cyrus the Great and Artaxerxes, helped to bring into being the arrangement between Jews in Palestine and Jews in the Diaspora that exists to this day — the arrangement of so-called post-Biblical Judaism.

Under Rome, in the West, that arrangement ran into difficulties — difficulties that were intensified during the Christian centuries. By contrast with their fate in the ancient and medieval Christian Western world, things were relatively always better for Israel in the "lands of the Persians," even after the Islamic conquest. But that "Eastern" advantage seemed to have ended definitively after the

emergence of a secularized modern Europe that sought a full assimilation of Jews as European nationals during the period of so-called
"Enlightenment," which led to acceptance in the late 19th century
of the Zionist idea for a resurgent Jewish state in Palestine supported by the "family of enlightened Western European nations."

1. Modern Israel and Iran
in U.S. Foreign Affairs

In the case of Israel, the first approximations of what can only
loosely be called international relations with the United States date
back no further than the start of World War I. In 1914, with Europe convulsed in war, the activities of the international Zionist movement, which was then only some two decades old, became largely
centered in the United States. It was then that Louis Brandeis and
Felix Frankfurter emerged as its politically most influential American leaders. A turning point was marked by President Woodrow Wilson's announced support of England's famous Balfour Declaration
of 1917 of a Jewish homeland in Palestine, a declaration that coincided with America's decision to enter World War I on the side of
the British.

American dealings with Israelis on a national basis intensified,
to be sure, during the years of Hitler's rise in Germany, when large
numbers of German and Eastern European Jewish refugees fled to
the United States. The Nazi persecutions had intensified feelings of
national-religious solidarity among the refugees, and it was therefore not surprising that in America most of them should have thought
of themselves primarily as Jews engaged in an international war of
self-defense. Even as they were seeking to enlist American support
in that war, many of them sought to encourage the closest possible
collaboration between the United States and the Soviet Union,
brought into alliance by the common enmity of Adolph Hitler.

During the late 1930s, the leading Jewish refugees in America
took statesmanly initiatives to arouse the American people to a willingness to assume the burdens of international warfare. Their ardor
for the struggle, the sympathy they attracted as victims of the Na-

zis, the great contribution their physicists made to the development of the American atomic bomb, coupled with the high trust placed in them by President Franklin D. Roosevelt, enabled some of those refugees and their like-minded American friends to exert a decisive influence on the public definition of American war aims. They contributed significantly to the post-war vision of a permanently enforceable world peace, based on perpetuating the war-time Soviet-American alliance. Having reduced Nazi Germany to unconditional surrender by military means, the victorious allies were to collaborate further, in the spirit of the prophesies of Isaiah and Micah, to put an end forever to the very possibility of war, as of all racial, religious, ethnic, and class oppression.

Even though that vision of a permanently enforceable peace soon gave way to the realities of a cold war among the Allied victors, the defeat of Hitler in 1945 proved to be a turning point in the history of the Jews on a par with ancient Iran's destruction of once-mighty Babylon in 539 B.C. Out of the ruins of Hitler's Europe arose the possibility of an exodus from Europe of enough Jews to establish a religious commonwealth that could vie in importance with that second Hebrew commonwealth of post-biblical times that marked the beginning of Iranian-Israeli international relations in the 6th century B.C.

It is well-known that the modern Jewish State of Israel which proclaimed its independence on May 15, 1948, did so under the joint auspices of both major victors in the war against Hitler. Within minutes of that proclamation, modern Israel was accorded *de facto* recognition as a sovereign nation by the United States; and within two days it received *de jure* recognition as such by the Soviet Union — even though by then the United States and the U.S.S.R. were already deep in the "cold war" relationship of the Truman administration's "containment" policy.

American dealings with Iran as a national entity pre-date the founding of Israel in 1948: They began on a significant political basis in the early years of World War II, and particularly in 1941. That was when England and the Soviet Union, as allies in the war against Hitler, invaded Iran to prevent its becoming a willing satellite of Nazi Germany. A German-Iranian alliance had been sought by Reza Khan, founder of the Pahlavi dynasty, as a means of freeing his country from English domination. That first Pahlavi Shah was deposed in 1941, to be succeeded by his more malleable 23-year old son, Reza Mohammed Pahlavi, who, as we all know, reigned continuously, except for a brief interruption in 1953, down to his fall in January 1979 at the hands of followers of Ayatollah Khomeini.

Reza Mohammed Pahlavi ascended his throne in 1941 with a clear understanding that he would not repeat his father's mistake. He was permitted, indeed, to continue his father's modernization programs for Iran, with but one notable change. As a recent historian has put it: "The main difference seemed to be that whereas Reza Khan wanted to modernize while eliminating actual foreign presence in Iran, Mohammed Reza Shah sought to do so while shoring up this presence." [Shahrough Akhavi, *Religion and Politics in Contemporary Iran: Clergy-State Relations in the Pahlavi Period* (State Univ. of NY Press, Albany, 1980), p. 72]

The Anglo-American concern in 1941 was to secure Allied control of the Iranian oil fields but, beyond that, also to open up a secure route for transporting American war supplies to the Soviet Union to sustain its Eastern Front against Hitler. But immediately upon Germany's defeat, it became a major Western concern to force the Soviets to pull out of their occupied sector of northern Iran — which they reluctantly did in mid-1946, the event marking the start of what would become America's successful strategy of containment pursued by the Truman and Eisenhower administrations.

Early in the 1950s, the young Iranian Shah, eager to further modernize his ancient state, found himself threatened by a faction of liberal, secularizing reformers, led by Dr. Muhammed Mossadegh. Dr. Mossadegh seemed to have the logic of modernization on his side. Why not follow the example of Kemal Ataturk in Turkey? Why not minimize Islamic tradition and relegate the pomp of an age-old pre-Islamic throne to museums catering to tourists? But, most important: Why not start to reconstruct Iran as a truly modern nation by ousting the dominant foreigners instead of doing their bidding?

Mossadegh had been made the Shah's prime minister for the purpose of implementing reforms. But, fearful of the rapidity with which reforms were actually being introduced, the Shah drew back.

Mossadegh then boldly inaugurated what amounted to a revolution. Refusing to step down on the Shah's orders, he made world headlines by seizing and nationalizing the British-owned and operated oilfields. That proved to be no more tolerable in British eyes than the first Pahlavi Shah's flirtation with Nazism. But this time, the offender was eased out without Soviet help, and the main burden of securing the Shah's hold on his father's throne was left to secret agents of the American CIA, sent in to act not only for President Eisenhower but also for England's Winston Churchill.

It had been observed that Mossadegh, with his intensified modernization programs, had even less support among the old-time Muslim religious leaders than the Shah had, and no support at all among the common people. Based on that estimate of the situation — so different from the gross misreading of things in 1978 — American secret agents undertook what the leader among them, Kermit Roosevelt, aptly called a *Countercoup* in his book on the subject, subtitled *The Struggle for the Control of Iran* (McGraw Hill) published in 1979, some twenty five years after the fact.

That countercoup occurred in April 1953, at the very start of the Eisenhower Administration. The young Shah and his wife had been sent off to Italy for a vacation while Mossadegh was doing his worst. But then, within a matter of hours, street riots orchestrated with the backing of the American CIA forced Mossadegh to leave his residence in his pajamas. The young Shah was restored to his throne within hours. A few days later, he celebrated his restoration in his royal palace in the company of Kermit Roosevelt. Over vodka and caviar, he toasted his guest, saying: "I owe my throne to God, my people, my army — and to you."

But, more importantly, when Kermit Roosevelt reported his achievement "at the White House to President Eisenhower, the two Dulles brothers [John Foster and Allen], Secretary of Defense Wilson, Admiral Radford, Chairman of the Joint Chiefs of Staff, and General Andy Goodpaster" on September 4, 1953, he stressed the importance of accurate intelligence. CIA intelligence had correctly assessed Mossadegh's lack of support among the people; it had also shown that, to succeed, Mossadegh would have had to gain Soviet support; and a logical conclusion had seemed to be that if the army, first, and then the people, were finally forced to choose "between their monarch and a revolutionary figure backed by the Soviet Union," they would overwhelmingly choose to support the monarch — which they did. But then Kermit Roosevelt admonished his Washington superiors:

> If our analysis had been wrong, we'd have fallen flat on our faces. But it was right. If we, the CIA, are ever going to try something like this again, we must be absolutely sure that people and army want what we want. If not, you had better give the job to the Marines.

Special Agent Roosevelt's point had been that the alternative to failed covert operations cannot be a wringing of hands and expressions of "sympathy" for crushed clients. It must be military action to secure the same end — and indeed military action of the kind the Eisenhower administration did not shrink from calling *massive retaliation* at places and times and with weapons of its own choosing. Eisenhower made that clear in bringing the fighting in Korea to an end by threatening such retaliation if diplomatic negotiations failed. And two years later, when Britain and France "secretly conspired with Israel, without informing Washington," to destroy Egypt's Nasser immediately after his seizure of the Suez canal, Eisenhower refused to lend his support, under constraint, to a scheme that was destined to fail without his support. He refused, in other words, to be tricked into having to send in American "marines" to salvage someone else's secretly concocted design. In all his major containment undertakings, Eisenhower apparently made it a criterion that nothing should be done covertly without plans to accomplish the same end overtly, which is to say, militarily, if the covert operation failed.

2. Linking U.S. and Israeli Interests in Iran

In his book of 1979 on the countercoup, Kermit Roosvelt also made a point of stressing the importance of the fact that Iran, although Islamic, "was *not* an Arab country." He and Allen Dulles, speaking for the CIA in high councils of the American government at the time, had been fully aware, he tells us, of the concern of all in those days to protect Israeli interests while dealing with Iran. He and Allen Dulles therefore "emphasized — separately, together, and as often as possible" — the fact that the Shah's Iran had "excellent although informal relations with Israel." Looking back on the event, Kermit Roosevelt could add in 1979: "These relations became closer in later years when certain Israeli friends discreetly joined the CIA in helping to organize and give guidance to a new Iranian security service. This informal Israeli action was 'entirely under the table,' essentially a clandestine operation — but it was of great value to the Iranians." [9-10]

One may say, indeed, that in the years immediately following the countercoup of 1953, the United States and Israel entered upon an extensive collaborative effort to strengthen the Shah's hold on the reins of government, not only by training his security forces or secret police on the American CIA and Israeli Mossad models, but even more by financial and technological support of his drive toward rapid modernization of the entire nation. What exactly was the Israeli interest here? Twenty-five centuries of uninterrupted and continuous association, no doubt; but more particularly the fact that, on the eve of the founding of the State of Israel in 1948, there had been some 160,000 Jews living in Iran, constituting one of the most successful communities of the Jewish diaspora in the entire world.

During the 1950s and 1960s, almost half of the 160,000 Jews in Iran emigrated to Israel, to enjoy the one thing denied them even in a land where they had so long flourished in comfortable dependance. By the mid-1970s, however, there were still over 80,000 Jews in Iran. The Israeli government was therefore much concerned to assist the United States in its design to build up the Shah's economy, together with his military, to make his nation the most powerful and reliable in the Middle East, second only to Israel, and perhaps surpassing Israel in some important respects, because of its tremendous oil resources and large population.

In fact, during the years of the Eisenhower administration, immediately following the countercoup of 1953, American policy seemed to favor Iran more than it did Israel. The American strategy seemed to be to restrain Israel — and England and France also, if need be — in order to build up in the Middle East an alliance for mutual security on the pattern of Western Europe's North Atlantic Treaty Organization (NATO). In the Eisenhower-Dulles scheme of things, the assumption was that the Jewish national state could best be rendered secure by means of pacts with Iran, first of all, and then with Saudi Arabia and Egypt.

The Israelis were eager enough, as already indicated, to enter into mutual security relations with Iran. Iran was an Islamic state, to be sure, but, as Kermit Roosevelt had stressed, *not* an Arab nation. And that was important, even though Islamic international pressures at the time prevented fully normalized Israeli-Iranian diplomatic relations. But prospects of dependable relations with Saudi Arabia and Egypt, back in the 1950s, were something else. In the Dulles-Eisenhower view, sparsely populated Saudi Arabia ought not to have presented any serious long-range difficulties. Calculating "per capita," it was the richest of the Arab oil-states; and it seemed obvious that the United States could rather easily secure its cooperation, since its government was altogether dependent for its survival on oil exports to the United States and its Western European and Japanese allies.

Populous Egypt, all agreed, was a more serious problem. So long as Egypt aspired to lead a more or less united coalition of Arab-Islamic states, there seemed little likelihood of improving Egyptian-Israeli relations. But there was always a hope that, in time, Egypt might tire of being just one among many Arab-Islamic states; that it might be induced, on the broad international scene, to want to glory once again in its pre-Islamic Egyptian past. That was not an ill-founded hope. Yet such a change of aspirations required time. The transformation came in fact only after Israel and Egypt had fought, from the 1950s into the 1970s, several bitter wars.

3. Iran, Israel, and the Kissinger-Nixon Doctrine

The year of the last of those bitter wars, 1973, was a major turning point in modern Middle Eastern history, radically transforming the kind of role the United States was to play in that history. Two years before, in 1971, as if mindful of a grand American-Israeli design for its future, the Shah's Iran boldly celebrated its pre-Islamic heritage at ancient Persepolis, declaring its royal throne to have been established by Cyrus the Great some 1,200 years before the birth of the Prophet Mohammed. Although not much noticed in the Western press, the exiled Ayatollah Khomeini had thundered out his rage at the very idea, calling upon Almighty Allah to show his anger. But, unlike the Ayatollah, President Richard Nixon and his chief foreign policy adviser Henry Kissinger smiled admiringly. Then, in 1972, after Nixon and Kissinger had gone to Moscow to negotiate a settlement of the Vietnam war by offering the Kremlin the virtually unbelievable material advantages of genuine detente with the United States, the Shah's great day arrived. Nixon and Kissinger flew down directly from Moscow to Tehran to offer the Shah what has come to be called a blank check, with which he was to buy whatever he needed to make his country a virtual superpower for the maintenance of peace and prosperity in the Middle East.

It needs to be noted that, between 1945 and 1972, Iran had spent $1.2 billion to import arms. When the new "Nixon Doctrine" made the country its regional proxy in the Persian Gulf, arms purchases for the next six years shot up to $18 billion, with the revenues from a four-fold increase in the price of oil providing much of the purchasing power. During the same years, American exports of arms to Israel increased at an even greater rate. The great air-lift of arms during the Yum Kippur war of 1973 was only the beginning. And while American foreign aid to Israel sky-rocketed in the following years, negotiations with Egypt proceeded, and Egypt in due course joined the ranks of Israel and Iran as a chief recipient of American arms.

According to Kissinger and Nixon, the so-called Nixon Doctrine for regional security to be sustained by regional powers was to get its consummate trial in Iran. In South Vietnam it had been called Vietnamization. It had meant that the South Vietnamese government would no longer be treated as an American client, but as an ally, charged to sustain itself, throughout the withdrawal of American military forces and afterwards. It was known that, in Southeast Asia, the doctrine could have a semblance of succcess only if the Kremlin agreed to intervene in restraining Hanoi, at least for a "decent interval." But, Iran was to be something else. Iran was to be given, in advance, everything she needed or thought she wanted, to go it alone, as chief keeper of the peace in the region. After Iran, Saudi Arabia would be similary assisted, though on a smaller scale. And then, after Henry Kissinger had fully succeeded, with his shuttle diplomacy, in bringing the Israeli-Egyptian fighting to an end, it would be Egypt's turn.

Before the Watergate crisis overcame him, President Nixon seemed to think he was putting into operation the Dulles-Eisenhower plan for the region. Once the 1973 war was settled, the entire Western world, but especially the United States, greatly enjoyed the spectacle of Egypt's following Iran's lead in looking beyond the Islamic heritage it shared with its Arab neighbors, to its millenial pre-Islamic heritage. The Shah had had his celebration of Iranian antiquities at Persepolis, with all the world invited to look on. Egypt of course had always had its great Pyramids and Temples on view.

But far more impressive, and much more directly instructive, was the grand "King Tut" exhibit mounted for an international tour with American cooperation. In America, the exhibit drew unprecedented millions of culture-minded Americans to local museums all across the country. Friends of Israel everywhere hailed the event as a great break-through. And so the ground was prepared for Israeli acceptance of leadership in a four-way Middle Eastern alliance based on the Nixon Doctrine.

The link between the already patently-failed Vietnamization policy and the Kissinger-Nixon plans for applying a more workable version of it in the Middle East after 1973 is ably traced by Francis Furuyama in an article for the American Assembly's volume on *East-West Tensions in the Third World,* edited by Marshall D. Shulman (New York, 1986). Furuyama writes:

> As a result of the Vietnam-induced constraints on the direct employment of U.S. combat forces, American policy in the 1970s began to search for proxies that would take over the burden of regional security. The most clear-cut application of the Nixon Doc-

trine occurred in Iran, where the Shah after 1972 was expected
to assume many of the responsibilities for maintaining regional
stability in the Persian Gulf in the wake of the withdrawing British.... To facilitate [the Shah's] doing so he was given virtually
free reign...with regard to arms purchases. The problem of this
approach was twofold: first, there were very few candidate proxies like Iran...; and second, the very act of conferring a regional security role on a state had disturbing internal consequences.
... In the absence of full-fledged proxies, the United States came
to rely increasingly heavily on military assistance as a policy tool
during the 1970s.... The substantial increases in the level of U.S.
arms transfers that took place during that decade are traceable
to four countries, all of them located in the Middle East: Israel,
Egypt, Saudi Arabia, and Iran. [194]

After the Shah's fall in 1979, American diplomats with long experience in the region marvelled at what President Nixon had done
and linked the later development of the Iranian hostage crisis directly
to the application of that so-called Nixon Doctrine. In his excellent
study, *All Fall Down: America's Tragic Encounter With Iran* (Random House, New York, 1985), Gary Sick, who was chief assistant
to Zbigniew Brzezinski on the National Security Council throughout the hostage crisis (and who went on to become Program Officer
for U.S. Foreign Policy at the Ford Foundation), has written:

> The decision by President Nixon in 1972 to subordinate U.S. secu-
> rity decision making in the Persian Gulf to the person of the shah
> was unprecedented, excessive and ultimately inexplicable. The sub-
> sequent erosion of an independent U.S. capability to follow in-
> ternal events in Iran was as unnecessary as it was unwise. This
> was the legacy of five years of prior policies — policies that were
> accepted and continued without challenge when the new [Carter]
> administration took office. [170]

"Ultimately inexplicable," indeed, if one takes the Nixon Doctrine seriously, if one assumes that Henry Kissinger hadn't the statesmanly prudence to know what Kermit Roosevelt had explained to his

superiors in Washington after his successful covert Iranian countercoup of 1953. According to Kissinger's explication of the Nixon Doctrine, when more or less covert aid to a client state fails, the alternative will be not to send in American fighting forces for the purposes of winning, but to pull such fighting forces out and constrain the client to act like a first-class ally, like it or not. Under the circumstances, the decision of 1972 to "subordinate U.S. security decision making in the Persian Gulf to the person of the shah" becomes something worse than inexplicable. And it is no wonder, therefore, that Kissinger led the parade of Shah-supporters who, after having assigned him an impossible task, insisted on America's "standing by," uselessly, after his fall.

4. The Religious Dimension

In *All Fall Down*, Gary Sick is content to say that application of the Nixon Doctrine in Iran is "ultimately inexplicable," and to leave it at that. He is then at some pains, however, to clarify what he had meant by an erosion of U.S. capacity to follow internal events in Iran. One has first of all to try to explain, as Sick puts it, why "all existing intelligence systems — from SAVAK to Mossad to the CIA — failed so utterly in the Iran case." Sick acknowledges that the functioning of the CIA in Iran had certainly been "allowed to deteriorate almost to the vanishing point," as part of the design to have the Shah's government stand on its own two feet, as a "sovereign ally," not a client. But even if the CIA had been allowed to operate, Sick feels constrained to acknowledge, it would probably have wasted its time looking in the wrong place for the source of the Shah's coming troubles. "Only in retrospect," says Sick, "is it obvious that a good intelligence organization should have focused its attention on the religious schools, the mosques and the recorded sermons of an aged religious leader who had been living in exile for fourteen years. As one State Department official remarked in some exasperation after the revolution, 'Whoever took religion seriously?' " [165]

In other words, the religious reaction to American efforts to implement the Nixon Doctrine in the Middle East — to transform a client into an independent regional superpower — had caught

American foreign affairs decision makers by surprise. Although the Israeli-Arab struggle in its many phases from 1948 to 1973 seemed so obviously to have been pitting the Messianic zeal of Biblical Judaism against an Islamic fierceness worthy of the Koran, it did not appear to Western observers that religion as such, however zealous or fierce, could prove to be politically decisive in the long run.

But then came the fall of the Shah in January 1979. It had been brought on by the preaching of religious leaders whom the West perceived as medieval fanatics. Unarmed masses succeeded in toppling what had appeared to be a government of the first rank in that part of the world, boasting of a military and police establishment second to none. Suddenly it had all been blown away, as by a desert storm. But the expectation of Western observers who simply could not take religion seriously was that perhaps even such an uprising might only be temporarily successful in its religious form, to be succeeded by a secular-reform government, at first, and then by either an equally secular military coup or a Marxist revolutionary anti-religious dictatorship.

The shock came when it appeared that the regime set up under the Islamic auspices of the Ayatollah Khomeini was by no means about to be blown away. The Ayatollah had predicted as much at the time of the Shah's celebration of the 2,500th "anniversary" of his throne at Persepolis in 1971. In a book published that same year and titled *For An Islamic Government*, Khomeini had said, among other things:

> We have the duty to protect Islam. It is an absolute necessity, more even than prayer or fasting.... If we do nothing but pray, the colonialists will leave us alone. But we must not let them take our riches and content ourselves with praying under the pretext that God will punish them.... Out of a series of 50 volumes of Moslem tradition, there are maybe three or four that deal with prayer or the duties of man toward God, a few that deal with morals, and all the rest deal with society, economics, the law, politics, and the state.

How could such a religious worldly-crusading attitude produce more than isolated acts of fanatical martyrdom in the second half of the 20th century? Mohammed the Prophet had boldly gone on horseback flourishing a sword to build the Kingdom of Allah on earth; his armies of religious zealots had swept all around the Mediterranean, and far inland in many directions, slaughtering and then converting and then taxing infidels. Not long after that, comparable religious-crisis statements had been heard in the West when medieval Popes battled Holy Roman Emperors or led crusades to the Holy Land. Next it was the turn of Protestant Reformers backed by powerful princes to utter comparable words from time to time, rousing pious hearts to fight with religiuos zeal for kingdoms of this world. Christianity and Islam with their diverse sects are after all but mighty branches of an ancient monotheistic growth of militant Judaism that has been advancing claims of earthly sway from the days of mighty Moses to those of Menachem Begin.

"Whoever took religion seriously?" In the Middle East and in the West, the answer through long centuries has of course been: Muslims, Christians, and Jews. What our foreign policy decision-makers in the West had failed to realize, while they were undoing 25-years of U.S. containment policy, following Henry Kissinger's lead starting in 1969, was that, in our own time, religion has managed to replace fear of war as the chief determinant of our foreign relations. Surely the Israeli-Egyptian war of 1973 was a religious war waged with contempt for those who viewed the cold war balance of nuclear terror with fear and trembling. Those who took the religious aspect lightly pointed out, of course, that in that war the oil resources of the Middle East had for the first time become a military factor on the Arab side, bringing the Egyptians close to victory. Why not a materialist, economic, secularist interpretation of the fighting on both Israeli and Egyptian sides? That was the line of pursuit dictated by the Nixon Doctrine. Remind the Egyptians that, like the Iranians, they have had a long and glorious pre-Islamic history. Remind the Saudi Arabians, if they need reminding, that their well-being depends not on their numbers or religious fighting spirit but on continued purchase of their oil by the industrialized free nations.

So much for the Arab zealots. What about the Israelis? Do they really take their religion seriously, in the Zionist messianic sense? Surely they know better. Surely they must realize, in this 20th century which is about to end, that those who take religion seriously enough to fight for it are destined to have rough times on this earth until they learn better — especially in this nuclear age, when preventing a nuclear holocaust ought to be everyone's chief concern, a concern that a zealous fighting spirit can only dim, to everyone's great peril.

That is the reason why the events of 1979 in Iran, starting with the Shah's flight from his throne in January and the seizure of the American Embassy in Tehran on November 4, took the entire American decision-making establishment by absolute surprise. "Whoever took religion seriously?" The answer was that, in the last decades of the 20th century, the Ayatollah Khomeini and his faithful followers did, and that the Israelis, who were accused in the Islamic world of hiding fanatical religious purposes behind their alliance with the United States, also did.

5. Antinomian Prerogatives of Religious Zeal

Iranians and Israelis, we started out saying, have indeed been doing business together, covertly or overtly, happily or unhappily, for about 2,500 years. At first the advantages of religious zeal had all been on the Israeli side, and the Israeli leaders of those early days, like Nehemiah and Ezra, were able to work wonders. The early Iranian rulers, with their Zoroastrian "God of Light," were essentially secularists, as Herodotus observed. And so were the Macedonian kings educated by Aristotle who succeeded the Iranians as arbiters of war and peace among the peoples of the Middle East. The Romans too, who studied with the Greeks, were secular-minded; and, in the early centuries of the Caesars, it was they who contemptuously brought the second Hebrew Commonwealth — the commonwealth of post-biblical Judaism — to a disastrous end.

As noted earlier, through all the centuries of Roman domination in the West, the cultural and religious life of the Jews flourished far more richly in the East, especially in the lands of the Persians. After the 7th century Islamic conquest, it proved to be utterly humiliating for a time for the Iranians to have to profess the conqueror's faith and use his Arabic script to write. But when they turned themselves into Shiite enemies of Islamic orthodoxy, the surviving Iranians were able to transform themselves basically into a proud religious people. The Jews in their midst looked on with admiration as well as, from time to time, fear. But they too survived and, from time to time, flourished.

Coming back to the present, the question is: How does one deal with Iranians who take their Islamic religion seriously, even when they don't seem to be living up to its moral precepts, or when their perception of the true good of their faith and of the means of attaining it may be obscured by cataracts of vice? It is a question that became urgent for Americans in January 1979, when the Iranian Shah, who had been given a blank check — for inexplicable reasons, as Gary Sick suggests — to make himself another Cyrus, was forced to abandon his throne by virtually unarmed supporters of an aged Islamic Holy Man.

In February 1979, it seemed that, from a foreign relations standpoint, the Israelis would be the chief losers, that the successor regime would seek normalized relations with the United States and the oil-consuming industrialized nations generally, while denying oil to Israel and shutting down its representation, as a nation, in Iran. On February 14, 1979, Iranian radicals had seized the American Embassy only to be forced to surrender it back to the Americans by commando forces of the Ayatollah. The Israeli equivalent of an Embassy in Tehran had also been seized; but instead of ordering its liberation and return to the Israelis, that same Ayatollah had transferred title to it over to Yassir Arafat in recognition of the legitimacy of P.L.O. claims against Israel.

In the months that immediately followed, relations between the United States and the Islamic Republic of Iran were rapidly normalized, while Iranian relations with Israel steadily deteriorated until they sank to their lowest level since the founding of the modern State of Israel. The best the Israelis could hope to do, it soon appeared, was to deal covertly with the Ayatollah's government, offering to supply it with urgently needed things, in exchange for assurances that Jews still living in Iran — still some 80,000 — would not be accused of being Zionist spies and treated badly.

Still, the normalization of relations between the Ayatollah's Iran and the United States during Carter's Presidency was a bitter pill for the Israelis to swallow. And so there was almost a sigh of relief in Israel when those normalized relations became strained almost to the breaking point by the seizure of the American Embassy and the taking of American hostages by radical Islamic and Marxist students on November 4. Even so, American-Iranian relations were not immediately severed. The justification for not breaking relations was, on both sides, acknowledgement that the hostage-takers had done their deed against the will and contrary to the interests of the Ayatollah's government, headed by Mehdi Bazargan. The radicals holding the American Embassy forced Bazargan to resign, and they scrutinized his successor to see if he too ought to resign. American observers realized that, so long as Washington would not authorize the Ayatollah's government to storm the Embassy at whatever risk of lives, that government would be in a worse bargaining position, with respect to the hostage takers, than the United States.

The Carter administration's efforts to sustain formal diplomatic relations with the Ayatollah's government broke down completely only in early April 1980, when it became obvious that the government really had no control over the fate of the Americans being held in the Embassy buildings. In retrospect, as Gary Sick has noted, that fact ought to have emerged as obvious from the start, when assurances were given by all Iranian officials that there would be a repetition of events like those after the first seizure of the embassy on St. Valentine's day. The Ayatollah Khomeini himself had given assurances to a papal emissary who visited him in Qom on November 10, 1979 that the hostages were being well-treated. As Sick reports it, the papal envoy had been promised "full access" to the embassy, "to see for himself." That promise was of course never kept, writes Sick, "raising doubts about Khomeini's actual control over the students in the embassy." [224] Indeed, by December 1979, Sick adds, the "students in the embassy" had clearly emerged as an "independent force that even Khomeini seemed unable to control."

That was an early development that ought to have been closely pursued by American negotiators but was not. Those who had an interest in prolonging or even deepening the crisis could not be counted on to help, of course, even if asked. At any rate, as Sick notes: "Reports were being received almost daily in Washington that in a showdown with the students, Khomeini could not be certain he would prevail. Consequently, he was avoiding any steps that might undermine his authority or bring him into conflict with the most radical elements of the revolution." [245]

The formal American diplomatic break with Iran in April 1980 coincided with the Carter administration's decision to launch its ill-fated desert rescue mission. Suddenly Israel and the United States were again, diplomatically, in the same boat. While the Americans were keeping up relations with the Ayatollah's government, the Israelis had found themselves isolated. Now, with diplomatic relations completely severed, such isolation was finally ended. One could have expected that the United States and Israel would act increasingly together in dealing with Iran. But that wasn't to be. It is known that when, in their concern for the well-being of Jews in Iran, the Israelis sought by covert means, right after the embassy seizure on November 4, to supply the Iranians with arms and other necessities, President Carter wouldn't hear of it — not even when it was suggested that such covert dealings might facilitate release of the American hostages. Carter had banned all such transfers, and that was that. The Israelis found themselves emphatically chastised and warned not to attempt any such thing in the future, or they would risk a discontinuance of America's liberal foreign aid practices with respect to Israel.

It is important to recall at this point that the American hostages in Tehran were finally released in January 1981 only after the Carter administration had facilitated the transfer of billions of dollars to the Iranian authorities; and even then, it was rather the threat of American punitive military action that proved efficacious, coming as it did from a new militantly "conservative" politician, with strong "born-again Christian" support throughout the country, who was just then being sworn in as President of the United States.

For most of the Americans involved in trying to deal with the Ayatollah Khomeini's government during the 444-day hostage crisis of 1979-1981, the experience amounted to a plunge into the dark. Many of those participants have written at length about the experience. There has been a tendency to want to dismiss it all with cliches about having to learn new diplomatic ways for dealing "with developing nations of the Third World." In our global village of this planet earth, dealing with developing peoples is like dealing with the underprivileged inhabitants of unruly slums in our great old cities. We are all familiar with the attitude and most of us are hardly prepared to recognize it as fundamentally our own, even when dealing with national cultures as ancient as that of Iran — or Israel.

Perhaps the best summing up of the lessons American diplomacy has tried to draw out of the Carter administration's experience is to be found in a collection of studies titled *American Hostages in Iran: The Conduct of a Crisis* (Yale Univ. Press, 1985), edited for the Council on Foreign Relations by Paul H. Kreisberg. Among the major contributors were Harold H. Saunders, who headed the State Department's Iran Working Group during the crisis; Warren Christopher, chief negotiator during its concluding stages; and Gary Sick, chief assistant to the National Security Adviser throughout the period. In his introduction to the volume, Warren Christopher points out that "one of the most controversial questions raised about U.S. policy on the Iranian crisis is whether it was right, as a matter of principle, to negotiate with the terrorists who took over the embassy." It ought not to have been forgotten, in assessing the prudence of the arms-transfers for hostages undertaken by relatively minor figures in the Reagan administration — transfers that added up to relatively small sums of money in all — that the negotiations for hostages pursued by the top people of the Carter administration involved billions actually transferred after a period of some fourteen months during which the Carter government was virtually paralyzed, incapable of much else besides deals designed to bring the hostages safely home.

Were any lessons of profit drawn from the Carter administration's dealing with the Iranians at the close of its term? Most of the contributors to *American Hostages in Iran* have hesitated to say that there were. In fact, in his chapter on "Lessons and Conclusions" with which the volume ends, Abraham A. Ribicoff, former Connecticut governor and senator, stressed the unprecedented difficulties of finding anyone in the Ayatollah's Islamic Republic of Iran willing and able to act responsibly in a diplomatic sense; and then, summing up the chief points made in the preceding chapters of the volume, Ribicoff concluded:

The Iran hostage crisis was a crisis of the future. It was a time when our antagonists refused even to acknowledge the existence of basic norms that all nations had hitherto considered sacrosanct. The very premises of traditional international diplomacy were thrown to the winds. There were neither precedents nor solutions for the urgent challenges. In similar crises in the future, it will be wrong and indeed dangerous to assume that the other actors are motivated by the kinds of forces that shape American behavior. [395]

Does that sort of conclusion add to our understanding of basic relations of war and peace in the Middle East? Is it not, after all, a region where almost all the existent states, including our special ally, the State of Israel, are theocracies? Do they not all, through their leaders, profess to take their laws and ultimate purposes as states from the Holy Writ of Almighty God? For all our unhappy experience with Iran, we still seem inclined to think that there ought to be some way of getting a theocracy to act as if God were not its ruler, in which case it could let itself be induced to play the game of international relations in the nuclear age the way secular states like our own play it. Still, our diplomats know in their hearts that the modern Jewish State of Israel is no more prepared to play the game by the standard of secular states now than its prototype in biblical times had been. Confronting the nations of the Middle East today, we have to ask ourselves: Have we truly understood what the international politics of religion really amounts to in our time? Do we dare to ask ourselves what it really means for a modern state to declare itself to be a genuinely Islamic or a genuinely Jewish political community, living by God's laws?

6. Guidance from Spinoza

Here it is possible that the great secular Jewish philosopher Benedict Spinoza (1632-1677) can provide some needed guidance. In his bold *Theological-Political Treatise* published in 1670, Spinoza devoted several chapters to a discussion of the advantages and disadvantages of religious commonwealths formed by "covenants with God" — of which the Hebrew commonwealth of *Old Testament* times appeared in his age to have been the prototype. A central chapter carries this heading: "Of the Hebrew Republic as it was during the lifetime of Moses, and after his death till the foundation of the Monarchy; and of its Excellence. Lastly, of the Causes why the Theocratic Republic fell, and why it could hardly have continued without Dissension." The next chapter's heading reads: "From the Commonwealth of the Hebrews and their History certain Lessons are deduced."

Explicitly excluded from Spinoza's discussion of religious commonwealths is any consideration of what he called the second Hebrew commonwealth of post-biblical times which, he says, was "a mere shadow of the first, inasmuch as the people were bound by the rights of the Persians to whom they were subject." Generalizing on the lesson to be "deduced" from the history of the first Hebrew commonwealth, he says: "Although the commonwealth of the Hebrews, as we have conceived it, might have lasted for ever, it would be impossible to imitate it at the present day, nor would it be advisable so to do." The "present day," for Spinoza, was that of Europe after the Thirty Years war which ended with the Peace of Westphalia in 1648, and of England after the so-called Puritan Revolution which ran from 1603 through 1649, and culminated in a civil war, the beheading of King Charles I on January 30, 1649, and the military founding of a "kingless commonwealth" or Republic by "men of religion" who had "left farm and merchandise at a direct call from God" and who charged and fought "singing psalms."[565]

It is by way of chastising English Protestants in their zeal to create an equivalent of the commonwealth of Moses that Spinoza reminds his readers of the major defect of states patterned on that Old Testament Hebrew model. Because it results from a covenant with God, and therefore needs the consent of God as well as of those "transferring their rights" to God, such a commonwealth necessarily finds great difficulties in trying to deal meaningfully with other peoples. Indeed, says Spinoza, "such a form of government would only be available for those who desire to have no foreign relations, but to shut themselves up within their own frontiers, and to live apart from the rest of the world; it would be useless to men who must have dealings with other nations; so that the cases where it could be adopted are very few indeed."

Certainly there is something shockingly modern about the words just quoted. The Ayatollah's Iran and the modern Jewish State of Israel are both constituted as religious commonwealths. Does Spinoza's observation apply? Needless to say, since its foundation in 1948, the religious State of Israel has had to deal incessantly with other states, some secular, like the United States and the Soviet Union, and some, like its Islamic neighbors, committed to upholding sets of religious laws very different from those of the Holy Books on which Israel bases its claims to a Palestinian homeland. The same is obviously true, although to a lesser extent, of the Islamic Republic of Iran founded early in 1979. Few of Iran's "foreign entanglements" have been with foreign "supporters," and certainly with none that have played anything like the role of the United States in Israel's founding or in the return of the Shah to his Iranian throne in 1953. Since its origins in January 1979, the Islamic Republic of Iran has had to deal mostly with professed enemies, even among the nations of Arabic Islam, to say nothing of the United States, the Soviet Union, and Israel.

In hostile relations, as Spinoza concedes, religious zeal can be a powerful resource. But what about deals with states seeking peaceful relations while presuming all the while to legislate sacrilegiously for themselves, or worse, claiming to have received their laws from their necessarily-false gods?

More particularly, we must ask with Spinoza: What is the meaning of pacts or international treaties entered into by the People of God with infidels? Can they be binding — *pacta sunt servanda* — if they depart in any sense from the True God's revealed Book of Laws? And what of the obligations of faithful Muslims condemned to live as second-class citizens among Christians in a professedly Christian commonwealth where there is no American-style wall of separation between Church and State? Or in a professedly Jewish environment, like that of the modern State of Israel? Perhaps their only peaceful recourse is to mutter some Muslim equivalent of that great medieval hymn of the Jews, the *Kol Nidre*, the literal meaning of which the Jews of the nineteenth century were obliged to fore-swear in order to be accepted as loyal citizens of some of the most liberal states of Europe — by foreswearing which they pledged not to remain true Zionists in their hearts while swearing national oaths of allegiance in non-Jewish states.

It was the ordeal of having to compromise one's faith for the sake of citizenship in secular European states that gave rise to the modern Zionist Movement — to create a truly religious Jewish State in which one can be wholeheartedly a Jew, believing faithfully in a Jewish commonwealth or kingdom of *this* world, and not of some more or less shadowy world beyond the grave. Although a kingdom of God which is *not* of this world has been part of the faith of most orthodox Christians since the beginning, it has plainly been anathema not only to faithful Muslims and Jews, but also to some Old Testament-style Christian sects, many of which are flourishing in 20th century America.

According to Spinoza's frank analysis, when professedly religious governments enter into accords with peoples of other faiths, or no faiths, they must either profess to be acting under constraint or run the risk of losing their religious authority at home. That is what Spinoza meant by insisting that genuinely religious constitutions "are useless for states desiring foreign relations." In recent times, the fall of the Shah of Iran, and the virtual impossibility of dealing with members of the Ayatollah Khomeini's government without bringing down its so-called moderate members, as happened during the 444 days of the American Hostage crisis, illustrate the point. So also does the assassination of Egypt's Anwar Sadat for having appeared to compromise, in the profoundest religious sense, by "going to Jerusalem" and accepting the Camp David accords with their manifestly rich material advantages.

The remarkable achievement of the leaders of the Jewish State of Israel since 1948 has consisted in their ability to deal with other states — with so-called friends as well as professed foes — without appearing to have actually compromised their "fundamental laws" as a religious state. Their friends, like the United States, have had to virtually identify their interests with Israeli national interests to qualify as friends, with no quarter given even in apparently small matters. All America, for instance, saw how Elie Wiesel boldly chastised

President Reagan in his own White House, giving no quarter as he denounced the President's visit to the Bitberg Cemetery in West Germany. By agreeing to make the visit, Professor Reagan professed to be respecting a Western tradition of civilized international relations dating back to the time of Homer. Wiesel, quite after the fashion described by Spinoza, would not hear of such a thing as civilized international relations in the special case of the grievances of Jews against the German nation which had spawned Hitler.

Even more notably, at the time of the Israeli invasion of south Lebanon, Prime Minister Menachem Begin had responded to President Reagan's criticism in a similar fashion. Ordinarily, Jews are forgiving. Ordinarily, they do not object to the chief of one state visiting the cemetery of another former enemy state after peace had been concluded. Ordinarily, Jews protest a seemingly useless slaughter of civilians in war, as so many of them, indeed, protested the slaughter inflicted on more or less innocent natives by the American military in Vietnam. But, in the case of enemies of Israel, other criteria apply. And that is because, with their old testament prophetic inheritance, the Jews are God's chosen people, charged to enforce His will, His laws in the world. Terrible things done for God's sake by his chosen people are not terrible. And, similarly, covert undertakings that might otherwise seem to qualify as just dirty tricks are rendered immaculate when pursued in the interests of a higher, absolute, divine law.

At the height of the war against the P.L.O. in Lebanon, Menachem Begin, that fiercest of Israeli prime ministers, heard that President Reagan was "losing patience" with him because of the alleged brutality of the Israeli assault. His response was quite in the spirit of Elie Wiesel's reproof of Reagan for deciding to visit the Bitburg cemetery. The word was going around at that time that, to Israel's critics in the West, the situation of the trapped Palestinians in Beirut seemed to parallel that of the Jews sealed up in Poland's great Warsaw Ghetto, awaiting the final onslaught of hate-filled Nazis. In complaining to Reagan, Begin boldly insisted on reversing the image — and let Israel's critics be damned. On his 69th birthday, replying to greetings from President Reagan, Begin did not hesitate to say: "I feel as a prime minister empowered to instruct a valiant army facing 'Berlin' where, amongst the innocent civilians, Hitler and his henchmen hide in a bunker deep beneath the surface.''

The P.L.O. guerrillas in Beirut numbered, at that time, some seven or eight thousand. They and their families — wives, children, grand-parents — constituted at best a rag-tag assortment of displaced persons, surely no better armed in spirit than the fighting men and women of the beleaguered Jewish Warsaw ghetto under the Nazi occupation. Yet Begin insisted on comparing them with "Hitler and his henchmen" entrenched deep down in their Berlin bunkers. Thus the Israeli invasion of South Lebanon was to be compared to nothing less than the final drive of the combined forces of the United States, England, and the Soviet Union, as well as France and other allied states, to close in on and annihilate another Hitler, reincarnate in Yassir Arafat.

But, the image with which he retorted to Israel's critics around the world was not, for Menachem Begin, at issue in his response to President Reagan's apparent criticism of Israel's war in Lebanon. Why should President Reagan be giving hints that he might be losing patience with Israel? Didn't he understand the absolute righteousness of Israel's cause? "My generation, dear Ron," the Israeli Prime Minister admonished, "swore on the altar of God that whoever proclaims his intent to destroy the Jewish state or the Jewish people, or both, seals his fate, so that what happened from Berlin, without inverted commas, will never happen again." As for Israel's blitzkrieg military successes against the hate-filled, Nazi-like foe hidden among the innocent people of Lebanon, Begin assured Reagan that lately he was turning ever more intently "to the creator of my soul in deep gratitude."

Begin's self-righteous fervor, as leader of God's Chosen People battling for God's Kingdom on Earth, had already drawn a response from the popular American Evangelical preacher Jerry Falwell that recalled the response of the early Iranian Kings, from Cyrus the Great to Artaxerxes, to similar pleas for support from Jewish leaders of the caliber of Nehemiah and Ezra. "I don't think," Falwell has typically said, "that America could turn its back on the people of Israel and survive. God deals with nations in relation to how those nations deal with the Jew." Virtually to the same purpose, Cyrus the Great had said back in 639 B.C.: "Since God Almighty hath appointed me to be king of the habitable earth, I believe that he is the God which the nation of the Israelites worship; for he foretold my name by the prophets, and that I should build him a house at Jerusalem, in the country of Judea." The prophet referred to is Isaiah, to whom God had spoken in a secret vision, saying: "My will is, that Cyrus, whom I have appointed to be king over many and great nations, send back my people to their own land, and build my temple."

After having been chided with prophetic zeal by Menachem Begin, and after having repeatedly said in public that he was not about to turn his back on Christian Evangelicals like Jerry Falwell, who had consistently supported him politically, President Reagan himself began to express an almost biblical approval of Israel's claims in the Middle East, as for instance, after he had received support from the American Israel Public Affairs Committee (AIPAC) in getting approval from Congress to keep American Marines in Lebanon after pressures had mounted to bring them home. In an October 1983 phone call to thank AIPAC's executive director, Thomas A. Dine, Israel's first-ranking lobbyist in Washington, for helping to "swing" a number of crucial votes in the Senate, the President said among other things, "I just want to thank you and all your staff for the great assistance you gave us on the War Powers Act Resolution.... I know how you mobilized the grassroot organizations to generate support."[29] But then, in words that help us to understand what may have prompted Cyrus the Great to look with wonder on the Israelites and their God, back in the 6th century B.C., the President of the United States added: "I turn back to your ancient prophets in the Old Testament and the signs foretelling Armageddon and I find myself wondering if...if we're the generation that's going to see that come about. I don't know if you've noted any of those prophecies lately but, believe me, they certainly describe the times we're going through." [246]

CHAPTER TWO

Current Israeli-
American Relations

1. The Israeli-American Mutual Security Alliance of 1983

President Reagan spoke in such terms to Thomas Dine in October 1983. During the next month he proved how far he was ready to go in behalf of a cooperative Israel by making a change in U.S.-Israeli relations almost as radical as that which occurred in U.S.-Iranian relations back in 1973. In 1948, when Israel declared its independence, its relationship to the United States had plainly been that of a client-state, receiving much and giving little, in accordance with its very limited means. Under Presidents Eisenhower, Kennedy, and Johnson, perception of the basic relationship hardly changed at all. President Johnson actually risked drawing a comparison between America's support of Israel and its support of the client-state of South Vietnam — neither of which, in his view, could survive without American support. But then came the Nixon Doctrine. All our client states were thereafter to be treated as allies and forced to stand on their "own two feet," or at least pretend to do so. Many of those client-states were reluctant to put on even a pretense of independence. But not Iran, as we have seen; and certainly not Israel.

In a "strategic cooperation agreement" signed by President Ronald Reagan and Israeli Prime Minister Yitzak Shamir in November 1983, Israel gained official recognition as having earned a status of complete equality as a military partner of the United States. That agreement amounted to a formal U.S.-Israeli alliance for mutual security, its underlying assumption being that while the United States continues to supply material support, in the form of arms and advanced technology, the Israelis will supply a fighting will, an unmatched international intelligence network, and covert daring. It was in the spirit of such a partnership, apparently, that President Reagan acted in giving his assent to American pursuit of covert Israeli initiatives to open up lines of communication with the government of the Islamic Republic of Iran, through the sale of arms, despite public avowals that the United States would not enter into such dealings with governments which, like that of the Ayatollah Khomeini, appeared to be sponsoring international terrorism.

How could an American government bring itself to think in terms of following Israeli initiatives in that regard? After the 1953 American intervention to sustain the Iranian Shah, Israelis secretly joined forces with the CIA to help in the future. But the initiatives had been unmistakably American. Why the change in 1985? Why should anyone in Washington have been ready to believe that the Israelis, in their Zionist religious state, might be better at such dealings than the heirs of Allen Dulles and Kermit Roosevelt?

That must remain a question of some urgency for the future conduct of American affairs in regions of the world where religion simply has to be taken seriously. From the standpoint of Spinoza's view of religious commonwealths covenanted on the Old Testament model, the explanation is perhaps to be sought in the absolute sense of righteousness in their cause that has consistently characterized the conduct of the Israeli leaders especially in times of crisis, when the fate of Israel might seem to be in the balance. It is an antinomian self-righteousness, appealing to an absolute higher law, for the sake of which all other laws must be sacrificed, if need be.

The Israeli statesmen with a strong sense of Jewish history had a keen impression of what the 1979 revolution, or, rather, counter-revolution, of the Ayatollah Khomeini meant. In the 2,500 years of continuous association with the Iranians, during the pre-Islamic and Islamic periods, the Jewish people had had experience enough with such changes. After the grand show at Persepolis, the Khomeini revolution had been like another Islamic conquest. The Israelis, in their millennial experience, had seen it all before. That is why, after the Shah's fall, they undertook to deal with the new regime, despite its professed anti-Zionist proclamations. There were still some 80,000 Jews living in Iran; and if supplying the regime's most pressing needs could make things better for those Jews, every effort should be made, it was decided, at least covertly, to accommodate the Shah's successor. As we have already noted, President Carter had emphatically opposed the idea. Still, a beginning had been made, and under what appeared to be the worst possible circumstances.

In that connection, we must remind ourselves that, not once, but twice before the much publicized and much scrutinized 1985-1986 arms transfers, Israel had engaged in similar covert deals with Iran. As Hirsh Goodman reminded readers of Israel's English-language *Jerusalem Post* in late November 1986, the first such Israeli arms "transfer" to Iran had indeed occurred during Carter's Presidency, "in 1979-1980, with Menachem Begin as prime minister, Ezer Weizman as defense minister and Mordechai Tsipori as his deputy." The object then was, first, as already noted, to try to protect the more than 80,000 Jews still living in Iran, and, more specifically, to ensure, as Goodman puts it, "the prolongation of the Jewish community." That was an arms deal in which Israel acted altogether on its own. Indeed, in Goodman's words: "This effort came to an abrupt end when President Jimmy Carter, who had imposed an ironclad embargo on arms sales to Iran during the American hostage crisis, discovered the covert channel."

The second Israeli arms "transfer" to Iran occurred in 1982, when Begin was prime minister and Ariel Sharon was minister of defense. The purpose then was strategic: Israel was eager to strengthen Iran as the lesser of two evils in the Iraq-Iran war. This second transfer, like the first, Goodman writes, "was carried out without American permission, and using middlemen (as opposed to government-to-government sales). The sales were mainly of munitions for Israeli-made systems that had been sold to the Shah, though there have been reports of Hawk anti-aircraft missiles, TOW anti-tank missiles and aircraft spare parts among the items sold."

Hirsh Goodman's account of the third Israeli arms transfers of 1985-1986 is a bit more interesting than most accounts in American newspapers. It was handled in Israel, he writes, "by Shimon Peres, Yitzhak Shamir and Yitzhak Rabin, through David Kimche, director general of the Foreign Ministry, and the prime minister's adviser on terrorism, Amiram Nir." Unlike the previous two transfers, which were either opposed or ignored by the United States, this third transfer saw a first American-Israeli collaboration, and, indeed, an American displacement of Israel in direct negotiations.

Goodman stresses the fact that the deal, in this third case, served Israeli interests and might well have served American interests, even if it didn't finally turn out that way. Like the United States, Israel, too, has been injured, for its trading with Iran has certainly embarrassed it in its relations with Jordan and Egypt. In the same issue of the *Jerusalem Post*, an editorial reminded readers of contradictions in the first responses of Israeli officials to suggestions that Israel had "led the way" in the joint U.S./Israeli arms transfers. As the editorial put it:

> The pretense that the arms were shipped only in response to an American request was contradicted by Mr. Meese.... The initiative for a shift in U.S. policy on Iran, he told the White House press, had come from Israel. If it was Mr. Meese who was not telling the truth, Mr. Peres would presumably have corrected him during his own impassioned reply to the Knesset debate on the arms deal yesterday. The fact is he did not. What the foreign minister — and former premier — did was to offer the first detailed rationale for the arms deal in public. Life is full of contradictions, Mr. Peres proposed. One moral imperative may conflict with another. But Israel acted in the Iranian matter out of purely moral considerations, getting not a penny out of it. (Oddly, Premier Shamir had only a night earlier described it on television as an economic necessity for an arms-producing country.)

In answering questions posed to him by members of the House Foreign Affairs Committee, Secretary of State George Shultz complained of having been by-passed, cut off from information, in the course of the arms transfer operations. The lesson to be drawn, he said, was that National Security Council people should not conduct operational activities "except in very rare circumstances." He noted that the example to the contrary of Henry Kissinger is often cited, particularly that of his "diplomacy in China," which was, of course, spectacular, Shultz conceded. "Everybody refers to it — and it was a wonderful thing," he agreed. "On the other hand," he said further, "to the extent that it causes other people to aspire to be Henry Kissinger, it can get you into trouble. There's only one. They broke the mold when they made him."

Secretary of State Shultz was of course proving with his remarks precisely the point that Robert C. McFarlane, former Special Assistant to the President for National Security Affairs, would make before the same House Foreign Relations Committee some two hours later, in testifying about American "errors" made in the transaction. The U.S., he said, — and, indeed, he himself — had erred in imagining that Americans today could deal with terrorists, or with nations supporting terrorism, with the sort of flexibility Israel had already displayed in arms deals with Iran and with other Islamic states. "If there was a mistake, and I probably made it," McFarlane said to the surprise of many, "it was this . . . ."

At that point, McFarlane seemed to be taking his cues from the chapters of Spinoza from which we quoted earlier. After characterizing with some care Israel's extraordinary capacity to shift gears in its dealings with foreign states, and especially with Arab and other Islamic nations generally perceived to be extremely hostile, McFarlane contrasted such high flexibility with what has increasingly been demanded of our leadership. "We are different," he concluded; "we are not Israel. Israel has a certain respect as being able to differentiate between terrorist states, to react violently or to negotiate." He erred, he reiterated, in imagining the American people were able to support nuanced dealings with enemy nations in the Israeli manner.

Could a Henry Kissinger have done better than McFarlane in McFarlane's position? McFarlane did not presume to challenge George Shultz's high estimate of Kissinger. He called attention, however, to Israel's past record with regard to arms sales. He was plainly well aware of Israel's declared policy of making itself a major arms-exporting state, with the help of United States material assistance, and of the considerable experience Israel has had in dealing with all sorts of governments, without internal difficulties of the kind that the United States has consistently experienced, even apart from the apparent illegality of the reported transfer of moneys received from Iran to support rebel forces in Nicaragua.

McFarlane's insistence on the long experience of the Israeli nationalists or Zionists in this regard, and on the error of his imagining the United States could follow Israeli practice and get away with it under our form of government, is important. There have been times in the past when the United States could and did follow such a course in difficult situations. But then it was done in keeping with Kermit Roosevelt's maxim: Never attempt to do covertly anything that you're not prepared to do overtly, using military power, if the covert operation fails.

From such a vantagepoint, Secretary of State Shultz was plainly wrong in his assessment of Kissinger's alleged successes with secret diplomacy and in covert national-security ventures. When Kissinger's secret ventures failed, there was obviously no intention on his part, or on the part of the Presidents he served, to pursue the same ends by military means. The alternative for dirty tricks that fail, on Kissinger's watch, was to leave our clients to take their lickings on their own — after having been elevated, willy-nilly, to the status of allies.

2. Traditional Anglo-American Success in Covert Warfare

For proper examples of what is required in dealing covertly with really difficult situations, we need to look back at least as far as Winston Churchill's collaboration with Franklin D. Roosevelt to get the United States into the war against Adolph Hitler despite the firmly expressed will of the United States Congress and a majority of the American people to resist the idea by every possible legal means.

Needless to say, it takes a great deal of *secular* maturity to attempt to do, illegally, what England's last great wartime leader was apparently always prepared to do for his England. "Madam," he is reported to have said when challenged on moral grounds for attempting to make a "deal" with Stalin, "I would make a friend of the devil himself if it would save England." Our Abraham Lincoln had of course said and done as much when he "broke the law" to save the Union for the American people in whose hearts his memory is enshrined forever.

It is a pity that English traditions make it relatively easy, whereas American traditions make it extremely hard, for an opposition party leader to keep secrets from governing officers whose judgment he does not trust. Churchill in opposition kept state secrets from Prime Minister Neville Chamberlain. Our President in office is apparently unable to keep secrets from the heads of certain congressional committees, which, because of the constitutional system of separated powers, can make a kind of carnival, if they so wish, of even the gravest presidential pretensions to secrecy.

We know that, in England, the House of Commons rules, through its committee of the whole, appointed out of its ranks by the Prime Minister, who is usually the head of the majority party in the Commons. Even so, there exists what the English call the "Crown," worn by its kings or queens, who are legally bound to sign a bill for their own execution if properly drawn up and passed through Parliament.

According to the best accounts left us by Churchill himself and his chief public and private supporters in plans to counter the official policy of the Chamberlain government in the late 1930s, Churchill had no "parliamentary authority" to do anything of the sort. His support came from the king. How that worked has been ably described in William Stevenson's *A Man Called Intrepid*, which was subtitled "The Secret War: The Authentic Account of the Most Decisive Intelligence Operations of World War II — and the Superspy Who Controlled Them." Discussing the 1939 secret mission of Colonel Colin McVeagh Gubbins to Warsaw, Stevenson writes:

> Mystery still surrounds it. The operation, like many others, was conducted in defiance of official British appeasement policy.... Gubbins, however unorthodox, was still a member of the British Intelligence Directorate. He came under Prime Minister Chamberlain's orders. Chamberlain seemed to think that by yielding to Hitler's demands, he could satisfy them. Gubbins was convinced that yielding to such demands did not terminate hostility, but excited it. The conflict [between Chamberlain's convictions and Gubbins's] was resolved by the fact that directors of British intelligence are confirmed in their appointment by the Crown. Their jobs are

'within the gift of the Monarch' by long tradition. This untidy
British arrangement baffles Americans accustomed to constitutional legalities. [47]

To help to clarify the British arrangements in such matters for
the benefit of Constitution-minded Americans, the story has been told
in Washington about a Chief of the Secret Service who was asked by
King George VI for classified information. As Stevenson reports the
tale, "the Chief replied: 'I must answer that my lips are sealed.' The
King said: 'Suppose I order "Off with your head"?' The Chief replied:
'In that case, Sir, I would lose my head with my lips still sealed'."

That story was supposed to remind Americans to whom it was
told of the family-like character of high level intelligence relationships
in the English government, relations built up upon centuries of experience. That experience served Churchill in good stead when, after
years of secret activity to reverse English policy while out of office,
he was finally made a member of the Government by being "maneu-
vered back into the Admiralty as First Lord after a quarter-century's
absence." He had become, in other words, an equivalent of our Secretary of Defense. Here is how Stevenson describes what would certainly have been a terrible dilemma for any American counterpart:

> Churchill, while still serving irresolute leaders, now had the pow-
> er to move great fleets over the oceans. He was also war lord in
> a field where Britain was mentally prepared — secret operations.
> From his Admiralty post he commanded weapons of intelligence.
> As companion, he had Admiral Sir Hugh Sinclair, known as 'C,'
> chief of the Secret Intelligence Service, and appointed by the King.
> Churchill and C were secure in the knowledge that they must act
> to help the king defend his people — against government policy,
> if necessary, although conflict was best avoided by forgetting to
> mention all that went on.

One could imagine Churchill called before an equivalent of our
congressional foreign affairs committees! Fortunately, the Allied
Powers defeated the Axis Powers in World War II, and the extralegal things done by Americans and Englishmen to assure Anglo-
American victory have not come under siginificant *governmental*

scrutiny, even though revisionist historians have been kept somewhat busy. Stevenson's account here is very plain:

"Thus the Prime Minister of Great Britian, so long as he was appeasement-minded Neville Chamberlain, was not taken into the confidence of the various intelligence groups, consisting now mostly of gifted amateurs, who were known in general as 'The Baker Street Irregulars,' after the amateurs who aided Sherlock Holmes. Like the methods of the great detective, their approach was unorthodox. They were reticent with their own Prime Minister, but agreed to confide in the President of the United States." [71]

When Franklin Delano Roosevelt became fully aware that, for reasons of state, the intelligence people in England associated with Winston Churchill had excluded the British Prime Minister from their plans for a secret war, and had included him in those plans, he was flattered. At one point he boasted: "I'm your biggest undercover agent." He was plainly serving the English national interest, as Churchill conceived it. But he believed he was also serving the American national interest, violating the letter of the law, indeed, but not his presidential oath, seeking by every necessary means to do the sort of things Lincoln had felt obliged to do during the Civil War, regardless of the letter of the Constitution. [136]

Lincoln, following the practice of crisis Presidents who preceded him, understood the second part of his oath to mean that, if it took a violation of part of the Constitution to effectively "preserve, protect, and defend" it as a whole, it was his sworn duty to violate it. He argued that to effectively defend the Constitution, it was essential to preserve the Union of which that Constitution was the organic law; since, if the Union failed, the Constitution would constitute nothing. Lincoln's often cited words are a reminder that, with the oath, our Constitution added something to the presidential powers not otherwise specified in it. That added something was our American equivalent of the prerogatives of the Crown in England — prerogatives that permitted Colonel Gubbins and Winston Churchill *in and out of office*, like McFarlane and his National Security Council colleagues in 1985 and 1986, to do things counter to the letter of the law, as well as above and beyond the call of duty, to save their country.

In an article on secrecy and foreign affairs, in which he contrasts the American and British situations, Anthony Sampson has noted: "The Congress committees (of the United States), with their large staffs geared to publicity, have no real equivalent in Britian." Congress committees in America are constitutionally authorized, as already noted, to frustrate a President in a way that could be done in England only "illegally" by a party leader opposed to the reigning Prime Minister, as in the case of Winston Churchill. With a touch of regret, Sampson adds: "No opposition leader since World War II has been able to command his own effective intelligence system, as Churchill could before the War through his own contacts and Staff." [221]

Sampson would have it otherwise, he seems to hint. Even so, we can probably survive the microscopic scrutiny provided by television of our constitutional system of separated and checked and balanced governmental powers. Of far greater urgency just now is the challenge of what we have earlier called the politics of religion.

3. Alternatives

Religion is daily filling a moral vacuum in the United States, now that secularism is generally on the defensive. We have for too long made the mistake of not taking it seriously, at home as well as abroad. We have paid dearly for that mistake. And we connot hope to undue it simply by *ad hominem* protests. Ex-Congressmen like Paul Findley, who boast of liberal voting records and consistently liberal stances on all major public matters — including support of World Government! — now claim that they have been overwhelmed politically by the pressure of religious lobbies. In Findley's view it has been in his case, apparently, a Jewish lobby that has driven him out of Congress. But there are also Moral Majority religious lobbies that many public office seekers complain of, not to mention Roman Catholic anti-abortion or "right-to-life" lobbies, and even some allegedly well-financed Islamic lobbies.

The United States must come to terms with the fact that, despite the so-called balance of terror in nuclear arms, there are people in all lands today who take religion very seriously. We noted above that Judaism, Christianity, and Islam have all, in the course of their histories, passed through phases when their primary religious concern has been to struggle to establish a "Kingdom of God" on earth. Much has depended on whether their adherents in any particular land constituted a ruling majority, or a tolerated or oppressed minority. That is not meant to suggest, however, any basic identity of Christian, Islamic, and Jewish traditional perspectives on earthly politics. The three differ markedly, as we shall show, though they have indeed enough in common to have earned them the common enmity of progressive rationalists and revolutionary materialists through the centuries.

At any rate, it would appear that we must as a nation begin to speak more frankly than we have in the past about the politics of religion. The alternative is plainly to run the risk of being overwhelmed by it.

PART II

Historical Patterns

CHAPTER THREE

Three Traditions of Monotheism in Our Times

Islam, Christianity, and Judaism are global religions. Of the three, only Christianity, in its traditional, catholic or universal orthodoxy, does not aspire to a kingdom of this world. All flourish, of course, as living branches of a single tree of monotheism, rooted in the ancient Middle East. They are alike in that each has adherents in diverse lands living under governments that either (1) persecute them, (2) tolerate them, or (3) establish them. And because they variously rule or are tolerated or oppressed (whether as strong or weak minorities or majorities), it is difficult to generalize about the political attitudes of their adherents, without seeming to contradict oneself and without giving offense to partisan apologists of one sort or another.

Yet one has only to leaf through the pages of any issue of America's leading newspapers — like the Washington *Post* or New York *Times* — for the past decade to realize that our world has long since crossed the threshold of an era that has brought the "politics of religion" to the most vital center of American international relations. During World War II and in the first three decades following that war, the only significant religious pressure applied on American decision-making for foreign affairs appeared to be Jewish. In the war itself, the Soviet Union, bastion of atheistic communism, had joined its despised, only nominally-Christian enemy, the United States, to crush a professedlly pagan Nazi Germany. In the midst of that catastrophic clash of minimally religious great powers, the long suppressed spirit of Jewish national identity and statecraft had its conclusive religious awakening. While its numbers in the American and Soviet diasporas increased, other millions of Jews gathered themselves out of the ashes of Europe to form a Zionist state in Palestine — a state to be defended by means of its own with or without the support of the superpowers which had collaborated in its establishment.

Until recently, Israel seemed to be the only really significant religion-based force in the politics of the Middle East. Only rarely in the 1950s and 1960s did the Islamic Arab peoples show signs of searching in their souls for sparks of the ancient, sublime carelessness of life which had once spurred the armies of Mohammed and his Successors to sweep like a desert whirlwind not only around the Mediterranean but deep into Central Asia and India as well. But since 1973, all that has changed. Mohammedanism now vies with Judaism as a religious alternative to the reigning Marxist and capitalist forms of irreligious secularism. Is there to be, soon, a comparable Christian response of the kind that Alexander Solzhenitsyn has been calling for?

1. Jewish Biblical Expectations

Divine governance of human history is an article of common faith in the three great monotheistic religions. Yet they differ markedly in their estimates of the role of the faithful in realizing the ends of that divine governance.

Judaism has been from its inception a rigorously national religion. So firm has it been in its national exclusivity that no form of political universalism, whether of the old imperial or of the modern capitalist, communist, or liberal supranationalist varieties, has come close to undermining it. The divine governance guarantees that, in the last days of the era of wars, Jews are to be the ultimate architects of mankind's fate, fulfilling literally the old prophecies of Isaiah and Micah:

> For the law shall go forth of Zion, and the word of the Lord from
> Jerusalem. And he shall judge many people, and rebuke strong

nations afar off; and they shall beat their swords into plowshares, and their spears into pruning hooks: nations shall not lift up sword against nation, neither shall they learn war anymore.... Now also many nations are gathered against thee.... Arise and thresh, O daughter of Zion: for I will make thine horn iron, and I will make thy hoofs brass: and thou shalt beat in pieces many people: and I will consecrate their gain unto the Lord, and their substance unto the Lord of the whole earth. (Micah, IV)

In his classic study, *The Jews Among the Greeks and Romans* (Jewish Publications Society, Philadelphia, 1915), the eminent juridical scholar Max Radin summarized what the ancient Jews conceived to be their national prerogative in the world, even when confronted by the might of Rome: "To secure the independence of a few square miles of semi-arid soil between the Jordan and the Sea was no deed to puff men with inordinate pride, however difficult of actual accomplishment it was. As a step toward larger deeds, however, it was notable enough. What was the larger deed, and how was it to be accomplished? However disproportionate it may seem to us, it was nothing less than dominion over the whole world, to be accomplished by sudden and miraculous conversion of men's souls for the most part, or by force of arms, if it should prove necessary." (73)

It was a vague Roman awareness of that "larger deed" (coupled with the zeal of many Jews whenever an eligible person among them advanced a Messianic claim) that led to the forced scattering of Jews in distant cities of the Empire. The Roman authorities had long before then overwhelmed the national exclusivity of all the other religions of the Mediterranean world. Roman armies had in fact become "collectors of gods," so that finally their great Pantheon came to serve as a sort of United Nations Assembly of traditional national "ideals," kept under lock and key as hostages of an enforceable world peace.

The other non-Roman people of antiquity, following the Greek cosmopolitan example, readily consented to "pool" their traditional values for the sake of peace; the Jews alone resisted, determined to wait in exile for millenia, if need be, till God chose in his own good time to fulfill their Messianic expectations.

In 1944, David Ben-Gurion characterized the modern Zionist drive for an independent Israel as a "Jewish Revolution" against a millenial destiny of exile. It was occurring, he acknowledged, in the midst of a more visible "world revolution" which, in both its liberal and communist manifestations, seemed to be moving in a reverse direction. While liberalism and communism were collaborating in an anti-nationalist crusade, here were the Zionists seeking a manifestly national fulfillment: "the complete ingathering of the exiles into a socialist Jewish state." To explain the apparent contradiction, Ben-Gurion raised the same question Max Radin had raised: Have the builders of Israel no larger deed in view? Is the establishment of a Jewish socialist state on a few square miles of semi-arid soil between the Jordan and the Sea to be the ultimate goal?

"This is not," was Ben-Gurion's frank reply in 1944, "our ultimate goal. . . . The ingathering of the exiles into a socialist Jewish state is in fact only a precondition for the fulfillment of the real mission of our people. We must first break the constricting chains of national and class oppression and become free men, enjoying complete individual and national independence on the soil of a redeemed homeland. After that we can address ourselves to the great mission. . . ."

Israel's renowned philosopher Martin Buber had adressed himself to the same theme back in 1939, in a letter to Mohandas K. Gandhi who, despite his long friendship with Jews in South Africa and England as well as India, had advanced the view that "it is wrong and inhuman to impose the Jews on the Arabs" in Palestine. In Johannesburg, Gandhi had known two kinds of Jews: the wealthy, who, for social ease, "shared the racist attitudes of the British and Boer aristocracies," and the impoverished immigrants from Poland and Russia, whose ghetto life in South Africa was very like that of Ghandi's Indians. In those days, ghetto Jews had Gandhi's full sympathy as fellow-sufferers. But later in India he came to feel that the fate of Jews and Indians in other lands was a "nemesis they had brought upon themselves by their exclusiveness." In discussions with Jewish friends he did not hesitate "to attribute the sufferings of the Jews to their self-regarding conception of themselves as a chosen people," even as he attributed the "treatment of Indians overseas to the caste-system, based on a distinction between Aryan and non-Aryan, of their homeland."

About the nationalist-religious designs of the Jews in Palestine, Gandhi had written in 1938: " I have no doubt they are going about it in the wrong way. . . . Let the Jews who claim to be the chosen race prove their position on earth. Every country is their home including Palestine not by aggression but by loving service. A Jewish friend has sent me a book called *The Jewish Contribution to Civilization* by Cecil Roth. It gives a record of what the Jews have done to enrich the world's literature, art, music, drama, science, medicine, agriculture, etc. . . . They can now add to their many contributions the surpassing contribution of non-violent action."

With exceptional frankness, the learned Martin Buber defended the uncompromising militancy of the Zionist national claim on Palestine. "We cannot," he wrote, "renounce the Jewish claim; something even higher than the life of our people is bound up with this land, namely its work, its divine mission." After the State of Israel was established in 1948, Buber did not hesitate to say that mankind the world over would thereafter have to choose between two forms of world socialism, one God-centered, on the Israeli model, the other Godless, on the Marxist model. And he concluded: "We must designate one of the two poles between which choice lies by the formidable name of 'Moscow.' The other I would make bold to call 'Jerusalem'." (p. 141, in W. Herberg's *Martin Buber*, 1956)

It is this Zionist vision of Israel as a major step toward ultimate fulfillment of Jewish Biblical expectations that underlies the fiercest forms of anti-Semitism in our time, particularly in the Soviet Union and the Arab-Islamic world. After the Six-Day War of 1967, Soviet anti-Zionist propagandists, including several Jews, began to ask in effect why it was that Zionists were now presuming to match their "Jerusalem" model of socialism against the Moscow model as the hope of the world. They presume it, Soviet propaganda alleged, because they know themselves to be the "invisible power which controls the great western powers, the international press, etc." On this theme, the Oct. 4, 1967 issue of *Komsomolskaya Pravda* published the following:

"The adherents of Zionism in the U.S.A. alone number from 20 to 25 million people. . .Jews and non-Jews. They belong to associations, organizations and societies which play the greatest role in American economy, politics, culture, science. Zionist lawyers comprise about 70 per cent of all American lawyers; 60 per cent of the physicists (including those engaged in secret work on weapons of mass destruction) are Zionist, and over 43 per cent of industrialists." And on that same October 4, 1967, *Za Rubezhom* added this: "Zionism in our days is the ideology, organizational system, and practice of the Jewish bourgeoisie. Its basic creed [as contrasted with that of proletarian Jews in the Soviet Union] is anti-communism." (See L. Kochan's *The Jews in the Soviet Union Since 1917*, Oxford 1970, p. 336)

During the American Embassy hostage crisis, and until recently, the Ayatollah Khomeini seemed to accept that line. In earlier days, he had been more willing to believe that the Zionists would seek to overcome Islam by means of the Marxist-materialist ideology. But in the flare-up about the Shah's presence in the United States — facilitated by Henry Kissinger and David Rockefeller — the stress was almost exclusively on Zionist-American connections.

During the late 18th and 19th century, Western-European attitudes toward the Jews turned largely on the assumption that the manifest longing of most Jews for a homeland of their own made them untrustworthy citizens. The most liberal of governments, indeed, felt that true Jewish civic emancipation was incompatible with Jewish nationalist ardor. And Jewish leaders seeking civic emancipation understood this. It was only after civic emancipation had been attained on an individual basis that nationalist or Zionist emancipation could be effectively pursued. By the late 1800s, as Getzel Kressel observes in a chapter on "Zionist Utopias" (*Zionism*, Jerusalem, 1973, p. 228), it finally became socially acceptable for Zionists to call upon liberal governments of the West to support them in their apparently utopian aspirations to build a national Jewish homeland in Palestine.

In this connection, Kressel cites as typical the standpoint of Theodor Herzl in both his *Judenstaat* (Jewish State) and *Altneuland* (Ancient New Land) as well as that of H.P. Mendes — "one of the first American Jews to respond to Herzl's call" — whose novel, *Look-*

ing Ahead (1899), "expresses the essence of the Zionist vision: the Jewish state and Jerusalem, its capital, would be the center of world peace, and by the creation of the state, the nations of the world would redress the wrongs they had perpetrated throughout the ages."

Of course, it is absurd for any enlightened government to insist that, because they are occasionally tempted to emigrate to Israel, most Jews in foreign lands can be charged with adhering to the Zionist vision of ultimate Biblical expectations. Against such insistence, G.W.F. Hegel wrote with severity over a century and a half ago, and his words certainly apply today: "To exclude the Jews from civil rights [simply for being Jews] would rather be to confirm the isolation with which they have been reproached — a result for which the state refusing them rights would be blamable and reproachable, because by so refusing, it would have misunderstood its own basic principles, its nature as an objective and powerful institution." (*The Philosophy of Right*, Knox trans., p. 169)

2. Christian Political Pessimism

Christianity very early distinguished itself from traditional Judaism precisely by denying the Jewish ideal of a religious national state. In the 5th century A.D., St. Augustine summed up the difference in his authoritative commentary on the response of Jesus to Pilate's questions about His alleged kingship of the Jews. The great African bishop quotes and interprets:

"Hear then, ye Jews and Gentiles; hear, O circumcision; hear, O uncircumcision; hear, all ye kingdoms of the earth: I interfere not with your government in the world. . . . 'My kingdom,' He said, 'is not of this world.' What would you more? And he confirmed this by saying further: 'If my kingdom were of this world, then would my servants fight, that I should not be delivered to the Jews'."

From the time of Constantine through its last days, the Roman imperial government tried, of course, to use Christianity as a spiritual prop for its world rule. During the Middle Ages, too, political rulers who were also Christians tried to do the same, aspiring to constitute a so-called Holy Roman Empire which would spread finally around the world. But through the ages the best Church leaders have rigorously resisted every variety of political universalism in the name of Christ. St. Thomas, Roman Catholicism's chief teacher in the Middle Ages, was an anti-imperialist. Christianity, he insisted, was a universal spiritual community which fared best in its earthly pilgrimage when political regimes were many and diverse, and respected one another as equals before God in their separate stations. For individual Christians as citizens of earthly kingdoms, the distinctively Christian political ideal was, of course, that of chivalry. That ideal is operative today, justifying Christianity's claim that its adherents can be loyal citizens of any and all nations that will have them, even when one such nation, for reasons of state, may be obliged to wage war aganist another that numbers Christians among its soldiers.

3. Mohammed's "Revolution of the East"

Islam, last of three monotheistic religions rooted in the Mosaic tradition, started with the Arabs of the desert. It represented a revolutionary return to the desert monotheism of Moses, after Judaism had long since submitted to the lure of the city. Mohammed on horseback was, in Hegel's apt phrase, the great "Revolution of the East" which swept before it "all limits, all national distinctions, so that finally no particular claim of birth or possession is respected — only *man* as *believer.*" Possessed by a desert-nurtured, sublime impatience with particularity, the Mohammedans longed, as Hegel says, "to establish an abstract worship, and they struggled for its accomplishment with the greatest enthusiasm. This enthusiasm was fanaticism, that is, enthusiasm for something abstract."

Fanaticsm is essentialy destructive. It cannot endure the assertion of values it has not created. But Mohammedan fanaticsm, Hegel concludes, "was, at the same time, capable of the greatest elevation — an elevation free from all petty interests, and united with all the virtues that appertain to magnanimity and valor. *La religion et la terreur* was the principle in this case, as with Robespierre, *la liberté et la terreur.*"

Islam swept across Asia Minor and deep into India; across North Africa, into Spain and Southern Italy, Southeastern Europe and even France, before its desert zeal diminished. Its kingdoms, before the coming of the stern Turks — Asiatic equivalents of Europe's Norsemen — were lightly built, with no inclination to tolerate the awakening of national political consciousness, whether among its own ruling classes or the subject peoples. The duty of the faithful Islamic leader was to annihilate — even as the Marxist revolutionaries of our time seek to annihilate — all established institutions and values of the ancient regime. First comes revolutionary destruction and conquest, then (as Professor Mahdi of the University of Chicago writes in summing up the doctrine of Islam's chief political philosopher of medieval time, Alfarabi, c.870-960), "having made use of the advantages of war and compulsion to establish his divine law and to suppress the wicked and incorrigible, the ruler must return to promote friendship among citizens, and to the peaceful work of persuasion and free consent."

That's how it was in Islam's early centuries. First comes a whirlwind of destruction, a churning up of seas in which nothing abides. It is true that in its conquests Islam founded many kingdoms and dynasties — yet "all of them contingent," as Hegel says in his *Philosophy of History*, "built on sand." They were dynasties "destitute of the bond of organic firmness," kingdoms that "did nothing but degenerate," composed of individuals who "simply vanished." But where "a noble soul makes itself prominent — like a billow in the surging sea — it manifests a majesty of freedom," writes Hegel, "such that nothing more noble, more generous, more valiant, more devoted was ever witnessed. . . . Never has enthusiasm, as such, performed greater deeds. Individuals may be enthusiastic for what is noble and exalted in various particular forms. The enthusiasm of a people for independence has also a definite aim. But abstract and therefore all-comprehensive enthusiasm — restrained by nothing, finding its limits nowhere, and absolutely indifferent to all beside — is that of the Mohammedan East."

It is true that, at first, the Islamic conquerors destroyed whatever confronted them, including the culture, the arts and sciences, of the conquered. Hegel notes that "Omar is said to have caused the destruction of the noble Alexandrian library. 'These books,' said he, 'either contain what is in the Koran or something else: in either case they are superfluous.' But soon afterwards the Arabs became zealous in promoting the arts and spreading them everywhere.'' Indeed, by taking in the inherited culture of the Hellenized peoples of the ancient Near East, the armies of Islam brought together a Greek-based civilization more enduring than their dynasties and kingdoms — a civilization destined to serve the developing nations of Europe as a bridge back to the precious learning of ancient Greece.

"In the struggle with the Saracens,'' Hegel concludes, "European valor had idealized itself to a fair and noble chivalry. Science and knowledge, especially that of philosophy were kindled among the Germans (at the Hohenstauffen court in Sicily) by the East — a fact which directed Goethe's attention to the Orient and occasioned the composition of a string of lyric pearls, in his *Divan*, which in warmth and felicity of fancy cannot be surpassed. But the East itself, when by degrees enthusiasm had vanished, sank into the grossest vice. The most hideous passions became dominant, and as sensual enjoyment was sanctioned in the first form which Mohammedan doctrine assumed, and was exhibited as a reward of the faithful in Paradise, it took the place of fanaticism.''

Hegel wrote those words in the 1820s, when Islam had indeed been "driven back into its Asiatic and African quarters, and tolerated only in one corner of Europe through the jealousy of Christian powers.'' But now, after a century and a half of new tumults brought on by awakened impulses of nationalism and resurgent religion, brought to a fever-pitch by the rise of an Israeli state in the Muslim-Arab quarter of the world, Islamic fanaticism has produced not only militant Arabic nationalists and terrorists, but also the towering figure of a holy man of Allah, an Iranian Shiite who has forced all the world to take him seriously.

The Ayatollah Khomeini's first call has been, of course, for the destruction and elimination of all things Western in the Iranian Islamic world. At the Faiziyeh School in Qom, on September 8, 1979, less than two months before the second seizure of the American Embassy in Tehran, he had admonished the faithful in these words:

"All of the problems of Easterners and, among them, our

problems and miseries, are caused by our losing ourselves. In Iran, until something has a Western name, it is not accepted. Even a drug store must have a Western name. The material woven in our factories must have something in the latin script in its selvedges and a Western name put on it. Our streets must have Western names. Everything must have Western color in it. . . . Writers put a Western name on the books they write. . . . If our books did not have these titles, or our material did not contain that script and if our drug stores did not have that name, we would pay less attention to it. . . . Our universities were at that time Western universities. Our economy, our culture were Western. We completely forgot ourselves. . . . As long as you do not put aside these imitations, you cannot be a human being and independent. . . . As long as these names appear on our streets and our drug stores and our books, and our parks and in all our things, we will not become independent. It is only the mosques which do not have Western names and that is because the clergymen, until now, have not succumbed.''

The ideal of modernization in most Islamic countries of the Middle East since the formation of modern Turkey as a sovereign national state has been most aptly formulated by the statesmanly teacher of Kemal Ataturk, the learned philosopher, literary scholar, and sage, Ziya Gokalp. In 1923, Gokalp had written of the Turkish people and their new literary culture: ''We belong to the Turkish nation, the Islamic community, and Western civilization. . . . Our literature must go to the people and, at the same time, towards the West.'' The founder of the Iranian Pahlavi dynasty had been receiving similar advice from learned advisers — mostly English and German, however. But he did not appreciate the difference between Turks and Iranians, between one non-Arabic people that took its Muslim faith and Arabic script as spoils of conquest and another that had had that same faith and script imposed on it by conquering Arabs.

The Turks had ''moved forward,'' voluntarily, to form themselves as an ''Islamic Community,'' retaining their native language, but gladly taking up the script of the conquered to write it. In exactly the same spirit, they decided, in the 1920s, to give up the Arabic script, but not the Islamic faith; by choosing to write their Turkish language in Roman characters, they very deliberately and successfully sought to Westernize their civilization. For reasons that need to be explored at length in a later chapter, nothing quite of the same sort was possible for the Iranian people under the modernizing Pahlavi Shahs. They dared not "move forward" like the Turks, by abandoning their Arabic script and writing their Farsi in Latin characters, for they liked to pretend that the Iranian language — like their dynastic name — had a glorious history running back to times long before there were any Roman characters to write in. And thus, when Roman characters came to be used in modern Iranian books, it was always only to indicate foreign Western things, mostly American. The Ayatollah Khomeini reflected on the basic difference in his "sermon" of September 8, 1979, marking the anniversary of the "Black Friday" massacre of the same day, the 17th of Shahrivar, a year before.

"Do not forget," the Ayatollah recalled, "that we had a 17th of Shahrivar and we must not forget that on that day, we had so many martyrs and so much blood and the nation rose against foreigners and their agents. Blood was spilt, but it was victorious. . . . Recall the days when they attacked us with complete cruelty and you, with complete courage, your men and women, stood against then. Someone told me, 'I saw with my own eyes, that a child 10 or 12 was riding a motorcycle and went toward the tanks. The tank ran over and killed him.' A spirit was born which prompted a child to do such an act. Empty handed, a monarchical empire of 2500 years, 2500 years of criminals, was done away with. Do not forget your honor. . . . Push away and turn your backs on things which pull you to the West and trample upon your honor." [209]

Once again, as in the 7th century A.D., Islam had been called upon to overcome a decadent Iranian monarchic state. It came first to destroy. Would there follow a return of holy power in another form, as Alfarabi had put it, "to promote friendship among the citizens," engaging in "the peaceful work of persuasion and free consent"? If we may judge from the fanaticism of the Ayatollah Khomeini's doctrine and the popular response, *la religion et la terreur*, which Hegel sets against *la liberté et la terreur* of the French Revolution, may once again inspire fear in the ruling councils of many nations. Conceivably, mankind may yet be asked to choose among three, rather than just between two prospective centers of an enforceable world peace. Perhaps a symbolic Mecca, desert capital of so much of the world's oil resources, will have to be added to Martin Buber's Moscow and Jerusalem.

And have our Western advocates of an enforceable world peace, with all the tax-exempt American foundation capital-resources lending support, no American alternative to offer? Has anyone, since the days of James Burnham's *Struggle for the World* or President John F. Kennedy's inaugural address of 1961, lately talked as if Washington might itself dare to vie with Jerusalem or Mecca as a believable rival to Moscow? If zeal counts for anything, Washington can hardly count at all. Perhaps after an Israeli Jerusalem and an Islamic Mecca have fought out there round, the winner may indeed — on the strength of biblical and Koranic expectations — want to challenge Moscow.

4. The American Religious Legacy

On the other hand, it is perhaps just as well that few American champions of an enforceable world peace now look to Washington D.C. as a suitable peace-keeping capital. That represents a return to the views of the American Founding Fathers who, in their Declaration of Independence, claimed for their new republic only a "separate and equal station" among the powers of the earth. Such a modest station sufficed, in their view, to secure the blessings of liberty to themselves and their posterity. They believed, indeed, with Aristotle and St. Augustine, with St. Thomas and Locke, that the state is, at best, a necessary evil. It is built up initially — they knew from their own revolutionary experience — to gratify a variety of passions. But they knew also that, if free men are to endure political government, they must sooner or later reconstitute it as a bastion of right and order against their own worst appetites.

The American political legacy of just over two centuries teaches that the passionate, selfish aims and appetites of individuals and factional groups are best checked and balanced in the internal rationality of states framed, like the American republic, with a mixed constitution. And it teaches further that the self-centered interests of states, which usually end up being proclaimed as universal ideals, are best checked and balanced in a system of sovereign nation-states, each of which recognizes the right of every other to perish in battle, if need be, rather than have an alien political will imposed upon it, in the name of universal peace, or any other suggestively-humanitarian, universal value.

In the tradition that brought the *New Testament* teachings down to our founding fathers, the most important political lesson was, without question, the one that emerges from Pilate's interrogation of Jesus in the Gospel according to St. John, earlier cited in St. Augustine's commentary. When the Founder of Christianity was arrested on the charge that he was planning to set up an independent state within the territorial jurisdiction of another state, the local Roman governor pointedly asked him what he thought of the traditional prerogatives of political sovereignty. And the answers Jesus gave were frank and unequivocal — quite unlike those we are used to hearing from the radical-chic advocates of civil disobedience and "creative disorder" today.

"Knowest though not," Pilate asked Jesus, "that I have power to crucify you, and have power to release you?" In response, Jesus affirmed that such powers as the governor claimed over persons brought before the bar were legitimately his and were, indeed, God-given. "Thou couldst have no power at all against me," he answered, "except it were given to you from above." Pressed to say whether he actually claimed to be an independent king within the Roman jurisdiction, again Jesus didn't mince words. He did not for a moment deny his Messianic Kingship. Rather, he denied only that he had ever claimed to be a king of the Jews in an earthly Zionist sense. "My kingdom," Jesus assured Pilate, "is not of this world." And then he went on to indicate how basic and unalienable, in his judgment, is the right of an earthly state to wage war to prevent its subjugation by a foreign or alien will. "If my kingdom were of this world," said Jesus, "then would my servants fight that I should not be delivered to the Jews."

There is a powerful truth of political pessimism in that response. Jesus acknowledges that, if his kingdom were of this world, his servants would fight for its safety, and for him as its head, even against his fellow Jews, if they sought to subjugate him. His kingdom not being of this world, his servants or supporters were not to fight as if it were. Sovereign statehood could remain a desire of the Jews, he taught, only in the measure that they declined to accept him as the long-awaited Messiah. Jews as Christians were urged by Jesus to pledge allegiance to whatever states they happened to inhabit. He urged them to pay their taxes willingly and to render unto temporal rulers what the law prescribes, even when, as was often the case, those rulers pursued domestic and foreign policies which ran counter to traditional Jewish interests.

St. Peter and St. Paul, who considered themselves loyal Jews, fully shared the wordly political pessimism of their Master; and through them his doctrine passed to the Church Fathers, the greatest of whom — St. Augustine of Africa — traced out all its implications in a rounded theory of politics that was destined to dominate Christian thinking for over a thousand years. The Protestant Reformers, Luther and Calvin, no less than St. Thomas Aquinas, were heirs of the Augustinian legacy; and it was their immediate disciples who gave that unflinchingly realistic doctrine the modern relevance with which it is expressed in the writings of Hobbes, Locke, and Burke, as also in the authors of the American *Federalist Papers*.

Surely St. Peter and St. Paul would have felt themselves at home in the political doctrine of our *Federalist Papers*. For those papers are saturated with the realistic convinction that political government is at best a necessary evil. It is necessary because greater evils would be unleashed without it: because, apart from its legal, customary, and educational restraints, men tend to behave worse than the wildest beasts, perverting even reason itself (which is God's image in man) to gratify their most vicious appetites. And it remains evil all the while because, even when it functions most effectively, it can do so only by placing certain human beings in offices of concentrated power which can readily be abused. Power by its very nature tends to corrupt; but the worst of it is that, in the spheres of criminal justice and foreign relations, the necessities of government actually oblige persons in positions of highest trust to commit, for the common good, acts of the very kind that civilizing society, with its laws and education, attempts to repress in the conduct of the mass of its members.

In *Federalist Paper* No. 51, where he argues simultaneously for a concentration of powers to preserve the Union and for a separation of powers to guard against domestic tyranny, James Madison wrote: "Ambition must be made to counteract ambition." And on that principle of political realism he proceeded to erect his renowned defense of our constitutional system of checks and balances. "It may be a reflection on human nature," he explained, "that such devices should be necessary to control the abuses of government. But what is government itself, but the greatest of all reflections on human nature?" Then come these momentous words, the pessimistic sense of which might well have been drawn straight out of the Gospels, St. Paul, and St. Augustine:

> If men were angels, no government would be necessary. If angels were to govern men, neither external nor internal controls on government would be necessary. In framing a government which is to be administered by men over men, the great difficulty lies in this: you must first enable the government to control the governed; and in the next place oblige it to control itself. A dependence on the people is, no doubt, the primary control on the government; but experience has taught mankind the necessity of auxiliary precautions.

Madison, Alexander Hamilton, John Jay, authors of the *Federalist Papers*, were all of a mind that the first necessity of legitimate government is to provide for the common defense. As to the industrial and military power that would have to be concentrated in government to meet that necessity, Hamilton had urged that no limit could reasonably be prescribed. Authority "to raise armies; to build and equip fleets; to prescribe rules for the government of both; to direct their operations; to provide for their support. . .ought to exist without limitation," he wrote, "because it is impossible to foresee or to define the extent and variety of the means which may be necessary to satisfy them. The circumstances that endanger the safety of nations are infinite, and for this reason no constitutional shackles can wisely be imposed on the power to which the care of it is committed."

That sums up the dilemma of all free government. Power must

be concentrated for defense, but divided, checked, and balanced, to prevent its abusive application to purposes other than defense. How the dilemma was resolved in practice, students of the exercise of sovereignty by our great statesmen, from Washington and Jefferson to Jackson and Lincoln down through the World War Presidents Wilson and Roosevelt, are fully aware. The monumental center of Washington, D.C., becomes increasingly an unanswerable graphic reminder. One starts with the solemn statue of Abraham Lincoln and the words inscribed in stone behind it: "In this temple, as in the hearts of the people for whom he saved the Union, the memory of Abraham Lincoln is enshrined forever." That temple viewed from the air is plainly the crown of a mighty cross in our nation's capital — a cross that has Capital Hill at its base and the White House and Jefferson Memorial at the ends of its cross beam. Washington's monument, rising near the point where the long and short beams intersect, is like a spear in the side of an invisible savior of our body politic, for whose ultimate agony Lincoln Memorial, with all its solemn words, will one day serve as a fitting crown.

Washington, Jefferson, Lincoln — each of them confirmed in word and deed that profoundest truth of our Western Political tradition, both secular and Christian, which is that coercive government is at best a necessary evil, and that when free men and women deny either its evil or its necessity they must soon cease to be free.

That was the truth that guided Lincoln in responding to Horace Greeley's plea as an Abolitionist that Lincoln should use all his powers to put an end to slavery at all costs. Distinguishing sharply between his unlimited prerogative powers to do the negative work of preserving the Union and his properly checked and balanced positive powers to perfect it according to his personal ideas, Lincoln replied: "My paramount object in this struggle *is* to save the Union and is *not* to save or destroy slavery. . . . What I do about slavery and the colored race, I do because I believe it helps to save the Union; and what I forbear, I forbear because I do *not* believe it would help save the Union. . . . I have here stated my purpose according to my view of *official* duty, and I intend no modification of my oft-expressed *personal* wish that all men, everywhere, could be free."

We have there a pessimistic view of politics and history that is thoroughly American and thoroughly compatible with traditional Christianity, if not with the expectations of traditional Judaism or Islam. According to the Gospels, Jesus Christ was unmistakably a political pessimist. He did not pretend that earthly states could survive without an organized willingness to restrain domestic lawbreakers and to wage war. He taught that poverty could never be completely eliminated by human provision and rejected as utterly vain the age-old expectation that the world's wise men would one day succeed, through their collective wisdom, in transforming this vale of tears into a regime of happiness for all mankind.

CHAPTER FOUR

Ancient Israel
and the Ancient
Imperial Superpowers

Pahlavi, as we shall have occasion to discuss later, was the name of the Iranian language actually in use just before Mohammed's conquest of the country in the 7th century A.D. That fact has tempted some friends as well as foes of the modern Pahlavi shahs to suggest that the dethronement of that dynasty in early 1979, by the followers of the Ayatollah Khomeini, amounted to a second "Revolution of the East" — a repetition of what had happened in 642 A.D.

It must be granted, however, that the original Islamic conquest of Iran in the 7th century was not nearly as "anti-Zionist" in inspiration as the Ayatollah Khomeini's revolution appears to have been. Here again friends and foes alike (extremes meet, as the saying goes) tend to agree on at least one important point, namely: that when the triumphant Ayatollah stripped the Israelis in Tehran of what had been their equivalent of an embassy and handed it over to Yasser Arafat for the use of his Palestine Liberation Organization (P.L.O.), the event marked a major turning point in the long history of Jewish-Iranian relations.

We glanced at the historical beginnings of those relations in the first chapter. Needless to say, the Jewish people can claim a sacred history that extends far beyond the founding of the Persian Empire in the sixth century B.C. Still, as was noted in passing earlier, there is a sense in which it can be said that Judaism as it exists today — with a large diaspora or dispersion that looks to Jerusalem as its undisputed spiritual center and supports it as such — owes its existence to the policies of the ancient Iranian King Cyrus the Great and more particularly to their implementation during the reigns of kings Darius and Artaxerxes. The nature of the debt of post-biblical Judaism to Iran for its institutional supports that have survived to this day — non-biblical supports — merits close study in our time, for there are signs of efforts in Judaism itself (as well as among its Zionist non-Jewish secular and Christian supporters) to arrive at a reassessment of their abiding importance.

1. Iranian Foundations of Post-Biblical Judaism

America's most eminent biblical archeologist, William Foxwell Albright of The Johns Hopkins University discusses the matter at some length, suggesting contemporary parallels, in his long chapter on "The Biblical Period" of Jewish history contributed to Louis Finkelstein's four-volume work already cited. He there admonishes his readers, however, not to imagine that the Jews themselves were passive while the early occupants of the throne lately vacated by the Shah Mohammed Reza Pahlavi were arranging a postbiblical future for them.

In the *Old Testament* books of Ezra and Nehemiah (Esdras I and II in the Roman Catholic versions) and in the related chapters of Chronicles II, we can read for ourselves the major documents of ancient Iran's initiatives in behalf of the "captive Jews" who became its subjects when mighty Babylon fell to Cyrus in 539 B.C., "without a battle and without fighting." As cited by Ezra, the Edict of Cyrus issued in that year reads in retrospect like an ancient unequivocal version of the Balfour Declaration of 1917 A.D. It authorized "all Jews throughout the kingdom to return to Jerusalem to rebuild the Temple of Jehovah," stipulating further that "those who do not go should contribute toward the expenses of those who do, and also supply them with clothing, transportation, supplies for the journey, and a freewill offering for the Temple." Yet back then too, there was much opposition in Palestine to implementation of such an order. The new Jewish Temple appears to have been finished by 516 B.C. But in fact an entire century had passed before the high priest Ezra could record that all was finally done "as commanded by God and decreed by Cyrus, Darius, and Artaxerxes, the kings of Persia."

Ezra's *Memoir*, documenting the sixth and fifth century equivalents of our Kissinger shuttle-diplomacy, Camp David accords and Geneva conferences, and providing ancient counterparts of contemporary P.L.O. and other Arab protests, makes fascinating reading. But the central figure on the Jewish side in those days was the prophet Nehemiah — a man "endowed with unusual energy and presumably with exceptional charm" (as Professor Albright characterizes him) who had risen to cabinet rank in the government of the Persian King Artaxerxes Longimanus (465-424 B.C.).

Nehemiah was almost certainly a eunuch, since the office of high intimacy he held as special assistant to the Iranian king "required a eunuch to fill it"; "love for his people was so great, however," writes Albright, "that his physical handicap became an asset and he was able to serve Israel with rare singlemindedness." In his *Autobiography* (Esdras II in the Roman Catholic versions), Nehemiah certainly displays singlemindedness, as well as charm and energy. As Albright summarizes: "It appears to have been in December, 445, that Nehemiah learned from his brother Hanani and other Jews who had recently come from Jerusalem how bad the situation there really was. He seems to have been particularly moved by the news that the walls were still in ruins, a fact which made it possible for Arab, Edomite or Ammonite raiders to attack the unprotected city almost at will."

When the news from Palestine was confirmed beyond any doubt, Nehemiah sat down and wept, he tells us, refusing to eat for several days. Finally, his heart torn with guilt for having "forgotten Zion" — like so many successful Jews in the Diaspora — he decided to risk his post in the Gentile kingdom to do something for his people. Raising a prayerful voice to God, he said: "Please help me now as I go in to ask the king for a great favor. Put it into his heart to be kind to us." And then, in a statesmanly "diplomatic" style anticipating that of Henry Kissinger in the very best pages of *The White House Years*, Nehemiah thus dramatizes the "Rose Garden" or private dining-room sort of conversation which, in the view of the most competent historians, marked the beginning of post biblical Judaism:

One day in April [Nisan], four months later, as I was serving
the king with his wine set before him, he asked me. 'Why so sad?
You aren't sick, are you? You look like a man with deep troubles'.
(For until then I had always been cheerful when I was with him).
I was badly frightened, but I replied, 'Sir, why shouldn't I be sad?
For the city where my ancestors are buried is in ruins, and the gates
have been burned down.' 'Well, what should be done?' the king
said. With a quick prayer to the God of heaven, I replied, 'If it
please Your Majesty and if you look upon me with your royal favor,
send me to Judah to rebuild the city of my fathers!' The king replied, with the queen sitting beside him, 'How long will you be gone?
When will you return?' So it was agreed! And I set a time for my
departure!

Nehemiah asked for letters to the provincial governors to
guarantee his safe passage to Jerusalem, and authorization to requi-
sition from the imperial stores all the timber needed for the city walls,
gates, and fortresses, as well as a suitable house for himself. The
Iranian ruler granted all of that, and more. By 440, attended by
armed guards and bearing the royal rescripts, Nehemiah arrived in
Jerusalem, and in 439, "almost exactly 148 years after its destruction by the Chaldeans," he began the work of rebuilding the great
city wall. Through Nehemiah's intercession, the high priest Ezra also
received a royal rescript at the Iranian court at Susa, granting him
"extensive powers," as Professor Albright writes, "to reform the
religious organization at Jerusalem." In all that Ezra and Nehemiah undertook to do in those days, there seemed to be an underlying
assumption that the Iranian imperial rule was destined to last forever
and that the "union between the altar in Jerusalem and the throne
of Susa was natural and indestructible."

The fact that Nehemiah the prophet and Ezra the high priest
were fully supported in all they did by the might of the Persian kings
has led some of the most learned scholars to conclude that the form
of Judaism that then came into being may properly be called "a
creation of the Persian Empire." Professor Albright reminds us
that precisely that conclusion was "brilliantly defended" by the
great historian Eduard Meyer in *Die Entstehung des Judentums*

(*The Origin of Judaism*, Halle, 1897) and that Hans Heinrich Schaeder had more recently supplied extensive analytical documentation in *Esra der Schreiber* (Ezra the Scribe, Tuebingen, 1930). But Albright, as we have already noted, warns against a one-sided reading here. The claim that "Judaism was created by the Persian Empire" has really neither more nor less validity, he writes, "than the corresponding statement, sometimes heard, that 'Zionism has been created by the British.' We need not depreciate the role played by Cyrus and Nehemiah, by Lord Balfour and Lord Samuel, to recognize that in general there was more opposition than support among Persian and British officials. Judaism and Zionism were both developed by the Jewish people, working against great odds—so great, in fact, that without benevolent assistance at critical moments from the Persian and British imperial authorities success might have been impossible, in spite of the faith of the leaders of both movements."

2. Bickerman on the Iranian-Judaic Legacy

Those words were published in 1949. The British had just given up their imperial dominance in the Palestine area; the cold war that was to divide new-born Israel's two superpower sponsors, the U.S.S.R. and the U.S.A., was just then beginning; and Henry Kissinger's efforts to build up Mohammed Reza Shah Pahlavi as a twentieth-century re-incarnation of Artaxerxes Longimanus were still a long way off. Granted that in the days of Nehemiah and Ezra there was "more opposition than support" of the Jewish cause among Iranian officials, why did the Iranian kings respond as they did? What did they perceive to be their imperial interest in the foundation of postbiblical Judaism?

Elias J. Bickerman confronts that question head-on in his chapter on "The Foundations of Postbiblical Judaism" which immediately follows Albright's account of "The Biblical Period" in Finkelstein's anthology. From a purely secular standpoint, it can be said that the Iranian kings of the sixth and fifth centuries B.C., longing to rule all the diverse peoples of the world, sought to use the Jews as a supranational bureaucracy that could be trusted to support rather than disrupt the Iranian imperial scheme. Professor Bickerman's perspective is by no means purely secular; yet, as an historian fully worthy of the high respect accorded him by Professor William L. Westermann (to whose post as Professor of Ancient History at Columbia University he eventually succeeded), he approaches the question of Iran's contribution to the shaping of postbiblical Judaism with absolute adherence to the highest standards of secular scholarship.

Bickerman starts his chapter with an affirmation of the fact that the "sacred history of the Chosen People ends chronologically with Nehemiah's prayer: 'Remember us, O God, for good'.'' He notes that "in the Wisdom of Ben Sira, composed in Jerusalem about 190 B.C.," the prophet Nehemiah's name "concludes the praise of the Worthies," signifying that after Nehemiah we are "beyond the sacred" and have entered into the profane or postbiblical period of Jewish history. "Thus, even before the Maccabean revolt," he writes, "the Jews recognized that after Nehemiah and his contemporary prophets, that is, toward the end of the fifth century, in the age of Socrates, the postbiblical period of Jewish history begins. That period is marked by a unique and rewarding polarity: on the one hand, the Jerusalem center and, on the other, the plurality of centers of the Diaspora. The Dispersion saved Judaism from physical extirpation and spiritual inbreeding. Palestine united the dispersed members of the nation and gave them a sense of oneness. This counterpoise of historical forces is without analogy in antiquity."

Other peoples had of course been dispersed in antiquity; but in time the offshoots almost invariably "lost connection with the main stock." Bickerman cites the example of the Phoenician and Greek settlements around the edges of the Mediterranean — adorning it, Cicero would later say, like the tassels around a Roman senatorial toga — which never dreamed of making a return to their lands of origin. Other peoples in antiquity had seen their homes and cities destroyed by conquerors and had returned to rebuild them as soon as that became possible. Bickerman cites the example of the Greeks of Thebes who, eighteen years after Alexander destroyed their city, returned *en masse* to rebuild it. "The exceptional feature of Jewish history," he emphasizes, "is the reluctance of so many of the exiles to go back.'' Though their return was authorized and facilitated by the Iranian kings, most of the Jews chose to stay where they were: "they remained in Mesopotamia, but, paradoxically, continued to care for the Holy City generation after generation, for centuries and millenia.''

More specifically, as Bickerman says, the scattered Jews "continued to consider Jerusalem as the 'metropolis' (Philo), turned to the Holy Land for guidance, and in turn, determined the destinies of its inhabitants. Men who established the normative Judaism in Palestine — Zerubbabel, Ezra, Nehemiah — came from the Diaspora, from Babylon and Susa.'' Looking at this unique counterpoise of nationalism and cosmopolitan tendencies from a theological standpoint, one needs to add, writes Bickerman, that the "polarity of Jerusalem and the Dispersion had its ideological counterpart in the paradoxical combination of universal monotheism and particularism, in the conception that the sole Lord of the Universe dwells on the hillock of Zion. This theological paradox held the Jews of the Diaspora together, and from all points of the compass they directed their eyes to the Lord's Temple in Jerusalem.''

Professor Bickerman then links the ethnic-religious concerns of Nehemiah and Ezra with the Iranian imperial-political interests "which unwittingly enabled Israel to develop into a people alike at home in the ancestral land as well as in the lands of the Dispersion.'' It was no small thing that Jews of the caliber of Nehemiah and Ezra, "born and reared in the fifth generation in the Diaspora,'' should have "risked disgrace to obtain royal favor for the Holy City.'' Professor Albright, as we saw, compares Nehemiah's post in Iran's Palestine of the fifth century B.C. with Sir Herbert Samuel's in England's twentieth-century Palestine; and similarly, in *Egypt Under Babylon and Persia* (Oxford, 1970), Professor P.R. Ackroyd suggests that Ezra might be viewed as "a sort of 'secretary of state for Jewish affairs'.'' Why should an Iranian "king of kings'' (*shahanshah*) have seen fit to appoint Iranian Jews to posts of ultimate authority in Palestine?

Scholars agree that, shortly before Nehemiah's assignment to the Jerusalem post, the whole province or satrap "Beyond the River'' had risen up in rebellion against Artaxerxes I, supported by anti-

Iranian forces in Egypt. "Palestine," Bickerman stresses, "is the bulwark of Egypt. As Napoleon observed, domination over Palestine is indispensable if one wishes to protect the valley of the Nile." Iran's empire included Egypt; Judah was thus "important for the approach roads to Egypt, and Egypt was a continuing source of anxiety." That would explain the choice of Nehemiah as *tirshatha* in Jerusalem. In the words of Professor Ackroyd: "A loyal governor there, who owed his position to the personal favor of the Persian king, could be a valuable support for Persian control of the west. . . . Similar considerations may apply in the case of Ezra."

Accordingly, for serious scholars the critical question that suggests itself at this point is this: How many of the "changes of great moment in the political, social, and religious life of the Jews" that Nehemiah and Ezra introduced owed their acceptance to the "force of Gentile law" that backed them, rather than to any intrinsic "Jewishness" of their own? Or, to put it in another way: From the point of view of the Jews of Jerusalem and the Diaspora upon whom they imposed it, could it not be said that the form of Judaism institutionalized by Nehemiah and Ezra was something essentially new — a substantively Iranian creation?

Max Radin, whose *Jews Among the Greeks and Romans* was cited earlier, stresses the continuity with the past. Evidence of such continuity, he acknowledges, is lacking; we can "only conjecture the stages of the process," since, from the standpoint of reliable sources, "the Persian period forms the largest gap in the history of the Jews." Certainly if we compare what the state of the Jews was in the seventh century with what it became after Ezra and Nehemiah, the contrast is impressive. Before Ezra and Nehemiah there had not been an institutionalized Diaspora or a fixed canon of the *Torah* or a prescription that the Five Books of Moses (Pentateuch) be read through, with expositional commentaries, in every Synagogue in the course of each year. Certainly the concept of the synagogue itself — with its threefold use as the House of Prayer (*Beth Tephila*), House of Study (*Beth Hamidrash*), and House of Assembly (*Beth Haknesset*) — was new, to say nothing of Ezra's draconic remedy against the sort of "religious apostacy which foreign marriages would bring."

On the contrast between the old and the new in this regard, Professor Bickerman is quite specific. The Jews of the Ezra-Nehemiah Restoration, he writes, remained "convinced that God set them apart from the nations (Lev. 20:24), but they called Him the God of Heaven, which was the title of Ahuramazda, the deity of their Persian rulers." They "imagined that they were living according to the Law of Moses," he continues, "while the synagogue, unknown to the Torah, became a fundamental part of their devotional life," so that the "congregation of the Lord" became institutionalized as the "basic element of the nation." But the innovation of perhaps greatest significance, he says, was the Ezra-inspired "democratization of the instruction in the Law" which "opened the way to the coming of the scribe, and imperceptibly compromised the supremacy of the priest. From now on, the superiority of learned argument over authoritative decree prevailed." In other words, the religious community of the Jews is in large measure secularized, at least to the point where "the model of happiness," as Bickerman writes, is no longer "the officiating priest in the Temple, but rather the Sage who meditates on the Torah day and night. Scribes and Sages, clergy and laymen, the Jews were expected to be 'saints,' holy unto the Lord (Lev. 20:26). But the Law of God which gave the standard of holiness was imposed upon the saints by the decree of their pagan sovereign."

Bickerman thus prepares us for his general conclusion about the "debt" of postbiblical Judaism to imperial Iran for the "unique and rewarding" Jerusalem-Diaspora polarity that thereafter characterizes it. Without a trace of equivocation, he writes: "The spiritual unity of the Jews could hardly be established around Jerusalem if the whole Orient, from the Indus to Ethiopia, had not been one world obeying the orders issued by the Persian king. By its influence at the royal court, the Diaspora in Babylonia and Persia could act in behalf of Jewry everywhere and impose a uniform standard of faith and behavior." That confirms Eduard Meyer's view, discussed by Albright, that postbiblical Judaism "was created by the Persian Empire." There is no denying, Bickerman continues, that "the reestablishment of normative Judaism after the Exile is connected by both Jewish tradition and modern scholarship" with the revered name of Ezra, the high priest "who restored the Law of Moses";

but he hastens to acknowledge that, "unlike Moses, Ezra's authority to promulgate and administer the Torah in Jerusalem was not derived from a Divine Revelation." Ezra, Bickerman reminds his readers, "arrived in Jerusalem as a Persian commissioner with a royal letter placing 'the Law of thy God' on the same compulsory level as the law of the king, and threatening the offender of Mosaic precepts with death, banishment, confiscation of goods and imprisonment. In this way the perpetual character of the Torah was established and the Divine Law made known and imposed on all Jewry under the Persian scepter."

Never before had the Chosen People relied on pagan rulers for their religious integrity as well as for their temporal security. In those days of intimacy between the Jerusalem altar and the Iranian throne, we hear nothing about the longed-for "Messianic age which was destined to come after the overthrow of the Persian world power." Armies, we are told, were "superfluous for Israel" under the circumstances, since "the Jews need not fight when the Lord is with them," bending the will of rulers of world empires to their cause. In those days, pagan Iran — Zoroastrian, Magian Iran — had no Islamic masses that might rise up resentfully, at the call of an Ayatollah Khomeini, to overthrow a "king of kings" who presumed to use Iranian force and revenues to support the cause of world Jewry. Bickerman, to be sure, wrote the words we are citing in the late 1940s, long before the current Israeli-Iranian crisis. Even so, he was able to provide this brilliantly suggestive summary of things to come for postbiblical Judaism after the days of Nehemiah and Ezra:

> When, after the dissolution of the empire of Alexander the Great, about 300 B.C.E., the unity of the political world of which the Jews were a part had been broken, their religious and spiritual cohesion remained firmly established on the foundations laid down during the Persian age by Ezra and Nehemiah, King Darius and King Artaxerxes. The imperial protection shielded the Palestinian Jewry from the Arabs and the Philistines, Edom and Moab. In the background of Jewish history in Palestine, from the time of the Judges, there was a constant drive of Aramaic and Arab nomads against the settled country whose comforts they envied.

Persian, and later, Macedonian, frontier guards secured from now on the peace of the Jewish peasant. If Jerusalem had not been part of a Gentile empire, the nomads would have driven the Jews into the sea or swallowed up Palestine, and the rock of Zion would have been the foundation of an Arabian sanctuary a thousand years before Omar's mosque.

We have cited the views of many eminent scholars — W.F. Albright, Eduard Meyer, Max Radin, and Elias J. Bickerman — on the still-controversial thesis that postbiblical Judaism (Judaism as it exists institutionally today) can perhaps be regarded as a "creation of the Persian Empire." The judgment of Professor Bickerman just quoted at length — noting that, except for the support of a Gentile empire, the ancient Jews might well have been driven into the sea by Arab nomads soon after the days of Ezra and Nehemiah — stands as a reminder of the contemporary implications of ancient Iranian-Israeli relations. It is impossible to study the history of those relations without thrilling to the parallels offered, for instance, by Henry Kissinger's account in his memoirs of his dealings with Shahanshah Mohammed Reza Pahlavi between 1972 and 1980.

Bickerman candidly notes that, as an alternative to driving the ancient Jews of Palestine into the sea, the Arab nomads of the surrounding lands, if not restrained by Aryan-Gentile empires, might simply have "swallowed up Palestine"; in which case, as he says, the "rock of Zion would have been the foundation of an Arabian sanctuary" a thousand years before the erection of the great Mosque of Omar.

But Gentile-Aryan empires seemed always to be at hand, eager to support the cause of the Jews against their ancient Arab-Semitic cousins. Indeed, during the thousand years before Muslim-Arab armies took possession of the rock of Zion, the Jews of Palestine saw diverse Gentile-Aryan rulers come and go. Alexander the Great who conqured the ancient Iranian empire in 333 B.C. started the succession. After his death in 324, his ambitious generals fought for his empire. But they succeeded only in dividing his "one world" into three parts, and with it the diaspora of the Jews, which was thereafter never again to be "under one law." The European successor state, Macedonia, ruled by the descendants of Antigonus, had no direct impact on the fate of Judaism in those days. But the new Kingdoms of Africa and Asia, ruled by the descendants of Ptolemy in Egypt and Seleucus in Syria, were soon struggling for possession of Palestine as the key to control of the Nile Valley.

During that century-long struggle, the cultural-political pressures on the Jews of Palestine mounted steadily. In the great cities of the Diaspora it was relatively easy for Jews to adapt themselves to the cosmopolitan environment. But in Palestine and particularly in Jerusalem, difficult choices had to be made, with some Jews favoring the Ptolemies of Egypt, others the Syrian Greeks, and still others trying to maintain a middle or neutral position. At any rate, it was only with the definitive triumph of the Syrians, around 200 B.C., that foreign rule seemed to become, for the first time, religiously insupportable. The crisis came under the secular-minded Greek King of Syria, Antiochus IV, who reigned from 175 to 163 B.C. In twentieth-century terms. Antiochus might have passed for a liberal humanist on the intellectual pattern of an Arnold Toynbee. Encouraged by some "progressive" Jews, he seems to have imagined he could push through a "crash program" of total modernization — a program far more extreme, to be sure, than the sort of thing attempted for traditional Islamic Iran by the Pahlavi Shahs of the twentieth century.

The result was a time of oppression that culminated in a revolt without precedent in Jewish history. At first, the upheaval was almost exclusively religious in character. A time came, however, when the Syrian officials tried to induce an aged priest of great spiritual authority to lead the way in abandoning the old worship. His name was Mattathias. The king's officers invited him to "bring his sons and brethren" to the new sacrifice, in the expectation that "the influence of his character and office, as a ruler, might induce others to follow his example; that he might thus be regarded as one of 'the king's friends'." No doubt with the stern prophetic aspect of an Ayatollah Khomeini, Mattathias thundered out his protests. But, while he was doing that, "he saw one of the apostate Jews come forth to the altar to offer sacrifice. . . . Inflamed with zeal, he ran toward the culprit, and, in the sight of all the people, inflicted on him the punishment which the law denounced against idolatry — he slew him upon the altar. He also slew the king's commissioner."

As soon as Mattathias with his son and supporters had retreated to a place of safety where they could lay plans for the future, there came upon them a realization that, for "reasons of state," Jews of their stamp would have to abandon at once the traditional "religious obligation to avoid all war like operations on the holy Sabbath." That was indeed — as the English Assyriologist George Smith astutely observed in his classic study of *The Hebrew People* (2 vols., London, 1859) — "a most important decision, and had a mighty influence on the results of the ensuing war." Not the traditional religious obligations of the Ezra-Nehemiah restoration, which had had the force of Iranian-Gentile law behind them, but the "safety of the nation," of the Jewish people as a potentially sovereign political community, would thereafter have to be the highest law.

Accordingly, old Mattathias marched grimly from town to town, imposing a "forced unity," a rigid conformity, on all Jews, as something indispensable for the safety of the whole. When finally he found his end approaching, he "exhorted his sons to devote their lives to the holy cause. . . . He advised them to regard their brother Simon as their counsellor, on account of his wisdom; and Judas he appointed the captain, because of his strength and bravery: him he surnamed Maccabeus, or 'the hammerer'," (Charlemagne's grandfather Charles, who halted the Muslim advance into Western Europe at Tours and Poitiers in 732 A.D., Smith noted here, has similarly been surnamed Martel, the hammer.)

The Hebrews had had their Exodus; now, under their "hammerer," they were to have their War of Independence. Putting the event in juridical-historical perspective, George Smith wrote: "From the time of their return from captivity the Jews had been always in entire subjection to Gentile powers. At first they were a part of the Persian Empire; they then passed under the dominion of Alexander; on the division of his kingdom they were subjected to Egypt; and, lastly, had been attached to the Greek kingdom of Syria. Nor is it probable that the Jews would have made any vigorous efforts to obtain self-government, if they had been ruled with tolerance."

But there was another side to that celebrated uprising of the Maccabees. Even the "insane impiety of Antiochus" might have remained endurable had it not been for the obvious decline and fragmentation of his kingdom. The Parthians, kinsmen of the old Persians, had already seized most of the provinces east of the Euphrates; but, of greater importance, to the west, as Smith phrased it, "the mighty power of Rome was steadily advancing, giving constant evidence of her great purpose and destiny — to govern the world. It was, therefore, the manifest policy of Rome to encourage, rather than suppress, efforts made by states, subject to the kingdoms of Syria and Egypt, for the purpose of obtaining independence. Under such circumstances Judas commenced his martial career."

With Rome's support, therefore, the Jews ousted their Syrian rulers and went on to enjoy several generations of *de facto* independence. In time, however, their self-rule lapsed into a tyranny of its own. Desperate struggles for power ensued. At last, appeals were made to Roman military commanders in the area to intervene, with a vague expectation that the new western empire might conceivably transform itself, before long, into another benevolent Iran. The Romans intervened; Judea was quickly incorporated in the emergent *pax Romana*; local rulers eagerly sought the good will of the Pompeys, the Julius Caesars, and the Augustus Caesars; and the Caesars, in turn, learned to make the same sort of use of the "unique and rewarding" postbiblical Diaspora-Jerusalem polarity that the Iranian kings and Alexander the Great had made.

But having acquired a taste for self-rule, some factions in Jerusalem began to look with displeasure on the willingness of Jewish leaders to collaborate with the keepers of the cosmopolitan peace of Rome. As the Jewish historian Josephus informs us, at the time of the suicide of Nero, in 68 A.D., when the "affairs of the Romans were in great disorder [at home, three emperors came and went in the course of a single year!], those Jews who were for innovations then arose" to challenge the Roman peace in Palestine, hoping that "all of their nation who were beyond the Euphrates would have raised an insurrection with them," backed by the armies of the Parthians. Unhappily, the Jews beyond the Euphrates didn't move, the armies of the Parthians didn't come. And so, in 70 A.D., the Zealots concentrated within the walls of Jerusalem had to face the imperial armies of Titus alone. In the end, the Holy City and its Temple were razed to the ground, and there occurred a second forced scattering of Jews, destined to last almost 2000 years.

3. Israel Under the Greeks and Romans: Toward a Portable Homeland

One has to stress, however, that the Jews of the late first century A.D. were far better prepared to deal with a forced scattering than their ancestors of biblical times had been. Nehemiah and Ezra had not labored in vain. The Diaspora administrative system created under Iranian auspices was functioning. And there had been added to it the tremendous impact of cosmopolitan Greek culture, which only the Jews and Romans in antiquity fully absorbed. Back in 280 B.C., long before the Syrian conquest of Palestine, the Greek King Ptolemy II of Egypt had urged the Jewish scribes of Alexandria to translate their Torah into Greek. This they immediately undertook to do; and, as Professor Bickerman tells it, for three centuries thereafter, Greek-educated Jewish scholars "did not cease from rendering their books into the world's common language" — a "venture of translating. . .unique in antiquity."

Had that venture not been made, the ancient scriptures in Hebrew characters might have suffered the same fate as the ancient Egyptian hieroglyphic and the Mesopotamian cuneiform writings. "By translating liberally its literature, sacred and profane, new and old, into the world language," writes Bickerman, "Judaism preserved its vitality. Moses and his law, or the revelations of the Jewish seers, entered and filled in the mental world of the proselytes as if the latter had been born in Abraham's posterity. The Jews became 'people of the Book' when this Book was rendered into Greek."

It was with a Diaspora shaped under the Iranians and a Book in the universal langugage of the Greeks that postbiblical Judaism faced up to the challange of irresistible Roman power. And then, in the very process of being overwhelmed physically by that power, it reached out for a third element indispensable for its survival —

what Judah Goldin and many other scholars have aptly called "a portable homeland." In the very midst of the fighting, so Professor Goldin writes, the great Rabbi Johanan ben Zakkai, leader of the Pharisees of Jerusalem, "perceived that arms could not save Judaism," and that "neither would pessimism nor spiritual timidity." He had "pleaded with the war parties to submit," but none would heed him; so he "had himself smuggled out of the leaguered city (in a coffin), made his way to the Roman camp, and submitted a petition — Would Rome grant him and his disciples refuge in the coastal city of Jabneh where he might establish an academy?"

Titus the conqueror would later have a coin minted with the inscription *Judea capta*. And the sculptures on his triumphal arch in Rome would vividly memorialize scenes of Jerusalem's destruction. Yet, while the fighting was still going on, despite the fanaticism of the Zealots, the Roman commander had granted the Rabbi's request. By the cosmopolitan Gentile grace of Vespasian's imperial son Titus, therefore, a Professor Goldin has been permitted to observe in our time that "the battle cries on Mt. Zion had not yet subsided when from Jabneh the voices of the scholars could be heard."

Almost as if to compensate for the destruction of Jerusalem, Rome greatly increased the sweep of the Jewish Diaspora in the West. In the East, however, the more prudent emperors had drawn a line at the Euphrates — a sort of watery equivalent of today's iron curtain — beyond which they really did not care to extend their legal jurisdiction. East of the Euphrates, as Josephus so pointedly stresses, the "upper barbarians" or Parthians ruled. They had displaced the Syrian-Greeks in the third century B.C., and for four-hundred years thereafter they "divided the world with the Romans," against whom they constantly waged war. Gradually, as they relaxed their discipline, their provinces broke away; and, by 226 A.D., all was finally lost to the Sassanid Persians who claimed direct descent from Cyrus, Darius, and Artaxerxes, and whose sway lasted until the Arab Conquest of 650 A.D.

Through all those centuries of Syrian, Parthian, and Sassanid-Persian rule east of the Euphrates, the Jews of the Babylonian Diaspora remained outsiders — mere onlookers — with respect to their brethren in the Roman Empire; and their fate was very different.

From the time of the Maccabees down to that of the Zealots who faced the army of Titus, it had been common knowledge in Palestine how well things had been going for Jews under the Parthians. As Professor Goldin relates, before 70 A.D., "contributions from the Babylonian Jews flowed steadily and liberally," in the form of Rabbinical learning as well as money. But money and learning had not sufficed, apparently, to set the Parthians on the march while there was still hope of saving the Temple.

At any rate, in the second and third centuries A.D., the scattered Jews of the West witnessed many marvels. They saw the Caesars respond again and again with fierce persecution to the rise of a Judaic "cult" called Christianity. Then they saw the Christianized empire divide itself into Western Latin-speaking and Eastern Greek-speaking (Byzantine) halves. And all the while, without relief, they had seen the symbol of the Crucified Messiah — "unto the Jews a stumbling block and unto the Greeks foolishness" — raised aloft on churches and imperial banners from the Atlantic to the Euphrates, as also upon the rock of Zion itself.

Fortunately, from the standpoint of the Jews, there was, all that while, Rome's more or less self-imposed barrier of the Euphrates, beyond which Babylonian Jewry flourished. As Professor Goldin observes in tracing the development of the Babylonian Talmud, "there were cities in that country — Nehardea, for instance — which were entirely inhabited by Jews." By the third century A.D., he elaborates, Babylonian Jewry could indeed "point with pride to its organized community life. There were courts, synagogues, schools, communal facilities; Jews filled public and commercial offices; the political representative of the Jews was actually a leading dignitary of the Parthian and Persian courts. He was known as the Exilarch, Resh Galuta, the chief or prince of the Exile; and. . .when the royal house was friendly or tolerant, Jewish communities were so self-sufficient as to justify the description of their being a state within a state."

For a brief time after the fall of the Parthians, the Babylonian Jewish community had indeed felt profoundly threatened. The Sassanid Persians undertook with much zeal to revive the Zoroastrian faith neglected by the Parthians. While other cults were being restricted, Zoroastrian priests were encouraged to write their commentaries on the sacred Avesta in the revived "national language": a mixed Persian dialect that came to be called *Pahlavi* — like the latest Shahs! — because it had been spoken by the Parthians (*Pahlavas* in Persian) who had not, however, reduced it to writing. But before long, the Sassanids took up where the Parthians had left off in waging incessant war against Byzantine Christendom. Once again Babylonian Jewry was drawn into public service and prospered; and once again, as in the days of the Zealots, a depressed Palestianian Jewry looked to the East for an army of deliverance. In the end, Rome's Christian soldiers were in fact driven out of the Holy Land: not by light-worshiping Iranians, however, but by the much feared Arabs of the desert whom the Gentile emperors, from Cyrus and Alexander down through the Caesars and the last of the Sassanids, had so long held in check.

CHAPTER FIVE

Iran After Mohammed's Conquest: A Nation of Shiite Martyrs

As we come to focus on Islamized Iran, we must, however, break off our historical narration and assume a present-day perspective. We earlier drew parallels between recent Israeli history and events of the times of Artaxerxes and Nehemiah. We must now remind ourselves that, if Henry Kissinger, in his dealings with President Nixon and the last of the Pahlavi Shahs, recalls the statesmanly labors of Nehemiah in the pre-Islamic Iranian capital at Susa, the Ayatollah Khomeini recalls, in no less striking a manner, the Islamic conquerors who swept across Iran in the 7th century A.D., burying its ancient civilization under the whirling sands of their desert faith.

1. Pahlavi Imperial Dreams and Shiite Alienation in the 1970s.

December 11, 1978, was surely a critical day in Islam's contemporary history. Fittingly, on that day, the very knowledgeable Israeli journalist Walter Eytan focused his "Dateline Jerusalem" column for the American *Hadassah Magazine* on the theme: "Israel's Oil Supply From Iran May End." In the days of Nehemiah, the Iranian natural resource on which the safety of Jerusalem Jewry depended had been timber for city walls, gates, and fortresses; now it was oil, to keep the most advanced military-industrial complex in the Middle East running. But the chief external danger was still what it had been then: the great Arab masses in the neighboring lands, always threatening either to drive the Jews into the sea or simply swallow up Palestine.

Eytan began by reminding his readers of the ancient links between Iran and Israel, and of the efforts of the Pahlavi Shahs, since 1925, to surround their throne with an aura of their country's pre-Islamic imperial grandeur. "In 1936," Eytan wrote, "the Persian 'King of Kings,' the usurper who was the father of the present Shah, decided to revive his country's primitive name of Iran. To this day, though the Persian tongue [the Sassanid *Pahlavi*] is written in Arabic characters, there are few things that will anger an Iranian more than to hear his country confounded with the Arab world." All of which, Eytan had hastened to add, "help explain why Iran, albeit discreetly, cultivated relations with Israel — so much so that thousands of Israelis are employed there today, mostly in development of the country's industrial infrastructure, and you can fly El Al nonstop from Tehran to Tel Aviv."

But on December 11, 1978, the searing question — and not for Israel alone, according to Eytan — was this: How much longer could such a situation last? How soon before the Muslim masses in Iran rise up against a Shah who bans traditional Shiite street processions [over 93% of all Iranians are Shiite Muslims] and plainly sides against the Palestinian Arabs by supplying Israel with virtually all the oil she uses? Eytan noted that, according to its lunar calendar, Islam was already deep in the "month of Muharram, whose first ten days are a period of mourning for Shiites," during which they "work themselves into a fury and frenzy in memory of the prophet Mohammed's grandson, the martyred Imam Hussein." In fact, that very day which had not yet run its course at the time of writing, December 11, happened to be, in 1978, the tenth of Muharram, the *Ashura*, Islam's high holy day of repentance when, in Eytan's words, "the massed faithful are particularly receptive to religious incitement."

Without mincing words, the Israeli journalist then added that, unfortunately, Iran's Muslim masses "are now viscerally anti-Israel, and it will be a miracle if this is not translated into persecution of Iran's own Jews." As leader of those masses, the Ayatollah Khomeini, already based in France, had called specifically "for 'rivers of blood' to flow in the streets on the 10th of Muharram . . . to topple the monarchy.'' Tape-recorded sermons smuggled into the country had urged the faithful to defy the Shah's ban on traditional Muharram processions. According to the aged exiled ''Imam,'' the Shah's blatantly secular modernization programs and his pro-Israel leanings were all of a piece. Since his shamelessly pagan display of ''Ozymandian megalomania'' at Persepolis in 1971, the man who now called himself ''Light of the Aryans'' (*Aryamehr*) as well as ''King of Kings'' (*Shahanshah*) had apparently become ''an easy dupe of Henry Kissinger and the Zionists.'' Charmed by Kissinger's almost biblical flattery, he had let himself be cajoled into sacrificing Iran's Muslim integrity and precious oil reserves to procure useless arms, conspiratorial intelligence services, and over-priced technology. He succumbed to the delusion, in brief, that he might become another Cyrus the Great or Artaxerxes, to be celebrated as such by tomorrow's Ezras and Nehemiahs.

Rivers of blood did flow in Tehran on the night of December 11, 1978. At an intersection now known as Martyrs' Square, the Shah's troops, ordered to enforce the law, fired into the teeming masses, ''killing more than a thousand people gathered at a mosque for the procession.'' The Ayatollah Khomeini called it a renewal in fact of Islam's greatest ''self-inflicted shame,'' for which all Muslims, Shia and Sunni alike, have traditionally done penance on that very day.

In the Islamic tradition, the term Shiite means ''factional'' or ''partisan''; and it is important to stress that, as distinct from Sunnite or ''orthodox'' Muslims, the Shiites are indeed partisans of an idea of governmental legitimacy that has a complex and radical bearing on the Middle East crisis today. Specifically, Shiites hold that the valid succession of leadership in Islam ran by direct blood line from Mohammed through his son-in-law and cousin Ali to his grandchildren Hassan and Hussein (sons of his daughter Fatima); and not, as the Sunnites hold, through the so-called orthodox successors — Abu Bekr, Omar, and Othman — who had become caliphs before Ali by right of election, not blood relationship.

When he was belatedly elected in 656 A.D., upon the death of Othman, Ali too became a so-called ''orthodox'' caliph. But he immediately faced uprisings by princes who declared themselves to be opposed on principle to claims or pretensions of blood. Ali was killed in 661. His son Hassan succeeded him, but was forced to abdicate at once in favor of Moawiyah, founder of the Omayyad dynasty. For a time Hassan received great public respect as head of the surviving family of Mohammed; yet in the end he was mysteriously poisoned and died. Defying tradition, Moawiyah then boldly designated his own son Yazid as heir apparent. But the ambitious Yazid, anxious to secure the succession, greatly feared the claims of Hassan's younger brother Hussein. We come thus to the event of "greatest shame in Islamic history."

2. The "Shame of Islam": The Kerbela Massacre of 680 A.D.

What is the event of "greatest shame in Islamic history"? For all Muslims to some extent, but for Shiite Muslims particularly, there can be no doubt that it was the brutal slaughter of virtually all the blood-descendents of Mohammed the Prophet on the plains of Kerbela (in modern-day Iraq) during the Muharram mourning period of 680 A.D. By that year, the distinction between Sunnite or orthodox Muslims and Shiite or unorthodox-partisan Muslims had already been sharply drawn. The orthodox were those who "espoused the ancient Arabic tradition of succession by election"; the unorthodox, those who "desired succession by inheritance, through blood-relationship to the Prophet." But, during the caliphate of Moawiyah (661-680 A.D.), as we saw, the Sunnites brazenly reversed themselves to claim succession by inheritance for Moawiyah's son Yazid, who then proceeded to secure his succession by mass murder of the Shiite descendents of Mohammed, with the Imam Hussein at their head.

　　　The best introduction to that "tragedy of Kerbela" (which just happened to have occurred during the Muharram mourning period) is still Edward G. Browne's account of it in his monumental *Literary History of Persia* (Cambridge, 1902-1924). Every serious student of Iranian political and cultural history is familiar with Browne's contributions in the field, which provide the indispensable base for further study. In his *Nationalism in Iran*, for instance, Richard W.

Cottam aptly identifies Browne not as a literary historian but as the "brilliant British Iranist" who, in his vivid account of *The Persian Revolution of 1905-1909* (Cambridge, 1910), proved that he "understood the emerging liberal nationalist movement more fully than any man, Iranian or foreign." Certainly Browne, who was a tireless scholar, enjoyed an incomparable mastery of the literary-cultural inheritance of modern Iran. And it was as a master of that inheritance that he studied the striking phenomenon of the annual commemoration, both ritualistic and theatrical, of the Kerbela martyrdoms during the Muharram period of mourning. Drawing on old Muslim historians for details, Browne had thus introduced the subject in his literary history:

> No name is more execrated throughout Islam, but most of all in Persia, than that of Yazid. A Persian who will remain unmoved by such epithets as 'liar,' 'scoundrel,' or 'robber,' will fly into a passion if you call him Yazid. . . . 'His reign,' says al-Fakhri, 'lasted three years and six months. In the first year he slew al-Hussein, the son of Ali (on both of whom be Peace!); in the second year he sacked Medina and looted it for three days; and in the third year he attacked the Ka'ba.'
>
> Of these three outrages, the first in particular sent a shudder of horror throughout the Mohammedan world. . . . It was not only a crime but a gigantic blunder. . . . The *Shia* or 'faction' of Ali had hitherto been sadly lacking in enthusiasm and self-devotion; but henceforth all this was changed, and a reminder of the blood-stained field of Kerbela, where the grandson of the Apostle of God fell at length, tortured by thirst and surrounded by the bodies of his murdered kinsmen, has been at any time since then sufficient to evoke, even in the most lukewarm and heedless, the deepest emotion, the most frantic grief, and an exaltation of spirit before which pain, danger, and death shrink to unconsidered trifles.
>
> Yearly, on the tenth of Muharram the tragedy is rehearsed in Persia, in India, in Turkey, in Egypt, wherever the Shiite community or colony exists; and who has been a spectator, though of alien faith, of these *ta'ziyas* without experiencing within himself something of what they mean to those whose religious feeling

finds in them its extreme expression? As I write it all comes back: the wailing chant, the sobbing multitudes, the white raiment red with blood from self-inflicted wounds, the intoxication of grief and sympathy. Well says al-Fakhri: 'This was a catastrophe than which naught more shameful hath happened in Islam. May God curse every one who had a hand therein, or who ordered it, or took pleasure in any part thereof!'

3. The Shiite Legacy of the Martyred Imam Hussein

According to an ancient Muslim tradition, the Imam Hussein, son of the Prophet's cousin Ali and of his daughter Fatima, had linked himself very intimately with Iran before his martyrdom. He had married Shahr-banu, "daughter of Yazdigird, last of Persia's Sassanian kings, whence Persia became specially connected with the house of Ali." Not all the children of that union of Islam and Iran died at Kerbela. Millions indeed now honor Shahr-banu as the "Mother of Nine Imams" — of all, that is, who came after Ali, Hassan, and Hussein. Many centuries were to pass before that tradition could be effectively exploited politically. But, as Edward Browne observed in his literary history, the potential had been there from the beginning. In this connection Browne had introduced and discussed the insightful remarks of Sir William Muir on the long-range political consequences of Yazid's fateful "blunder" of 680 A.D.

"The tragedy of Kerbela," Muir wrote in his *Life of Mahomet and History of Islam* (4 vols., 3rd ed., London, 1895),

> decided not only the fate of the Caliphate, but of Mahometan kingdoms long after the Caliphate had waned and disappeared. Who that has seen the wild and passionate grief with which, at each recurring anniversary, the Muslims of every land spend the livelong night, beating their breasts and vociferating in wailing cadence the frantic cry — *Hassan, Hossein! Hassan, Hossein!* — can fail to recognize the fatal weapon, sharp and double-edged, which the Omayyad dynasty allowed thus to fall into the hands of their enemies?

The first to take up that weapon were the founders of the Abbasid dynasty who, claiming descent from Mohammed's uncle Abbas, thereby qualified for Shiite support against the Omayyads. But, once in power, the new dynasty became even more orthodox than its predecessors. In the words of the eminent Arabist Louis Amelie Sedillot: "Born enemies of the Omayyads though they were, the Abbasids, fearing to let the Shiites gain too much power, were avowedly on the side of the Sunnites and persecuted all who opposed their views." Shiite Iranians who could not adapt themselves to the inevitable orthodoxy of Arab successors either lapsed into fanatical opposition once again, or concealed themselves to await the rise of new political contenders, regardless of origin. In fact, only with the prospects of a genuinely Iranian bid for power, many centuries later, did Shiite Islam finally come into its own politically.

That happened with the Safavid kings of the sixteenth century who, it has been said, "were the first dynasty to gain power through the power of religion." An excellent account of the political use the Safavids made of the Muharram observances in this regard is provided by Peter J. Chelkowski of New York University in his introductory articles for the "proceedings of an international symposium on Ta'ziyeh held in August 1976 at the Shiraz Festival of Arts, Shiraz, Iran," which were later published with the title *Ta'ziyeh: Ritual and Drama in Iran* (New York, 1979).

"In the first years of the sixteenth century," Professor Chelkowski writes, "the Safavid dynasty brought Iran back onto the political map of the world and made Iran a superpower in the area. The Shiite order of Islam was established by the Safavids as the state religion. This has had a significant and lasting effect until the present day, not only upon religious life but on political, cultural, and social life as well. It was a turning point in Persian history, and a new phase in the history of Islam." From an ethnic-national standpoint, Shiite Islam proved most effective, Chelkowski stresses, as a force to "unify the country, especially against the aggressive Ottomans and Uzbeks who were adherents of Sunnite Islam. The Muharram observances received royal encouragement; commemoration of Hussein's martyrdom became a patriotic as well as religious act."

A number of European "envoys, missionaries, merchants and travelers" of the sixteenth and seventeenth centuries who witnessed the Muharram observances as they developed under the Safavids have left us detailed descriptions. Obvious similarities were noted "between the Muharram processions and the European medieval theater of the Stations of the Cross." But there was also the notable difference that during the Shiite ceremonies "the spectators remained stationary while the tableaux moved and in the theater of the Stations the tableaux were stationary while the viewer-penitents moved."

One eye-witness account of 1618 tells us that, "with the arrival of the tenth of Muharram, the day of the martyrdom of Hussein, large processions appear from all directions...carrying flags and standards. A variety of armed and turbaned horsemen accompany the processions. In addition to these there are several camels bearing large boxes, in each of which there are three or four children representing the captured children of the martyr Hussein. Besides these, every procession carries biers wrapped with black velvet and upon which a single turban, usually green, and a sword are placed." Another traveler of the same period adds: "Processions of people shouting 'Va Hassan, Alas Hussein!' roam the lanes and chant dirges. Some of these processions are armed while others are not. A lot of the people carry bludgeons five or six cubits long and frequently they split into groups and attack one another.... Next a company of armed men passes, shooting their guns into the air. Then come coffins followed by the mayor of the city and other notables; and all finally enter the great mosque...where a mulla mounts the pulpit and recites the eulogies, and all weep."

4. Mourning the Martyrs Through the Centuries: Ceremonial Catharsis

As to the political implications and uses of all this, one of the leading Iranian religious scholars of the late nineteenth century Muhammad Rafi Tabatabai, drew a parallel between the Muharram processions, with their ritualistic dramatic development, and the ancient Greek and Western European tragic theater. As he explained in his authoritative book on the "philosophy of the sufferings and mourning for Imam Hussein," published in 1906, the aim of the Safavids in transforming those ceremonies into a kind of *theater* had obviously been to provide a healthy catharsis of emotions. When well-presented, whether in theaters or in the streets, Tabatabai concluded, the re-enactments of the martyrdoms at Kerbela and related cruelties serve to "kill two birds with one stone: both as relief for tempers and as a means of gaining popular support.... In any event Ta'ziyeh had considerable impact on the minds of both upper and lower classes."

What exactly the politically-charged emotion was that the Muharram observances were supposed to call forth and purge, Tabatabai indicated rather dramatically at the very close of his book by quoting "the verse from the Koran which is the justification for the mourning ceremonies of Muharram: 'Those who do wrong shall surely know by what overturning they will be overturned'."

Here it might be appropriate to take note of the extraordinary impression the Muharram observances made on the common English soldiers who witnessed them in India during the nineteenth century. It was one thing to hear what Indians (whether Muslim or Hindu) said when their purpose was to communicate with their British masters and quite another to hear their voices when they seemed to be giving irrepressible expression to what they evidently felt most passionately in the depths of their souls. For the English soldier, most typical of the latter was the cry *Vah Hassan! Alas Hussein!* of the Muharram processions — a cry which he appears to have rendered in his own argot (recollected in tranquility, no doubt) as something like *Hobson Jobson*.

The brilliant Sir Henry Yule, at any rate, had insisted that nothing better typified the rank and file English soldier's perception of the soul of Muslim-Hindu India than that phrase. For that reason, as he took pains to explain, he chose to set it "up front" in the title of his incomparable *Hobson-Jobson: A Glossary of Colloquial Anglo-Indian Words and Phrases, and of Kindred Terms, Etymological, Historical, Geographical and Discursive*, which he jointly compiled with A. C. Burnell over a hundred years ago (London, 1886; 2nd edition, revised by William Crooke, 1903; reissued, 1968).

When we turn to the phrase in the Glossary itself, as Yule whimsically advises us to do in his Introductory Remarks, we find:

> HOBSON JOBSON,s. A native cry of excitement; a *tamdsha* (see TUMASHA); but especially the *Moharram* ceremonies. This phrase may be taken as a typical one of the most highly assimilated class of Anglo-Indian *argot*, and we have ventured to borrow from it a concise alternative title for this Glossary. It is peculiar to the British soldier and his surroundings, with whom it probably originated, and with whom it is by no means obsolete, as we once supposed. My friend Major John Trotter tells me that he has repeatedly heard it used by British soldiers in the Punjab; and has heard it also from a regimental Moonshee. It is in fact an Anglo-Saxon version of the wailing of the Mohammedans as they beat their breasts in the procession of the *Moharram* — YA HASAN! YA HOSAIN! It is to be remembered that these observances are *in India* by no means confined to the Shias. Except at Lucknow and Murshidabad, the great majority of the Mohammedans in that country are professed Sunnis. Yet here is a statement of the facts from an unexceptionable authority:
>
> 'The commonality of the Mussulmans, and especially the women, have more regard for the memory of Hassan and Hussein, than for that of Mohammed and his khalifs. The heresy of making Ta'ziyehs (see TAZEEA) on the anniversary of the two latter imams is most common in India: so much so that opposition to it is ascribed by the ignorant to blasphemy. This example is followed by many of the Hindus, especially the Mahrattas. The Muharram is celebrated throughout the Dekhan and Malwa, with greater enthusiasm than in other parts of India. Grand preparations are made in every town on the occasion, as if for a festival of rejoicing rather than of observing the rites of mourning, as they ought. The observance of this custom has so strong a hold on the mind of the commonality of the Mussulmans that they believe Mohammedanism to depend merely on keeping the memory of the imams in the above manner.' Mir Shahamat Ali, in the *Journal of the Royal Asiatic Society*, XIII, 369.

Toward the end of the nineteenth century, after it had fascinated the interest of many Western scholars and critics — among them

Matthew Arnold, Ernest Renan, and the Count de Gobineau — the Ta'ziyeh of the Muharram observances had been on the verge of giving rise to an "art form" in the strict sense which, in Iran at least, would have helped to make it politically neutral. But attitudes changed in the twentieth century. A culturally-obtuse determination to "westernize" as quickly as possible blinded many high-placed Iranians to both the political utility and the cultural promise of the old tradition. During the 1920s and 1930s, and increasingly after World War II, public support of Iran's equivalent of Christendom's Passion Play declined rapidly. Some foreigners intervened in its behalf; but by and large in Iranian ruling circles the whole thing was "misconstrued" — so Professor Chelkowski writes — "as an unworthy ritual and a crude spectacle."

When he first came to power in the early 1920s, but before taking the title of shah, the first of the Pahlavis, Reza Khan, had been tempted to break abruptly with all tradition and follow modern Turkey's example of modernization by a process of virtually instant and total de-Islamization. That proved impossible. Yet even after he had apparently made peace with Shiite Islam to secure his dynastic position in 1925, he still wavered back and forth in his attitude toward the traditional street processions. His son who succeded him in 1941 did the same at first; and then, during the decades following World War II, with his intensified longing for a renaissance of pre-Arabic Iranian grandeur, did much worse — until, by the mid-1970s, it was too late. The weapon of the Muharram observances forged back in the seventh century slipped from his loosened grasp into the waiting hands of the Ayatollah Khomeini. Thus, instead of safely crossing the threshold that would have made it a pure art form (an "indigenous avant-garde theater of Iran," as Peter Chelkowski phrased it), the Ta'ziyeh suddenly retreated back into the streets of its origin — and this time with a vengeance!

The Muharram-Ashura processions of 1978 in the streets of Tehran were nothing like the grand and colorful spectacles of the seventeenth century described by Western travelers. A ban had in fact been placed on them in 1978 and, to facilitate its enforcement, martial law had been declared. The crowds that assembled illegally were mostly country people, new to the city. Yet the spirit of the so-called Muharram verse of the Koran seemed to echo and re-echo among them all the more intensely because of their shabby clothes and crudely-fashioned banners, standards, and posters: "Those who do wrong shall surely know by what overturning they will be overturned." And when the Shah's troops finally fired into the crowds to enforce the law many voices were heard, even among the wounded, shouting boldly that the Shah was the treacherous Yazid of our time and Khomeini its righteous Hussein.

But already back in 1976, while the Shah (secure in his possession of billions of petrol-dollar revenues and matching credits) still seemed to have his Iranian masses under complete control, other potentially explosive parallels between contemporary events and the villainies at Kerbela were being drawn. One of the papers read at the Shiraz Festival of Arts, for instance — Professor M. M. Mazzaoui's "Shiism and Ashura in South Lebanon" — took note of the increasingly political use being made of the Muharram commemorations. The focus was on the Ta'ziyeh performances or ceremonies of the "closely-knit Shia community of Jabal Amil in south Lebanon" which borders on Israel directly to the south and which has provided a home, in recent decades, for "a large community of Palestinians." In due course the author was able to observe that, "aside from the religious fervor which is common to Ta'ziyeh both in Lebanon and in Iran, the situation in Jabal Amil has certain peculiarities" due quite obviously to the immediacy of the Israeli-Palestinian Arab struggle.

"Over the past three decades," the author added, "the assimilation between the Amils and the Palestinians has reached a degree whereby, as a modern Lebanese sociologist puts it (in French, of course!): 'Husayn, c'est la Palestine; Yazid n'est qu'une prefiguration du Zionisme!' It is a total identification of Hussein, the martyr of Kerbela, with the tragic fate of the Palestinians; and of the archenemy Yazid with the alien Zionist movement responsible for the tragedy." And then venturing a contrast soon to be invalidated by events in Iran, the author concluded:

> These conditions should be seen within the framework of a
> highly confused but essentially 'free society' in Lebanon, as

compared with say, the more centrally stable and somewhat more uniform political and social conditions in Iran. If one is permitted to make a final judgement, one would like to say that in Iran Ta'ziyeh will safely develop...within the relative safety of art forms. This is politically neutral ground. In Lebanon, on the other hand, I would venture to guess that Ta'ziyeh will remain for a long time to come an expression of 'opposition, martyrdom, and revolt.'

That is how things looked from the perspective of lovely Shiraz in 1976. It is significant that, after the Israeli invasion of south Lebanon some six years later, the hostility of the Shiites there toward Israel was intensified, as one would have expected. But, as was soon apparent, the retreating Palestinians, who had been the direct target of the Israeli attack, made the mistake of presuming that they could freely return to the south Lebanese area after Israel's withdrawal. That was not to be. The Shiites of Lebanon broke with the Palestinians, who are not Shiites, and have ever since tried to resist their return and oust their remnants.

But the graver miscalculation on Professor Mazzaoui's part back in 1976 lay in his expectaction that in Iran "Ta'ziyeh will safely develop." Ta'ziyeh did indeed develop in Iran after 1976, but not safely. By the end of 1978, as a matter of fact, political and social as well as religious conditions in Iran had abruptly and radically changed. At their center was the public celebration of the Ta'ziyeh. The Shah had come to be perceived as Yazid — but a Yazid acting for Israel and for a "Zionist dominated America." He was perceived as a mere puppet, unworthy of the Islamic faith which he could, it was charged, only hypocritically profess at best. The Shiite masses of Iran, relatively unarmed, boldly sought martyrdom in confronting that Shah with cries of *Vah Hassan, Alas Hussein* on their lips. The theatrical catharsis which had been the promise of Islamic Iran's medieval Ta'ziyeh was thus prepared for a final bloody performance, destined to be viewed by millions in Tehran, and by hundreds of millions throughout the world, when it played before television cameras in the streets in front of the American Embassy after its compound of official buildings was seized on November 4, 1979.

An Islamic year before the seizure of the American Embassy — indeed, during the same period of religious commemoration of the Kerbela martyrs late in 1978 — Iran's Mohammed Reza Pahlavi, King of Kings, and Light of the Aryans, had often appeared on international TV newscasts to discuss his mounting domestic difficulties. And, commenting on several such appearances, Walter Eytan had observed in his insightful article of December 11, 1978:

> Anyone who has seen Shah Mohammed Reza Pahlavi on television in recent weeks must have been struck by the grief and tension in his face. He is obviously at bay, and there are few who believe he can hold out indefinitely against the furious mobs seeking to de-throne him. The Shah, disingenuously or otherwise, has been admitting his past mistakes; it has been embarrassing to hear his fresh *mea culpa* daily. But it is doubtful whether any amount of liberalization, or denunciation of the corrupt practices he tolerated for so long, can save him now. There is not much point in arguing whether Iran is today, December 1978, in a revolutionary or prerevolutionary stage of political evolution. It is hard to see how the Shah can win, as he alternates between concessions to a disaffected people and the use of brute force against them. His vacillations are those of a man who does not know from one day to the next which way to turn.

Eytan's conclusion at the time stressed the implications for Israel of the Shah's manifest disorientation. Admonishing Jewish readers of his "Dateline Jerusalem" column, he observed that, "even if the Shah survives, he can hardly afford any open alliance, however indirect, with Israel. Indeed, a total breach with Israel could be one of the inescapable conditions of his survival, just as it would almost surely be a consequence of his fall." Underlying the pathos of the general impression made by the Shah's TV appearances were reminders of happier times past, and especially of past difficulties overcome. The Pahlavi Shahs had had their ups and downs, but, after World War II, at any rate, the Western powers, and particularly the United States, had almost always acted to save things in the nick of time. How had it become possible for street crowds led by medieval-minded clerics to shake the foundations of a throne that claimed a 2,500-year imperial inheritance?

5. Pahlavi: A Name for Modernizing Shahs to Conjure With

From the founding of the Pahlavi dynasty by the last Shah's father, the policy toward the Islamic faith had been more or less clearly defined. As Professor Shakrough Akhavi aptly put it in his previously cited *Religion and Politics in Contemporary Iran: Clergy-State Relations in the Pahlavi Period* (New York, 1980), the "position of the Pahlavi dynasty from its origins" had been, plainly enough, "to separate religion from politics," in gradual stages. Certainly, when he became military dictator in 1921, the first Pahlavi Shah seemed determined to sustain that position aggressively. For his first two years in power, his obvious plan had been to model himself on Turkey's Kemal Ataturk. Persia would be declared a republic with Reza Khan serving as its first president. Kemal Ataturk had abolished the Ottoman sultanate and then the caliphate itself. On his orders, a republican constitution had been drawn up that made no mention of Islam. And a few years later, the republican parliament was to rule that the Turkish language itself would no longer be written in its traditional Arabic script but in the religiously neutral (because pre-Christian) characters of the Roman alphabet.

Reza Khan had very seriously contemplated such a course of modernization. But he soon realized that, historically, Persia's status as an Islamic country was really the opposite of Turkey's. The Turks had taken their Islamic faith and their Arabic script by conquest, the way the Scandinavian Norsemen took up French after they conquered northern France, and later gave it up to speak English, and even to call themselves Englishmen, after they had conquered and ruled England for several centuries. Conquerors can be cavalier with their spoils of war. It is otherwise with the conquered. The Turks, moreover, had been illiterate barbarians before their conversion to Islam, whereas the Persians, as we have seen, claimed a glorious heritage from the remotest times. The faith of Islam and the Arabic script had been imposed upon them in the seventh century, and their ancient pride had never quite sufficed to overthrow that double yoke. Yet it had sought and found an outlet *within Islam itself*. As we have seen, the Iranian national attachment to Shiism, as against Sunni orthodoxy, provided just such an outlet, with its fullest expression reserved for the annual commemorations of the martyrdoms of Kerbela.

Having recognized that he could not possibly follow Kemal Ataturk's direct course, Reza Khan had promptly reversed his plans. There would be no republic, there would be no attempt to cast off the Arabic script. If, for the sake of complete modernization, the yoke of Islam was ever to be lifted, it would have to be done indirectly. And the obvious means seemed to be to emphasize and celebrate the "continuity" of the imperial office, from Cyrus the Great through the Qajars (and their successors), without in any way suggesting that it made a serious difference for the cause of modernization whether the mass of Iranians remained faithful Shiites or not.

As a sign of his intentions when he first proclaimed himself Shah in 1925, Reza Khan very deliberately assumed the dynastic name of Pahlavi, but without any explicit clarification. In *Mission For My Country*, his son suggested a clarification only parenthetically, writing: "The present Pahlavi dynasty (called after the name of an ancient form of our Persian language)...." And there he let the matter drop. Reza Khan's biographer, Donald Wilber, tells us a bit more. The choice of the name was apparently suggested to the military dictator in the early 1920s precisely to serve as a link between pre-Islamic and Islamic Iran, since it was already being used by European linguists as the name for the Persian language as it had been written just *before* the Arab conquest of the seventh century A.D.

Our best authority on the meaning of the term, however, remains Edward G. Browne, whose *Literary History of Persia* we cited earlier. Browne wrote long before the founding of the Pahlavi dynasty, and his concern is therefore not with the dynastic name as such. Still, he very significantly stresses that in modern Persian the term has several meanings, some popular, some scholarly, all of which have, however, distinctly pre-Islamic connotations. In its various cognate forms, it always suggests the heroic days of Iran before the Arab conquest. Persia's greatest epic poet, Ferdusi, tells us that it was the language of the great pre-Islamic kings; and the celebrated Omar Khayyam, in his most pagan mood, says that the language in which "the Nightingale sang to the Rose" in olden times had indeed been the "divine high-piping Pahlavi."

But Browne's primary concern is with the stricter use of the term by modern linguists. There is a sense, he writes, in which "the Persian language of today, *Farsi*, the language of *Fars*, is the lineal offspring of the language which Cyrus and Darius spoke," and which is preserved for us in the inscriptions engraved on the cliffs of Behistun and on the walls and columns of Persepolis. The celebration at Persepolis in 1971 had been intended, as we shall see, to stress an unbroken continuity from those times to the present. But Browne reminds us of the two great gaps in that continuity. The first came with the conquest of Alexander the Great. It was a gap in writing, if not in speaking Persian, that lasted more than 500 years. Then came the revival under the Sassanid emperors. That was when, as we mentioned before, the Pahlavi form of writing was developed. It is now represented for us, Browne writes, by "inscriptions on monuments, medals, gems, seals, and coins, and by a literature estimated as, roughly speaking, equal in bulk to the Old Testament. This literature is entirely Zoroastrian and almost entirely theological and liturgical."

That explains why the conquering Muslim Arabs abruptly cut off its use. For a time, spoken Persian ceased to be written in Iran. The Zoroastrian priests and their flocks either went into hiding or, as in the case of the Parsis, sought refuge in distant lands where they continued to write their Pahlavi, but only for religious purposes, expounding the doctrine of their sacred Zoroastrian Avesta in it. Meanwhile, in Iran, when things calmed down, spoken Persian came to be written in Arabic. And here Browne gives us this important clarification. As used to designate the Persian of the Sassanids, the term Pahlavi, he writes "applies rather to the script than to the language," for, apart from the script, that language was really "little more than an archaic form of the present speech of Persia devoid of the Arabic element."

Devoid of the Arabic element! There we have the key to the choice of the dynastic name. But, since the Arabic element in Persian is essentially also the Islamic element, we are obviously treading — religiously — on dangerous ground. "In the East," as Browne explains, "there is a tendency to associate written characters much more than language with religion. There are Syrian Christians whose language is Arabic, but who prefer to write their Arabic in the Syriac characters; and these *Karshuni* writings (for so they are called) form a considerable literature. So also the Turkish-speaking Armenians and Greeks often employ the Armenian and Greek characters when they write Turkish. Similarly the Jews of Persia have a pretty extensive literature written in the Persian language but in the Hebrew character, while the Moors of Spain who had forgotten how to speak Arabic wrote Spanish treatises in the Arabic character." The Pahlavi script was thus more closely linked in the Eastern mind with the "Zoroastrian religion than was the Arabic character with the faith of Islam; and when a Persian was converted from the former to the latter creed he gave up, as a rule, once and for all a method of writing which was not only cumbrous and ambiguous in the highest degree, but also fraught with heathen associations." Browne concludes:

> Moreover, writing (and even reading) was probably a rare accomplishment among the Persians when the Pahlavi character was the means of written communication.... It had no intrinsic merit save as a unique philological puzzle; and, once deprived of the support of religion, ancient custom, and a conservative priesthood, it could not hold its own against the far more legible and convenient Arabic character.... But the fact cannot be too strongly insisted upon that the peculiarity of Pahlavi lay in the script only.

In other words, there had been true continuity of speech for the Iranians after the Arab conquest. But the pre-Arabic script had been too "cumbrous and ambiguous" to survive on its own. Had Reza Khan attempted to revive it as an instrument of de-Arabizing modernization, it would have meant condemning a majority of modern Iranians to permanent illiteracy. There remained the possibility of a switch to Roman characters. But, with foreign scholars showering rich praise on the Iranian legacy in those days, such a venture was equally out of the question. What remained was but a suggestive name: Pahlavi. It didn't change much. But it clearly indicated a dynastic determination to de-Arabize and de-Islamize the nation, even if for the moment the means were inadequate.

Or we should say, rather, that the means seemed inadequate until the 1970s. Then, in quick order, came the 2500th anniversary celebration at Persepolis and Henry Kissinger's first visit. That was followed immediately by a sky-rocketing rise in the price of oil which seemed to make all things possible. Henry Kissinger, like a latter day Nehemiah in reverse, laid the whole design out for Nixon, first of all, and then for the Shah, already far-gone in what would later be called his "folie des grandeurs."

With a pre-Islamic imperial name like Pahlavi and a full supply of the most modern American arms, why couldn't the son of Reza Shah the Great aspire to heights of imperial grandeur comparable to the times of Cyrus, Darius, and Artaxerxes? The last thing that Mohammed Reza Pahlavi could have suspected when he began his Middle-East strategy discussions with Kissinger in 1972 was that Persia's Shiite faith would bring him down — and that it would do so largely on the strength of the wailings of millions of uprooted peasants gathered in the streets of Tehran for the traditional Muharram commemorations.

PART III

Making and Breaking a Shah

CHAPTER SIX

Puppet-Masters of Mohammed Reza Pahlavi's Career, 1941-1973

What exactly was the social force that stood up against Iran's Shah so effectively in December 1978 as to drive him into exile the following month? Walter Eytan, loading his assessment rather heavily on one side, had put it this way just before the fall.

> Arrayed against him are the Marxists and the mullahs — 'those priests,' to quote Edward Gibbon, writing of Persia in the eighteenth century, 'who had so long sighed in contempt and obscurity.' Marxists are of course traditionally anti-religious, but they know how to play on religious feelings; and the two opposites do not sit with one another as uneasily as one might assume, especially in the Muslim world.... Iran, for centuries a poverty stricken nation, is now paying the price for its sudden oil wealth.... The Shah would claim he has done his best. He has worked to modernize his country...but modernization inevitably has its social consequences.... The Shah had apparently not reckoned with the force and fanaticism of the mullahs' resistance to his initiatives and reforms. Precisely because of his paternalism, he never succeeded in gaining acceptance as the father figure he wished his people to love. But how could he have forgotten that he had been dethroned and expelled once before?

Of course, the temporary expulsion of the early 1950s, about which we must say more later, had been brought about by secularizing, modernizing reformers. The young Shah had not had to contend, at the time, with what Eytan calls, "the conservatism of a

103

hidebound priesthood and its hold on the prejudices and superstitions of the masses.'' Back in 1953, it had really appeared to most observers of political developments in the Middle East that the Israelis, who had just founded their Socialist national state according to the ancient prophecies, would retain their monopoly on the old zeal of the ''politics of religion,'' of which we have spoken before. Certainly there had not yet been seen in the Muslim world — as Eytan puts it — anything like a ''resurgence of Islam tending to literal application of the Koran and a return to practices once thought out of keeping with the twentieth century.''

Yet, if we are to gain some clarity in our study of Iran's recent Islamic revolution, it is important to start with the Shah's own perspective on the major turning points in his relatively long career. And here the best vantage point is perhaps his book, or governmental ''white paper'' of 1967, titled *The White Revolution*. In the preface to that book, he reminds his imperial subjects that, although he had succeeded to his father's place in 1941, he had, for reasons of state, delayed his actual coronation until 1967. Before that time, he wrote just after the event, Iran had been so insecure politically and socially, so impoverished economically, that he could not bring himself to the point of assuming the title of monarch in such a land. The worst moment, the absolute low point, had occurred in 1953. The years immediately following were years of muddling through. The long awaited turn for the better, he recalled, really began only a decade later, in January 1963. That was when, in defiance of the old unholy alliance of the entrenched nobility and the conservative clergy — Iran's *rouge et noir* — the common people, called upon to manifest their will in a national referendum, voted overwhelmingly in favor of his ''six-point program of reforms'' which he called the White Revolution, or preferably, the ''Revolution of the King and the People.''

In the Shah's own words: ''When I came to the throne, on September 16th, 1941, the machinery of government had, as a result of foreign aggression, completely broken down. . . . For a period of more than twenty-one years, until January, 1963, my country and I were subject to frequent vicissitudes of fortune and witnessed artificial scenes played for our benefit by actors who were manipulated like puppets from the outside.'' In *Mission For My Country*, published in 1960, the Shah had tried to maintain an Olympian attitude of "fairness" in writing about the man who had succeeded, for a brief time in 1953, in deposing him: the aged Dr. Mohammed Mossadegh, who for a time was given almost as much TV "exposure" in the United States as the Ayatollah Khoemeni has had more recently — though the men are hardly comparable otherwise. The Shah pointed out that, in 1940, the last year of his father's reign, Mossadegh had been arrested and that he personally as crown prince had interceded to gain his release. And than he added:

> In 1953, when Mossadegh was convicted of treason, I wrote to the court saying that I forgave him for all wrongs he had done me. Because of this letter and his advanced age, he escaped the death penalty which in this and most other countries is normal for proved traitors, and received only a slight sentence of three years' of imprisonment. Thus for the second time my intervention saved his life. When he was released in 1956, he retired to his country estate near Tehran, for he is a weathy man. As this book is published (1960), he is still living a peaceful and uneventful life at home with his family.

The Shah could never bring himself to deny that, as he said, "on paper much of Mossadegh's career sounds eminently respectable." In fact, back in those days it was the view of many impartial observers that, if events in Iran then had the aspect of a puppet show, Mossadegh had in fact been the puppet the most difficult to maneuver from the outside, while the young Shah seemed to be the easiest. Mossadegh's purpose had been to drive the British, primarily, but also other oil-dealing foreign countries out of Iran. He was anything but a religious fanatic. Taking his cue from Gandhi's "Quit India" movement, he had gained support for a movement to force the British out regardless of the immediate economic consequences. Here the Shah, ready to accomodate the oil companies, reasoned weakly: "His special weakness seemed to be economics. I am in no sense a professional economist...but in all candour I must say that rarely have I met anyone in a responsible position who matched Mossadegh's ignorance of the elementary principles of production, trade, and other economic factors."

1. First Major American String-Puller:
Kermit Roosevelt and the Countercoup of April 1953

We all know that, when the United Nations attempted to "solve" the hostage crises in Iran by undertaking an inquiry into the charges advanced against the Shah as a puppet of American oil interests, the old events of 1953 were daily re-examined, or at least reviewed, in our newsmedia. Bernard D. Nossiter's very long article for the *New York Times* on "Khomeini v. Shah: What the record shows" (Nov. 26, 1979), for instance, called attention to the words of Iran's President Bani-Sadr to Kurt Waldheim. "Iran," Bani-Sadr had written, "is a country that, since the coup d'etat of 1953 until the fall of the regime of the Shah, was placed under the domination of the United States that is to say on the road to political, social and economic decadence." Nossiter in turn asks more pointedly: "Did the United States pull all the strings for 25 years in this land of 35 million people?" That question, interestingly enough, is raised in the closing paragraphs of a narrative that begins with these words:

> On Aug. 18, 1953, a disconsolate Shah Mohammed Reza Pahlavi and his wife were shopping on the Via Veneto in Rome. They had just fled Iran, where a nationalist Prime Minister, Mohammed Mossadegh, had ignored the Shah's order to resign and won nationalist acclaim for seizing the British-run oil fields. Yet the next day, street crowds and soldiers, organized by Kermit Roosevelt of the Central Intelligence Agency, drove Prime Minister Mossadegh from power. While the old man fled in his pajamas, Mr. Roosevelt personally escorted his successor, Fazlollah Zahedi, from his hiding place to office. A few days later, a grateful Shah, back in his palace, told Mr. Roosevelt over vodka and caviar, 'I owe my throne to God, my people, my army — and to you.'

Publication of Kermit Roosevelt's own account of the *Countercoup* or *Struggle for the Control of Iran* was delayed, as we noted in the introduction, for reasons of public reserve and honor until 1979. One of its jacket blurbs noted that its author's "effectiveness as an agent and organizer was attested to by Kim Philby, the British agent turned Russian spy, who called the author 'the quiet American...the last person you would expect to be up to his neck in dirty tricks'." His book of 1979 confirms what had been the contemporary impression. The fact that he and his group were able to restore the Shah to his throne in *a single day* proved, it was said, that the Mossadegh clique of modernizing reformers really had no popular base in Iran. They were even further removed in spirit from the Shiite masses than the Pahlavi Shahs had ever been, despite their name. What the local CIA chief — grandson of Theodore Roosevelt — then proceeded to do was set up an internal security system designed to protect the Shah's government against infiltration by Mossadegh types who would covertly work for its overthrow. The instrument designed at that time for the government's security was of course the once-dreaded SAVAK, consisting of 30,000 secret policemen. Kermit Roosevelt, wrote Nossiter, has himself acknowledged that "his agency helped 'organize and give guidance' to the new Iranian security force, with the help of Israeli 'friends'," and that, before long, "SAVAK agents were allowed to operate in the United States, watching Iranian students here."

On the matter of the CIA's initiatives in the coup d'etat of 1953, it is important, from a revisionist standpoint, to recall the installment of a long serialized article titled "The Mysterious Doings of CIA" that appeared in the November 6, 1954 issue of the *Saturday Evening Post*. It was written by Richard and Gladys Harkness, and it celebrated the care with which the people above and below Kermit Roosevelt handled the chore of saving the Shah's throne for him. The authors gave Allen Dulles his due. But they also stressed the roles of "a diplomat, a princess, and a policeman" in the "Stranger-than-fiction circumstances" of the coup. The diplomat was Loy Henderson, U.S. Ambassador to Iran at the time; the princess was the Shah's dynamic sister who often put her brother to shame with her political daring; and the "policeman" was Brig. Gen. H. Norman Schwartzkopf who, years earlier, as head of the New Jersey state police, had conducted the Lindberg kidnapping investigation of 1932. On Schwartzkopf's role, the Harknesses wrote:

> From 1942 through 1948, Schwartzkopf was detailed to Iran to reorganize the Shah's national police force. His job in Iran was

more than the tracking down of routine criminals. He protected the government against its enemies — an assignment requiring intelligence on the political cliques plotting against the Shah, knowledge of which army elements could be counted on to remain loyal, and familiarity with the Middle East psychology. . . . Schwartzkopf returned to Iran in August 1953, he said, 'just to see old friends again.' Certainly the general will deny any connection with the Shah and Maj. Gen. Fazlollah Zahedi, his colleague on the police force. But as Mossadegh and the Russian press railed nervously at Schwartzkopf's presence in Iran, developments started to unfold in one-two-three order.

As the crisis peaked, Allen Dulles, the diplomat, and the princess found opportune reasons for separate journeys to Switzerland, to be safely out of the way. The young Shah stayed behind at first. But finally it was decided that he too had better leave. The actual fighting, however, lasted only about nine hours. The claim of the Harknesses, in those days when public support of the idea of the Agency was complete, was that the CIA had intervened only to prevent Mossadegh from defying the will of the Iranian people. "Thus it was," they concluded, "that the strategic little nation of Iran was rescued from the closing clutch of Moscow. Equally important, the *physical* overthrow of Mossadegh was accomplished by the Iranians themselves. It is the guiding premise of the CIA's third force that one must develop and nurture indigenous freedom legions among captive or threatened people who stand ready to take personal risks for their own liberty."

Even so, the restored Shah proceeded very slowly in reasserting his royal prerogatives. There were still many self-seeking politicians, he would later say, who "played a double game and betrayed their country in the guise of nationalists and liberals." Besides such "false" nationalists and liberals, there were the "feudal lords who had created autonomous local governments, and, in order to protect their own interests, competed among themselves to serve foreign designs." Of less importance in his view at that time were the "self-styled religious leaders who, ever since the establishment of constitutional government in Iran, were generally known to be at the beck and call

of one foreign power in particular.'' Such groups, he had concluded in his retrospective assessment of 1967, ''acted as deterrents to
Iran's progress,'' keeping the country in a permanent state of anarchy that served only to facilitate foreign exploitation.

Such groups, he further protested, had learned to use the
processes of constitutional, parliamentary government to their own
selfish interest. His remedy, finally, was to proceed over their heads
as parliamentary factions with direct appeals to the people. Like the
last king of the ancien regime in the earliest phase of the French Revolution (and like America's F.D.R., but far less successfully), the Shah
proclaimed himself to be the leader of a popular revolution against
entrenched privilege. His revolution was to consist, in fact, of a six-
point program of modernizing reforms to be imposed autocratical-
ly, from above, after receipt of a democratic mandate in the form
of a national referendum.

2. From the "White Revolution" (1963) to the "Imperial Coronation" (1967)

The call for a national referendum on the so-called White Revolution — white, because bloodless — permitted the Shah to denounce
all opposition to his reforms as reactionary. The votecount on January 26, 1963 proved to be overwhelmingly in his favor. And so he
set about at once to implement the six basic reforms, which called
for (1) land redistribution, (2) enfranchisement of women, (3) an all-
out assault on mass illiteracy, (4) nationalization of the forests (the
old timber resource of the days of Nehemiah!), (5) profit-sharing
for workers in major industrial enterprises, and (6) sale of
government-owned factories to the private sector to help defray the
costs of the other reforms.

It took the Shah some five months, after the referendum, to
destroy or silence all opposition. Most of it he was able to eliminate
by strategic compromises, balancing new gains for many, through
governmental largesse, against old losses. By showing that what he
took from the upper-classes with one hand they might find restored
to them, in a modernized form, with the other, he quickly built up

a new upper-class consensus. A more enduring opposition came from the religious leaders; but the ulamas, as they were called, were by no means united. As Professor Shahrough Akhavi notes in his study of clergy-state relations in the Pahlavi period, previously cited, the *ulama* had traditionally been among the "largest landholders in the society"; yet, more importantly, the projected reforms threatened their traditional hold on the educational system, especially in the rural areas. They saw the merchant and professional classes, and the governmental bureaucrats, being advanced at their expense by the modernization programs. Professor Akhavi then adds this important clarification:

> But the political reasons for the opposition of the clergy were equally fundamental: arbitrary rule, the granting of extraterritoriality and, more generally, foreign control over certain aspects of the economy; the nation's policy in the Arab-Israel conflict, according to which oil was sold to Israel and cooperation between the two countries' intelligence apparatuses took place.... Relations with Israel were later to become a powerful source of conflict between the Shah and Ayatollah Khomeini after the mid-sixties. But...even though the riots of 1963 [against the Shah's revolution, during the Muharram mourning period] were led by Khomeini [as emergent spokesman of the Qumm religious establishment], he was at that time an unknown figure to the National Front organization in Tehran, which had continued to operate off and on after the coup that overthrew Dr. Mossadegh. As a consequence, despite the fact that extensive demonstrations took place in dozens of Iranian cities that spring, the Khomeini faction among the clergy and the National Front failed to coordinate their activities.

Professor Akhavi's point is that the Ayatollah Khomeini had never really been part of the modernizing, liberal opposition to the Shah. Thus, while the Shah had been trying to win that opposition to his side by means of modernizing reforms, he had left himself unprepared for *principled* criticism on the part of the truly *faithful* clergy. It was something like the dilemma of the Renaissance popes who, after having been attacked by Christian humanists for their dogmatic attachments to tradition, took the lead cultivating arts and letters and science and discovery, and even rationalizing philosophy. And then suddenly came the cry of undermined "purity of faith" that Luther raised, and renaissance was abruptly rent through with reformation. Khomeini proved to be the Shah's Luther.

The Ayatollah's intervention came at a time when most of the clergy seemed prepared to compromise, to accept the Shah's projected largesse in exchange for state control of education and even of the preparation of the clergy. In Professor Akhavi's words:

> There were signs of further compromise...in June 1963, when the government released some 27 *ulama* who had been arrested in the course of the last few months. Among those whom the regime arrested, albeit for a brief time, was the grand *mujtahid* of Qumm, Shari at-madari. Khomeini, himself, was arrested in the wake of a series of fiery speeches at the Fayziyah Madrasah in which he articulated practically all of the grievances of the *ulama*.... He was seized at his home in the early morning hours of 15 June 1963 in order to avoid the Qumm crowds that surely would have attempted to restrain the authorities from arresting and dispatching him to Tehran. Thence, he was sent to exile in Turkey where he stayed until October 1965, when he took himself to Iraq and resided in Najaf until the early fall of 1978.

In those days, the Shah frequently spoke out against the claims of religious leaders like the Ayatollah Khomeini that they were privileged spokesmen for the faith of the Shiite masses. Insisting on the equality of all Muslims in God's presence, he made bold to say on one occasion: "No one can claim that he is closer to God or to the *imams* than I am." Yet, paralleling his persistent democratization of religious relationships was his constantly accelerating drive to raise his *political* authority to transcendent heights. In 1967, he staged his long-delayed grand coronation. His father then became Reza Pahlavi the Great, and he himself became King of the Kings of all the world, as well as Light of all the Aryans. Four years later the representatives of all the *lesser* kingdoms and principalities of the world, from Peking to Moscow and Washington, were gathered at Persepolis for the grand fete of 1971. And quickly after that came the visit of Henry Kissinger, the Disraelian flatterer who set the Shah up for his mighty fall.

3. Persepolis (1971): A 2,500-year-old Pre-Islamic Throne?

In October 1971, the Shah of Iran had initiated the celebration of what he called the "2500th Anniversary of the Founding of the Persian Empire" by the Zoroastrian king Cyrus the Great more than a thousand years before the birth of Mohammed. To be sure, strict chronology had not dictated the choice of that particular year for the celebration. As the Shah himself had written in *For My Country* (New York, 1960): "Already I have mentioned that our monarchy has reached some 2,500 years of age. I do not intend this to be an exact figure, because it depends on how you do your own arithmetic. Cyrus the Great became king about 2,506 years ago [dating back from 1960], but it took him a few years to unify the country and to consolidate our first empire."

By stricter chronology, however, 1971 would have been a most suitable year to celebrate two other anniversaries. There was first of all the 50th anniversary of the military coup of 1921. That was when the Shah's father, Reza Khan, made himself military dictator. More significantly, it was also the 30th anniversary of the Shah's accession to the throne in 1941, the year his father was unceremoniously ousted by the Allied Powers for having supported Hitler. But why celebrate military coups and ignominious successions when it is possible, with a little loose arithmetic, to look back 2500 years to the founding of "our first empire" by kings whose fame is secure wherever the Old Testament is loved and read?

For the occasion of the celebration of the pre-Arabic, pre-Islamic glories of Iran's ancient imperial past in 1971, a "Royal Tent City" was built just beyond the majestic ruins of ancient Persepolis. The intention was to "house heads of state and royal guests" there in a style surpassing Hollywood's most extravagant fantasies. Yet the tourist brochures took pains to explain that Persepolis itself was not, as Western scholars used to believe, "a group of impressive palaces built on the capital city of a great empire in order to express political might and gratify royal pride." Not at all. Starting with Darius I, who founded it in 518 B.C., the ancient kings had assembled their people there only on the most solemn occasions: to offer prayerful thanks to their "Great God, Ahura Mazda," by whose grace they "overcame all enemies and established the world empire which was planned to bring peace, order, and prosperity to a chaotic world."

Unfortunately, the western newsmedia didn't think much of the "$100 million fete" at Persepolis. They spoke of the Shah's "Ozymandian megalomania," and never tired of pointing out that his father had, after all, started his climb to the top as an illiterate teen-age private in the Russian-trained Persian Cossack Brigade whose main charge had been to guard the old Qajar shahs (primarily against their own subjects) and to protect the foreign embassies and consulates that ultimately paid for everything. Leftward-leaning critics added that the reigning Shah really owed his throne (which he had briefly lost in 1953) much more to the machinations of the great American oil companies and the CIA than to the traditions of Persepolis.

And then there was the voice of the Ayatollah Khomeini, altogether unheeded in the West in those days. In his Iraqi exile, Khomeini denounced the Persepolis festivities with their utterly pagan, anti-Islamic panegyrics to the traditions of Zoroastrian kings — all staged with incredible extravagance, as he said, "while famine was raging in that part of the country" among the faithful masses whose "true religion of Islam" was again suffering a martyrdom like that of Hussein on the plains of Kerbela, at the hands of a modern-day Yazid.

4. From Persepolis to the American *"Blank Check" of 1972*

But the extravagances of Persepolis in 1971 were soon reduced to insignificance by a shift of fortune the following year that abruptly made the Iranian Shah one of the chief beneficiaries of American largess in all the world — second only to the State of Israel. We have already taken note of the role Henry Kissinger was to play in the fortunes of the Iranian Shah, starting in 1972, by drawing a biblical or post-biblical Judaic-Iranian parallel. But, of course, it was as an American, rather than as a Jew, that Kissinger approached the Shah in that fateful year — though the Shah, recalling the glories of Israeli-Iranian relations in the times of Cyrus, Darius, and Artaxerxes, may have thought otherwise.

In fact, before he could think of playing Nehemiah for a modern day claimant to the throne of Artaxerxes, Henry Kissinger had first to play the more likely role of a latter-day Disraeli in the service of Richard M. Nixon's presidency. Back in December, 1968, when Nixon first announced his choice of Kissinger for the coveted post of chief presidential national security adviser — a post held by McGeorge Bundy and Walt Rostow during the Kennedy-Johnson terms — newsmen had expressed surprise. He was known by fellow academicians to have been decidedly liberal in his foreign policy views, as well as in his political preferences. For years he had been employed as an adviser by the leading Republican liberal politician in the country and had served Democratic Presidents, while protesting in public that there were no Republicans with whom he cared to serve, other than Rockefeller.

During his first interview in office for *Time* magazine, Kissinger was asked about his ideological orientation and what he hoped to accomplish as Nixon's chief foreign policy adviser. He replied cryptically: "If I were in 19th century Great Britain, I might be a Disraelian Conservative in domestic affairs, but not in foreign policy." Paraphrased by the *Time* reporter, his own clarification read: "Disraeli was an unabashed imperialist. Kissinger, by contrast, believes that U.S. power must not be spread too thinly, especially in politically underdeveloped areas that America little understands." Years later, that Disraelian reversal of Disraelian expansionist foreign policy came to be defined as the "Nixon Doctrine," better known in its first major application in Southeast Asia, as "Vietnamization" — a policy of turning clients into allies and of reaching out for local proxies, in order not to spread American power "too thinly, especially in politically underdeveloped areas."

It was in 1972 that Kissinger brought the Nixon doctrine to Iran. From the vantage-point of the Shah, it was as if God Himself had intervened to renew the grand old times of Iran's collaboration with diaspora Jews of a high statesmanly character. In the first volume of his memoirs, covering his service as national security adviser, and therefore titled *The White House Years*, Kissinger gives us a retrospective view of his first official meeting with the Shah — who had by then already been driven from office; and he therefore writes about him, of course, with his usual melancholic admiration for poseurs who fall. Fresh from his Moscow "triumph" of that same year, where he had failed to get the Kremlin leaders to restrain Hanoi in her plans to conquer South Vietnam militarily (but had negotiated the Soviet-American detente accords anyway), President Nixon's foreign policy adviser had dashed off to Iran to set up another local bulwark against "Communist aggression." Kissinger's idea in those days was to pursue "peace at all costs" on a direct basis with Moscow while at the same time financing useless local struggles (always *insufficiently* supplied) in peripheral areas, as a gesture of Disraelian conservatism to avoid a "Middle America" backlash on the homefront. In Kissinger's words:

> From Kiev, we flew to Tehran on May 30, [1972], to be greeted by one of America's closest allies, the Shah of Iran. At the airport stood a slight, erect figure, Mohammed Reza Pahlavi, Shahanshah Aryamehr, imperial by title, imperious by bearing. America has little to be proud of in our reaction to his overthrow many years later. History is written by victors; and the Shah is not much in vogue today. Yet it hardly enhances our reputation for steadfastness to hear the chorus today against a leader whom eight Presidents of both parties proclaimed — rightly — a friend of our country and a pillar of stability in 2 turbulent and vital areas.... Without doubt the Shah was an authoritarian ruler. This was in keeping with the traditions, perhaps even the necessities, of his society. It was for a time the source of his strength just as it became later a cause of his downfall.
>
> As time went on and I got to know the Shah better, I realized that he was not by nature a domineering personality.... I could

never escape the impression that he was a gentle, even sentimental man who had schooled himself in the maxim that the ruler must be aloof and hard, but had never succeded in making it come naturally. His majestic side was like a role rehearsed over the years. In this he was a prisoner, I suspect, of the needs of his state, just as he was ultimately the victim of his own successes.

We have there an example of Henry Kissinger's well-known penchant for successes that have ruinous consequences. In his doctoral dissertation, *The World Restored* (New York, 1957), for instance, he had said of the old Austrian statesman with whom he himself has been compared: "The success of Clemens von Metternich made inevitable the ultimate collapse of the state he had fought so long to preserve." Kissinger's White House boss had a comparable success, as we all know. Under the ex-Harvard professor's Disraelian direction, the old cold-war warrior had "succeeded" in reversing the Soviet-American coldwar relationship of twenty-five years standing. The evidence was unmistakable — documented repeatedly by the *New York Times* and *Washington Post* — that Kissinger was the true architect of that reversal. Walter Lippmann, however, had boldly urged his readers to be "grateful" to Nixon for having made it possible. "Only Nixon, among the available public men," he had written, "could have made such a reversal." The rule, he explained, has been well-known to political operatives since the days of Benjamin Disraeli: "You always get conservatives to do the liberal things. . . . In Nixon's case it's very dramatic because he was such a violent and unscrupulous anti-communist, but nevertheless it's in the correct order of political progress that it's happening."

We have there the key to Nixon's "inevitable collapse" in the Watergate cover-up scandal of his second term. Disraelian reversal-politics is in essence unprincipled. It is by intent a betrayal of the faith of the Disraelian's old-time supporters; and yet it purports to be "dishing" those whose policies it surreptitiously advances and can therefore never gain their open approval. Nixon realized how desperate his plight was only after he had already thrown Spiro Agnew to the wolves and was plainly prepared to sacrifice everyone else to his right in his administration, if need be. But by then it was too late. In the end, with "Middle America" looking on in disbelief, he found himself standing alone, completely at the mercy of his old intellectual foes who, of course, showed no mercy. Desperately he looked to Kissinger for salvation. He made his White House assistant the nation's Secretary of State. Surely Kissinger's friends would intervene at the last minute to "save Henry" by saving his despised boss. But in that he proved to be as self-deluded as, in comparable circumstances years later, the Shah of Iran would prove to be. Nixon fell alone. He handed his letter of resignation to his former assistant. In what amounted to a White House coup d'etat, the ex-Harvard professor managed the extraordinary feat of dumping the captain of our ship of state and staying on as its pilot.

The fall of Iran's Shah from the heights of success has been, to be sure, a far less complex phenomenon than the collapse of Richard Nixon. In fact, the Shah's "success" had never been a reality. It had been from the beginning a staged success, a juggler's trick, concocted largely as a consequence of decisions taken by our government at about the time of Kissinger's first visit to Tehran in 1972.

A little later on we must examine in some detail Henry Kissinger's contribution to the Shah's dilemma, which consisted in his arming Iran to the teeth, uselessly, at the very same time that our fighting forces were being unilaterally withdrawn from Vietnam and detente at all costs was being negotiated with Moscow. Here we need to stress only that, just a few months before Kissinger's visit in 1972, the Shah had made a great show of pride in his country's pre-Arabic, pre-Islamic past, an ill-omened show (as we noted in passing earlier) that gave the foes of pan-Arabic Islam a clear signal. Although the Pahlavis had for fifty years professed loyalty to the traditional Shiite faith of Iran, what the Shah said and did with much public fanfare in 1971 proved that his intention was to bring about a reversal in the religious-political priorities of his land even more shockingly Disraelian — if he could get away with it — than the Kissinger-Nixon reversal of the Soviet-American cold-war relationship.

CHAPTER SEVEN

Kissinger's "Deal" With the Shah and Its Consequences, 1973-1979

We earlier quoted Gary Sick's words in his authoritative insider's study *All Fall Down: America's Tragic Encounter with Iran* (1985), where he says: "The decision by President Nixon and Henry Kissinger in 1972 to subordinate U.S. security decision making in the Persian Gulf to the person of the Shah was unprecedented, excessive and ultimately inexplicable." Our implied promise, when we first cited that last phrase — itself not easily explicable — was that we would in due course offer a rather obvious explication.

For guidance, one has only to look back to Walter Lippmann's analysis of the importance for American foreign policy in the 1970s of the previously unexpected Kissinger-Nixon alliance which literally shocked the American northeastern establishment intelligentsia when it first surfaced in December, 1968. Kissinger's appointment, announced at that time, as President-elect Nixon's national security adviser had instantly converted Walter Lippmann from a contemptuous critic of the new President into what can only be described accurately as a contemptuously ardent admirer. Lippmann — we must here repeat — had seen at once the *Disraelian* potential of such an alliance. "The theory when I was young and just learning about politics," he told his official biographer Ronald Steel, "was that you always got conservatives to do the liberal things, and liberals to do the conservative things."

In his review of Richard Nixon's *The Real War* (1980), Ronald Steel updated his account of Lippmann's reasons for taking up with enthusiasm the promise of a Kissinger-Nixon alliance in the name of traditional, hardline American conservatism. Steel singled out for praise the Kissinger-Nixon foreign policy initiatives which, after 25 years of cold war, led to "the restoration of ties with the communist rulers of China, the SALT treaties on nuclear weapons, and the first real movements towards detente with the Soviet Union," and added: "All of these were Nixon's accomplishments, however much help he got from Kissinger." Echoing his mentor Lippmann, he then proceeded to explain: "Only Nixon had the political skills — and, it should be stressed, the anticommunist credentials — to pull them off. Even the duplicitous 'Vietnamization' program, with its heartless bombing campaign and its cynical prolongation of the war for four years with great agony and no apparent gain, could be called a political success for it diffused domestic opposition and masked defeat."

1. Retrospective Inquiries During the 1980 Presidential Campaign

But of greater relevance here are the links Lippmann's biographer Steel drew in 1980 between the Kissinger-Nixon detente initiatives and the sudden build-up of the Iranian Shah after 1972, as America's "anointed gendarme in the Middle East." Steel recalled that, "under a secret agreement in May 1972," Kissinger and Nixon "personally gave the Shah permission to buy any conventional weapon in the American arsenal"; and that, "in the four years beginning in 1973 the Shah spent $15 billion on weapons, making him the world's leading arms buyer." What it also did, of course, was to make the Shah's "ultimate collapse" — to borrow Kissinger's phrase — "inevitable, despite his successes."

When Steel wrote those words in 1980, what was to become the 444-day hostage crisis under Carter had reached its exacerbating climax. As the election in which Carter was to suffer an ignominious defeat approached, the newsmedia undertook almost daily reviews of details of American Iranian relations since the countercoup of 1953. But the primary focus was inevitably on the apparent futility of the military build-up of the Shah that started with the secret Kissinger accord of 1972. In due course, highly publicized inquiries were pursued that focused primarily on Kissinger's initiatives in (1) the decision of 1972 to sell the Shah all the conventional weapons he could afford to buy, (2) the OPEC decision to raise the price of crude oil high enough to make the Shah's regime the largest arms purchaser in the world, and (3) the maneuvers, both in our country and in Iran, to prevent normalization of relations with the successor regime after the Shah's fall.

How Kissinger defended himself against such inquiries was determined, in 1980, entirely by his high political hopes and expectations. Eager to earn a place for himself in a victorious Republican administration, he quickly made clear his readiness to play his old Disraeli-conservative game to the hilt for Ronald Reagan against the hostility of the establishment newsmedia, as he had done for Nixon early in his first term. His admirers in the media hastened to oblige him, representing him as a foreign-policy hawk. Even Jack Anderson obligingly wrote several columns on the subject, pointing to Kissinger's purposive ambiguities as examples of "conservative duplicity." But he was outdone in this by a segment of the highly rated "60 Minutes" TV news program, with Dan Rather serving as interviewer and commentator. The central theme of the segment was a charge that, with respect to Iran, Kissinger had, with Nixon's nodding consent, circumvented "the will of Congress" by "raising great sums of money" to finance the build-up of Iran under the Shah as a staunch anti-communist, right-wing, authoritarian force. In retrospect, we have an apparent parallel there with what Colonel Oliver North would later be accused of doing on an incomparably smaller scale in 1985-1986.

With Kissinger "under fire" as a "conservative hawk," William F. Buckley, with his characteristic noblesse, hastened to take up the defense. Summing up the case that Dan Rather's segment of "60 Minutes" and other newsmedia personalities had mounted against the ex-Secretary of State, Buckley wrote these prescient words:

> Dan Rather put together a program the thesis of which was that Kissinger, while serving as secretary of state, searched out means of financing one of his, and Nixon's objectives namely, to trans-

form Iran into a first-class military power. To do this required the purchase of highly specialized and extremely expensive equipment, notably aircraft. Congress was not about to give the Shah free planes, and Iran didn't have the financial reserves to buy them. So? Why not suddenly encourage the Shah to raise the price of oil? That way, from the increased revenues, the money would be there to buy the arms. Rather got together, to document the thesis, James Akins, who had been ambassador to Saudi Arabia during the period when the oil prices first went up, George Ball, who while doing special work on Iran for President Carter got to review the cable traffic back in 1973 and 1974, and William Simon, former secretary of the treasury under Nixon and Ford.

In other words, in an election year that favored a Republican victory, Kissinger was getting himself conveniently charged with having engaged in dirty tricks to help a right-wing "authoritarian" regime in Iran! The ex-Secretary of State had at first agreed to appear personally in the segment of "60 Minutes" titled the "Kissinger-Shah Connection," but had later declined. He would appear, he said, only if certain "terms" were met. He wanted several persons who worked with him to be called in as witnesses, to discount the "testimony" of Akins, Ball, and Simon against him. The terms were rejected on the grounds that the witnesses suggested had acted as Kissinger's agents and not on their own. Instead of appearing, Kissinger sent a letter explaining that, "immediately after the OPEC decision [to raise the price of oil] on December 28," he had written a "strong letter of protest to the foreign minister of Saudi Arabia and to President Sadat." He explained further that, "on the basis of my recommendation and draft," President Nixon, in turn, had "sent a strong letter of protest to the king of Saudi Arabia." Finally, "on December 29," he took the "decisive" move of sending "an even stronger protest to the Shah." Off the record, Kissinger added that the American Ambassador Akins "is lying," and is "engaged in a personal vendetta against me." George Ball, he said, "is jealous of me" and wants to "destroy me"; and the whole thing, including William Simon's part in it, was to be dismissed, he said, as "malicious, ridiculous, and untrue."

Yet it is a fact confirmed by the Shah himself that he "cleared the huge 1973-74 oil price increases — the first such boosts — with Henry Kissinger, who was Secreaty of State." And Ambassador Akins' letter on the subject is a matter of record. The Shah had insisted, in dealing with the reluctant Saudi Arabian leaders, that he had received a go-ahead signal directly from Kissinger. The Saudis, Akins wrote, had begun to suspect "quite correctly, that Kissinger wanted to enrich the Shah in order to build him up as the guardian of the Persian Gulf." Paraphrasing the words of Sheikh Ahmed Zaki Yamani, the Saudi oil minister, Akins added: "He said that the talk of eternal friendship between Iran and the Unites States was nauseating to him and other Saudis. They knew that the Shah was a megalomaniac, that he was highly unstable mentally, and if we didn't recognize this, there must be something wrong with our powers of observation. Furthermore, if the Shah departs, we could have a violent, anti-American regime in Tehran."

2. J.C. Hurewitz's Analysis of the Corruptive Force of the Deal

In *The White House Years,* Henry Kissinger gives us this pathetically cosmopolitan eulogy of the kind of transnational, transreligious concept of government the Shah of Iran had been induced to entertain for himself: "The grandeur of Persian aspirations and culture imposed its own consciousness, transcending the national origin, race, or purpose of the invaders [in the course of centuries]. The result was not a nation state in the European sense but a potpourri of Persians, Kurds, Baluchis, Afghans, Jews, Turkomans, Arabs, and many others. For twenty-five hundred years Iran has been governed as an empire even as the dynasties changed; the state needed a unifying principle beyond that of the many nationalities composing it. In one of the ironies of history, the most individualistic peoples and centrifugal societies sometimes create the most absolute forms of rule, as if only the most exalted authority could justify subordination. In Iran, whatever the dynasty, the authority of governance ultimately resided in the remoteness of the emperor."

Missing in that passage is any significant reference to the Islamic faith of the overwhelming majority of the people of Iran. How does a ruler who has no inherent religious or national ties with his subjects sustain himself? The answer from the remotest times has always been: by isolating himself from his subjects, and by relying upon a virtually alien police and military force for his protection. The Shah had built up the necessary police force, starting in 1953, with the help of the CIA and Israeli friends. But it was not until after the meetings with Henry Kissinger in 1972 that he began an effective building up of his military force. J.C. Hurewitz, professor of government and director of the Middle East Institute of Columbia University, has summed up the situation for us in *The Persian Gulf: After Iran's Revolution* (New York, 1979). "Between 1945 and 1972," he writes, "Iran had spent a total of $1.2 billion on arms imports. Over the next half-dozen years, the Shah entered into commitments for the purchase of more than $18 billion worth of weapons, among them some of the most sophisticated systems in the inventories of the Unites States and its Western European allies — including F-14 Tomcat fighters with Phoenix air-to-air missiles that give the fighter its 100-mile reach, P-3F Orion antisubmarine patrol planes, Chieftain tanks, Spruance-class destroyers, and the AWACS (airborne warning and control system), a plane which even major allies of the United States found too expensive."

What was Kissinger's role in this massive Iranian arms buildup? Professor Hurewitz, who is by no means a critic of Kissinger's long-range aims in the Middle East or elsewhere, put it this way: "The Shah was able to do this becauise the United States in May 1972 had agreed to sell him virtually any conventional military hardware he wanted. The decision was taken by President Richard M. Nixon and his national security adviser, Henry A. Kissinger — at a time, it should be noted, before anyone foresaw the monumental rise in the price of crude oil that was about to take place in less than 20 months, placing in the Shah's hands more money than he could have anticipated in his wildest dreams. It proved a rash decision which lifted all normal U.S. restraints on the transfer of the most advanced conventional weapons to third world countries."

The question that we have to pose here immediately suggests

itself. Is it true that, when the "rash decision" was taken in 1972 to enable the Shah to arm himself, *no one* foresaw that there would be a monumental escalation of the price of crude oil to supply him with money to pay for the buildup — so manifestly useless in terms of America's real interests? The evidence is piling up to prove that Kissinger, for one, very clearly foresaw how the large sums to be paid to American arms manufacturers were to be raised, and that he, perhaps more than anyone else, facilitated the Shah's fund-raising drive to transform Iran into at least the *semblance* of a "first class military power."

3. A Shaky Throne: Illusory Support of the "Nixon Doctrine"

There was little doubt that the Shah's vast expenditures for arms after 1973 aroused widespread opposition in Iran. The major catalysts were an ever increasing presence of American technical experts and manifestly closer ties with Israel. Writing in early 1979, Professor Hurewitz thus summed up the situation:

> To these gathering forces of resistance the Shah's answer was threefold. He sought to outweigh them by the new military and economic classes which he rapidly created, and to whom he looked for loyalty. He sought to inspire and awe them with a cult of personality built around his imperial person and the ancient, pre-Islamic Persian heritage of kingly rule. Finally, what he could not outweigh or inspire he sought to repress through the all-too-familiar apparatus of the police state. His secret police, known as SAVAK, became for the opposition the most hated force in Iran. The list of political dissidents abroad lengthened....
>
> Until 1977 there were no untoward signs that the Shah's system was in danger. The first symptom of possible internal disorder, visible in retrospect, was his sudden, unexplained dismissal in August 1977 of the government of Prime Minister Amir Abbas Hoveida after a dozen years in office. But...the first overt sign of serious opposition, and of its probable source, came in Janu-

ary 1978. Out of a blue sky the government had inspired the publication of a letter accusing Ayatollah Khomeini, then in his 14th year of exile, of collaborating with the Communists in a conspiracy to overthrow the Iranian monarchy. On January 9, in reply to the letter, opponents of the Shah staged a protest demonstration in the shrine city of Qumm. Although the demonstrators were met with force, the opponents of the Shah grew progressively bolder as 1978 wore on.

The paradox of the situation was that, with his feared secret police, the Shah had dealt quite effectively with the internal Communist opposition. His direct deals with Moscow, paralleling Kissinger's detente negotiations (and no doubt facilitated by Kissinger), had in fact deprived the local Communists of Soviet support. His success there led him to make his singularly grave mistake, which was to try to dispose of the austerely religious Shiite-Islamic opposition by linking it with the Communists. Had he not been such a determined modernizer, had he not been so hostile to the traditional street processions commemorating the martyrdoms of Hassan and Hussein during the Muharram mourning period — which is to say, had he not borne the name Pahlavi — he might have guarded himself against such a mistake. At any rate, by the time of the Muharram observances of early December 1978, it was too late to reverse things.

What was the professed American justification for Henry Kissinger's military build-up of the Shah after the start of Soviet-American detente in 1972? It was the so-called Guam or Nixon doctrine which, in its initial application in Vietnam, was called "Vietnamization." Kissinger had explained the doctrine, with his characteristically Disraelian ambiguity, in a *Foreign Affairs* article of January 1969, titled "The Vietnam Negotiations," written before he went to work in the White House basement. Its underlying idea was that, in seeking a "global resolution" to its inherited cold-war of 25 years standing, the Nixon administration should cease to treat its cold-war client-states as clients, and begin to treat them as allies. America, such former clients were abruptly to understand, helps those who help themselves. We would be generous. But eventually the Saigon government, for instance, would have to manage to defend itself on its own. If, after a "decent interval," that proved to be impossible, it would simply have to collapse in the face of persistent Communist aggression.

What about the relationship of the Viet Cong to Hanoi? In the closing pages of his January 1969 article, Kissinger insisted that the Viet Cong, the NLF in the South, were indeed true clients, not allies, of the Hanoi regime. "Hanoi," he wrote, "cannot be asked to leave the NLF to the mercy of Saigon." The relationship was one of total dependence — quite the opposite of the Washington-Saigon relationship. "As for the United States," Kissinger concluded, "if it gains a reasonable time for political consolidation, it will have done the maximum possible for an ally — short of permanent occupation."

The monstrous misrepresentation there is that the Thieu government in Saigon was ever in any sense an "ally" rather than a creature of the American government. The Diem regime had been, in some measure, an ally, for it had resisted the Communist aggressors while there were never more than 14,000 American troops on Vietnamese soil. But, after Washington gave its order to "dump Diem," the successor regime was pure and simply a client, an agent, on a trifling scale, of America's limited-war commitment to resist local Communist aggression in the third world. President Johnson had understood this. That is why, to the very end, he refused to reduce the American troop level in South Vietnam by even a single soldier. The reversal came with Kissinger. As he explained things to Nixon, detente with Moscow and normalization of relations with Peking would permit the United States to leave its third world clients to fend for themselves, with a fair chance of surviving, since, in their eagerness to enjoy the advantages of detente, the Communist world leaders would willingly restrain their clients, in Southeast Asia and elsewhere.

4. The Vietnamization of Iran

In an article titled "Should U.S. Create a Quick-Strike Force?" (December 1, 1979), *New York Times* correspondet Robert Burt explained in some detail why the "crisis in Iran" had brought to a head the long-mounting criticism of the Kissinger-Nixon decision of 1969 to treat our third-world clients as allies — in the expectation that Soviet-American detente would suffice to deter local aggressors from taking advantage of the new situation. The United States, Burt pointed out, has indeed had the "ability to intervene in military conflitcts around the globe since World War II." The Marine Corps is "equipped and trained for fighting in small 'brush fire' wars," and our military still assure us that "a large fraction of the Army's 82nd Airborne Division," which is kept on continuous alert, "could be flown anywhere in the world within 24 hours." But that is beside the point. In Burt's very candid words:

> Since the end of American involvement in Indochina, successive administrations have followed the so-called Nixon Doctrine of 1969, which said that local military forces, rather than American troops, had the primary responsibility for deterring aggression in the third world. Under Shah Mohammed Reza Pahlavi, Iran emerged in the 1970s as something of a regional policeman, giving military help to neighboring countries, such as Oman, that faced threats from insurgent groups. But the collapse of the Shah's reign in Iran and its replacement by a fiercely anti-American Islamic Government have prompted a thorough review of the Nixon Doctrine.

Yet why hadn't there been a "thorough review of the Nixon Doctrine" back in 1975, after its application in Vietnam had "made inevitable" the Thieu government's collapse and the total humiliation of our embassy staff which was literally "run out of town" by the conquerors? As Secretary of State, Kissinger had insisted to the end that his detente "back-up" system would work: a last-minute Kremlin call would abruptly restrain Hanoi's violence, so that the surrender of Saigon could be peacefully negotiated as "inevitable." In *The White House Years*, Kissinger quite brazenly reminds us that, at the time of his famous "tilt" toward Pakistan, on the eve of the India-Pakistan war of late 1971, he had been counting on Soviet intervention to restrain Indira Gandhi from waging war. Had he tilted toward Pakistan to prevent the separation of East Pakistan —

which has since come to be called Bangladesh? No. As he now acknowledges: "There was no question of 'saving' East Pakistan. Both
Nixon and I had recognized for months that its independence was
inevitable; war was not necessary for its accomplishment.... The
Soviet Union could have restrained India; it chose not to." But that
had happened in late 1971, before the March and April Summit Meetings in Moscow to negotiate Soviet-American detente. One of the
arguments that Kissinger pressed on Nixon in favor of detente was
that, to enjoy its advantages, Moscow would indeed thereafter pull
the reins on its clients.

Of course, nothing of the sort ever happened. After our unilateral troop withdrawal from South Vietnam, we continued to pour
countless quantities of arms and equipment into the area; and, in
the end, it all passed into the hands of the conquering enemy. Meanwhile, the same doctrine was being implemented in Iran. Obviously
the arms and technology poured into Iran starting in 1973 served
only to conceal momentarily another aspect of the American global
retreat from power architected by Kissinger. Yet, after the Shah's
fall, he brazenly based his bid to gain a post for himself in a prospective Republican administration on seemingly hardline proposals
designed to "tilt" the country once again in the wrong direction,
committing it to "stick with the Shah." By doing that — given the
almost conspiratorial media support he received as a "private person" — he supplied the forces of the radical left in Iran (as well as
agents of foreign governments anxious to prevent normalization of
Iranian-American relations at this time) with a series of golden op-
portunities.

5. *Foreign Stakes in the Shah's Fall and Israel's Special Dilemma*

Even before the Shah set off on his extended vacation on January 16, 1979, many of the major oil-importing countries were making plans to negotiate new trade deals with a successor regime
enjoying the full support of the Ayatollah Khomeini. On this theme,
Walter Eytan had observed back in early December 1978 that the

Western nations and Japan would have been foolish and irresponsible had they acted otherwise. Obviously, once the Shah fell, Moscow and its revolutionary agents in the area would try to fish in troubled waters. But the Shah had in fact consistently lived up to his treaties with the Soviet Union. He had not been above using his "flirtations with Moscow" to blackmail the West (particularly the United States) into giving him ever more generous support. A genuinely Islamic republic might be less apt to play such a game. And, as for continuing oil sales to the West, Eytan — who brings to his prescient journalism the support of well-informed service as a former director general of the Israeli Foreign Ministry — had thus summed up the prospects as of December 11, 1978:

> Western countries, including Israel, have certainly been as interested in buying Iranian oil as Iran has been in selling it. They naturally have sought to insure their interests by shoring up the Shah whenever they could. When the Shah decided he had to build up the mightiest armed force in the area, he found willing suppliers — who of course had an interest, as well, in recovering at least some of the money they had paid out for Iran's oil. However, as Professor Geoffrey Barraclough has recently pointed out in *The New York Review of Books* (November 9, 1978): 'One has only to look at recent events in Iran to see that lavish investment in sophisticated American military hardware is no guarantee against a population goaded by poverty and oppression.'
>
> With France and Britain each following its own scenario in Iran, the United States has been seeking, apparently for the first time, to make contact with the forces [opposed to the Shah]. The Iranians are Shiite Muslims by religion, with their fiery leader, Ayatollah Khomeini, living in exile (conveniently for the French government) in Paris, and directing his followers to mutiny and revolt from there.... Besides Khomeini, in Iran itself there is the National Front, which long sought in vain for American understanding and support. No new Iranian regime will be freer than the Shah has been from fear of the Soviet Union, for whoever comes to power knows that it is not the USSR who will buy up the country's oil. Thus there are objective conditions which sug-

gest that the West will not have to write off Iran as wholly as it has had to write off Afghanistan.

But then Eytan had added these ominously candid words: "None of this, however, is applicable to Israel." Israel's age-old presence in Iran, he explained, was a factor here. As of December 1978, there were 80,000 Iranian Jews still living in Iran and another 80,000 that had settled in Israel. That balance had helped to maintain close ties under the Shah. But, even with the mounting "anti-Israel" feeling among the Shiite masses, the "average Jew in Iran belongs to the business and professional classes and cannot see his way to uprooting himself, even in the disastrous situation that prevails today." Yet the status of Jews remaining in Iran is one thing; the interests of the state of Israel, Eytan urged, "are a different story." And he proceeded to explain:

> Whatever links to the West a new regime may preserve, these are not likely to extend to Israel.... Israel has for years bought most of its oil imports from Iran. This source could easily be shut off by a new Iranian regime, especially since it represents only a miniscule part of Iran's total production. Israel would then have to find new and probably more costly, because more distant, suppliers.
>
> There is another vision which seems to be fading, even if the Shah remains. Political planners in the United States have seen an Israeli-Egypt peace pact not only as an asset in itself, but as a cornerstone of future stability.... Given peace with Egypt and Israel's sturdy footing in Iran under the Shah, added to the powerful pro-Western interests of the Saudis, it looked at last as if some truly solid bulwark could be built up against Soviet encroachment. Now this dream must vanish.

Israel, Egypt, and Iran are, as already noted, the three powers of the Middle East that can boast of glorious pre-Islamic, non-Arabic, ancient cultural heritages. The Shah's Iran celebrated its pre-Islamic heritage at Persepolis in 1971. More recently, Egypt has seen all of culture-minded America flock to local museums to view its pre-Islamic "King Tut" exhibits. And with Saudi Arabia — rich in oil and sand but sparsely populated — so manifestly dependent on the oil-consuming West for its well-being: why not make it a fourth side of America's solidly *tetragonal* interest in Middle East security?

Still, the Kissinger-Nixon-Ford build-up of the Shah, Eytan had acknowledged, proved to be counterproductive. The man on the Peacock Throne, it had to be acknowledged, gave off an "unwholesome image in the world as a whole." For the time being, he concluded in 1978, Washington "is stuck with him, just as it was stuck for so long with General Anastasio Somoza in Nicaragua. But just as it has been doing its best, however belatedly, to disengage from Somoza, it has begun as well to seek new allies and a new leverage in Iran." That will mean, however, at least a temporary strain in US-Israeli relations. "Iran," wrote Eytan in his final sentence of December 11, 1978, "is at Israel's door — and at Washington's too."

CHAPTER EIGHT

Kissinger's Man in Iran: William H. Sullivan

When the Shah was forced to give up his Peacock Throne in January 1979, Henry Kissinger had been "out of office" for two years. But, with his Rockefeller connections, and the vast network of power interests that he brought with him out of his government service, the ex-Harvard professor was able, in his apparently private capacities, to affect the course of public events far more profoundly than most top-level wielders of official power — not excluding the new President, Jimmy Carter. During his White House years, Carter was to have many direct confrontations with Kissinger, in all of which the President plainly lost. From the point of view of this study, the most significant of those confrontations had to do with U.S.-Iranian relations, starting with the controversy over the admission of the fallen Shah to the United States during the spring and summer of 1979, and the consequent "hostage crisis" that started with the seizure of the American Embassy in Tehran by radical factions on November 4, 1979.

Yet, to be really effective as a political force, Kissinger out of office needed the help of a least a few high-placed inside collaborators; and so, during his last weeks in office, he worked frantically to gain Carter's acceptance of the services of two men who had indeed been his closest collaborators in winding down the war in Vietnam. The two were General Alexander M. Haig who, at the time of Carter's election was serving as Supreme Allied Commander in NATO, and William H. Sullivan, U. S. Ambassador to the Philippines. Before leaving office, Kissinger managed to get Carter to

133

nominate Sullivan to succeed Richard Helms as U.S. Ambassador to Iran, and to look favorably on the idea of appointing Haig to a second two-year term as NATO commander, which Carter in due course proceeded to do.

Haig and Sullivan had both been recommended to Henry Kissinger, originally, by public officials with impeccable Democratic-liberal credentials. In the case of Haig, the strongest recommendation had come from that leading liberal counsellor of the Kennedy and Johnson presidencies, Joseph Califano, with whom Haig had served under Robert McNamara and Cyrus Vance. (It was Califano, and not any "Reaganite," who sat at Haig's side as counsel and confidant during the Senate hearings on Haig's confirmation as Secretary of State.) In the case of Sullivan, the chief sponsor had been no less a Democratic-liberal establishment figure than W. Averell Harriman, who had early groomed him for high office, advancing him through the foreign-service ranks, during the 1960s, almost as rapidly as Henry Kissinger would later advance Haig up through the highest military ranks in the early 1970s.

President Carter evidently mistook Haig and Sullivan for bureaucratic loyalists. He imagined they would work for him as loyally as they had worked for Kissinger in a Republican administration, and for Kissinger's predecessors in earlier Democratic administrations. But in that view he proved to be gravely mistaken. By mid-1979, it was patently clear that all through Carter's presidential term, Kissinger's international "strategic" interests had been far better served by Sullivan and Haig than Carter's had ever been.

The Haig/Kissinger connection is, of course, well-known. Here we want to point out that, for Kissinger, it has always been a self-protective connection. Roger Morris, who was a member of Kissinger's inner-circle in the Nixon White House basement when the connection started, has given his studied opinion about it in his *Uncertain Greatness: Henry Kissinger and American Foreign Policy* (New York, 1977). After stressing the fact that he approved completely of Kissinger's *ends* in reversing the American cold-war policy of 25 years standing, Morris expressed fears about the *means,* and about the measures Kissinger was constrained to pursue to protect himself in Nixon's hostile White House. The most notable of such measures, according to Morris, was the close relationship with Haig. As Morris puts it:

> Kissinger needed Haig to provide reassurance, as well as to act as a litmus test on the right in a government where Kissinger was unlikely to be attacked successfully from the left. For the most controversial policies Kissinger planned — initiatives in arms control and ending the war — he would be, he believed, most vulnerable to criticism. Haig the decorated combat veteran, the leathery soldier of stern opinions, would help clothe those actions. Jealous of the relationship as well as of Haig's power, Helmut Sonnenfeldt would joke in acid terms that Kissinger the German-Jewish immigrant kept on Haig, the all-American colonel from Philadelphia to testify at some imagined right-wing trial, if Henry went too far with detente.

Just how much acid there was in Sonnenfeldt's "joke" about the Kissinger-Haig relationship is made abundantly clear in Seymour Hersh's comment on it in *The Price of Power: Kissinger in the Nixon White House* (New York, 1983). Confirming Roger Morris's account, Hersh adds that "Kissinger's reliance on Haig was a constant topic of conversation among ambitious men in the National Security Council." Evidently, Sonnenfeldt "often theorized to other staff people that Kissinger wanted Haig around to testify in his defense at a war-crimes trial," the Sonnenfeldt thesis being that, since Kissinger's "real fear was a reaction from the right," Haig was "needed to testify to Kissinger's patriotism." [116] Hersh and Morris were both acknowledging the patently Disraelian dissimulation in Kissinger's hawkish pronouncements on national security affairs. His deeds would betray him in the end, Kissinger feared; and it seemed prudent, therefore, to "buy protection," while there was still time, by facilitating Haig's meteoric rise through the ranks from colonel to four-star general in little more than three years.Haig's original appointment by President Ford to the NATO command-post created for 5-star General Eisenhower owed much to Kissinger; and his reappointment to it in 1977 was almost entirely due to Kissinger's intervention. In due course, Haig amply paid back his sponsor by taking up Kissinger's position in his attacks on President Carter's Iran policy.

1. Introducing Sullivan

Kissinger's long-time links with Ambassador Sullivan have been less publicized or commented upon, but they run much deeper. And perhaps the best brief introduction to them — if we are to avoid preliminary bias — is that provided by a *Time* magazine biographical profile published in its February 26, 1979 issue. By that date, the Shah had already fled into exile, and the interregnum of his last Prime Minister, Shapour Bakhtiar, had abruptly collapsed, to be replaced by the triumphant Ayatollah Khomeini's first revolutionary administration, headed by Bakhtiar's old friend and colleague of the Mossadegh days, Mehdi Bazargan. In that chaotic period of new beginnings for the revolution, a band of heavily-armed radicalized militants, acting on their own, had stormed the U.S. Embassy in Tehran, taking the American Ambassador, William H. Sullivan, and most of his staff captive.

That "embassy seizure" of February 14, 1979 (St. Valentine's Day) has, of course, been totally eclipsed by the "second embassy seizure" of November 4, 1979, which went on and on, with pathetic consequences for the Carter administration; but, even more, for the Ayatollah's first ministries, all headed by pro-American "moderates," and all toppled by the threats from the embassy attackers that they would "kill hostages" if the Ayatollah didn't instantly dismiss the governments they disapproved of. But, at the time of its occurrence, that earlier St. Valentine's Day attack had been big news, featured in all the papers and other newsmedia of the "free world." The February 26 issue of *Time* presented the event as its cover-story, which it supplemented with a colorfully-boxed biography of the Ambassador in charge, under the title: "Sullivan — Cool Salesman." Included with it was a picture taken some years back showing the cool salesman with Henry Kissinger, both of them smiling broadly, while the accompanying text emphasized that Sullivan had indeed been Kissinger's chief collaborator in drawing up the terms of the Paris Accords of January 1973 which, as the *Time* biography stressed, "brought peace to Vietnam."

That profile also reviewed Sullivan's diplomatic service before he joined Kissinger — and Haig — in the Vietnam peace negotiations. We are told that, back in 1962, Sullivan had had the good fortune to be "tapped as deputy of the American delegation to the Laos neutrality conference in Geneva by then Assistant Secretary of State W. Averell Harriman." Harriman, the profile explained, had reportedly admired what he described as Sullivan's ability "to see the other fellow's point of view." Thereafter, Sullivan "was regarded as a Harriman protege and as an expert on Southeast Asia," and he was quickly moved up in the diplomatic service. His "five-year assignment (1964-1969) as Ambassador to Laos," soon followed; and it was then, as the *Time* profile noted, that "he caught the eye of Henry Kissinger."

Linking Sullivan's prior service under Harriman and Kissinger with his service in Iran, the *Time* reporter noted first that Sullivan's ambassadorial appointment to Iran in the spring of 1977 had been "among the first made by the new Carter Administration," and that Senate approval had come easily. But, since the theme of the short biography was that Sullivan was not only cool but also tough — like his past sponsors Harriman and Kissinger — the *Time* reporter went on to observe that, had he been "proposed later" for the same post, "there is some question as to whether Sullivan would have been approved by the Senate Foreign Relations Committee," since several of the "liberals on the committee" had recently expressed "reservations about his role in Vietnam and his reputation for favoring authoritarian regimes." As a further indication of "toughness," there was an added comment that Sullivan had "also earned the enmity of antiwar activists, for he had directed the secret U. S. bombings of Pathet Lao targets in Laos," about which he "later admitted withholding the truth...from visiting members of Congress."

Those final evidences of toughness served, to be sure, to mark Sullivan as a "neo-conservative" of the special Disraelian breed nurtured by Kissinger. What has to be stressed, however (and we mean to stress it in due course), is the fact that, like Kissinger, Sullivan clearly favored authoritarian rulers only after they were hopelessly undermined and in their death throes. The *Time* profile on Sullivan had been written *after* the revolution that toppled the Shah was over. And, before the Shah, in Sullivan's career, there had been Diem and Thieu. That Sullivan was by then an old hand in dealing with collapsing autocrats was made graphically clear by the *Time* reporter's account of his first visit to Sullivan's embassy residence:

> The spiral staircase leading to the ambassador's office on the second floor of the American mission in Tehran is lined with photographs of the Shah with every President from F.D.R. to Jimmy Carter. In the ambassador's own living quarters there hangs a lacquered painting of a peaceful Vietnamese peasant scene with a simple inscription: "To my friend Bill Sullivan." The signature is that of South Vietnam's ex-President Nguyen Van Thieu.
>
> William H. Sullivan, 56, who played a major role in shaping U.S. policy in Southeast Asia, has been Washington's man in Iran since 1977. Last week, as he was held hostage in his own embassy, the irony of those mementos was apparent. "They shot up my home, my office and the chancery — an interesting Valentine's Day," said the ambassador. "You win some, you lose some."
>
> Sullivan's *sang-froid* was characteristic; he is known in diplomatic circles as a self-assured salesman of policy, cool under stress and adroit in coping with diplomatic delicacies. "I think he's got water for blood," says Eugene Lawson, a former State Department colleague who is now director at Georgetown University's foreign service school. "He's a collected, shrewd guy who always seems to land on his feet."

The same profile indicated that, for the first eighteen months of his two years in Iran, Sullivan had followed the example of his predecessor, former CIA Director Richard Helms, in requiring that his embassy staffers "avoid contact with the Shah's opposition." But then, as the *Time* account phrased it, late in 1978, he abruptly "reversed that position when the dimensions of the protest became apparent." He didn't do so officially, however. As the *Time* account explains: "American businessmen in Iran have found the silver-thatched envoy approachable and friendly, but many complain that he kept them in the dark about U.S. plans and perceptions." In fact, it was only rather late in December 1978 that he took the step of "asking Americans whose presence was not essential to leave Iran"; and it was not until there was a visibly widespread "fear of a tide of anti-American sentiment" that the further step was taken of "encouraging subordinates to open a dialogue with the Khomeini forces."

When Sullivan first arrived in Tehran as ambassador in June 1977, he was reportedly "asked about parallels between Tehran and Vientiane," the capital of Laos, where he had earlier served as ambassador. According to the February 1979 *Time* profile, his reply back in June 1977 had been "oddly prescient." He had said: "We ran Laos, but in Iran, which is tremendously important to us, there's not much we or anyone else can do." That had been a puzzling response. By June 1977, Laos had long since succumbed, like Cambodia and South Vietnam, to the might of our Communist enemies in Southeast Asia. Had it perhaps been Sullivan's intention in 1977 to suggest that, because we couldn't "run" Iran the way we had earlier "run" Laos, Iran might be spared a comparably harsh fate? Hardly. Functioning as Kissinger's man in Iran, Sullivan was from the start busy doing there what his long apprenticeship under Harriman in Geneva (1962-63) and Kissinger in Paris (1972-73) had prepared him to do.

2. Apprenticeship: Dumping Diem for Harriman and Thieu for Kissinger

In *The Best and the Brightest* (New York, 1972), David Halberstam has dwelt on the Harriman-Sullivan relationship, providing details not readily available elsewhere. The relationship began, we are told, after President Kennedy had assigned Harriman the job of getting a Laotian settlement in 1962. The "old man" had hastened to Geneva, writes Halberstam, where he was "appalled by the size of the mission and by the amount of deadwood." But then he spotted Sullivan, "a thirty-eight-year-old officer way down the list in seniority," whom he immediately liked. Halberstam explains why:

> Bill Sullivan had served in Asia as a young man and did not seem to spout the cliches of most of the mission, and Harriman immediately offered him a job as his deputy. Sullivan declined, noting that there were a dozen people senior to him in the mission. Several days later Harriman called Sullivan in again and offered him the

same job; by this time he had sent home everyone senior to Sullivan. This did not endear him to some of the departed who were connected with the Department's traditionalists, and, as he continued to negotiate with the Soviet delegate, G. M. Pushkin, there were mutterings that he was giving away too much of Laos, that great bastion. "I think the next cable will be signed 'Pushkin'," said one high-level official. Harriman's reaction when he heard of the remark was swift and devastating (he was not called "The Crocodile" for nothing), he decided that the man be transferred to...he thought for a minute and then chose...Afghanistan. [115]

In what he did for Kissinger during the Paris negotiations with Hanoi that culminated in the Paris Accords of January 1973, Sullivan clearly put the experience he had gained with Harriman, and as Ambassador in Laos, to work once more. The principle that had guided Harriman in Geneva has been called the principle of "fingertip feelings," and its application has been described in detail in a book by one of Kissinger's former students at Harvard, Dr. Allan E. Goodman. The book is provocatively titled *The Lost Peace: America's Search for a Negotiated Settlement of the Vietnam War* (Stanford, 1978). And it comes with a Foreword provided by William H. Sullivan, who was then already serving as ambassador in Iran. The book's author explains that Sullivan was asked to write the Foreword in recognition of the fact that he had been from the beginning the central figure in that search. In the author's preface, Sullivan is introduced with these precisely factual yet highly suggestive words:

> The secret search for a negotiated settlement in Vietnam actually began with a meeting between U.S. and North Vietnamese representatives in 1962.... The President authorized W. Averell Harriman and his deputy William Sullivan (later a deputy assistant secretary of state deeply involved in the negotiations during the Johnson and Nixon administrations) to approach the North Vietnamese delegates at the Geneva Conference with an offer of secret talks. The President wanted Hanoi to know that Washington regarded the conflict in South Vietnam as an internal Vietnamese affair. Harriman and Sullivan were to suggest that the Laos

Accords could serve as a model for an agreement guaranteeing Vietnam's neutrality.

This diplomatic overture to Hanoi had to be kept secret because, as one of Washington's emissaries put it, "To broadcast our meeting with North Vietnam would have alarmed the South Vietnamese who opposed such contacts. We knew if we were successful with Hanoi, we would have to bring Saigon around." The meeting and the site were arranged by the foreign minister of a neutral country attending the conference, and Harriman and Sullivan took an elaborate detour through Geneva alley-ways in order to avoid being seen by any of their South Vietnamese colleagues. They met with the former minister of North Vietnam and his military assistant, Colonel Ha Van Lau, who like Sullivan, later participated in the secret Paris Talks.

The so-called Geneva accords negotiated by Sullivan in 1962 were supposed to have provided an international basis for making good on President Kennedy's pledge to guarantee the safety of South Vietnam. Harriman was optimistic about them. But the syndicated columnist Joseph Alsop had wryly observed that such optimism reminded him "of the White Queen in *Alice in Wonderland* teaching herself to believe six impossible things before breakfast." [116] President Diem, who had to sign the accords, shared Alsop's view — to put it mildly. But, he couldn't simply mock them; for, if he signed those agreements, he would be expected by his patrons in Washington to live up to them: *pacta sunt servanda!* He was therefore furious, protesting "that the terms would tie South Vietnam's hands but not the Communist's hands." And he predicted correctly that, free from the kinds of restraints Washington would impose on his Saigon government, the Hanoi leaders would soon be intensifying their "use of the eastern part of Laos to move supplies and troops from North Vietnam to the South."

When he learned of Diem's recalcitrant outbursts, Harriman became something far worse than an old crocodile ready to snap off the legs of subordinates in our own government. For all his anger, poor Diem remained the head of a lowly client state. Out of sight of his Washington patrons, he might occasionally roar like an oriental tiger; but, in their presence, he had at best to play the fox. So he accepted the Geneva accords as drawn up by Sullivan, though he winced and whined in the process, like a dog who knows the difference between being stumbled over and being kicked. For that, Harriman refused to forgive him. Before long a full scale "dump Diem" crusade was unleashed in the American newsmedia and in the corridors of the foreign service where Harriman was still a power. In due course, the "dump Diem" movement built itself up into a Washington-backed coup d'etat which culminated, on November 1, 1963, in the brutal murder of Diem and his brother Ngo Dinh Nhu.

At some point, Harriman and John F. Kennedy had decided between them that continued American involvement in Southeast Asia affairs would be best served by removing President Ngo Dinh Diem from the South Vietnamese scene, and Sullivan's cool expertise was called upon to bring the necessary pressures to bear. He did such a thorough job of it that, when Henry Kissinger and Richard M. Nixon made a parallel decision regarding President Nguyen Van Thieu, Kissinger hardly hesitated for a moment before calling on the same Harriman protege who, by then, had had a lot more experience in the arts of breaking recalcitrant client governments in the course of five years service as American ambassador in troubled Laos.

Thus, when he joined Kissinger to negotiate peace with North Vietnam over Thieu's head in Paris, it was, for Sullivan, like old times once more. Only now there would be added the incalculable advantage of applying the old Harriman "fingertip feeling" under the far more protective cover of Richard Nixon's "indelible" reputation as a hardline, uncompromising anti-Communist.

On this point, Professor Goodman reminds us that, as far back as his 1969 article titled "The Vietnam Negotiations," published in the January 1969 issue of *Foreign Affairs,* Kissinger, who hadn't yet been sworn in as Nixon's chief national security advisor, had urged the application of an updated Harriman "fingertip-feeling" approach to negotiating a Vietnam peace. He called it his new "bargaining principle"; and, as Goodman observes, Kissinger was at pains there to explain what peace negotiatiors, since the time of Harriman and Sullivan in Geneva, had been neglecting to do. They had, according to him, persisted in the seemingly inevitable mistake of trying to reach a settlement by getting Hanoi to change its ways — to compromise on its declared aims. That hadn't worked, and couldn't work, Kissinger had argued, because Hanoi's Communist ideologues couldn't publicly compromise and survive domestically. As Dr. Goodman phrases it in retrospect, Kissinger's alternative, his new "bargaining principle," was this: "That an agreement would only be possible if the negotiations were aimed not at changing Hanoi's behavior — behavior that was incompatible with a long-term peaceful settlement of the conflict — but at changing Saigon's."

That is how Harriman and Sullivan had operated back in 1962 in Geneva. To make their deals with the North Vietnamese, they had had to take "elaborate detours" through Geneva's alleys so as not to betray their readiness to compromise to their South Vietnamese colleagues. Back then, the North Vietnamese had consistently maintained that "there was basically nothing to negotiate," that they weren't about to give up their basic demand for a total withdrawal of American forces from South Vietnam. Now, with Sullivan summoned back from Laos to serve as his chief deputy, Kissinger was proposing to let the North Vietnamese have their way for the sake of peace while getting Thieu's Saigon government to do all the necessary compromising.

The question for the North Vietnamese back in 1969 was: Could Kissinger get away with doing under Nixon what Harriman and Sullivan had attempted to do under Kennedy after the Geneva Accords were pressed on Diem? Diem had been struck down for refusing to go along with Harriman's "fingertip-feeling" strategy. But then Kennedy, too, had been struck down, and, for a long time there was no ruling authority in Saigon secure enough to do any compromising. What about now? Had President Nixon, with his "indelible" anti-Communist hardline reputation, really agreed to an application of Kissinger's new "bargaining principle"?

Three years were to pass, after publication of Kissinger's January 1969 article, before any serious evidence surfaced that Nixon was prepared to follow such a course. Then, in January 1972, when he was looking forward to his "journey for peace" to Moscow, scheduled for later in the year, Nixon surprised the American people (and Hanoi) by revealing that secret talks with the North Vietnamese enemy had indeed been going on, under Henry Kissinger's direction, since the early months of his presidential term. Kissinger's January 1969 article had been, in other words, a veritable blueprint for actualities to come.

Then came the Nixon trip to Moscow, prepared for at a secret meeting of Kissinger with top Soviet leaders in the Kremlin a few weeks earlier. It was Kissinger who laid the ground work for the agreements later reached by Nixon in the much publicized Moscow meetings. Strategies for peace in the Middle East were proposed and basic agreements were apparently reached with respect to peace in Vietnam. How all of that led to subsequent "break-throughs" in the Paris negotiations is thus summed up by Dr. Goodman, drawing directly, as he explains, on the substance of long interviews with Sullivan and Kissinger:

> The origin of the Paris Agreement [negotiated mostly by Sullivan] lies in the four sessions of the May 1972 Moscow Summit. Kissinger indicated to Soviet foreign minister Gromyko that Washington was at last prepared to be responsive to Hanoi's insistent demand that any agreement embody a political as well as a military solution: the United States was willing to sign an agreement calling for the creation of a tripartite commission to govern South Vietnam after the war. This idea provided the foundation for a conceptual breakthrough in the deadlocked secret negotiations; it permitted Le Duc Tho to propose a three-party "National Council of Reconciliation and Concord" with little fear that it would be rejected by Washington. For Kissinger, the essence of the conceptual breakthrough was that he could see an agreement that, from Hanoi's point of view, embodied a political solution while, from Washington's point of view, it embodied a solution ambiguous enough to forestall the charge that the United States had overthrown Thieu.

We begin to get a sense of what Kissinger valued in Sullivan when we take note of the fact that the terms of the Kissinger-Sullivan draft agreement had been kept from President Thieu until after Nixon had been prevailed upon to assure Hanoi that the terms "were acceptable to the United States." Nixon had, however, added the proviso that Saigon would "have to be consulted, of course." That did not mean, as Kissinger explained it to Hanoi, that Thieu would in any sense have a final veto in the matter. Thieu would be treated not as an ally — despite the rhetoric of "Vietnamization" — but as the client he in fact was. Still, there was the serious risk that, not Thieu, but "hardliners" in Washington — men around Nixon like John Erlichman and H. R. Haldeman (whom Kissinger regarded as personal enemies) — might try to exploit Thieu's objections in making a case of their own against the accords. It therefore became a matter of utmost urgency, from the standpoint of Sullivan and Kissinger, as architects of the Paris Accords, to get Thieu's at least nominal assent to them on the record as soon as possible. In Dr. Goodman's words: "What Kissinger feared most was a delay that would encourage every agency still seeking military victory in Vietnam to critique the agreement and to bring to bear on the President pressure (which he knew would be well orchestrated by Haldeman and Erlichman) to push for more than the North Vietnamese had already agreed to."

Sullivan was charged, at that time, with assuming full responsibility for the agreement's terms of supervision, while Haig was given the more onerous task of putting a personal squeeze on Thieu, to get him to accept the accords. Part of that was to make sure that other Americans who had access to Thieu would give him "no hope" — to cite the words of one of Haig's top colleagues at the time — "that there was any exploitable difference between Nixon and Kissinger on the cease-fire-in-place issue or that, with the election over, the President would change his mind about wanting the agreement."

The terms under discussion here were, of course, the same that prompted the notorious "peace-is-at-hand" Kissinger news conference of October 26, 1972, on the eve of Richard Nixon's landslide reelection to the Presidency. Hanoi radio had unexpectedly made those terms public the day before — a fact of which Kissinger became aware when Alexander Haig called him about it at 2:00 A.M. Fearing that things might get out of control, Kissinger immediately summoned Haig and Sullivan to the White House, and for the next three hours — as Bernard and Marvin Kalb have noted in their biography of Kissinger — "Kissinger, Haig, and William H. Sullivan, the State Department official who had been assigned to the negotiations...discussed ways of responding" to minimize the media damage.

During the news conference that followed later in the day, Sullivan's name came up in a conspicuous way for the first time. When reporters insisted on asking questions about the "portions of the agreement dealing with supervision" of the cease-fire, Kissinger sought to deflect them; and so, in his deepest professorial voice, he explained that the "details" of supervision were of a complexity and length which "will no doubt occupy graduate students for many years to come, and which, as far as I know, only my colleague, Ambassador Sullivan, understands completely."

It wasn't easy to get Thieu to make a public statement accepting such terms. Sullivan's diplomatic finesse, Haig's arm-twisting, and Kissinger's mounting contempt, made increasingly obvious, did not suffice in themselves to move him. Kissinger appealed to Nixon to teach Thieu a lesson. The result was the so-called Christmastime carpet-bombings of North Vietnam during the last two weeks of 1972 — the "biggest bombing campaign in the history of warfare" — with General Haig on hand in Saigon to spell out the lesson. President Thieu was to understand that, while Hanoi's vast invading army, entrenched in South Vietnam since the time of its Spring Offensive of 1972, was safely out of harm's way, the Christmas pounding of the North would appear to most Americans as positive proof that Nixon was keeping his word to Saigon. If, after that, Thieu persisted in holding out, he would have only himself to blame for any subsequent American loss of patience with him. Haig then handed Thieu what was plainly an ultimatum from President Nixon — no doubt drafted by Kissinger — informing him that he had "four days to make up his mind."

After four days, Thieu had said to Haig: "I have two choices: to be a short-term hero like Diem, who was done in by friendly Americans, or think of the long-range fate of my country." By that, Thieu could have meant only that he would give the Nixon ultimatum an appropriately-oriental reply. Taking advantage of Sullivan's skillfully-ambiguous phrasing of the settlement terms, he was choosing to save face temporarily, while knowing full well that his words of acceptance would at once be read by both Kissinger and his counterparts in Hanoi as a total "cave in."

Yet there was something more. Thieu finally yielded in the matter only after Kissinger produced for him, in writing, a solemn American presidential assurance that, "should the settlement" he was urged to sign "be violated by North Vietnam," the United States "would respond with full force" to secure the integrity of South Vietnam. Unfortunately, that presidential assurance had been given in secret. And we must suspect that, in procuring it for Thieu, Kissinger had been at pains to keep it secret not only from the American people and their Congress but also from Hanoi.

That was the opposite of what had occured at the time of President Eisenhower's "secret threat" that brought the fighting in Korea to an abrupt close in 1954. Eisenhower had made his secret threat directly to the enemy in North Korea, and to its supporters in Peking and Moscow. And he had disclosed its substance to the Congress, if not to the American people. Nixon, born-loser that he was, had, on the contrary, given his assurance of a full scale response to enemy aggression only to our South Vietnamese clients. It was the fact of its secrecy from Congress, and the rest of the Federal government, that permitted Kissinger — Nixon's partner in the secret — to get away with what he subsequently proceeded to do. After Nixon's resignation, in an obvious dereliction of duty, Kissinger failed to transmit the document to Congress.

President Thieu produced the officially-signed letter addressed to him by the President of the United States at a press conference only after he had fallen from power, in the last days of the North Vietnamese conquest of South Vietnam. Kissinger then sheepishly acknowledged that it had indeed been given; but he pretended that Nixon's resignation had somehow deprived it of juridical efficacy — which was utterly false. Then Kissinger, the great Disraelian pretender, indulged himself in the further pretense, persisted in to this day, that, had Nixon not been "forced to resign" by his political enemies at home, North Vietnam would not have ventured its military conquest of 1975, completed just 20 months after Nixon left office. What makes that a pretense is Kissinger's suggestion that he would have approved of Nixon's recourse to "massive retaliation" on the Eisenhower-Dulles model to defend the political integrity of South Vietnam.

In fact, Kissinger's entire career as a civilian national security strategist had been based, as we have seen, on criticism and rejection of the Eisenhower doctrine. Kissinger, as Secretary of State, therefore persisted in discounting the validity of Nixon's pledge to Thieu committing our country to wage all-out war, if need be, to secure South Vietnamese independence. As former chief of naval operations Admiral Elmer Zumwalt summed it up on May 1, 1975, after the final Saigon collapse: "The Nixon-Kissinger administration must bear a large share of the blame for the fact that Congress failed to honor those commitments that had been made in the name of the country." Needless to say, when Nixon lost his high place in that administration, the responsibility or blame devolved entirely on Kissinger, his *de facto* successor as "President for Foreign Affairs."

One final point needs to be stressed before moving on. President Nixon's pledge to Thieu remains significant, despite the fact that nothing came of it, for this reason: although he had been for years under Kissinger's tutelege, when the chips were down, even President Nixon, the self-proclaimed neo-pacifist, had finally joined Truman, Eisenhower, Kennedy, and Johnson in refusing to be the first popularly elected American President to deliberately lose a war. To gain even a semblance of American acceptance of our negotiated defeat in Vietnam, Kissinger had to content himself in the end with a non-elective Presidency — the *interregnum* of Ford and Rockefeller — something without precedent in American History.

3. Supervising Saigon's Surrender from the Philippines

The February 1979 *Time* biography of Sullivan noted that, after the Paris Accords of January 1973 had been negotiated and signed, Kissinger's favorite Southeast Asia troubleshooter — his cool salesman — had been abruptly appointed Ambassador to the Republic of the Philippines. As Frank Snepp informs us, in his much-publicized book *Decent Interval: An Insider's Account of Saigon's Indecent End Told by the CIA's Chief Strategy Analyst in Vietnam*

(New York, 1978), "veteran diplomat William H. Sullivan" had at that time "been slated to replace [Ambassador Ellsworth] Bunker in Saigon," but had "turned down the job." [71] Why had he turned down Saigon? There, he could have directly supervised the cease-fire he had helped to negotiate.

For Sullivan's own account of his options and preferences at the time, we can turn to his autobiography, *Obligato 1939-1979: Notes on a Foreign Service Career,* published in 1984. He there says nothing, of course, about having been offered the ambassadorship to Saigon; but, as for his acceptance of the Manila post "in the spring of 1973," he assures us that it had not been "designed to mean a clear break with the tentacles of Vietnam." On the contrary, "it was the intention," he writes, "that I should concurrently serve as the first American ambassador to Hanoi." He confides that, "after the Paris negotiations," his name had been "informally proposed to the North Vietnamese and had been accepted." No doubt it was Kissinger who proposed his name for the Hanoi post, even as he would later urge it on Carter for the ambassadorship to Iran. Poor President Thieu was being squeezed to accept a treaty that committed him and his country to unconditional surrender; and here were Kissinger and Sullivan making plans for normalized diplomatic relations with Thieu's and our own professed enemies in the north! Sullivan thus explains what he calls "the concept":

> The concept had been based on the premise that the Paris agreements would be observed and that the relations between Hanoi and Washington would be moved toward normalization. This would have meant the establishment of a small mission in Hanoi, to be permanently directed by a chargé. Because our Air Force had small executive jet transports located at Clark Field in the Philippines, I would be able quite literally to commute between Manila and Hanoi.... After I had been in Manila a short time, it became apparent that the Vietnam dimension of my duties would not materialize.... As [the North Vietnamese] came to sense how badly the Nixon administration had been wounded by Watergate. .. all thought of "normalizing" our relations with Hanoi through the establishment of an embassy evaporated. [248, 250]

Thus, the parallel with the Harriman-Sullivan scheme for dealing with Hanoi over the head of President Diem back in 1962 was complete. Back then, Sullivan and Harriman had advanced plans to gain Hanoi's cooperation in "settling" Vietnam's domestic controversies peaceably. But, when Diem crossed Harriman with his recalcitrance, and was purged as punishment, Hanoi perceived it as an abandonment of American whole-hearted support of the South, and therefore of any need to cooperate. Just so, the plans to peaceably establish an American embassy in Hanoi evaporated, as Sullivan says, once Hanoi realized that Kissinger had no intention of validating Nixon's pledges to Saigon as the "law of the land," by officially transmitting them to Congress.

In due course, during the so-called "decent interval," President Nixon got himself threatened with impeachment and was forced to resign, as we all know. He had tried to appease his critics by making foreign-born Henry Kissinger his Secretary of State — that being the first time an American Jew had held such high public responsibilities since the days of Judah Philip Benjamin in the Confederate government of Jefferson Davis. After Nixon's fall, Kissinger was apotheosized in the newsmedia and in the northeastern foreign policy establishment — where the cry had been: "Dump the Captain, save the Pilot!" — and he remained in place through the ignominious fall of Saigon in April 1975, during the Ford-Rockefeller interregnum.

Without Nixon, however, it proved impossible to get the American people to accept the "final solution" for the Vietnam war that he and Sullivan had projected. Refugees from South Vietnam came pouring out, many of them headed for the Philippines, where Sullivan was lodged, his dreams of going to Hanoi as ambassador rapidly fading. In a desperate effort to save at least a few of the hundreds of thousands of South Vietnamese employed by the U. S. from certain death at the hands of their conquerors, the American command had inaugurated an airlift to Clark Field in the Philippines. Most of those coming in were "undocumented Vietnamese," and when the flood became a tidal wave, the Philippine government pressed Sullivan to do something about it, and, as Frank Snepp reminds us, Sullivan was soon sending

cables to Washington and Saigon, demanding a halt and proposing that all the illegals be sent back to Vietnam. His messages
caused considerable unease at the state department, since no one
wanted to backtrack as he suggested. Finally. . . a compromise got
approved: no more illegals were to be "detained" and "processed"
until a special immigration parole could be worked up for
them. . . . When [the American Ambassador in Saigon, Graham
Martin] received the directive. . . he tore it up. . . . He resented Sullivan's imperious tone. . . . [334]

Graham Martin had been called in from retirement in Italy, after
his tour of duty as ambassador there, in late 1972, to take the Saigon post after Sullivan had turned it down. That is why Sullivan had
presumed to use an imperious tone with him. Still, with no prospect
of making it to Hanoi according to Kissinger's plans, Sullivan was
bitterly disappointed. He had turned down the ambassadorship to
Saigon to escape the worst sights of its "indecent end," as Frank
Snepp called it. But now, there was no denying that the "shadow
of the Vietnamese war" had stretched out to envelop Sullivan's embassy compound in the Philippines. All Americans alive at the time
will remember, of course, that, when the U.S. prisoners of war were
released by their Hanoi captors, the major TV "homecoming ceremonies" took place at Clark Field in the Philippines; and, in 1975, it
was not only South Vietnamese refugees who were ferried in, but
also the last of the Americans who all "had to go," before the Hanoi
leaders would so much as hint at talks about the ultimate fate of
the conquered South. Sullivan has registered his surprise, for instance, about how the last contingent of American marines to leave
Saigon behaved at Clark after they had completed their assigned mission of supervising the final evacuation of American personnel from
the totally devastated and humiliated South Vietnamese capital.

The link here with Iran is important, for when Robert McFarlane
gave his testimony at the televised joint Senate-House Iran-Contra
hearings in 1987, he recalled his experiences as a marine in Vietnam.
He recalled that he had led the first contingent of marines to actually engage in combat in Vietnam, at the start of the "Americanization" of that war, and that he had been sent back, at the war's abject

end, to help to supervise the final marine corps evacuation to Clark Field. McFarlane said that it was the experience he and other combat marine officers, like Oliver North, had had in Vietnam, witnessing America's betrayal of literally hundreds of thousands of South Vietnamese clients left behind to face their conquerors on their own, that made them vow never to let a comparable betrayal of faithful clients occur again, if they could possibly help it.

The disciplined character of the marines who saw the curtain come down on the American involvement in Vietnam has been accurately reported by Sullivan in his memoirs of 1984, though that was hardly his intention, since he didn't appreciate it in the least. From his Manila vantage point, Sullivan recalls the last days, when the Americans — forced to abandon their once thriving, oversized embassy in Saigon and their vast "Pentagon East" at the nearby air base — finally came pouring into the Philippines. He writes:

> When, in 1975, the final assault was mounted from Hanoi, the Philippines were the first to feel the effects. The panicky evacuation of the Americans from the path of the military onslaught was carried out in ships, planes, and helicopters that landed at American facilities in Philippine military bases. Indeed, as our officials arrived in Subic Bay aboard evacuation ships, they were then flown by helicopter literally into our front yard at the Embassy.... We sheltered the ambassador [the same Graham Martin he had earlier abused with his imperious tone!] and his immediate group at our home in Manila and, for a period of rest, at our summer place in the hills of Bagio.

But the ambassador's plane had not been the last. Still to come, after the "panicky evacuation" of all the others, was the last contingent of marines, whose arrival Sullivan characterizes as "an anomaly." They had, of course, witnessed from the compound and roof of Saigon's embattled American embassy the entire "panicky evacuation," supervising it from beginning to end — their unit serving, in Sullivan's words, as "the rear guard that had closed up the evacuation." Most of them had originally arrived in Manila, not too many days before, on a transport ship moored at a Manila pier. From there they had proceeded to Saigon in full combat readiness.

In the heart of Saigon, those marines had then accomplished their pathetic combat mission, while Soviet-made tanks were waiting at the outskirts of the city to move in and storm the Embassy gates once the last Americans were gone. Those marines saw, of course, the thousands of abandoned South Vietnamese clients, who were left behind on the ground, as also those who perished before their eyes, when they lost their grip on the helicopter landing gear to which they had clung, and fell, or were dutifully shot by marines on orders not to permit any delay of the evacuation. When all other Americans were out, the last marines were finally transported back to the Philippines, on orders to proceed directly to their transport ship moored at a Manila pier. The idea was to begin and complete the pathetic evacuation mission as the thoroughly disciplined military unit they indeed were. Sullivan describes what he saw of the return of those Marines to his front yard at the Embassy in these terms:

> Suddenly, another large camouflaged helicopter loomed out of the sky and circled for an approach to our landing pad. Instead of making a normal landing, the big craft, which carried the insignia of the U.S. Marines, executed a "dust off," with its nose in the air and its rotor blades turning, as a company of combat marines in full battle gear tumbled out of its tail. We watched in astonishment as the big ship moved off again in the direction of Subic and the marines began to form up into a column of twos, their rifles at the ready. It appeared they were going to make a rapid march somewhere. [251-252]

Sullivan got his Manila embassy security officer to find out who the marines were and what they were doing. His own embassy "marine guard unit" was quickly sent out to "ascertain intentions," as he says. It was learned that the captain of that marine unit had intended to march his men fully armed back to their quarters on the moored transport ship from which they had earlier departed. The captain couldn't have been Robert McFarlane, for by then McFarlane had already become a major. But one can be sure that the captain who ordered his men to tumble out of the last evacuating helicopter, in full combat readiness, felt like McFarlane and Oliver North about the strategems of the Harrimans, Sullivans, and Kissingers, who had for so long been trying to teach the United States how to lose "limited wars" to prevent their escalation into general wars. But Sullivan, ever mindful of diplomatic decorum, confronted that captain and his unit to administer what he calls "a little quiet explanation about Philippine sovereignty and the impropriety of forced marches on foreign boulevards."

Sullivan, co-author of the humiliating terms of unconditional surrender forced on President Thieu back in January 1973, seemed anxious to impress upon that marine captain and his men the fact that the Vietnam war was indeed over. He literally disarmed what he called "these slightly bewildered young men," and saw to it that they were seated on a nice bus "with their helmets in their laps and their rifles following in an Embassy station wagon." What else than that, as a fitting ending to a war fixed from the beginning to be lost by the American clients fighting in it? *Sic transit gloria mundi!*

All of that was witnessed by President Ferdinando Marcos of the Philippines. Wherever American combat troops had served in Southeast Asia since the early 1960s, disaster had followed for the American clients, like Diem and Thieu in South Vietnam. Certainly, with Sullivan in place as ambassador, Marcos had good reason to fear for his own future. He had kept himself closely informed about developments in South Vietnam; and when he had seen the United States stand idly by, in the spring of 1972, while over 300,000 regular North Vietnamese troops marched into South Vietnam, he saw plainly what was coming. A peace settlement, he recognized, was about to be imposed on the Thieu government — a settlement which would back that government into a corner, leaving no way of escape. Fearing that Communist-backed local factions in the Philippines might try to force him into a similar corner of unreliable dependence on American power, Marcos, on September 22, 1972, had boldly imposed martial law, and proceeded to effectively suppress all serious Communist opposition, without American intervention.

Marcos had for years supplied a significant contingent of soldiers for service in South Vietnam. He knew first hand, therefore, what an American military presence, purporting to help in a fight against local Communist aggression, could mean to the host country. He saw how civilian Washington had insisted, first with Diem and then with Thieu, that the enemy be allowed his inviolable sanctuaries, his secure harbors, and safe inland supply stores, as assurances that the American object was not to try to defeat him — at the risk of superpower intervention — but merely to discourage his local aggression. As Marcos saw it, if similar political restraints on his government were to be the price of renewal of the Clark Air Force Base and Subic Naval Base leases, he'd much prefer to do without the economic advantages of having such bases.

In the end, Marcos got his way. He saw Thieu's government in South Vietnam conquered militarily by the North Vietnamese occupying army that had been left in place in the South as a direct consequence of the Paris Accords earlier negotiated by Kissinger and Sullivan. But by then the focus of Kissinger's strategy for peace through defeatist interventionism on the losing side had already shifted Westward to post-colonial Africa and the Persian Gulf.

4. The Tehran Build-Up: Eighteen Months as the Shah's "Staunchest Supporter"

Sullivan remained at his Manila post, as we noted, through the end of the Ford-Rockefeller interregnum. He was, with Kissinger, part of that interregnum, which had made the abject defeat of our Vietnamese clients in April 1975 endurable for a generally disoriented American people. Had President Ford won an elective term in the White House in 1976, Kissinger might have taken up the challenge of turning even stubborn Marcos into another Diem or Thieu. But with Ford's defeat, that prospect passed. Kissinger turned his attention to the Shah. And Sullivan in Manila must then have welcomed the news that, in his last days under Ford, Kissinger was pressing for his nomination as Ambassador in Tehran.

But, the political question at the time of Sullivan's nomination in 1977 was this: Why had Carter, who had criticized Kissinger rather severely during the election campaign, agreed to nominate a man who was so obviously a Kissinger favorite? The answer is that he had also been, strictly speaking, a Brzezinski favorite, and therefore a favorite of *both* teams making up the powerful Rockefeller-brothers American political lobby. In the 1976 presidential election, it will be recalled, Nelson Rockefeller had backed Ford and Kissinger even as his brother David backed Carter and Brzezinski. At least at the outset, Sullivan was acceptable to both. The Senate confirmation hearings on Sullivan's appointment made this bipartisan consensus clear. There was virtually no Senate criticism on either side of the aisle. Which is to say, Sullivan had, on a lower level, to be sure, exactly the same sort of bipartisan establishment support that Kissinger enjoyed. Like Kissinger, he had managed to earn points for himself as a "conservative" during the Nixon-Ford years, while remaining true to the Democratic establishment that had nurtured him in his early years as a foreign service officer.

In the newsmedia, only Anthony Lewis of the New York *Times* was in the least disturbed by Carter's "choice" of Sullivan. In a column dated April 14, 1977, Lewis posed the question in these terms: "If Gerald Ford were President now, and he picked for a vital ambassadorship a man who had directed secret bombing in Indochina and said Richard Nixon had the right to make war without authority from Congress, would Democratic Senators silently accept the choice?... Not likely." But Jimmy Carter, he reminded his readers, had lately made just such an appointment, "and so far, there has been little reaction except approving murmurs."

Lewis noted that, when Sullivan was nominated Ambassador to the Philippines in 1973, Democratic Senator Stuart Symington had dutifully reviewed Sullivan's Laos record. The nomination had been sent up by a Republican President, and sc Symington tried to make things at least a little hard, as a gesture of party loyalty. Still, Symington was perhaps more admiring than critical back then in observing that, in Laos, Sullivan had served virtually as a "military proconsul," during years that "coincided with the secret American war," for which he had "personally picked the bombing targets." Lewis further noted that Sullivan had concealed all of that from Congress at the time, and that, when it later became known, he had persisted in denying that civilian targets had ever been attacked.

In those same 1973 hearings, Senator Symington had reminded the nominee that, back in 1969, when he was asked whether the President could, on his own, order the bombing of a foreign country, he had replied, "Yes, sir." The Democratic Senator had then pressed the point, asking what legal authority Mr. Nixon might conceivably have for his more recent bombing of Cambodia "in the absence of any authorizing statute or treaty." Sullivan reportedly answered: "For now, I'd just say the justification is the reelection of President Nixon."

Needless to say, nothing of the sort had come up during the 1977 hearings, with a Democratic President making the nomination. Anthony Lewis righteously chided the Democratic senators for their silent approval, concluding, with respect to Sullivan's responses in past hearings: "It is not just the contemptuous cynicism of Mr. Sullivan's views on law and Presidential power that symbolizes another era. He is also identified with a disregard for human rights that Jimmy Carter has seemed to be changing." There, Lewis had indeed touched on a sore point destined to sour President Carter's attitude toward Sullivan — but that was to happen, as we shall see, under circumstances the very opposite of any that Lewis might have anticipated.

Except for Anthony Lewis's complaint about Democratic silence, Sullivan's appointment received easy confirmation. And little was said about him thereafter in the American newsmedia, until after the Shah's fall in January 1979, and, more particularly, as we have already indicated, after the first seizure of the American Embassy in Tehran by local militants the following month, on February 14, St. Valentine's Day.

But, we want to review briefly the record of Sullivan's two years in Tehran. In late 1976, when he was about to leave office, Kissinger could still argue convincingly that his deal of 1972 with the Shah was working to the good — that Iran was indeed becoming, militarily and industrially, a regional superpower. With an "experienced diplomat" like Sullivan on the scene, representing "American interests" as he had previously represented such interests in Laos, in the Paris peace negotiations with Hanoi, and in Manila, one could hope, surely, to give the Kissinger-Nixon doctrine (for turning dependent clients into independent but cooperative allies) at least one more successful trial, contributing, even if only by paradoxical means, to the prevention of global conflicts over ideologies in the nuclear age.

As we have already indicated, the Kissinger "blank check" issued to the Shah in 1972 had made the years 1973 through 1976 seem exceptionally prosperous — at least for most upper-class Iranians. For the millions of peasants and small town people who left the countryside for the first time to crowd into Tehran, however, things were very different. They found themselves hired as industrial helpers in great numbers that far exceeded the city's housing potentials. All about them, in booming Tehran, they saw great streets being paved and buildings rising daily, with conspicuously American and Israeli businessmen and technicians everywhere, often lording it over native Iranians. As is often the case when billions of dollars are poured into a backward economy, crowded shanty-neighborhoods flourished, their millions of inhabitants suffering a sense of social alienation that quickly turned them into a Muslim equivalent of what Marx, and Hegel before him, had called a *Lumpen-proletariat* or *Pöbel*. It was mostly a mass of illiterates utterly incapable of so much as hearing, much less heeding, the calls for patience constantly addressed to them by the Shah's people and their better-intentioned American and Israeli advisors. All they could effectively hear were the complaints against modernization addressed to them by their religious teachers who had either journeyed with them to Tehran, or been waiting in place to receive them as new parishioners.

We have already taken cursory notice of the consequent developments; but we want now to review them from Ambassador Sullivan's perspective. In May, 1977, just before he went off to assume his post in Tehran, Sullivan formally met with President Carter requesting guidance on the continuing arms sales to Iran and other issues, like charges of human rights violations. Carter had assured him, at that time, that relations with Iran were to remain what they had been under several administrations before his. But, during his first year as ambassador, Sullivan repeatedly but diplomatically indicated his continued disapproval of Carter's emphasis on human rights, making no secret of his support of Kissinger's view that, next to Israel, the Shah's Iran was "our most reliable ally" in the Middle East, and should not, therefore, be threatened with curtailment of arms sales, as if it were just another Third World client-state.

Sullivan boldly encouraged Carter to make his agreement with all of that clear. Plans were then made for a Carter visit to Iran by the end of the year; and, as the American TV newscasts showed, on New Years Day, 1978, Carter expressed the highest confidence in the Shah's efforts to bring about genuine democratic reform, reaffirming Henry Kissinger's representation of the Iranian leader as a "uniquely wise and farsighted ruler whose vision of a strong, prosperous and modernizing Iran was far ahead of his advisers and his people...leading his fractious and often reluctant nation into the twentieth century." [48-49]

That speech of "lavish praise" for a "modernizing ruler" — largely drafted for Carter by Sullivan — marked the start of an all-out imperial campaign to discredit the religious opposition to the Shah as reactionary and unworthy of a "great modern nation." In rapid succession, through the first weeks of the new year, the leading organs of the official media and often the Shah himself attacked Khomeini as a reactionary fanatic preaching such things as "sexual apartheid," against the ignominy of which the nation had to be protected. Yet, even while he engaged in such attacks on the Muslim clerics of the opposition, the Shah seemed to encourage the impression that he was merely using it as a device to rally public support and elicit public praise for his modernizing achievements. For a time, the city crowds responded to the Shah's appeals, and, indeed, the pro-Shah assemblies reached a peak on January 26, 1978, which was the 15th anniversary of the Shah's White Revolution of 1963. But, after that, there was a perceptible decline in public enthusiasm, and before long a point was reached when it was not the Shah but his clerical opposition alone that could assemble large crowds in the streets.

In that same January 1978, there had indeed occurred a series of religious demonstrations in the holy city of Qom, precipitated by a government-sponsored article ridiculing the Ayatollah Khomeini as a "communist dupe." After that, there were mounting "signs and signals," as Gary Sick would later call them, of brewing troubles for the Shah's government. Many observers became convinced at the time that "a revolution had begun." The demonstrators in Qom had been mostly religious students who, with their clerical mentors, were starting to "denounce the Shah's government as anti-Islamic."

The government responded in force; there were shootings and much bloodshed. In Sick's words, the "shooting in Qom set off a series of demonstrations at forty-day intervals, eventually culminating in the Shah's departure." Yet, the "initial outburst in Qom," he adds, "was ovelooked entirely in embassy and other official government reporting until much later." [34-5]

Gary Sick has also made the point that our intelligence services, which had been allowed to "deteriorate almost to the vanishing point" with respect to assessing the realities of domestic conditions in Iran, would probably have failed to read the signs of the times correctly even if they had been at full strength. They "would probably have looked in the wrong place," Sick tells us in a passage we cited earlier, where he adds with candor:

> Only in retrospect is it obvious that a good intelligence organization should have focused its attention on the religious schools, the mosques and recorded sermons of an aged religious leader who had been living in exile for fourteen years. As one State Department official remarked in some exasperation after the revolution, "Whoever took religion seriously?" [164-165]

Beyond that, we have the evidence of Sullivan's persistent playing down of adverse reports on the Shah's rule by members of his embassy staff, and specialists sent from Washington. There had been, for instance, a report by the economist Theodore Moran — a social-impact assessment of the 1972-1976 military-industrial modernization program that came out of Kissinger's Iran initiatives. That report showed that in Iran, as in other American client-states where vast sums of money were poured into the military-industrial support sectors, other sectors suffered apparently irreparable consequences. One consequence was the transport of millions of peasants from the countryside into chaotically-overgrown cities.

When Sullivan saw that memorandum, he rejected its "bleak prognosis" out of hand. His own view, conveyed to President Carter in late 1977, was that, as a consequence of the economic and social advances made since 1972, "the Shah had gained full political control of his country for the first time in his long rule." Offering a confident "counter-prognosis," Sullivan had added: "Not to have to be concerned with an opposition or recalcitrant legislature, the Shah tends to look well into the future to assess current events against broad historical trends.''

Besides Moran's bleak economic prognosis, there had also been a series of reports by a high ranking member of Sullivan's own embassy staff: Michael Metrinko — the same Metrinko who would later be numbered among the hostages seized on November 4, 1979. Metrinko was fluent in Farsi, the Iranian national language, as well as in Turkish. From his post as consul in Tabriz, he had reported that there seemed to be an ''ingrained hatred of the Shah spreading throughout the society.'' Sullivan's response was a complete rejection. He told Metrinko to ''talk to more Iranians,'' which Metrinko, no doubt with impatience, proceeded to do.

Metrinko talked to hundreds of merchants, students, workers, and clergymen. But nothing came of his lengthy report at the time. Sullivan ignored it, and it was not sent on to Washington. On the contrary, as late as June 1, 1978, Sullivan was telling Washington that his ''embassy soundings among religious leaders suggest an underlying basis of loyalty to the monarchy and to the independence of Iran as the Shah envisions it.'' What about the religious demonstrations recurring at forty-day intervals since the shooting at Qom in January 1978? All through the subsequent months, the Shah's people who witnessed them were insisting that they were the work of a ''few saboteurs,'' imported from opposition sanctuaries on the ''other side of the border.''

It is ironic that while the Shah was manifestly losing his capacity to assemble supportive crowds in the streets, Ambassador Sullivan, who could have seen the beginnings of the change with his own eyes, should have gone on an extended vacation that was to keep him out of the country for almost three months, from mid-June through late August 1978. Just before he left Tehran, Sullivan reportedly met with Israel's official representative there, Uri Lubrani, who later recalled having discussed his own ''gloomy prognosis'' of those days (based on observations of current events) with Ambassador Sullivan. Lubrani's views were sent to the Israeli embassy in Washington, but Sullivan certainly did not bring them up in reporting to his superiors while on extended leave. [37]

During his three months in the United States, Sullivan made several visits to Washington, on one of which he had lunch with Gary Sick and a subsequent meeting with Zbigniew Brzezinski. Sick had just lately drawn up a very somber report on Iranian affairs for Brzezinski, reflecting the views of British, French, and Israeli intelligence. But Sullivan proved to be "so optimistic and so certain of his assessment" that Brzezinski gave Sick more than one "quizzical glance," and Sick himself suffered, as he says, "a few pangs of regret for the shrill tone that had crept into [his] own reporting" to Brzezinski. [46]

Meanwhile, much was happening in Iran tending to confirm the gloomier estimates. Ignored by Sullivan's embassy staff, reports of those happenings had nevertheless reached Gary Sick's desk at the National Security Council. On August 19, a terrible fire in Abadan's Rex Cinema took the lives of some 477 people. The fact that many of the cinema exits were found locked suggested foul play. The Shah's government blamed the "Abadan holocaust" on Muslim fundamentalists allegedly protesting Western influences — even though it had been an Iranian film that was being shown, in a theater not frequented by Westerners. Critics of the Shah countered that SAVAK agents had probably set the fire to "generate opposition to the fundamentalist causes." To counter widespread belief that it was so, the Shah had instituted reforms. The entire cabinet headed by Prime Minister Jamshid Amuzigar had resigned on August 27 (a few days after Sullivan's return to Tehran). But even then it was pretended that events in the streets had *not* forced the resignation.

Still, the facts were undeniable. The Shah had already replaced the head of SAVAK — a veteran of some fifteen years of service as director of the secret police, and much criticized, to be sure, by the opposition leaders. To replace Amuzigar, the Shah selected a former prime minister who had served in "happier times." He was Ja'far Sharif-Imami, at that time grandmaster of Free-masonry in Iran, a symbolic focus of the Shah's anti-religious campaign of imperial modernization. Though they were hardly believable coming from him, the new Prime Minister immediately instituted anti-modernization reforms, like abandoning the "imperial calendar," dating things from the time of Cyrus the Great, and reintroducing the official Muslim calendar, dating things from Mohammed's flight from Mecca in 622 A.D. Gambling casinos were closed, and much else was shut down that challenged traditional Islamic values. But it was all perceived by the opposition as expressing the Shah's fears and vulnerability.

When Sullivan finally returned to Iran in late August, he met with the Shah and, after reading embassy staff reports on local events, sent a cable to Washington suggesting that the Shah, still far ahead of his nation in his progressiveness, needed encouragement. His cable included the draft of a letter he thought Jimmy Carter should send to the Shah over his presidential signature. The letter was flatteringly, even embarrassingly obsequious. But the State Department, defending "one of its own," resisted White House efforts to change Sullivan's draft. Even after the frightful Jaleh Square Massacre of September 8, when the Shah's troops shot into a crowd of unarmed protestors, killing some three to four hundred and wounding ten times as many, Sullivan kept up his optimism, reporting that the Shah "looked the picture of health, confident, almost feisty," when he met with several American businessmen, and that he definitely had things under control.

Sullivan met again with the Shah on October 24, and was surprised to find that the Shah had also invited the British Ambassador Anthony Parsons. In his cable on the meeting, Sullivan acknowledged that the Shah had expressed concern about the "progressive breakdown of public order" and wanted to review "his options" with the American and British ambassadors. Should he impose a military government — even though the military seemed reluctant to do what had to be done to keep the oil industry from closing down because of strikes? Or should he try a coalition government, assigning high offices to moderate opposition leaders — even though he had little confidence in the idea? What did the ambassadors recommend?

Sullivan's response was to argue that the situation "was not quite as dark as the Shah had depicted it." He advised against installing a military government, backing the idea of "bringing some opposition leaders into the present government." In his cable to Washington, Sullivan commented that he "thought the Iranian military" were feeding the Shah misinformation, making things seem much worse than they actually were, so as to pave the way for their own ascendancy. Back home, reports were coming in to the State Department that things might be getting out of hand for the Shah. A policy paper was prepared and sent on to Sullivan for his comment. The response from Sullivan was that the information reflected in the paper was mostly incorrect. He repeated his previous warning against the "plots" of the military who had a stake in making things seem worse than they were, and he rejected out of hand suggestions of an overture to Khomeini's forces. At this point Gary Sick elaborates on Sullivan's pledge of loyal support for the Shah briefly cited earlier. Khomeini, Sullivan flatly asserted, "should be firmly quarantined. Our destiny is to work with the Shah." Sick's point is this: As the full record would later show, Sullivan had already gone far in the very direction the State Department was recommending, but he had been doing it all on his own, and for purposes quite different from what Washington decision-makers could have imagined. Writing about Sullivan's response of October 24, 1978 to the State department policy paper, Sick says:

> To any seasoned observer, Sullivan's message is clear. He had his own game plan, which he was actively pursuing; in the meantime, he could kindly do without interference and kibitizing from Washington. The State Department seemed inclined to accept this rebuke and quietly shelved its policy paper. As a consequence, neither the State Department paper nor the ambassador's response was ever passed to the White House, and President Carter never saw it. [60]

October 26, coming two days later, was the Shah's fifty-ninth birthday. No public festivities were scheduled in troubled Iran, but the Iranian embassy in Washington thought it important to mark the occasion by bringing the Iranian crown prince, the Shah's 18-year-old son, to Washington as an occasion for reaffirmation of the Carter Administration's support of the dynasty. The boy was flown in from his flight-training school in a Texas airbase, and he in fact met with Brzezinski and other high ranking Washington officials at a small dinner party in the Iranian ambassador's residence. The crown prince had a birthaday of his own on October 31st, on which day, on the urging of Ambassador Sullivan, President Carter received him in the oval office, where, after a photo session, the President emphatically reaffirmed the American Government's support of the Shah and the importance of the American-Iranian alliance and friendship.

5. Imperial Indecision and Sullivan's "Opportunity"

As a high-level "member of the Iranian political hierarchy under the Shah," Gholam R. Afkhami would later observe in his *Iranian Revolution: Thanatos on a National Scale* that, at the time of the Ambassador's return to Tehran in late August 1978, the Shah found himself in a predicament that he was unable to confront decisively. In Afkhami's words:

> The monarch had come to face the moment of truth. In reality, he had only two choices: either he must don his military uniform and charge against his enemies in the name of honor, nation and history, accepting the full consequences of his decision; or he must take his chances and allow a man or a group of men, who could forge an independent following of their own, to take the reins of government and act as a political buffer between the Iranian monarchy, symbolizing an historically significant reality, and the people's anger, representing a fleeting moment in the painful process of sociopolitical development. By following either path, he would probably have stopped Khomeini and brought himself and the country a breathing spell to rearrange the future political policy and structure. Instead, he opted for the worst possible alternative: piecemeal and gradual appeasement. [95-96]

The Shah had asked Sullivan for guidance on that choice. In fact, on the very day that his son had been receiving President Carter's pledges of unwavering American support, Sullivan had met with the Shah once more to reconsider the choice. Sullivan, completely opposed to a military regime headed by the Shah, encouraged him to pursue the other course: admit moderate leaders of the opposition to his government — men of the "liberal" stamp of old Mossadegh, though much the worse for wear. But while the Shah made plans to give that alternative a try, other liberal leaders out of the Mossadegh past had already taken the initiative on their own. Ignoring efforts to get their old Mossadegh party, the National Front, to join a coalition government under the Shah, a group led by Karim Sanjabi had gone off to Paris with overtures to the exiled Ayatollah Khomeini. They asked for his support of a limited monarchy of the kind that had briefly existed before the Pahlavi era. The Ayatollah would not, however, so much as begin to consider such a possibility if the present Shah was not first removed. And his "liberal" supplicants succumbed. There was no chance, in other words, of saving the Shah by means of a coalition government.

That development had been made known to Sullivan and the British Ambassador Parsons on November 1. The Shah was then under pressure to try to save the throne rather than himself — which led to a consideration that, to do so, he might have to abdicate in favor of his son, in the dim expectation that that might be acceptable at least to moderates in the opposition. And that was the moment when, from the perspective of President Carter, Zbigniew Brzezinski, and Gary Sick in Washington, Sullivan seemed suddenly to have undergone a complete conversion. From having been the Shah's "staunchest supporter" in the Carter administration for eighteen months, he suddenly abandoned that role to rush to the opposite extreme. He began to talk of the urgency for U.S. action to force the Shah out and to make preparations for dealing with a revolutionary successor regime.

That, for Washington, was an altogether new, an unknown Sullivan. Writing of a so-called plan that Sullivan submitted in late November, vaguely intimating how the ends he was then advancing might be implemented, Sick pointed out that, in the past, every time Washington had "raised with Ambassador Sullivan the possibility of a more active role in attempting to halt political deterioration," Sullivan had "flatly rejected the idea." What was to be made of the abrupt reversal of early November 1978?

Ever since, students of Sullivan's conduct in those days have been either asking or trying to answer the question: Was it a true "conversion" that Sullivan underwent, or had it all been part of a game-plan stubbornly being pursued by Sullivan in secret? Gary Sick, at any rate, suspected the latter alternative. "Despite my normal immunity to conspiracy theories," he would later write, "I was forced to ask myself whether Sullivan, in line with his scenario outlined in early November, was saving all his efforts for a last-second deal between the opposition and the military *after* the Shah was finished. In the meantime, he was prepared to wait and watch as the Shah went down for the third time." [119]

Sick had evidently had no dealings with Sullivan in the days when he worked with Harriman and Kissinger, watching first Diem and then Thieu go down for the third time; he therefore doesn't draw the obvious comparison. But, after having reviewed Sullivan's long apprenticeship for his Iran job, we must draw it. And we shall in the next chapter.

CHAPTER NINE

The Shah's Ouster: Sullivan vs. Carter, Huyser, and Brzezinski

In reviewing Dr. Allan E. Goodman's account of Sullivan's role in the 1972-1973 Vietnam peace negotiations that started with the famous "October breakthrough" of 1972, we noted that it had required less than four months to bring President Thieu down from the high hopes for a true "peace with honor" of those days to the depths of despair of January 1973, when he was forced to accept the Paris Accords, recognizing them to be only slightly disguised terms of surrender. Years later, Sullivan was to have a parallel four-months experience with the Shah of Iran. It had been on October 27, 1978 — six years plus a day after Kissinger's peace-is-at-hand news conference of October 26, 1972 — that Sullivan, as we have seen, affirmed in no uncertain terms his long-standing commitment to support the Shah. We quoted his cable to Washington of that date, in which he said flatly: "Our destiny is to work with the Shah." The Shah's equivalent of the January 23, 1973 Paris Peace Accords forced on Thieu was, of course, his final flight into exile, which he was forced to make on January 16, 1979. [S. p. 59]

But to get a clear impression of how self-consciously and deliberately Kissinger and Sullivan worked together to bring President Thieu crashing down to his final humiliation, we need to recall a long news item that the *New York Times* ran on November 2, 1972. It was headed, "Kissinger Negotiates Washington Reception," and it told of Henry Kissinger's having "descended upon" the South Vietnamese Embassy in Washington, on November 1, "like some great musical comedy star...trailed by a huge entourage of male and female report-

169

ers, generals, and diplomats, as well as his usual National Security Council 'pack'.'' It was, the news item went on to say, "another sudden Kissinger mission, this time to demonstrate publicly the Administration's support of the Saigon government, which was celebrating its National Day." With Alexander Haig at his side, Kissinger, we are told, "inched his way through the crowd shaking hands with such officials as Gen. Creighton W. Abrams, former commander of United States forces in Vietnam, and now Army Chief of Staff, and William H. Sullivan, the Deputy Assistant Secretary of State for East Asian Affairs, who is charged with the details of the Indochina settlement."

Continuing to inch his way through the reception crowd, Kissinger repeatedly "nodded as ambassadors and others congratulated him on his negotiating successes" that had made possible his October 26 "breakthrough" announcement. At one point, he had observed "with a smile, 'I'm uniting Vietnam and both halves are screaming at me'." Of course, South Vietnam was screaming louder at that precise moment because its leaders feared that Kissinger was indeed trying to "unite" Vietnam when, in their view, he ought to have been making sure that the integrity of the South would be sustained after the American troops were all gone. At that reception, Kissinger had started to prove that his maneuver to laugh off President Thieu's life and death opposition to the terms of the Sullivan-Kissinger Paris Peace Accords, as they came to be revealed, could be managed as a colossal theatrical success.

Sullivan would get his chance for similar "theatrics" in Tehran immediately after the first attack on the U.S. Embassy there, which occurred on February 14, 1979. In the course of events that brought down Thieu in four months, Sullivan's role had been secondary. During the parallel four months that brought down the Shah, he was, of course, completely in charge and virtually on his own. Not that he did not enjoy the constant support of Kissinger and Haig. He had that, but neither of them was then a White House "power"; on the contrary, they were both all the while busy trying to undermine President Carter's authority, hoping, no doubt, to see him defeated in his 1980 bid for reelection.

Yet, apart from their opposition to Carter, all three in diverse roles — Kissinger with his determination to "stick with the Shah" in defeat, Haig with his presidential ambitions, and Sullivan with his duplicity in dealing with Khomeini over the head of the Shah — clearly labored toward the same end: to add Iran to South Vietnam as a successful application of Kissinger's doctrine of "defeatist interventionism," so as to teach Americans how to "take defeat" for the sake of peace in the nuclear age. In both countries, the task successfully completed by the Sullivan-Haig-Kissinger *troika* had been, plain and simply, to "negotiate" the regime of a client-ally out of existence, peaceably, if at all possible, by means of agreements secretly made with his enemies.

1. Sullivan's "Conversion" and First Reports of a Mysterious "Huyser Mission"

We spoke, at the end of the last chapter, of Ambassador Sullivan's meeting with the troubled Shah on November 1, 1978, and of the questions the Shah had raised at that meeting about his choices for the future. Two messages about that meeting had been promptly sent to Washington by Sullivan the next day; and, to stress their central importance, Gary Sick has made them the point of departure for his book *All Fall Down: America's Tragic Encounter With Iran.* The book's opening words are:

> Early on Thursday morning, November 2, 1978, the White House received two messages from U.S. Ambassador William H. Sullivan in Tehran. The first was a straightforward account of his most recent meeting with the Shah. This message, though highly classified, was intended to satisfy the curiosity of the foreign policy establishment and to divert attention from the shorter message that followed. The second message was a bombshell, and its distribution was limited to the inner circle of foreign-policy decision makers at the Department of State and at the White House.

The second message was a bombshell because, in its opening line (as paraphrased by Sick), Sullivan had said that, "during his meeting with the Shah on Wednesday evening [Nov. 1, 1978], he had

detected the first signs that the Shah might be considering abdication."
That was news indeed for Washington. Just a few days earlier, Sullivan had been asked by the State Department what he thought about suggestions of a "possible overture to the Ayatollah Ruhollah Khomeini in Paris"; and he had reaffirmed his eighteen-month old practice and policy of forbidding all embassy contact with the opposition. That had been the "familiar" Sullivan, close friend and protege of Henry Kissinger, whose estimate and support of the Shah he had consistently echoed.

Sullivan's point in sending the message was to inform his superiors that the Shah would no doubt soon be asking for official American advice on whether to abdicate or not; the ambassador was therefore asking Washington for guidance. Sick observes that Sullivan had thus deftly "turned" a corner. He was presenting the Carter administration with an unanticipated crisis, and telling it that it had less than forty-eight hours to make up its mind. "What," he seemed quite plainly to be asking, "do you want me to do?"

But, the truth was, as documents later revealed — documents supplied by friends and foes of the Shah — that Sullivan had already proceeded very far with his own plans for handling that crisis, which he had not only anticipated but worked strenuously to bring on. It would later seem evident that his intention had been from the beginning to confront his nominal bosses in Washington with a *fait accompli,* contrary to anything they had previously envisioned. Gary Sick's account of Sullivan's daring challenge to his Washington superiors is that of a principal insider — top Iran operative, as we have indicated, in the White House's National Security Council, headed by Zbigniew Brzezinski. Sick had seen an abundance of evidence about a mounting crisis. But, as he says, the "sustained, high-level policy attention characteristic of a genuine crisis had been curiously absent." Sullivan had seen to that. For "harried decision makers in Washington," therefore, "the real policy crisis began that Thursday morning with Ambassador Sullivan's skillful reversal of field." [3-4]

Sullivan was at that time a "cool salesman" indeed. Throughout the early stages of his turnabout, he consistently behaved as if it had been the most natural thing in the world. What was happening, he seemed ready to argue, had the logic of Kissinger's blank-check deal of 1972 behind it. For Gary Sick, as we noted earlier, that 1972 deal to "subordinate U.S. security decision making in the Persian Gulf to the person of the Shah" was "ultimately inexplicable." [170] And he says pretty much the same about Sullivan's "deal" of November-December 1978 for settling the Iran crisis on his own. Although he was repeatedly pressed by both the State Department and the White House to "make the call" on the Shah, to "sound a warning," Sullivan had persistently refused to do so; he attempted instead, as Sick puts it, "to walk a perilous line between declaratory support of the Shah in his reporting cables while conducting private negotiations with the opposition" [172] — negotiations never reported to his Washington superiors until it was too late to deal intelligently with them on an official level. But more needs to be said. Just as we have sought to explain the apparently inexplicable side of Kissinger's blank check deal with the Shah back in 1972, so we intend to explain what seems inexplicable about Sullivan's conduct.

Repeatedly in his insider's account, Gary Sick touches on the link between Kissinger's original deal with the Shah and Sullivan's conduct. For him, Sullivan's "declaratory support" of the Shah was but a superficial reaffirmation of attitudes that had "become official U.S. dogma after 1972, when the president and his national security adviser formally relinquished control of U.S. arms sales decisions to the Shah." [48-49] Sick reviews in detail the substance of Sullivan's dealings with the Shah during the year that culminated in the "bombshell" message of November 2, 1978. And we must draw on his account to guide us in retracing the major steps of the build-up of the Shah that went on uninterruptedly through all those months, with Sullivan pulling the strings as final puppet-master.

It is clear in retrospect that, before November 2, 1978, Sullivan had been careful to keep Washington in the dark as to what was developing in Iran. His prolonged absence all through the summer had meant that, as Gary Sick says, "there was no high-level contact with the Shah for nearly three months." Then came his reports that "studiously avoided setting off alarm bells in Washington," so that he could continue to control events on the scene as long as possible. That situation abruptly ended on the evening of November 2, after receipt of his "bombshell" message, when the Special Coordination Committee (SCC) of the National Security Council met for its first formal review of U.S. policy in Iran. Out of that meeting came a special communique to Sullivan, asking him to assure the Shah of continued U.S. support "without reservation," and urging him to take "decisive action" to restore order with guarantees of full U.S. backing "whether he chose a coalition or a military government" as the means. An expression of hope was added that, once things were brought under control, the Shah "would resume prudent efforts to promote liberalization and eradicate corruption." After that message was sent, Brzezinski himself followed up with a direct call to the Shah, attempting "to convey a sense of U.S. steadfastness and the need for the Shah to exert tough leadership." [72]

That was the first indication received by the Shah that the United States would support *which ever* choice he might be ready to make. He then explicitly asked Sullivan to transmit to President Carter his gratitude for the expressed "willingness to support him in any decision, including a decision to form a military government." But, since that expression of willingness had come in a personal phone call from Brzezinski (and Sullivan had been "voicing doubts" about Brzezinski), the indecisive Shah asked Sullivan if he could have "official confirmation" of its substance. Sullivan apparently did not transmit that request to Washington. Indeed, the fact of its having been made came out only much later, in the exiled Shah's memoirs. There we find him complaining that, whenever he asked Sullivan for official confirmation of messages, Sullivan would reply that he had "received no instructions." The Shah characterized that as the American envoy's "rote answer," which "had been given me," he observed, "since early September, and I would continue to hear it until the day after I left the country." The truth is, says Gary Sick, that, after November 2, Sullivan got plenty of instructions from Washington, but they were obviously not what the Ambassador "wanted to hear." At any rate, as Sick sums it up:

> Both the Shah and Ambassador Sullivan later asserted unequivocally that the Ambassador repeatedly found himself in the position of answering the Shah's queries with the same response:

"I have no instructions." In view of the voluminous reporting out of Tehran, it is difficult to understand why policy-makers in Washington had to wait for their memoirs [the memoirs of Sullivan and the Shah] to learn of these exchanges.

But, even without a reply from Washington, the Shah had had to act. Once it was clear that the old National Front leaders, who had gone on their own to Paris, had accepted Khomeini's demand that the Shah must go before serious discussions about the future could be pursued, he gave up, for the moment, on the choice that Sullivan had been pressing on him. On November 6, 1978, four days after Sullivan had sent his "bombshell" to Washington, the Shah "announced the formation of a military government." With that decision he seemed to have taken a hardline stand. Rumors immediately surfaced that the head of the military government would be Gholam 'Ali Oveisi — long-time first ranking general of the Iranian armed forces. Instead, the Shah named General Gholam Reza Azhari, "the benign and genial chairman of the Supreme Commander's staff."

It was Azhari's government which, in a "superconciliatory" gesture, began to arrest former officials of the Shah's government, including long-time Prime Minister Amir Abbas Hoveyda and the former chief of SAVAK, General Nematollah Nasiri, both of whom had earlier resigned their offices. All of Iran knew that those two men had been "extensions of the Shah himself and instruments of his rule," that "their sins and failings" were his sins and failings. Thus, as Gary Sick puts it, so far from proving otherwise, their arrest and imprisonment merely "sent an unmistakable message to the opposition that the Shah was on the run, while the Shah's associates could only conclude that it was every man for himself." [77]

At any rate, the military government quickly revealed itself to have been such in name only. In fact, it served to facilitate the breakdown of the governmental structure precisely because it had the name of military government. There was a new show of uniforms in high places, but the capacities for decision making previously weakened were now wholly lost. In Gholam R. Afkhami's words: "General Azhari shattered hopes that the government would regain those capacities by showing the dreaded force behind the throne to be chimerical, since the will to use it simply did not exist." [105]

By the closing days of December, the Shah called on Shahpour Bakhtiar to set up a new coalition government. Bakhtiar had been a young man during the days of Mossadegh, and was no doubt honored to have been appointed vice-minister of labor in the Mossadegh government. But he had never risen to any significantly high rank as a leader of the National Front. The Shah turned to him, indeed, only after the list of "so-called older and more recognized leaders" of the Front, including Mehdi Bazargan, "had been exhausted." [107] The irony of the Shah's turning to the National Front survivors for support of his throne in 1978 is clear. Viewed historically, he then appeared to be offering to undo all that had happened to displease Iranian "liberals" since 1953. The propaganda, used to court Western and especially American liberal support, was that Iran would now finally be reshaped, abruptly, to match the image old Mossadegh had designed for it; and the heirs of Mossadegh — at least those who had not already "gone to Paris" — would thus become the nation's first line of defense against the "extreme conservatism" of the Iranian Shiite masses or the counter-revolutionary mullas, headed by the Ayatollah Khomeini.

Word of Bakhtiar's appointment reached Washington, together with reports of panic in high places in Tehran, on December 27, 1978. Sullivan was asked to supply clarification on the appointee's "Understanding with the Shah"; but, in the meantime, contingency plans were immediately updated, focusing on what had to be done "in the event of a total collapse of order." U.S. forces from Spain to Singapore were put on alert. The drafting of instructions for Sullivan quickly highlighted a division of views — between the State Department and the White House — that had to be compromised before a final version could be sent. According to the instructions actually sent, a long list of alternatives was again to be presented to the Shah, any one of which, he was to be told, would have American support, provided it was *decisively* taken and pursued. The alternatives ranged from a coalition government, that was moderate but able to maintain order, to another military government capable of truly ruling with an "iron fist." If the Shah felt that none of the alternatives in that range was feasible, then, it was urged, he ought to "make way" for a Regency Council to govern in his place and make the hard decisions.

The Shah talked the new set of alternatives over with Sullivan and reached the correct conclusion that an "iron fist" alternative was being offered by Washington only as a resort of absolute necessity, "to end bloodshed," but not as a means "to retain his throne." The Shah immediately told Sullivan that if that particularly painful alternative were to be tried, "he would in any event leave the country," since he "did not have the heart for it," and "would not wish to be associated with it." Dictators, he observed, had to try to save themselves in a crisis by such means. They had no other. He was not, however, a dictator. He occupied a dynastic throne which was saved by the action of others in World War II and again in 1953. The dynasty's life was important, not the individual's tenure. With all of that, the Shah was indicating plainly enough that he had decided to leave Iran when he named Bakhtiar to head up a new government.

In his first "address to the nation" as Prime Minister, delivered on January 1, 1979, Shapour Bakhtiar at once made clear that he intended to govern without direction from the Shah, whom he did not mention at all in the entire address — though he was at pains to boast of his service thirty years before in the government of Mohammed Mossadegh. On January 3, he announced that his new cabinet would be made up exclusively of persons "who had not held office in the past 25 years of the Shah's rule." That was supposed to mean that the slate would be wiped clean, that all the antiliberal excesses of the years since Mossadegh's fall were now to be undone — and with the Shah's belated yet full consent. The proposed cabinet was supposed to have included, as minister of war, a retired general who had once been chief of staff but had resigned in a dispute with the Shah "over the use of the army to put down domestic dissent." For years he had been living in London in more or less voluntary exile. This was General Fereidoun Jam, a man much honored for his professional integrity. He turned the job down. But it was later learned that he did so because the Shah, to whom he had sworn his military oath, had refused his request to have, as war minister, full control over the military.

Despite Bakhtiar's failure to place such a man in his cabinet, or perhaps because of it, there was much talk at the time of a military coup which would restore the Shah, even if only as a figurehead for the army. Naturally the talk was that the United States would be behind the coup. And in apparent confirmation of such talk, on the day after Bakhtiar had projected plans for his independent cabinet, a "high-ranking American military officer" had quietly appeared on the scene, to serve, it was said, as "a liaison officer with the Iranian military." Quickly the rumor spread that a new chapter was to be added to the old tale of the adventures of Kermit Roosevelt and General Schwarzkopf. The officer in question was in fact U.S. Air Force General Robert Huyser, commander of all American forces in Europe, and chief deputy, serving directly under General Alexander Haig, in NATO's Supreme Allied Command.

What specifically had General Huyser come to do in Iran? He had arrived unannounced on January 4. News accounts surfaced back home a few days later. What they reported seemed fairly explicit. The general had been sent down from NATO, it was said, not to stir up a military coup, but to prevent one. The idea was, according to Washington insiders, to give the Shah's new government, headed by Bakhtiar, every possible chance to succeed, since the Shah really had no other significant civilian support in the country. As the February 12 issue of *Time* magazine put it, with a touch of skepticism: "General Huyser has forcefully argued that an army takeover would only lead to anarchy, but U.S. diplomats are uncertain as to whether the military is really listening."

General Huyser's mission to Iran proved to be brief and mysterious, from beginning to end. Both the pro-Shah and the anti-Shah forces regarded him as working against them — the former charging that he had been sent down to Tehran "with the clear purpose of neutralizing the Iranian Army so that it would not fight for the Shah's beleaguered regime," while the latter insisted that his secret orders were the very opposite: "to push the Army into power and place the Shah back on the Peacock Throne." That contradiction has never been resolved. But there were other perceptions of Huyser by key people. Bakhtiar, for instance, seemed to welcome General Huyser's intervention as a peace-keeper. The Prime Minister knew he had accepted a virtually impossible assignment — like agreeing to be captain of the Titanic *after* it had begun to sink! His purpose, he said, was to try to prevent a bloody massacre of unarmed civilian masses in the streets in a futile attempt to restore the unrestorable. To spare the nation that calamity, two things would have to be done. The first, he seems to have concluded, was largely in the hands of General Huyser, the second, in his own hands. While Huyser labored to contain the military, his own task would be to prevent an untimely return of the Ayatollah Khomeini. Bakhtiar's "greatest fear," wrote a *Time* correspondent on the scene, was that, if Khomeini arrived prematurely, "the event would trigger more bloodshed and perhaps a military coup" which would have only a Pyrrhic effect at best, since the rank and file of the army would not for long obcy orders to fire on their brothers, sisters, and parents.

That Bakhtiar was the one man still in Iran who could most be trusted to serve the Iranian national interest in such a time of crisis was acknowledged as much by partisans of the Ayatollah Khomeini as by those of the Shah and the military establishment. No one denied that he had had a "long and honorable record of opposition to the Shah," and that he would probably have been Khomeini's first choice to head a transition government, had the Shah not beat him to it. The Shah had boldly put Bakhtiar on his honor by asking him to take command of the sinking ship. Bakhtiar might have refused to collaborate with the Shah. He could then have gone in triumph to Paris to head up Khomeini's government in exile. Instead, to spare his country excessive bloodshed, he took up his thankless task under the old regime. It was a statesmanly gesture.

Bakhtiar's government lasted from January 4 to February 11, 1979. It was in his more or less firm grasp that the Shah left the reins of his imperial government when he finally took flight into exile, on January 16, 1979. The Shah had, to be sure, taken a similar flight in August 1953 — and that, as we have noticed, had a happy ending. But the intervening quarter of a century had clearly brought changes — up to and including the appointment of a protege of Mossadegh as Prime Minister! — that made a happy ending for the flight of January 1979 most unlikely.

3. Blaming President Carter: The Attacks of Kissinger, Haig, and Sullivan

Gary Sick makes the important point that educated Iranians have consistently found it difficult to believe that the Carter administration had not deliberately worked to bring down the Shah and clear a way for the Ayatollah's successor regime. As he says in *All Fall Down:*

> Thus, long after Khomeini returned to Iran and U.S.-Iranian relations lay in ruins, it was common to meet sophisticated, well-educated Iranians whose inevitable question would be, "Why did the United States want to bring Khomeini to power?" The logic behind this question was inexorable. All the power was in the hands of the Shah, who relied on the United States. Yet Khomeini had succeeded in overthrowing the Shah. The only explanation was that America had withdrawn its support from the Shah and had transferred it to Khomeini.... American officials, who were baffled and frustrated about the breakdown of Iranian society, found these elaborate rationalizations so patently absurd that they tended to dismiss them out of hand. Yet some version of this story was accepted by virtually every Iranian, from the Shah down to the unemployed construction worker swelling the ranks of the anti-Shah demonstrations. [34]

That the Shah fully accepted a version of that story he indicated quite clearly at the time of his flight into exile, on January 16, 1979. Just before his plane's take-off, an "authorized spokesman" told a gathering of the international press in Tehran that the Shah "blamed his downfall on Jimmy Carter's human rights campaign." Then, over a year later, in the first installment of his Royal Memoirs, published in late 1980, he charged that the Carter administration had deliberately "helped to overthrow him by working behind the scenes to make sure that the Iranian army would do nothing to save him." More specifically, the Shah added a damaging clarification that Alexander Haig's NATO deputy, General Huyser, had indeed been sent down to Tehran in early January 1979 — less than two weeks before the Shah's flight — "with the clear purpose of neutralizing the

Iranian army so that it would not fight for the Shah's beleaguered regime." If the Shah drew much of that conclusion out of the "logic" of U.S.-Iranian "power relations" at the time, as Gary Sick suggests, it is also a fact that he found confirmation of it in the views repeatedly expressed to him in those days by such notable American public figures as Henry Kissinger, Alexander Haig, and, of course, the U.S. ambassador on the scene, William H. Sullivan.

By the time the Shah started writing his memoirs, Kissinger had long-since emerged as his leading sponsor and protector in the United States. During the nine months following the first attack on the American Embassy in Tehran — an attack quickly brought under control by the successor regime — relations between the U.S. and Iran were very nearly normalized, only to be repeatedly undermined and almost completely severed by Henry Kissinger's persistent interventions to get the Shah admitted to the United States, and by Senator Jacob Javits's success in inducing the U.S. Senate to approve unanimously a resolution condemning the Ayatollah Khomeini's conduct in punishing supporters of the deposed imperial regime and seeking the Shah's return for a public trial.

But that is the subject for another chapter. Here we want merely to take note of what Kissinger was saying about the "Iran crisis" shortly after the second attack on the American Embassy — as, for instance, in a speech delivered before a meeting of the Republican Governors Association in Austin, Texas, on November 20, 1979. Despite the total loss of South Vietnam to Hanoi by military conquest, in April 1975, while he was Secretary of State, Kissinger there made a prolonged attack on the Carter administration, rising to this utterly partisan conclusion: "The biggest foreign policy debacle of the United States in a generation was the collapse of the government and of the Shah of Iran without support or even understanding by the United States."

Yet one needs to read those words with care. Kissinger's distinction, so neatly drawn, between the "collapse of the government," on the one hand, and "of the Shah of Iran," on the other, must not be passed over lightly. The pre-revolutionary government in question was gone for good; it was the Shah, as distinct from that government, who, in late 1979, was still alive. Kissinger was, in fact, suggesting for the record that an acceptable alternative to actually supporting *either* the government *or* the Shah in a decisive way would have been for our government to have followed Kissinger's personal example in showing at least an "understanding. . .of what was involved."

Understanding of that kind was what Kissinger had demanded of the American Congress in 1975, during the last weeks of the Thieu regime in Saigon. He had at that time called for additional military aid — not enough to prevent defeat, to be sure — but only as a gesture of some sort, for old time's sake! And it had been the same in the case of his subsequent appeal for a symbolic pittance of further support for "our side" in the struggle of Marxist factions in Angola. That appeal for token aid — which permitted Kissinger to cavort like a hawk when the outcome was a *fait accompli* — enraged conservative Republican Senator Jesse Helms at the time at least as much as it enraged liberal Democratic Senator Adlai Stevenson III.

Alexander Haig appears to have agreed completely with Kissinger's judgment ascribing the "biggest foreign policy debacle of the United States in a generation" to the Carter administration. Yet, like the "good soldier" he has always shown himself to be, he had never openly criticized the conduct or policies of his Commander in Chief while in active service under him. But then, after his resignation from the army in June 1979, and later, when he announced his intention to "run for President" as the Republican Party's nominee, Haig began voicing his criticism of Carter not only privately, among friends, but also publicly, with reporters. The first notable result had been a column by the famous journalists Roland Evans and Robert Novak, published on November 26, 1979, and titled provocatively: "Did Carter Send a General to Hasten the Shah's Fall?"

According to the syndicated columnists, Haig was then telling prospective political backers privately that his involvement in the "Iran crisis" had started with a phone call he received at his NATO headquarters in Mons, Belgium, on January 1 or 2, 1979, from General David Jones, Chairman of the Joint Chiefs of Staff. It had indeed been a call about his NATO deputy, General Robert Huyser. The Carter administration, Jones had told Haig, "planned to dispatch Huyser, who had exceptional contacts with the Iranian military and the royal palace, to Tehran.'' Huyser, as Jones explained it, was to try "to keep the Iranian military united and effective," while urging them, in the process, "not to attempt a coup against the shaky new regime of Shapour Bakhtiar.''

There was no news in that, to be sure. But presidential-hopeful Haig, in his private talks, went on to say that what Jones had reported to him was just "a smokescreen." Behind it, according to Haig, there had to be a Carter decision — urged on him by Secretary of State Vance over Brzezinski's objections — to have the Shah removed from power as quickly as possible, in such a way as to enjoy the good will of the successor regimes, starting with that of Bakhtiar, but by no means ending there.

As reported by Evans and Novak: "To Haig, the Huyser mission promoted this plan. He informed Jones on the telephone that night that he did not want himself, his deputy or the U.S. military involved in what he viewed as a specious undertaking. The next morning, word came to Mons from Washington that Haig would have to live with it, like it or not." With soldierly self-discipline, Haig kept all of that to himself right down to the time the columnists broke their story. Now he was giving it as "a major reason" for his having resigned his command and retired from the army. Evans and Novak observed, however, that as recently as the week before, when asked by newsmen "why he had left NATO and the Army, Haig had never mentioned the Huyser mission." What had drawn him out in late November 1979? Had he perhaps come more directly under Henry Kissinger's high pressure influence once more, as the controversy over Kissinger's successful efforts to get the Shah admitted to a New York City hospital began to peak?

At any rate, that was the highly-charged political context in which Haig first accused the Carter administration of "assigning his NATO deputy to hasten Mohammed Reza Shah's fall as Iran's ruler a year ago." Then the Evans and Novak column went on to conclude that, "whether or not Haig's interpretation of Carter's motives is accepted," there can be no doubt that "his private chats have fired the opening round of a battle with profound political implications: 'Who lost Iran?' "

Kissinger had briefly summed up his judgment on those implications in his Austin speech, cited earlier. Haig and Kissinger were certainly of one mind in blaming the Iran debacle on Carter. Yet it must be stressed that Haig didn't in the least share Kissinger's view of the Shah as a far-sighted statesman, worthy of being treated by the United States as a loyal and powerful "ally." That is not how Haig would have treated him. Haig has in fact insisted that the Shah was really never anything more than "an American creation," and that our government was wrong in trying to make him appear capable of pursuing a meaningful regional defense strategy on his own. "We confuse the Shah terribly by the inconsistency of our views," Haig has explained. "I don't think his was a case where we should have used military power. No, definitely not. That would have been a definite mistake. But we should have used our influence. The Shah was waiting for a signal from us, and it never came. He was a ward of the United States and Great Britain from the beginning. He was susceptible to our guidance."

That is poles removed from what Kissinger was saying. Kissinger, we must recall, had encouraged the Shah to think of himself as worthy of the 2,500 year tradition of Iranian imperial rule. Playing on his "royal" megalomania, Kissinger had let him quadruple the price of crude oil so that he could dream of "surpassing England and France as a military power by the 1990s." Thus, through heeding Kissinger's fulsome praise, echoed in Ambassador Sullivan's obsequiousness, and while at the same time "cashing in" on the blank-check deal Kissinger had arranged for him in 1972, the Shah had let himself be set up for a fall. Kissinger made his collapse inevitable by forcing him — a "ward of the United States and Great Britain from the beginning"! — to assume the responsibilities of an ally.

But we must turn, finally, to Ambassador Sullivan's version of the sort of blame that is to be placed on President Carter for the Iran debacle. Sullivan has explained it all in a series of publications, consisting of articles and books, that amount to "white papers" in the strict diplomatic sense of that term. The most important of those papers is surely the first, an article published in *Foreign Policy* (Fall 1980, pp. 175-186), and titled "Dateline Iran: The Road Not Taken."

As the title suggests, Sullivan is writing about "Washington's interference" with his plans for managing the course of the Iranian revolution. Alexander Haig's name is quickly introduced and we get a sense that it has been brought in to establish a "Haig-connection" of the self-protective kind that Kissinger had earlier established. Haig is soon called upon to bear witness to the fact of Washington's interference with Sullivan's plans because, as Sullivan explains, it had indeed been his NATO deputy, General Robert Huyser, who was designated by President Carter himself as the more or less unwitting agent of that interference.

According to Sullivan's account, General Huyser had been in recent years almost as much a deputy of Sullivan himself as of Haig. "I had used Huyser frequently in the past," writes Sullivan, with a perhaps deliberate emphasis on the word *used*, "to help us guide the Iranians in the restructuring of their armed forces' command-and-control system so that they would be able to utilize some of the sophisticated equipment we had sold them." It had been a *use* of Huyser with which General Haig had generally been familiar, for, as Sullivan proceeds to explain: "When it was proposed that Huyser come to Iran at the time of the Shah's departure, Haig called me on the secure line to say that he was opposed to the mission and would resign if it were undertaken. It was undertaken, and he resigned."

That brief representation of the Huyser-Haig connection is misleading in several respects. It certainly seems to suggest that Haig immediately resigned his command upon learning that the Huyser mission had actually been undertaken. In fact there was a gap of at least months, in the course of which Haig said nothing about it. But far more serious is the suggestion one gets from the passage that Haig's reasons for objecting to the mission might prove to be more or less identical with Sullivan's. Haig, as we have seen, objected to the mission in the belief that its purpose was to facilitate the Shah's ouster. In fact, at the time of that mission — as we shall be at pains to show — the only person in the Carter administration trying to "hasten Mohammed Reza Shah's fall" was Ambassador Sullivan. President Carter, Zbigniew Brzezinski, and certainly General Huyser, were laboring to salvage the Shah and keep the Iranian military loyal to the Shah's government headed by Prime Minister Bakhtiar.

Sullivan alone, as we shall see, was seeking to transfer the loyalty of the armed forces to the incoming revolutionary regime of the Ayatollah Khomeini, despite his previous eighteen months of representing himself as a stalwart, unwavering supporter of the Shah.

In his first "white paper," Sullivan plainly agrees that it was not Carter or Brzezinski but he alone who had sought in the end to do to the Shah what the Kennedy administration had done to Diem in South Vietnam and what the Nixon-Kissinger-Ford administration had later done to Thieu — matters of which he had had extensive firsthand knowledge!

What we mean to do in the rest of this chapter is to contrast Sullivan's account of his dealings with the Shah and the Iran military, during the last months of the Shah's rule and the first weeks following the Ayatollah's return, with the accounts of President Carter and his top White House expert on Iran, Gary Sick. The contrast, we believe, will highlight the fact that President Carter was tragically ill-served by his recalcitrant ambassador in Iran — about which, regrettably, there has never been a congressional investigation. It is something that deserves attention, for its consequences are still with us, determining events in our time — like the conduct of relations with the Islamic Republic of Iran, brought to a virtual standstill by the wholly partisan so-called Iran-Contra congressional and special-prosecutor investigations.

3. Sullivan and Iran's Armed Forces

What sort of a man was Robert Huyser? Why did he agree to undertake an assignment that his colleague and commander in NATO reportedly objected to strongly enough to resign over it in protest? Those are questions that Sullivan seems to be inviting us to ask where he writes: "Huyser, every inch a straightforward good soldier, arrived in Tehran somewhat flustered by the nature of his mission and by Haig's resignation." One finds no evidence of that in anything that Huyser has ever said regarding his mission, about which he was anything but frustrated — having eagerly volunteered for it. Certainly he was not informed at the time of any Haig decision to resign his command over it. But Sullivan's point is that, having a flustered emissary of President Carter on his hands, he was determined to play the gracious host in the finest tradition of the diplomatic service. Huyser "moved in with me," he writes, "and we shared all our message traffic and our common concerns. We did not always agree. But when we differed, we did so openly and with due respect to our differences."

In other words, Sullivan is determined to have no quarrel with the agent, in Huyser's case; his quarrel is reserved for the agent's "principal," the President of the United States. We learn next that Huyser and Sullivan had received basically identical orders as to how they were to respond to projected turns in the mounting governmental crisis in Iran. Where they differed was in their willingness to act as instructed. Without immediately disclosing what he himself had been up to before Huyser's arrival, Sullivan proceeds to make this point: "Huyser's mission as described in the official order he received, was to assist in maintaining the integrity of the armed forces and in transferring their loyalty from the departing Shah to the Bakhtiar regime." That is plain enough. As for his own specific assignment, Sullivan writes: "Parallel to this order, I received terse instructions telling me that the policy of the U.S. government was to support the Bakhtiar government without reservation and to assist in its survival." Those were not complex instructions. And it is reasonable to conclude that if Sullivan had not already been deep in the implementation of a counterplan of his own, he could easily have accepted them as given, agreeing to work in tandem with Huyser on essentially the same assignment. But, evidently it was much too late for that. He could not in his heart, in his conscience, accept the instructions sent to him. Thus, he informs us, he had replied to them

> by pointing out that the Bakhtiar government was a chimera that the Shah had created to permit a dignified departure, that Bakhtiar himself was quixotic and would be swept aside by the arrival of Khomeini and his supporters in Tehran. Moreover, I argued that it would be feckless to tranfer the loyalty of the armed forces to Bakhtiar because this would cause the destructive confrontation between the armed forces and the revolutionaries that

we [meaning, no doubt, "I"] had hoped to avoid. It would result in the disintegration of the armed forces and eventually in the disintegration of Iran. It would be directly contrary to U.S. interests.

Sullivan still pretended to believe that, in receipt of such a reply from him, the Carter White House might conceivably "reconsider" its chosen course of action and turn control of things back to him, to resolve matters as he saw fit. He therefore expresses disappointment in discovering that was not to be the case. We again get an invocation of his "Haig connection" where he writes:

> By this time, my exchanges with Washington had become increasingly acerbic. The reply I received to this message, in my judgment, contained an insulting aspersion upon my loyalty and instructed me, in no uncertain terms, to support Bakhtiar no matter what reservations I had. At this point, I decided, like Haig, to resign. However, I still was responsible for protecting about 15,000 remaining Americans in the face of enveloping chaos. I therefore quenched my Irish temper, sent my wife out of the country, prepared for the worst, and delayed my resignation until after the anticipated holocaust.

What Sullivan had done, in other words, was to tell his superiors in Washington that he was refusing to carry out their official orders. Gary Sick, we noted, had called Sullivan's "second" message of November 2, 1978, a "bombshell." It had asked for instructions on what to say when the Shah called for guidance about possible plans to abdicate. What about Sullivan's reply to the message of "parallel instructions" he received from Washington after Huyser's arrival? Sick informs us that "Sullivan received this message in the middle of the night," and that he had then "dashed off an outraged message" of his own, "which, among other things, characterized the President's decision as 'insane'." With that message, Sick says further, Sullivan "burned his last bridge. Washington was fairly on notice that the rebellion in Iran now extended to the person of the U.S. ambassador." [138]

President Carter has, to be sure, supplied his own account of the same events in his 1982 presidential memoirs *Keeping Faith*. Less

than ten pages of that book are devoted to Sullivan and his dealings
with the Iranian armed forces and Huyser, but the judgments offered
are severe and sharply pointed in their revelations. President Carter
notices, first, that as late as October 28, 1978, Sullivan was still of
one mind with "all my other advisers and me in believing that the
Shah was our best hope for maintaining stability in Iran." As evidence of that, the President cites a cable sent by Sullivan on that date,
saying that "the Shah is the unique element which can, on the one
hand, restrain the military and, on the other hand, lead a controlled
transition.... I would strongly oppose any overture to Khomeini."

In less than a week, to President Carter's complete surprise, that
view of the Shah was abandoned by Sullivan — in the two messages
of November 2 which we have already examined. As Carter puts it:
"By early November, Ambassador Sullivan had become convinced
that opposition leaders would have to be given a much stronger voice
in Iran's affairs than the Shah was willing to consider." Carter says
that he "could not disagree with this," but that he wanted to assure
the Shah that, in whatever arrangements he chose to make, he would
have the complete backing of the White House and Secretary Vance's
State Department. By then, Sullivan seemed to be insisting that the
Carter administration ought to tell the Shah that, in the present crisis, American support would be predicated on his "acquiescence to
suggestions from the American Embassy." In other words, Sullivan
wanted the President to tell the Shah to do "what Sullivan asks you
to do — or else." That parallels exactly what President Thieu had
been told in Saigon, in December 1972, to force his acquiescence
to the terms of the Paris Accords negotiated by Sullivan! [438-440]

Through late November and early December 1978, Sullivan
seemed to become more and more adamant in his reversed estimate
of the Shah, until, finally, by the year's end, he was recommending,
as Carter says,

> that we oppose the plans of the Shah, insist on his immediate depar-
> ture, and try to form some kind of friendship or alliance with
> Khomeini. I rejected this recommendation because the Shah, Bak-
> htiar, and the Iranian military leaders needed consistent Ameri-
> can support. Reports in the Washington press, however, indicated

deviations within the State Department from my policy of backing the Shah while he struggled to establish a successor government. [443]

It was at that point in his exchanges with Ambassador Sullivan
— exchanges which had indeed become, on Sullivan's part, "increasingly acerbic" — that Carter turned to Secretary of Defense Harold
Brown to see if some arrangement could be made to get what he called
"adequate reports from the military" in Iran, with whom Sullivan
seemed to have lost effective touch. In Carter's words: "Secretary
Brown and I concluded that we needed a strong and competent
American representative in Tehran to keep me informed about the
military's needs." Brown immediately recommended General Haig's
NATO deputy Robert Huyser, who quickly agreed to take the assignment, a major responsibility of which would be, in Carter's
words, "to strengthen the resolve of the military leaders and encourage them to remain in Iran in order to maintain stability even
if the Shah decided to leave." Carter adds that, at the same time,
"we made arrangements for the Shah and his immediate family to
use the Walter Annenberg estate in California if he later decided to
'take a vacation in a foreign country'."

Those are important revelations, in the light of what Carter's
severest critics, led by Henry Kissinger, would later be saying, so
as to misrepresent Carter as an "enemy" of the Shah and completely opposed to his being admitted to the United States! With that,
we are brought up to the moment of Huyser's arrival in Tehran on
January 4, 1979, and the parallel instructions subsequently received
by Huyser and Sullivan. "My instructions had been," the President
writes,

> to do everything possible to strengthen the Shah, but during these
> days I became increasingly troubled by the attitude of Ambassador
> Sullivan, who seemed obsessed with the need for the Shah to abdi-
> cate without further delay. He was getting quite nervous, and some-
> times reported that the Shah would not see him. I was still relying
> on some of his reports, which I later realized were not accurate or
> balanced. Sullivan insisted that we should give support to Khomei-
> ni, even if it meant weakening Bakhtiar and the coalition govern-

ment he was trying to form. The Iranian military leaders still supported the Shah and had no inclination to strengthen Khomeini's influence in any way. Sullivan's reports about the military's attitude were often at variance with those of General Huyser.... I wanted more than one opinion. Over time, however, I came to trust Huyser's judgment.''

We have already reviewed Sullivan's reply to President Carter's parallel instructions for coordinated implementation by Huyser and Sullivan. Characterizing that reply of January 10, 1979, Carter writes that it was ''a cable bordering on insolence,'' making use of ''such phrases as 'gross and perhaps irretrievable mistake', 'plea for sanity', and 'incomprehensible'.'' It had been obvious to the President, by then, that, previously, Sullivan had been carrying out his directives only ''halfheartedly, if at all.'' But now, with Sullivan's obvious change of mind ''in recent weeks about the Shah,'' even the least show of compliance with presidential orders ceased. Carter had promptly told Secretary of State Vance to ''get Sullivan out of Iran,'' but ''Cy'' — as Carter writes — ''insisted that it would be a mistake to put a new man in the country in the midst of the succession of crises we probably faced.'' Though he pleaded with the President to let Sullivan stay on, Vance offered no defense of Sullivan's manifest recalcitrance. Carter ''reluctantly agreed'' not to fire Sullivan instantly. But from then on, as he says, he ''relied primarily on General Huyser, who remained cool and competent.''

The pattern of conduct displayed by Sullivan in all of this must remain inexplicable, unless one realizes what Sullivan had actually been doing by the time Huyser ''joined him'' in Tehran. In his 1980 *Foreign Affairs* white paper, Sullivan declines to go into detail on the matter; but the paper nevertheless reveals that, at the time of his reply to the President's instructions, he had already gone a long way in carrying out a contrary plan of his own for dealing with the Iranian military. His plan was, of course, the ''road not taken'' in the article's title. He had proposed that ''road'' to Washington, he there explains, as a course of American action that would have salvaged all that was still salvageable in Iran at the time, from the perspective of genuine ''American interests.'' His was a plan, he professed to believe, that would have "saved the day" for America — if only the White House, heeding Zbigniew Brzezinski's counsels, hadn't blundered ahead on a mistaken course.

According to Sullivan, by late December 1978, all that could be salvaged in Iran that might be of real use to the United States in the future was not the Shah, or any "moderate government" headed by the likes of Bakhtiar, but simply the Iranian armed forces themselves. His argument was, therefore, that he should have been permitted to act on his own "to preclude the armed forces from being chewed up in the revolution. Because of our special relationship, we should determine whether we could broker an arrangement that would enjoy the support of groups that would prevail after the success of the revolution and that would have the blessing of Khomeini."

That had been the message he had sent to Washington — though by no means in such frank terms — back in late November, for a reply to which he had waited in vain through the first weeks of December. No reply ever came, he says: "Instead, it soon became apparent that my views were no longer welcome at the White House. Emissaries of various types began to arrive from Washington to assess the situation de novo and to encourage the Shah to use force." That, according to Sullivan's retrospective account of 1980, was what lay behind the acerbic exchanges with Washington about which President Carter complained, as we have seen. What should a "good ambassador" do under such circumstances? No doubt falling back on the "fingertip feelings" of the Harriman days and the "purposive ambiguities" of the Kissinger days, Sullivan decided to take the Iranian bull by the horns, so to speak, and present the Carter administration with his "accomplished fact," as we have earlier noted. He "began to steer the embassy," as he says, "through a series of actions that sought to establish the ground rules under which the Iranian armed forces, purged of some of their more controversial leaders, would be accepted by a [Khomeini appointed] Bazargan government."

How far had Sullivan managed to pursue that design to first purge some of the leadership of the Shah's army and then arrange for its transfer, otherwise intact, to the victorious revolutionary regime? Sullivan doesn't keep us in suspense. In a most extraordinary paragraph, worthy in itself of a very lengthy congressional inquiry, he puts his "high expertise" in such matters on display, writing:

> At the same time, we sought to determine on what terms the armed forces would accept such an arrangement. Because many of those who engaged for patriotic reasons in these conversations are still in Iran, and because their patriotic motives may be suspect in the highly charged atmosphere there [Fall 1980], I shall not go into details about these various discussions. Suffice it to say that detailed understandings were reached between the armed forces and revolutionary leaders in Tehran. A number of senior officers would have been allowed to leave the country with the Shah, and a tranfer of allegiance of the remaining armed forces would have been made in a way that would have preserved their integrity. Because the United States controlled the logistics of all sophisticated elements of the armed forces, there were means to assure the implementation of these agreements.

There, indeed, we recognize the voice of Sullivan in the role of "military proconsul" once more, as in the days when, as Ambassador to Laos, he "had directed the secret bombings of Pathet Lao targets in Laos." But, at least in those days, it was all done with the full knowledge of the White House, which gave the orders, if not of the U.S. Congress, from whose members Sullivan had diplomatically withheld the truth, when several of them paid him a visit in the field.

Gary Sick has supplied a detailed assessment of Ambassador Sullivan's "plan" for preserving the "integrity" of the Iranian military. After observing that the plan, which "involved a fundamental shift in policy," to say the least, had been "prepared without the knowledge of the President and was then presented only at the last minute as the situation become desperate," Sick observes that Carter's rejection of it was a foregone conclusion. Sullivan had, "in effect, asked the President to buy a pig in a poke." But the question is, could the plan have worked even if Sullivan had obtained White House approval and support?

Gary Sick answers that question with an emphatic no. It was, he says, from beginning to end a flight from reality. Sullivan had been trying to have it both ways. He talked publicly the way Henry Kissinger and Alexander Haig were always talking. It was always, "Stick with the Shah; don't deal with his opposition." But his secret plan, already far advanced toward implementation, had been to do in fact the opposite. And, after he had started his "detailed arrangements" to have the military leaders talk with the Ayatollah's people, the contradiction became only too obvious to hundreds and perhaps thousands of Iranians who counted. "In the end," Sick writes,

> this policy produced the worst of both worlds. His support for the Shah was perceived in Washington and Tehran as equivocal, thereby undercutting his credibility in both capitals. As a result, when the moment arrived to implement his plan for a brokered deal between the "moderates" and Khomeini, he no longer had the confidence of the President, and his last-minute proposal was rejected. The likelihood that the "moderates" could ever have bargained effectively with Khomeini about the terms of a post-Shah political arrangement was never very high. However, if U.S. support for such a plan was to have any realistic chance of success, it had to be carefully planned in advance with the knowledge and support of the White House. The way the plan was developed and presented virtually guaranteed its failure. [172-3]

Gary Sick seems almost to be suggesting there that Sullivan's plan had remained but a plan. Elsewhere, however, he is at pains to stress that its implementation had been carried a long way by the time of the Huyser mission. That is a fact. He had set things in motion and the wheels were already in high gear — which, says Sick, helps "to explain why Sullivan was so upset by the arrival of General Huyser," and why he hastily made a "last-minute effort through Vance to stop Huyser from initiating talks with the Iranian generals." What Sullivan had been designing and implementing, Sick observes, was what has to be called, at best, a "cynical reversal of roles." At worst, needless to say, it would have to be taken as an elaborate deception of the kind Kissinger called for toward the close of his first year in the Nixon White House.

At that time, quite like Ambassador Sullivan in his Tehran post,

Kissinger claimed to be motivated by the hard necessities of *Realpolitik,* which made him impatient to hear himself being criticized by outsiders with no political responsibilities. Academic colleagues, especially, had been very critical of the means he and Nixon had chosen to pursue in avoiding a populist "middle America" backlash while withdrawing American combat forces from South Vietnam at a precipitous pace. In December 1969, Kissinger gave such critics this seemingly frank yet utterly Disraelian reply: "Anybody can end the war. Our problem is to keep the society together." He had then gone on to warn that a settlement of the war in Vietnam arrived at without carefully planned "displays of American firmness" could turn our society "into a group that has nothing left but a physical test of strength, and the only outcome of this is Caesarism." "Upper-middle-class college kids," he further warned, "will not take this country over. Some more primitive and elemental forces will do that if it happens."

In his *Foreign Policy* article, Sullivan asserts that his intention in pursuing *Realpolitik* initiatives with the Iranian military and the anti-Shah forces of Khomeini was to hold Iranian society together for its own sake and to "save the military" for America's sake as well. Because of the Carter administration's interference, the result was, in Sullivan's words,

> ...that chaos descended on Iran. The armed forces disintegrated, their weapons fell into the hands of all those disparate elements in the revolution who in turn fell to fighting among themselves once the Shah was gone. Bazargan [the Ayatollah's first prime minister] and his government had no means to enforce order; and Khomeini, in his desire to remain the nominal leader of the revolution, would issue no directions that would be substantially disobeyed. This meant that the extremists would be able to set the pace, and in most matters, that has been the pattern ever since. The disintegration is well-advanced and there is a growing dependence on the Soviet Union.

All of that, Sullivan would have us understand, could have been prevented had he been permitted to execute his plan to deliver the military over to the Ayatollah's new regime intact. It was exactly what Kissinger had had a mind to do in negotiating with Hanoi over the head of President Thieu and arranging for Sullivan to become the first American ambassador to North Vietnam, once the "decent interval" required to unite Vietnam's two halves was complete. One recalls the words of Kissinger to that effect back on November 2, 1972, when he "crashed" the South Vietnamese Embassy's National Day reception in Washington with his theatrical entourage, as a gesture of "support" for Thieu's government which he had just sacrificed to Hanoi.

At any rate, one is left breathless not so much by the audacity of that Sullivan plan for the Iranian military (which was already being implemented when he proposed it to his Commander in Chief), as by the fact that there has been no congressional or special prosecutor's investigation of his conduct in having dared to do such a thing, directly contrary to orders in hand. But of course, in those days, the two Houses of Congress and the White House were all in the hands of the same party. And it apparently takes partisan *division* to sustain such investigations.

Still, we must ask: How could an Ambassador of Sullivan's rank, who had served under Harriman and Kissinger in peace negotiations with Hanoi kept secret from our clients in South Vietnam, have failed to await a word of support from his President before attempting to execute such a plan? In his *Foreign Policy* white paper, his excuse is that, in his dealings with the Carter White House, he had early been persuaded that his superiors there lacked the ability to govern in difficult times. When the time of true crisis came for the Shah's regime, he concluded, they must all have been overcome, at least momentarily, by a paralysis of will. In his words; "As far as I could determine, the United States, on the eve of the Shah's departure, was left with no policy." That is why he had presumed to act in the "American interest" without White House approval, intending to provide his superiors with the *results* of sound policy, which they would finally be forced to accept, out of necessity, in spite of themselves. After such rationalizations, he feels constrained to add, with some pathos: "However, I overlooked the Brzezinski factor. It appears that he had a plan in mind."

Writing as if he believed that President Carter might be less to blame, personally, for America's "mishandling" of the Iran crisis than his national security adviser, Sullivan insists that, starting in November 1978, Brzezinski had not only "begun to make his own policy," but had also "established his own 'embassy' in Iran". That "embassy," to be sure, consisted of single individuals allegedly "sent" by Brzezinski to serve as intermediaries between him and the Shah, without going through the U.S. Embassy. The first Brzezinski emissary was the Shah's own Ambassador to Washington, Ardeshir Zahedi. As Sullivan tells it, "Brzezinski reportedly encouraged Zahedi to urge the Shah to use force" to contain organized mass demonstrations. In early January, it was, again, Brzezinski, and not President Carter, Sullivan says, who had by then "already sent General Huyser to Tehran" as his direct emissary to the Iranian military, rather than to the Shah.

Using Huyser as his intermediary, Brzezinski, to no purpose that Sullivan could grasp, managed to interfere with Sullivan's "plan" for a peaceful transfer of the Iranian military from the control of the Shah's government, headed by Bakhtiar, to the projected government of the Ayatollah, which would almost certainly be headed by Mehdi Bazargan. In Sullivan's words:

> As the confrontation between Bakhtiar and Khomeini quickened, Huyser received continuing instructions to prepare the armed forces for conflict in defense of the Bakhtiar regime. On the basis of his observations, he offered to Washington his opinion that in such a confrontation the armed forces would prevail. But he always tempered his observation by stating that I disagreed and that I believed the army would disintegrate when ordered to fire on revolutionaries, some of whom were relatives of the soldiers. As a result, their arms would be dispersed throughout the whole tangled and conflicting fabric of the revolutionary forces, making it impossible for the Bazargan government to assume quick and effective control when it inevitably took power. [185]

It is a ruse, on Sullivan's part, to suggest, as he does there, that what is at issue is a conflict between a Brzezinski plan, privately advanced by Brzezinski, and a rival Sullivan plan that had, somehow a "higher justification." The truth is that Brzezinski's plan had long since become the plan of President Carter, the nation's Commander in Chief. Instructions for its implementation had been sent through channels to all concerned, with special directives to Sullivan and Huyser. What stood in the way of implementation of *that* plan were the prior arrangements Sullivan had *already* made with the Iranian military, which undermined Huyser's mission in advance, since most of the top military had already been thoroughly compromised, not to be further trusted by either side in Iran's tremendous domestic struggle.

4. The Shah's Flight: Out Like a Mouse?

The Shah's removal from his Peacock Throne in January 1979 proved to be a pathetic rather than a tragic event. He was not, as many maliciously said, "thrown out like a dead mouse"; but, given the facts about what the American Ambassador in Tehran had been up to during the preceding six weeks, the truth came close to that. In the flight of 1953, arranged for him by the American CIA in the days when it had just emerged as the chief instrument for the overseas exercise of presidential emergency powers under President Eisenhower, the young Shah had been accompanied by his second wife, the beautiful Soraya Esfaudari, whom he had married in 1948, after his first marriage, to Princess Fauzia, a sister of Egypt's King Farouk, had ended in divorce. That first marriage, of 1939, had been loveless: prearranged by the royal families of Egypt and Iran before the betrothed had so much as set eyes on one another. The love-filled marriage to Soraya also ended in divorce ten years later (1958), but only because she failed to bear a royal heir. Back in 1953, however, when they were forced to flee temporarily, the Shah and his beloved second wife were perceived everywhere as a truly romantic couple; and there was broad rejoicing in European social circles when word was received that joint Anglo-American undercover efforts had restored them to their throne.

But the flight of 1979 with the Empress Farah Diba — a third wife who had given the Shah an heir — had nothing of the old romance about it. On December 27, when painful decisions were being taken, Sullivan's embassy report to Washington noted that, "at the urgent request of the palace, the U.S. consulate in Tehran issued visas to the Queen Mother and her entourage, who listed their destination as Los Angeles." After being briefed by Sullivan on Washington's view of his "last alternatives," the Shah had asked whether, in the event that he chose to hand over the reins of effective government to a "Regency Council," Washington would "expect him to go abroad," to which question he quickly saw that the answer would have to be yes. Such a council could function only in his absence or total incapacitation. As Gary Sick summarizes: "The Shah then said there was the problem of where to go, and Sullivan related that 'there was a long pregnant silence while he stared at me.' Finally Sullivan said that he had no instructions but that he was confident the Shah would be welcome in the United States. The Shah seemed enormously relieved to hear this. . . ." [125-7]

Thus, in 1979, the Shah was only too well aware of the difference a quarter of a century had made. There was now not the slightest prospect that a Kermit Roosevelt or a General Schwartzkopf (to say nothing of their less publicized British counterparts) would intervene to set things right for him in his absence. In 1953, he had clearly been but a client of the United States. There had been no pretense that he could stand on his own. In his report to his superiors, Kermit Roosevelt had stressed that, if the Shah hadn't the support of the army and the people, restoring him to his client-throne could not be done by the CIA but would have to be left to the U.S. Marines. Back then, in other words, the Shah had been respectfully treated as the client he was. But, after the Kissinger deal of 1972, that had ceased to be the case. As we have several times noted, with the American "blank check" in hand, he was declared to be a full-fledged ally. And so, in the view of Kissinger's man in Iran, he could be left on his own, to face an altogether different kind of opposition that had the people on its side. In 1979, his opponents of 1953 — Mossadegh's National Front "liberals" — had ended up being his only possible, and never more than half-hearted civilian supporters. And they, of course, had remained notoriously unable to sustain themselves by force or other means against determined foes.

At any rate, late in January 1979, after the Shah's departure, the government of his last prime minister, already purged of all recent supporters of the Shah, began hasty preparations for a peaceful return of the Ayatollah Khomeini. That was basically the task it had assumed. Dealing with the military had been left to General Huyser, as we saw. There were no strong reasons for believing that the Ayatollah would agree to support Bakhtiar's "reform" administration. Still, as against an alternative of engaging in wholesale slaughter, a carefully-staged peaceful yet officially-sanctioned welcome for Khomeini seemed to be the only feasible means of maintaining a semblance of tranquility among the millions of unarmed Shiite Muslims who crowded the streets of Tehran daily, crying for the return of their exiled "Imam."

But what of the Iranian military? Ambassador Sullivan, as we saw, had "sorted things out" for his "final solution": he had prepared two lists of top officers, some to go, and some to stay. The lists had been kept from Sullivan's Washington superiors, but the names were known to the individuals listed, and to the agents of the Ayatollah, who had been asked for their approval or disapproval of the choices. When the regime of Shapour Bakhtiar collapsed some four weeks after the Shah's flight, and less than two weeks after the Ayatollah's return, the military officers involved in Sullivan's plan — those who were supposed to leave with the Shah, of course, but also those who were supposed to remain behind and "cooperate" — found themselves condemned all around. Their end — pathetic, where it was not truly tragic — was to be destroyed ignominiously. Sullivan's fate, when he finally left his post, proved to have been far less taxing, physically, than that of his compromised generals, though it was hardly less ignominious.

5. General Huyser's Report and the Last Days of Bakhtiar's Interregnum

It should be noted that General Huyser didn't stay in Iran very long. He had arrived on January 4, 1979, and left on February 3. He had done what he had come to do, and had, of course, learned something of what Sullivan had been attempting. In his report to

President Carter on February 5, he could point out that it had been hard to deal with the top Iranian military as a unit, because, from the start, the Shah had never permitted his top generals to function as a unit, with combined staffs. On the contrary, "each service chief had always reported independently to the Shah, with virtually no coordination between themselves." It had been the Shah's way of preventing conspiratorial leagues among his generals.

That was an old imperial tradition. When German kings, after the fragmentation of the Carolingian empire, succeeded in unifying Germany, they very intentionally divided their German command into some twelve subcommands so that, when they went on to reconstitute a "Holy Roman Empire," with Italy serving as the "imperial garden," they could remain more or less confident that no subordinate left behind in Germany would be able to make himself king in the imperial-king's absence. The scheme had less justification under the Pahlavi Shahs, to be sure; but the last of them did, after all, call himself Shah-an-Shah or King of Kings, and apparently dreamt constantly of ruling over regions as vast as those commanded by Persian rulers at the time of the Persian wars with the Greeks.

Huyser was repeatedly questioned about how his view of the military situation in Iran differed from Sullivan's. There was no concealing the fact that Sullivan had, long before Huyser's arrival, come to the conclusion that neither the Shah nor Shapour Bakhtiar could effectively hold the armed forces together. In Sullivan's view, they both had to go, together with many old generals, before anything positive could be done with the military establishment. Huyser lamented the fact that the generals he knew had had no experience acting together on their own; yet he believed that an American presence could supply what the Shah himself had supplied by way of a unified command, and supply it better.

Comparing Huyser's reports with what Sullivan had been saying and doing, Carter was forced to draw some painful conclusions about what must have been going on all along in Vance's State Department where, among the many officials that Henry Kissinger had left in place, he had few real supporters. Huyser's reports proved that there had been a large measure of "reluctance in the State

Department in carrying out" the President's directives "fully and with enthusiasm." That was an important result of the Huyser mission. Summoning all the State Department Iranian desk officers to the White House, "I told them," Carter has written, that "if they could not support what I decided, their only alternative was to resign — and that if there was another outbreak of misinformation, distortions, or self-serving leaks, I would direct the Secretary of State to discharge the officials responsible for that particular desk, even if some innocent people might be punished. I simply could not live with this situation any longer, and repeated that they would have to be loyal to me or resign."

That occurred, Gary Sick observes, shortly after Carter had told "Cy" Vance to fire Sullivan; and we can be sure that, had Carter ordered the firing of all personnel at the State Department's Iran desk, Vance's response would have been equally protective. The people Carter complained of were Vance's people as well as Kissinger's, though Kissinger's guidance was no doubt more valued all around. Like Lyndon Johnson before him, President Carter came to feel that he was surrounded by people who obviously thought that they owed greater loyalty to the major pre-Carter directors of American foreign policy. Kissinger had said, in his final year, that he hoped to "institutionalize" his foreign policy "successes," especially those aimed at preventing a nuclear holocaust at all costs. He had apparently succeeded; it had become very difficult to get people trained and placed by Kissinger to do what a mere President wanted and asked them to do. Carter, to be sure, was especially concerned with the links between Sullivan's activities and Kissinger's with respect to presidential policy in Iran. And, in retrospect, we can see that he had every reason to be concerned; for Kissinger out of office had greater control over Sullivan than Director William Casey of the CIA could conceivably have had over his so-called loose cannon in President Reagan's White House. As Gary Sick sums things up in this regard, for the period just before and just after the Shah's fall:

> Throughout the crisis, the discipline within the U.S. government had been deplorable at almost every level. Policy was constantly contradicted or undermined by leaks, unattributed comments by

"insiders" who had a particular axe to grind, and bureaucratic sniping. Public reports from the Shah's party in Egypt and Morocco increasingly blamed the Shah's collapse on the lack of support he received from Washington, and Henry Kissinger was beginning to launch a political campaign against the President based on the theme that Carter's policies had "lost" Iran for the West. [154]

By February 11, 1979, General Huyser, having completed his reporting, had left Washington for his permanent station in the U.S. European Command. On that day, during an emergency meeting called by Zbigniew Brzezinski, word had come in that the Iranian military, which had kept up a fight in its ranks to continue support of Bakhtiar's government through the whole previous day, until midnight, had, in a later meeting early on February 11, decided not to "confront the people," and therefore declared their neutrality. Emergency calls were placed, to Sullivan in his Tehran Embassy and to Huyser in his Stuttgart post, for their estimates on what could be expected or done. Brzezinski wanted to know if it were still possible to effect a military coup of some kind.

The responses from Huyser and Sullivan came soon enough. Sullivan, still wrapped up in his own plan for an "orderly transfer of allegiance" by the military to the Ayatollah's side, gave a plain enough answer. The military, he said, "was in the process of making its accommodation with Bazargan [the Ayatollah's replacement for Bakhtiar], and was too beleaguered to undertake any action." Huyser gave a purely military response. He said he thought the military would act positively "only if the United States was prepared to pledge full moral and political support, up to and including combat support." [Sick, 155-156]

Huyser's was the sort of response Kermit Roosevelt had given back in 1953. In dealing with a client-state — and Iran was, as Haig himself recognized, never anything more than a client-state — the patron state must assure the client that if it can't do the thing expected of it, the patron will, of course, intervene to do it! Did Huyser think the United States was prepared to do what the situation required? Had it done so in Vietnam, after expending so much American blood on the scene? No. The American policy had been to insist that its clients were allies. The United States would "help" its allies, of course; but, in the end, the allies would have to prove themselves self-reliant. It would depend on them, finally, whether their enemies would prevail or not. Since, in the cases of South Vietnam and Iran, the allies were not really allies but wholly dependent clients, any such American policy meant a thinly-veiled surrender, perfectly transparent to the enemy, though not to the mass of Americans. Summing up what happened in Iran on February 11, 1979, Gary Sick provides this somber paragraph:

> The best epitaph of the day's events — and perhaps of this entire period — was written by Air Force Colonel Tom Schaefer. Colonel Schaefer was the U.S. Defense attaché in Tehran, and was later to be one of the hostages. At the end of a long message report summarizing the developments of February 11, he concluded with admirable military brevity: "Army surrenders; Khomeini wins. Destroying all classified." [156]

PART IV

Religious/Political Dilemmas Since 1979

CHAPTER TEN

Khomeini's New Iran: Anti-Zionist But Not Anti-American

February 11, 1979 — the day the government of Shapour Bakhtiar fell — soon came to be celebrated by the Ayatollah Khomeini's successor regime as "the day of the revolution." One year later, after the November 4, 1979 hostage crisis had entered its fourth month, a Khomeini message to the people of his new Islamic Republic, in commemoration of the event, was read by his son Ahmed. It contained this notable passage:

> I have said many times and once again declare that Iran must pursue its decisive struggles until the end of all its political, military economic and cultural dependence on America.... Later, provided that our alert and noble nation grants permission, we will establish our very ordinary relations with America just as with other countries. [261]

Despite the November 1979 seizure of the U.S. Embassy in Tehran, that course of conduct had indeed been pursued by the new regime through the entire year since its inauguration in February 1979. But, as we must later examine in some detail, there had been all along powerful forces at work, in the U. S., Iran and elsewhere, seeking to prevent any diplomatic "meeting of minds" between the U.S. and the Ayatollah's Iran. In America, Henry Kissinger and Jacob Javits had emerged as leaders of the political opposition to normalization; in Iran, an undefined opposition finally found its focus with the November American Embassy seizure initiated by four "young radicals"; and elsewhere, it proved to be the Israelis who took the lead,

207

doing all they could, with considerable success, to upset any such normalization processes for as long as Israel continued to be excluded from them.

We spoke near the end of the last chapter of the preparations made by Bakhtiar to give the returning exiled Imam a more or less "peaceful" reception. Long-range preparations had consisted in domestic reforms, like excluding all recent Shah supporters from the government, and foreign-relations reforms, like severing the Shah's de facto ties with states whose national goals or ways of life offended the "universal ideals" of Islam, especially Shiite Islam. In the same message of February 11, 1980, Khomeini had added these harsher words: "Never compromise with any power.... Topple from the position of power anyone in any position who is inclined to compromise with the East and the West." By the time of that message, several heads of administrations appointed by the Ayatollah had already been toppled because of charges that they were compromising with Washington — charges made by the captors of American hostages who threatened to kill those hostages if the accused "pro-American compromisers" were not instantly ousted.

Still, apart from the evil of "compromising," the Ayatollah was insisting in that message that "very ordinary relations with America" should indeed be pursued, "as with other countries." Very different, however, was the attitude toward Israeli Zionists, for instance, and South African *apartheid* racists, for, in their cases, the ideals of Shiite Islam were more directly assaulted. That is why, back on January 3, 1979, in attempting to adapt his practice to Khomeini's ideal of Islamic temporal governance, Shapour Bakhtiar had announced that, while Iran would continue to "sell oil to countries requesting it," exceptions would have to be made. "Given the conflict that opposes us in a religious context to Israel, and in another context to South Africa," he had declared, "I think my government will not do that."

Those were long-range but very important accommodations made by Bakhtiar to "please" Khomeini. But, of greater urgency were the contemplated short-range accommodations. At the beginning of the last week in January 1979, Bakhtiar wrote a letter to the Ayatollah in his temporary Parisian residence-in-exile, addressing

him as "Your Sacred Eminence," and offering "respects and greetings to a great warrior striving for rights." But the point of that conciliatory approach was to ask Khomeini to delay his return to Iran
by three weeks — carrying the event into the middle of February.
"This request," said Bakhtiar, "is made to prevent incidents which,
if they occur, will be unpleasant events and will make everyone mourn
eternally." A premature return, Bakhtiar was indicating, would result
in fratricidal bloodshed throughout the country and especially in
Tehran. The Ayatollah refused to heed the request, which was repeatedly made, even after his return to Iran. Refusing to see Bakhtiar's
official emissaries, he said: "The former Shah was illegal; the two
assemblies [of his government] and Bakhtiar are illegal; and I won't
receive an illegal official." His stand would be that the only act he
would accept as legal from Bakhtiar was an act of resignation —
after which there might be discussion of a possible reappointment
to a position of authorized power.

Because Khomeini had refused to delay his return, attempts were
made to prevent a landing of his plane — loaded with reporters as
well as aides — at Tehran's Mehrabad airport. But those failed. Air
force technicians (*homafars*), turning on their commanders, seized
the airport facilities at the nation's capital and kept them operating
to receive the Ayatollah on February 1, 1979. And the arrival, writes
Sick,

> generally followed the script worked out between the government,
> the military and the revolutionaries in the previous weeks. The
> army stood back, and security was handled by the revolutionary
> forces. The Ayatollah was greeted by joyous mobs in the millions,
> and during his visit to the martyr's cemetery his helicopter was
> nearly swamped by the crowds trying to catch a glimpse of him.
> He took up residence in a small austere building in the south of
> the city. [150]

It was clear from the start that, in keeping with an ancient Shiite
tradition, the Ayatollah planned not to rule directly, but rather to
serve as "an arbiter of last resort," leaving the details of government to professional politicians." Having refused to accord Bakhtiar even "caretaker status while a referendum was conducted,"

the Ayatollah proceeded on his own to name a provisional government, to be headed by Mehdi Bazargan. Like Bakhtiar, Bazargan was a liberal moderate, "viewed by Washington as a patient conciliating figure" who could be expected to "get the oilfields pumping and possibly harness the disparate opposition forces as well as the nervous pro-Shah elements within the military leadership." It was understood, to be sure, that Bazargan would continue to "make an exception" of Israel, as well as South Africa, in his otherwise conciliatory approach to international relations. And from the standpoint of the central focus of this book, the significance of that "exception" is clear. The wedge that Bakhtiar's government had already hammered into place separating U.S. and Israeli interests in Iran was to be hammered in still further.

1. First Seizure of the U.S. Embassy in Tehran: A Conspiracy Against Khomeini?

Walter Eytan, the distinguished Israeli diplomat and journalist whom we cited at length earlier, had seen such a separation of U.S. and Israeli interest in Iran as inevitable, even if the Pahlavi dynasty could have been enabled, somehow, to retain its throne. From Israel's vantage point, it was significant, however, that there were evidently forces in revolutionary Iran which, for a variety of reasons (some not easily explicable), were as much opposed to normalized relations with the United States as they were eager to break off all ties with Israel. At any rate, as *Time* magazine reported it shortly after the event: on February 14, 1979, three days after the fall of Bakhtiar's government, and one day after "the Ayatollah Khomeini exhorted his followers to lay down their arms" — a "band of 100 Iranian leftists attacked the U.S. Embassy in Tehran," at ten o'clock in the morning.

That attack must have come as a relief to many Israelis resident in Iran, for, during the previous two days, Israel's mission in Tehran, which served as its equivalent of an embassy, had been similarly attacked; and the event had seemed to be part of the "exception" in Iran's international relations previously indicated by

Bakhtiar. The Ayatollah Khomeini's response to the attack on the
Israeli mission had been to congratulate the attackers and immediately hand it over to Yasser Arafat and his P.L.O., to serve as an
embassy for the projected P.L.O. government in exile. These are
Gary Sick's words on the matter: "When the Shah's regime collapsed
in February 1979, Israeli diplomats were trapped in Tehran and had
to request emergency evacuation on U.S. aircraft after their mission
was occupied be the P.L.O." [345]

That the United States could have been in a position to provide
emergency evacuation for the trapped Israelis seemed proof enough
that the Islamic Republic of Iran meant to maintain at least "ordinary relations" with the United States. That would have verified
Walter Eytan's prediction that the U.S., with its control of so much
of the marketing of Iranian oil, would not suffer much, economically, because of the revolution. Though they appreciated U.S. help
when their people were trapped in the Israeli Tehran mission, the
Israeli leaders were obviously dejected by the prospect of being excluded where U.S. officials were included. But then came the attack
on the U.S. Embassy on February 14 — St. Valentine's Day — which
seemed to balance accounts for the dejected Israelis, at least for the
moment.

We've mentioned the obvious; that that first attack on the U.S.
Embassy in Tehran was destined to be totally eclipsed by the second
attack of November 4. Yet we must insist that the second attack will
hardly be correctly understood (and will almost certainly be grossly
misunderstood) if the circumstances of the first attack, and of the
consequent conduct of the Ayatollah's government, are not clearly
recalled.

When, on February 13, Khomeini ordered all his followers to
lay down their crude arms, millions upon millions of them faithfully obeyed. The group that attacked the Embassy the next day had
obviously not obeyed. At one point in its eye-witness account of
events of that morning, *Time* magazine reported: "Barrages of
machine-gun and automatic-weapons fire raked the compound. Two
Marine guards were wounded and an Iranian embassy employee was
killed. After two hours of skirmishing, the attackers seized the embassy and took its occupants, including Ambassador William H. Sul-

livan, as prisoners. It is likely that only the intervention of forces loyal to the Ayatollah, who responded to Sullivan's desperate call for help, prevented even more mayhem.''

That brief account is accurate enough. Yet to grasp the importance of that first attack as a key to the tactics pursued in the second, one needs to fill in some details. There is first of all the fact that, through all the weeks of turbulence in the streets of Tehran starting in December 1978, the ''force of 19 lightly armed Marines at the embassy compound had not been beefed up.'' American officials, in other words, had all along been counting on the Iranian government, before and after the Shah's flight, for ultimate protection. The small Marine contingent, needless to say, ''proved no match for the invaders, who were later identified by State Department experts as members of the left-wing Cherkhaye Fedaye Khalq (People's Sacrifice Guerrillas).'' The extended eye-witness account in *Time* continues as follows:

> Shortly after 10 a.m., the attackers cut loose with machine guns, pistols and automatic rifles from rooftops across the street. As the first volleys of the surprise attack hit the building, Sullivan and Colonel Leland Holland, the defense attaché, took up a position at the command post in Sullivan's second-floor office. The Marine guards, clad in flak jackets and under instructions from Sullivan to refrain from firing back with their shotguns, lay down a cloud of tear gas. Attackers, surging against the locked gate like a human battering ram, burst into the compound. Others scaled the embassy's 12-ft. brick walls. From their posts, the Marines appealed over walkie-talkies to Sullivan (code-name ''Cowboy'') for permission to use their shotguns. His instructions: ''If you need to protect yourselves, you may fire. If you can arrange to surrender, do so.''

We interrupt this eye-witness account to recall that Sullivan had admittedly negotiated with the top people of Khomeini's regime, while Khomeini himself was still in exile, to arrange for a peaceful transfer of the allegiance of the Shah's top military leaders to their side. One can imagine the attitude of the governing officials of the new Islamic Republic when they received a ''desperate call for help'' from their old "collaborator," the American Ambassador, who, in Gary Sick's words, had himself joined the "rebellion in Iran" on January 10, 1979! The *Time* eye-witness account continues:

> A squad of invaders crashed into the embassy commissary and disarmed three Marine guards. Sergeant Kenneth Kraus, 22, was wounded in the forehead and eyes by pellets from his own shotgun, which had been taken by one of the leftists. At that, Kraus was lucky. "When they burst in, one of our Iranian employees stepped in front of me," said Kraus from his hospital bed. "He took a machine gun bullet in the chest. I guess he was hurt pretty bad." Overwhelmed by the assault, 18 Americans trapped in the embassy compound fell hostage to the attackers. They were frisked and paraded around the compound.

In the embassy building itself, about 70 staffers and a considerable number of other people sought refuge in the second-floor corridor outside Ambassador Sullivan's office, while the Marine guards covered their retreat. When the attackers finally broke into the building, a group of Americans rushed to "the building's east wing, where the communications equipment was housed." Some of the staffers simply crowded into the locked communications room just to get out of harm's way, perhaps; but a "dozen employees" very conscientiously started shoving "classified papers into burn bags that were thrown into an incinerator." One of them, a radio operator, "used a heavy sledgehammer to pulverize electronic gear and coding machines." The *Time* account then notes that, just as surprisingly as the attack had begun, it abruptly ended. "Almost unnoticed by the terrified Americans," we are told,

> a band of commandos wearing armbands with the legend ISLAMIC ARMY entered the room and quietly took over the attackers. "You are our brothers. Don't worry," they told the Americans, before politely frisking them, escorting them down the stairs to the compound and eventually setting them free. But the rescuers, who had been dispatched to the embassy in response to Sullivan's repeated, desperate phone calls, were not able to fend off the mob that had gathered in the compound. Among others, Ambassador

Sullivan was jostled, though not seriously injured, before the pro-Khomeini forces managed to clear the compound.

To bring the attackers to order, a spokesman of the acting Prime Minister, Mehdi Bazargan, shouted into a bullhorn: "Don't shoot. Orders from Khomeini. This shooting is a conspiracy against Khomeini." Before long, Deputy Prime Minister Ibrahim Yazdi, an American-educated Iranian well-known in the United States as a pro-American moderate, arrived on the scene; the embassy attackers laid down their arms, and all was calm once more.

An obvious question at this point is: What if the heavily-armed "band of 100 Iranian leftists" who attacked the embassy on St. Valentine's day had refused to lay down their arms, and had instead shut themselves up in the embassy compound, threatening to kill the many hostages they had seized if "pro-Khomeini forces" attempted to force their way in? That is an important as well as obvious question, for, of course, when many of the same people who had seized the embassy on February 14 returned to seize it again on November 4, they proceeded to do exactly that: they refused to surrender the embassy to the Ayatollah's government and defied it to try to repeat what it had so successfully done ten months before.

2. Cui Bono?

It is significant that, in disarming the band that attacked the U.S. Embassy on St. Valentine's day, the spokesman of the Ayatollah's government should have shouted through his bullhorn: "Don't shoot. Orders from Khomeini. This shooting is a conspiracy against Khomeini." Obviously, had the attackers not laid down their arms at once, they would thereby have proved themselves to have indeed been conspirators.

Who exactly were those attackers? We noted earlier that, in its eye-witness account, *Time* magazine had identified them initially as members of the well-known radical left-wing group, the "People's Sacrifice Guerrillas." Later, in an article on the subject for *The New Yorker* (June 9, 1980), Robert Shaplen described the attackers as a "random mob of students and workers"; but he then cited Ambassador Sullivan as having said that their ranks "included some young men wearing scarves that resembled those worn by members of an extreme group of Palestinian terrorists." Had the attackers really been Palestinian terrorists (Sullivan is careful to says there might have been just "some" in the group wearing such scarves), the response of the pro-Khomeini commandos would have become all the more significant. For in the case of the parallel seizure of the Israeli mission, which occurred at about the same time, all the media of the Western nations widely publicized the fact, with pictures, that Khomeini had personally turned the mission over to Yasser Arafat, as we earlier noted. As for the majority of the attackers, Sullivan hastened to acknowledge that they had quickly been identified as members of the Mujahedin — "Muslim activists who, though claiming to be loyal to Khomeini, were organized into vigilante squads and were meting out 'Islamic justice' as they saw fit." Such groups had seized arms from the forces of the ancien regime early on and had not surrendered them when the call to do so came from Khomeini.

Fortunately, much light is thrown on the question of the identity of the attackers by the interviews which American newsmen held with some of their leaders shortly after the event. *Time* magazine's eye-witness account previously cited stressed that, almost without exception, those interviewed expressed shock at having been abruptly disarmed by the pro-Khomeini commandos. The consensus among them, as reported in the *Los Angeles Times* a few days later, was that the militants greatly regretted having made it "all so easy," as they put it, "for Bazargan and the Americans." A typical response was that of American-educated Mariam Nazarour, who was to surface again in the second embassy seizure of November 4, 1979. "Mary" reportedly said: "I'm not happy with the Bazargan government. It's like the Pahlavi regime, but with a different name. We don't accept the Cabinet, and if everyone listens to the Ayatollah, we won't have a revolutionary republic." Summing things up from her obviously radical secular perspective, she had added: "Iran is not just for the mullahs." We will notice, later, how differently she responded to similar questions when repeatedly interviewed during the extended hostages crisis that brought down the Bazargan government and several successor governments — all of them authorized by the Ayatollah, until he was forced to chose between their continuance and the lives of the hostages.

"Mary" and most of the other militants interviewed after the St. Valentine's Day attack did not hesitate to say that, like the Shah's Prime Minister Shapour Bakhtiar before him, the 71-year old Mehdi Bazargan — appointed by Khomeini to head the new government — was basically a pro-American traditional republican politician, not a revolutionary. It was charged, for instance, that, instead of treating the deposed Bakhtiar as a fallen enemy, Bazargan treated him as a friend (which he had, of course, long been!), providing him with a "secret refuge in Tehran," at first, and then arranging for his safe departure from the country when the Shah's supporters were being brought to trial.

Another radical leader well-known to American reporters (who asked not to be identified) complained further that Bakhtiar and Bazargan were like Tweedle-dee and Tweedle-dum, equally eager to play up to Washington, as if there had never been a serious anti-American aspect to the revolution. Yet, the important thing about those interviews with radical leaders after the failure of their first seizure of the American Embassy — interviews which are on the record — is this: almost without exception they declared themselves determined not to permit the Bazargan government appointed by the Ayatollah to "get away with" its professed intentions of normalizing relations with the United States as soon as possible.

After the fact, reporters asked: What exactly was the group that attacked the embassy in February trying to achieve? "The best guess," the *Time* correspondent on the scene commented, "is that, having fought with Khomeini's forces against the Shah, they were trying to cause friction between Khomeini and the United States. If that was the case, the maneuver failed." And American authorities, it was said, had breathed a sigh of relief at the failure. They had just been through a comparable crisis in Afghanistan, where militants had seized the American Ambassador Adolph Dubs. Washington had asked the Afghan government and its Soviet masters to do "everything possible" to save the Ambassador's life. The requests were ignored. Ambassador Dubs was killed when the Soviet-backed authorities, which had given his captors an ultimatum, stormed the embassy despite American objections. Washington had then feared that the same would happen in Tehran. Thus, when word came that the Ayatollah's commandos were shielding the American compound, reasoning with the captors, there was great relief. "The cooperation shown by the Khomeini forces," it was reported, "fortified the delicate bonds that had been nurtured in recent days as U.S. diplomatic envoys pursued clandestine talks with Bazargan and his advisers."

From that moment on — right down to the start of the frantic Kissinger-Rockefeller efforts to get the Shah admitted to a New York City hospital — relations between the United States and the new Iranian Islamic Republic were steadily normalized, as we shall see. There were, to be sure, no prospects of a return to the sort of "deals" Kissinger had worked out with the Shah. And, despite Khomeini's personal assurances to the Iranian Jews (still numbering some 80,000), and to the more numerous Armenian-Iranian Christians, that there would be no religious discrimination in the Islamic republic, it could hardly be supposed that oil shipments to Israel would soon be resumed or that Israeli experts would soon again be called in to build up the economy, much less to sharpen the "efficiency" of the Iranian police and military intelligence services.

One cannot doubt that, from the beginning, the Ayatollah's government had been at great pains to try to drive a wedge between the United States and the State of Israel with respect to Iran. Its spokesmen repeatedly warned that the United States could not attempt to advance Israeli interests in Iran and maintain its own superpower interests there at the same time. Israeli agents and pro-Israeli Americans, it was charged, were at that very moment doing all they could to sabotage the otherwise constantly improving U.S.-Iranian relations.

One should not forget the sort of charges Khomeini had raised against the State of Israel before the Shah's fall. From the Shiite religious standpoint, Israel was by far a more dangerous enemy than the secular, materialist powers like the United States and the USSR. Israel had proven itself capable of making those superpowers collaborate in its founding as a state in 1948. And, ever since, it had shown itself capable of squeezing all the material support it needed out of the coffers of a "Jewish-dominated" American government. As to the extent of Israel's participation in the Shah's cruelties against the faithful Islamic Iranian masses, the Ayatollah had not hesitated to charge, at the time of the so-called Jaleh Square massacre of early September 1978, that the whole thing had been the work of Israeli conspirators or worse. The Shah's troops had fired on some 20,000 people gathered in Jaleh Square for the end of Ramadan Shiite mourning commemorations. Several hundred and perhaps a thousand Shiite faithful had been killed and tens of thousands wounded. The Ayatollah said he could not bring himself to believe that "good Iranian boys" in uniform could really have been induced to fire willingly on their "brothers and sisters" in the square. As Gary Sick later noted, the Ayatollah "told a visiting American that the troops who fired in Jaleh Square were not Iranian at all but rather Israeli troops imported by the Shah."

Initially, no comparable charges were directed against the United States. The worst said was that the United States was letting itself be played internationally as Israel's "dupe." Whatever criticism was directed against the great superpower of the West seemed always intended to vex it into resisting Israeli pressure on its conduct of international relations. It was urged that, if the United States were to retain any possibility of protecting its superpower interests in Iran peaceably after the Shah's fall, it would have to distance itself perceptibly from what were viewed in Iran as essentially Zionist concerns.

Still, as *Time* magazine noted in its February 26, 1979 issue, there had been some paradoxically "upbeat signs" in Israel immediately following the fall of Bakhtiar's government — perhaps because that government had already pledged itself to cut off the oil supply. Though they were "deeply concerned that the unrest in Iran could spread within the Arab world," Israeli officials "also feel," the *Time* account emphasized, "that the collapse of this once staunch Muslim (but non-Arab) ally of the West ought to enhance Israel's own strategic importance in Washington's eyes." Many of the Israeli leaders indicated that they were ready to "take their chances" with the new regime, whatever its initial declarations against Israeli-sponsored "international Zionism.'' They anticipated that its needs, especially if conflicts occurred with neighboring non-Shiite Muslim states, would force it to accept the kinds of deals that Israeli statesmen were well equipped to make, even with fanatical governments like that of the Ayatollah — as events through the 1980s would amply prove.

What stood in the way of all that, from the standpoint of Israeli hardball politics, or *Realpolitik*, as the Germans called it, was the prospect that the Ayatollah's government might succeed in its apparent intentions to make deals for needed supplies directly with the United States without Israelis serving as intermediaries. That is what had made the different treatments accorded the seizures of the Israeli mission and the U.S. Embassy such a bitter pill to swallow in late February 1979. Was it conceivable — many were asking themselves in the United States as well as in Israel — that the Carter administration might be ready, like the major European powers, to pursue normalized relations with Iran at Israel's expense?

It is certainly true that, during the first days under the Ayatollah Khomeini's government, American and Israeli relations with that government moved rapidly in opposite directions. Israel and Khomeini's Iran behaved towards one another from the beginning as religiously constituted states, under the sort of restraints in their "foreign" relations with one another that Spinoza had long ago so aptly characterized. The United States, on the contrary, was initially treated by the Ayatollah's regime as the purely secular state that it is defined to be in its fundamental law, while Israel was dealt with as a thoroughly Jewish religious state that could claim to be a Western-type secular state — a Western "democracy," for instance — only figuratively or for antinomian propaganda purposes.

At any rate, after the seizure and release of its embassy on February 14, 1979, the United States not only retained full, *de jure* diplomatic relations with the successor government, but also asked for and quickly received, as we shall see, additional Iranian military and police protection that rendered its embassy compound far more secure from street violence than it had been during the last months of the Shah's long reign.

3. Sullivan's Last "Happy Months": Khomeini's Commandos as U.S. Embassy Guards

We have examined at length the cover-story in the February 26, 1979 issue of *Time* which celebrated Ambassador Sullivan as a hero of the the first seizure of the American Embassy in Tehran on St. Valentine's Day. Sullivan had, in effect, been fired by President Carter in mid-January, and had been permitted to stay on temporarily only because of the special pleading of Secretary of State Cyrus Vance. Even so, he presented himself quite theatrically to the newsmedia as the American Envoy on the scene charged with protecting U.S. interests and the lives of Americans put at peril by the violence of the Iranian revolution.

When the St. Valentine's Day attack occurred, Sullivan, as we saw, had sent out frantic calls for help to the Ayatollah's government, and help was promptly sent. And why not? As Gary Sick reminds us, Sullivan had done all he could to enable the forces of the revolution to triumph without resistance, and, despite interference by the Carter administration, he had very nearly succeeded. At any rate, by January 10, 1979, there was no denying that, in Sick's words, "the rebellion in Iran" — a rebellion against the Shah and his American backers — "now extended to the person of the U.S. Ambassador."

In the final revolutionary struggle, it must be said, the side of the Ayatollah (backed by Sullivan) had clearly triumphed over the side of the Shah and Bakhtiar (backed by President Carter, Zbigniew Brzezinski, and General Huyser). In that defeat, the United States lost all it had in Iran except its embassy compound in Tehran; and that could hardly be deemed a secure position, since the ambassador in charge had himself reportedly "joined" the revolutionary opposition. One feels constrained to ask: Did Ambassador Sullivan enjoy at least some of the fruits of the victory he had helped the revolutionaries to gain? The evidence is strong that he did, through all of at least two happy months.

Sullivan has written with considerable frankness about his final weeks under the Ayatollah. The last chapter of his autobiography *Obligato* titled "The Iranian Revolution" reaches a climax with

Sullivan's description of the "hopeless fear" he had experienced while he crouched under a table during the embassy seizure of February 14, 1979 — hopeless, in the sense that he had had absolutely no expectation of surviving the tremendous barrage of firepower brought to bear by the militants. That experience, Sullivan says, led him "to make an unorthodox decision" about the "immediate future" of the American Embassy in Tehran. Because the embassy had proved so vulnerable during the attack, he decided, as he says, that he "wanted some Iranians inside our compound to mitigate our danger." He therefore asked the acting Foreign Minister, the American-educated Ibrahim Yazdi who had commmanded the embassy rescue on February 14, to "provide us with eighty guards, forty of whom would be stationed inside our compound, in contravention of all normal diplomatic practice." [275]

The guards inside the compound were to serve as a deterrent to further shooting from the outside; and they could serve also to assure the revolutionary government that the embassy people were not engaged in any "nefarious practices" against that government. But Sullivan says he was also pleased with the opportunity their presence, close at hand, afforded him to "get a closer look at those who had toppled the Shah." The guards were of three different kinds. Ignoring the group of forty posted outside the the embassy compound, Sullivan tells us of one inside contingent that was assigned as a personal bodyguard, detailed to guard his residence, and another whose task it was to guard the compound's perimeter from the inside. Of the first internal group, he says:

> It consisted of university graduates, most of whom spoke English and had traveled abroad. Several had close relatives in the United States. They were members of a left-wing mujahadin, but proclaimed a vigorous religious fervor. Their leader, a young man who had recently returned from the United States, said his ritual prayers with great ostentation. He was a dedicated follower of Ayatollah Khomeini. This group set up a command post in a small cloak room off the main foyer of my residence. The room was equipped with a telephone and had lavatories and toilets. It had previously been used as a guard post for U.S. Marines during my

predecessor's tenure. In its new capacity, it served as a place for the young men to meet for endless political discussions, [and] to organize their defense against the nightly hit-and-run raids that came from the streets.... I met from time to time with the leader of this 'bodyguard' group and discussed his political observations. Although he pretended to a deep piety, it was hard for me to assess its sincerity. Some of our younger Farsi-speaking officers who spent more time with the group gave them somewhat more credit as genuine political moralists.

Sullivan had early acknowledged that his arrangement to have such guards stationed inside the embassy compound was "in contravention of all normal diplomatic practice." But, after President Carter's clearly expressed desire to get his recalcitrant Ambassador out of Iran, it could be said that his own presence in the compound was in contravention of the same practice. One wonders whether, in his discussions with the leader of his "bodyguards," Sullivan ever brought up the matter of his plan for sending 100 or more of the Shah's senior generals out of the country with the Shah or that of his frustrated scheme for an orderly transfer of the rest of the military to the Ayatollah's forces. Those plans or schemes were, of course, fully known to the Ayatollah's people, because they had already been in large part implemented, before the White House sent in General Huyser to call a halt. Perhaps many of his guards had participated in summary executions of some of those compromised officers.

But, in many respects, Sullivan seemed to enjoy a status with the successor revolutionary regime like that of the celebrated Roman General Aetius at the court of Emperor Honorius in the fifth century A.D. Aetius had been held hostage among the Huns of Attila for some three years, and had won their loyalty to himself by proving he was a "better" Hun than they were, riding horses bareback in their fashion better than they, and fighting with seemingly more barbaric abandon. After his return to the Roman imperial court, Aetius had at his command — at what amounted to a snap of the finger — as many as 60,000 Hunnish horsemen ready to ride into Roman territory to do his personal bidding. No emperor dared to defy Aetius's will; and Aetius was to go down in late Roman imperial history, with Count Boniface of Africa, ranking as the "last of the Romans." Faithful Roman that he was, Aetius had to chose at last whether to permit the Huns to take Rome or run them into the northeast European woods, and he chose the later alternative; after which the Emperor Honorius, no longer fearful of Aetius's Huns, strangled the aging general with his own hands, thus depriving the empire of "its right arm" — Count Boniface had been the left arm — and assuring its military collapse.

We get a sense of how much like another Aetius Ambassador Sullivan must have felt from his account of the second group of revolutionary guards stationed within the American embassy compound. That second group was also leftist-radical in composition, "but made no pretense," Sullivan writes, "to the political sophistication of my bodyguard." It had been the nucleus of the "rescue force" that had liberated the embassy on February 14, 1979, and it was headed, Sullivan tells us, "by a huge hairy butcher named Marshallah, who was armed to the teeth and who occasionally administered discipline to his unit through a sharp cuff to a young man's head. This group had a somewhat vague relationship with Ayatollah Taleghani, who was an associate of Khomeini but considerably more enlightened."

That second group's original charge was, as already noted, to guard the compound perimeter from the inside, functioning under the general supervision of the embassy's military attaché, who "developed a close working relationship with them." They came, says Sullivan, to identify themselves with the Americans running the embassy, and especially with Sullivan himself. As Sullivan puts it without a blush: "I became 'their' ambassador. Hence, when I went out to travel around the city, they accompanied me in 'chase cars'. . . . I recall one Saturday when I went for brunch at the residence of my Dutch colleague and arrived accompanied by two carloads of these bearded, thuggish-looking characters armed with G-3 rifles and strung with bandoliers. They swarmed over the compound and took up guard positions in strategic points, their weapons pointed at nearby apartments."

Sullivan acknowledges that the scene "sent something of a shiver through the other guests, all of whom were ambassadors and their wives." When Sullivan "finally assured them that the group was friendly, their curiosity got the better of them," he says, "and the day finished with photo sessions, in which the fashionably dressed diplomatic ladies posed with the guerrileros for albums of their future progeny." That was a Saturday brunch at the Dutch embassy in Tehran, with a "hairy butcher named Marshallah" playing the part of Atilla for a latter-day Aetius to enjoy his last days in the Foreign Service of the United States!

One recalls Sullivan's words at the time of his decision to resign his ambassadorial post because of the Huyser mission back in January 1979. He spoke then of having to protect some 15,000 Americans in Iran, and therefore delaying his resignation "until after the holocaust." For him personally, the triumph of the Islamic revolutionary forces was hardly a holocaust, as we have seen. It brought him, on the contrary, a taste óf the life of a latter-day Aetius. The holocaust was reserved for the supporters of the Shah who were in effect offered up for sacrifice by the American Ambassador in open defiance of U.S. national policy and direct orders from the President. The worst victims were the literally hundreds and perhaps thousands of top ranking military officers. Their end, as previously indicated, was to be denounced by both sides in the conflict and to be destroyed ignominiously. Sullivan finally left his post, a few days after that Saturday brunch at the Dutch embassy in Tehran, to begin writing his "white papers," and to supplement his pension by getting himself placed safely among admirers in the academic community.

That he was proud of his performance in Iran, overseeing the fall of the Shah, as well as of his prior performances in negotiating the ruin of Diem and then Thieu in Vietnam — to say nothing of his tours of duty in Laos and the Philippines — he makes clear in the introduction to his autobiography where he boasts of having belonged throughout his public career to what he calls a "cohort of centurions" who, while not constituting an "Eastern Establishment," had in fact, in his words, "dominated the execution of our country's international affairs during those four middle decades of this century." There were never, he says,

more than a few thousand in this cohort. Most of us had been
junior officers in World War II and chose to stay in government
service out of some vague sense of responsibility for avoiding a
repetition of that catastrophe. We were deployed in the Cabinet
and Congress, in the Armed Forces, in the Foreign Service, and
occasionally in such private areas as the press; and we knew each
other through mutual association or by reputation. We had an
unspoken assumption that we shared the same civilized objectives
and that the only question at issue concerned means rather than
ends. [12-13]

At the book's close, Sullivan permits himself to say that, when he
retired from the Foreign Service after forty years, and largely out
of disgust with the Carter administration, he was "among the last
and among the most senior of our shrinking cohort of centurions.
Secretary of State Cyrus Vance, who was indeed our most senior,
did not last much longer. Now [1984], just about all of us have left
the public service." [278-279] His forty years, Sullivan assures us,
"was a time of turmoil, but also a time of many satisfactions."

4. Sullivan the "Centurion": Home, at Last

When he finally left the Foreign Service, William Sullivan retained, to be sure, the good will of that "cohort of centurions" to
which he understood himself to belong. Before he left, arrangements
had been made for him to serve at once as president of the American Assembly, an educational foundation funded by the Averell Harriman foundation and linked to Columbia University — an institution
that "arranges for experts and eminent people to study American
problems." In a New York *Times* column headed "Ex-Envoy to Iran
Tells of His Frustrations," *Times* reporter Bernard D. Nossiter wrote
of having interviewed Sullivan in "a Spartan eighth-floor office on
the Columbia campus, mulling over domestic American issues and
relieved to be free of foreign concerns." He had been at his new post
for some months and rated an interview because his "white paper"
had just appeared in the Fall 1980 issue of *Foreign Policy*.

At the time of the interview, columnist Nossiter wrote, Sullivan "had just added another State Department refugee, former Secretary of State Cyrus R. Vance, to the governing board of his new institutional home." Cyrus Vance, it will be recalled, had been asked by President Carter to "get Sullivan out of Iran" because of his recalcitrance with respect to General Huyser's mission. Vance had asked the President to hold off for the moment, and the President had agreed. Over a year later, in April 1980, Vance would object to the President's desert rescue mission, and he would resign because his advice was not taken. It was then that Sullivan welcomed his old boss — last of the grand "cohort of centurions" in government and the media to which they both belonged — to the governing board of the American Assembly over which he presided.

Nossiter's column reviews many of the charges advanced by Sullivan against Carter and Brzezinski for frustrating Sullivan's designs during the last weeks of the Shah's rule. He ascribes to Sullivan a comment that Brzezinski was able to "ruin things" in the end largely because, at one time, he "had the President down fishing," suggesting, as Nossiter puts it, "that things were settled in Mr. Carter's Administration in that fashion." The journalist is at pains to stress an inherent contradiction in what the ex-envoy to Iran had to say about the Shah's admittance to the United States despite the warnings of the American Chargé d'Affaires Bruce Laingen, who had succeeded Sullivan as head of the American Embassy in Tehran. Linking Sullivan's last newsworthy experience in Iran with the events of the second embassy seizure in November 1979, Nossiter writes:

> Mr. Sullivan, who had to lead his staff out of the beleaguered United States Embassy in Tehran [in February 1979], was careful not to criticize the event that led to the seizure of the embassy last November: the admission of the deposed Shah to the United States for an operation. "That was a genuine humanitarian action," the former envoy commented. He did criticize the Administration for failing to take adequate steps to deal with the repercussions of a move that "led every Iranian to assume some sort of political collusion to put the man back on the throne." Mr. Sullivan said the Administration's acceptance of "casual assurances that the

embassy was safe was rather reckless." Instead, he suggested, the United States should have "closed down the embassy or taken protective measures."

Nossiter is evidently puzzled about Sullivan's view of the admission of the Shah to the U.S. as a genuinely humanitarian act and at the same time an extreme provocation of ill-feeling on the part of "every Iranian" against the United States. And he is puzzled, too, by Sullivan's characterization of the Carter administration's acceptance of the Iranian government's assurances about the safety of the embassy; Sullivan would have had some sort of massive American show of force in support of the "genuinely humanitarian action" of admitting the Shah as an alternative to precautionary closing down of the embassy altogether!

It may very well be that Nossiter's notes for his column on Sullivan helped the New York *Times* to formulate its editorial of September 12, 1980, on Sullivan's article in "the current issue of *Foreign Policy*," objecting rather severely to its timing, attitude, and substance. The editorial was headed "Replaying Iran," and it began:

> Here we go: who lost Iran? Not me, says William Sullivan, the last American Ambassador in Tehran. Not the Shah, either; he only refused some American advice to shoot Iranians. Not the State Department, says Mr. Sullivan, though its human rights bias tainted the counsel of Secretary Vance and other hard-headed diplomats, like himself. Not even Jimmy Carter, the Ambassador implies in the current issue of *Foreign Policy;* the President was merely the dupe of a reckless National Security Adviser.
>
> Zbigniew Brzezinski's to blame for it all — defeating Vance, ignoring Sullivan, blinding Carter, astounding the Shah and offending Khomeini. And what did Brzezinski do? He gambled that an Iranian named Bakhtiar, on whom the fleeing Shah conferred his power, might join with Iran's armed forces to abort the revolution, create a pro-American regime and keep the Ayatollah in Paris. As this gamble collapsed, according to Mr. Sullivan, Mr. Brzezinski even dared to ask over an open phone whether a military coup could be arranged. The Ambassador recalls an unprintable reply.

The *Times* very accurately summarizes Ambassador Sullivan's version of the events. It then tries to fathom Sullivan's purposes in producing such a self-serving account of things on the eve of the 1980 presidential election. And it concludes by supporting the President and Brzezinski against the obviously recalcitrant ambassador. "Whatever their misjudgments, Mr. Carter and Mr. Brzezinski cannot now [September 12, 1980] debate Mr. Sullivan without further embarrassment and jeopardy to the hostages. The record of this Administration's messy response to the Iranian revolution is known. The parts played by individual actors in the drama, including Mr. Sullivan, will be judged in time — by others."

The editorial drew a number of responses. Republicans kept their peace, leaving it to Democrats to cut one another to pieces. The editors of *Foreign Policy* protested that they had not expected to publish Sullivan's account of the matter before the election, but were able to do so only because Sullivan managed to get a draft to them much earlier than expected. They noted that the *New Yorker* and the *Washington Quarterly* had already published "insiders' accounts" using White House and State Department sources; so they thought it only fitting that the Ambassador on the scene should have his chance to reply in person.

But it was Arthur Schlesinger, Jr., who led the academic defense for Sullivan — revealing how ready the old anti-Truman/anti-Johnson Democratic elitists were to "dump" Carter in 1980, even if it meant electing Ronald Reagan. Schlesinger said in part: "I am astonished by *The Times'*s editorial castigation of Ambassador Sullivan for the horrid crime of offering the American people an informed version of the events leading to the disaster in Iran. . . . The sarcasm about Ambassador Sullivan's motives is cheap and unworthy."

The chief Republican initiatives against the Carter administration started right after the Shah's fall in early 1979. Henry Kissinger and other key members of the Rockefeller establishment, including the Rockefellers themselves, led the major campaigns. But Kissinger's purposes clearly transcended mere electoral politics. From the beginning, he made it his task to compound Ambassador Sullivan's offense. Sullivan had seen to it that the Iranian military, which was prepared to support the Shah's Prime Minister Shapour Bakhtiar, in the event of the Shah's departure, was totally compromised and destroyed. Kissinger then saw to it that the United States was nevertheless "stuck" with the exiled Shah, even though the Carter administration was fully engaged in trying to maintain full *de jure* diplomatic relations with Khomeini's revolutionary Islamic Republic. Between them (with a slight assist from General Haig), Sullivan and Kissinger gave the United States its second greatest military defeat — considering all the arms and money that had been poured into the Shah's Iran — since the end of World War II, the first having been the Vietnam war defeat, in which all three had previously collaborated.

5. Obstacles to Normalized Relations: From Sullivan to Cutler to Laingen

We have quoted the Ayatollah Khomeini's words of February 11, 1980, at the height of the hostage crisis, affirming that, once its "political, military, economic and cultural dependence on America" was effectively ended, the new Islamic Republic of Iran would "seek to establish our very ordinary relations with America just as with other countries." [261] On the American side, although there was no one person who could speak for the nation as a whole with anything like the autocratic authority of a Khomeini, still, after the fall of the Bakhtiar government, there quickly emerged a consensus, among the leading American diplomats involved, that postrevolutionary Iran had by no means lost its "objective importance" in U.S. foreign policy and national security concerns.

In his introduction for the volume *American Hostages in Iran: The Conduct of a Crisis* (ed. by P. H. Kreisberg, 1985), Warren Christopher, chief negotiator for the U.S. in the concluding stages of the hostage crisis, for instance, calls attention to Washington's readiness to try to normalize relations with revolutionary Iran. "All things considered," he writes, "American interests argued strongly against giving up on Iran." The official American presence in the country was to remain considerably reduced after the revolution; but still, a decision was soon taken to keep up diplomatic relations, as Christopher puts it, "in order to continue communications and to promote a mature and correct, if considerably cooler, relationship with the revolutionary government." In sum, Christopher concludes, "we were not prepared to walk away from the situation, and we should not have been. At the same time, businesses and banks with commercial contacts in Iran had begun to reassess their operations and prospects there and to adjust to the new environment." [2]

Gary Sick, who headed the White House group on Iran throughout the crisis, makes a similar point in *All Fall Down*. In addition to the reasons reviewed by Christopher for maintaining relations with revolutionary Iran, Sick points out that the process of normalization after the Ayatollah Khomeini's return on February 1, 1979, was "further stimulated by pressures from groups in the United States to reestablish full consular relations as quickly as possible so Iranian Jews and Baha'is, who felt threatened by the new Islamic regime, could get visas to leave the country." [190]

But, as already noted in passing, there were groups, factions, interests in both the United States and Iran strongly opposed to normalized relations. At first it seemed that the most serious opposition in Iran would come from diehard supporters of the Shah, or of the Pahlavi dynasty, who hoped or dreamt that, if the U.S. saw the Khomeini regime as fanatically anti-American enough to sponsor attacks on the U.S. Embassy, there might be a restoration of the Pahlavis effected directly by the U.S. Besides that group, there were also the diehard partisans of the Iranian military, who felt that the Shah had betrayed them by asking them to support Bakhtiar's government rather than stage a coup, while that was still possible. Thus, when he was put on trial by the Ayatollah's government, Air Force General Amir Hussein Rabii especially criticized General Huyser for restraining the Iranian military under Bakhtiar, all for the sake of trying to legitimize the succession of the Shah's son to the Pahlavi throne. It was General Rabii who, before being sentenced to death, uttered the much quoted phrase, charging that, in early January 1979, Huyser simply "came and picked up the Shah like a dead mouse by its tail and threw him out." But, we can be sure that neither the right-wing military leaders nor the Shah's partisans were in any condition to participate in the first attack on the American Embassy.

Ambassador Sullivan had suggested that P.L.O. agents or sympathizers might have participated in or even led the attack. Yet that hardly seems likely. The aims of the P.L.O. would obviously be better served by keeping U.S. and Israeli interests at odds, as the Ayatollah's government had clearly sought to do by liberating the U.S. Embassy after it had turned the Israeli mission over to Arafat. Much more likely candidates were, to be sure, Iran's "impatient young Marxists eager to expand and control the revolution," as also the ever-present covert agents of foreign governments — Marxist as well as non-Marxist — who favored a complete Iranian break with the U.S. And one should not, of course, discount the ambitions of political factions eager to discredit the Bazargan government and make room at the top for themselves.

Finally, there was the strong possibility, noted earlier, that Israeli agents recruited out of the large Iranian Jewish community, working undercover, had brought on the first embassy attack as part of Israel's unconcealed determination to somehow place Israel and the United States in the same boat — *excluded together* from normalized relations with revolutionary Iran so long as they could not be *included together.*

At any rate, the interviews with the leaders of the first embassy seizure revealed that they were virtually all members of radicalized factions (some of them no doubt operating as "moles" for other factions) ready to criticize not only the patently pro-American leadership of the first government appointed by the Ayatollah, but also the Ayatollah himself, as too "religious" for their progressive Marxist purposes. As we saw, they boldly told their American interviewers that, if they had it to do over again, they would not have surrendered their prize — the American Embassy — so easily to Khomeini's commandos, led by an American-educated deputy prime minister who appeared to have enjoyed American citizenship for a time!

Yet, none of the groups indicated had nearly as much clout in Iran, with its autocratic religious leadership, as the chief American opposition groups had in the U.S. — at least until one of those Iranian groups attacked the American Embassy a second time, managing to retain hold of it, with dozens of American hostages, for 444 days. In Iran, as in most other Third World countries, the effective opposition to normalized relations with the United States, it must be stressed, invariably takes its cues from publicized American internal divisions. During the nine months following the first attack on the American embassy, the two major manifestations of public dissent faced by the Carter administration were those of the Kissinger-Rockefeller faction outside of government, and the Jacob Javits initiatives inside.

We reserve for later an account of the activities of the Kissinger/Rockefeller establishment to force the Carter administration to admit the Shah to the United States despite its clear perception that it might provoke the seizing of American hostages in Iran. We must stress here the almost universal recognition that Kissinger had become the focus of all opposition to Carter in the American political arena at this time; and that his was a power that rapidly increased in the course of the developing Iran crisis of the Carter administration. On August 5, 1979 — three months before the second seizure of the American embassy — one of the nation's leading civilian national security strategists, Richard Burt, in fact wrote:

> There can be little doubt that Mr. Kissinger, as a private citizen, has succeeded in maintaining much of the power and prestige accumulated as the White House National Security Adviser and then Secretary of State during the Nixon-Ford era. He has emerged as a one-man institution, influential internationally and a political force nationally. [For instance], when the Shah of Iran was deposed early this year, Mr. Kissinger sent a personal bodyguard to insure that his old friend was adequately protected from assassins.... With his access and visibility, Mr. Kissinger may actually possess more power at the present than he ever did in government.

Coming from Richard Burt, that last part of the passage quoted is highly significant. Burt does not rank as a friendly admirer of Kissinger, as does Max Lerner who, on August 8, 1979 — three days later — confirmed Burt's estimate, and concluded that Kissinger's "is the ultimate achievement — to remain as much a star after leaving office as he ever was when he held it. It is hard to find a parallel in American history."

But let us proceed chronologically, examining, first, how the Carter administration's efforts to pursue normalized relations with the new Iran were repeatedly and increasingly obstructed by a handful of powerful persons in and out of office during the nine months that separated the first from the second seizure of the American Embassy. We have reviewed what Ambassador Sullivan had been up to during his final two months in Tehran, guarded by revolutionary commandos not only when he was in the embassy compound but also when he went out into the city. We described him as a latter-day Aetius surrounded by Iranian equivalents of Aetius's Huns. Reviewing his conduct during those two months, one gets the impression that, had President Carter attempted to remove him by force, in those days, Sullivan's guards would have rallied to his defense. It appears that President Carter actually called Sullivan back to Washington in early April 1979 for "consultations," although it was generally known that a replacement had already been named.

Carter's choice of an ambassador to succeed Sullivan was Walter L. Cutler, and his name was quickly sent up to the Senate for approval as Ambassador Extraordinary and Plenipotentiary of the United States to Iran. The formal announcement of his nomination, made on April 24, 1979, indicated that Lloyd Cutler had joined the Foreign Service in 1956 and had served as Ambassador to the Republic of Zaire since 1975. Newspaper accounts indicated further that Cutler had already gained full acceptance as ambassador by the Ayatollah's government. Thus, the appointment had seemed to be settled to the satisfaction of all. In Tehran, after Sullivan's "resignation," the Embassy had been headed by chargé d'affaires Charles W. Nass, who maintained regular contacts with Iranian officials. But Tehran as well as Washington was eager to establish fully normalized relations, and both were pleased that Cutler, already approved by the Senate, would soon be on his way to assume his new post. But then, suddenly, a movement of opposition surfaced, not to the appointment itself, but rather to the very idea of normalized relations between the United States and the revolutionary government of Iran.

In those days, the newsmedia had been full of reports of trials and executions of "enemies of the revolution" in Iran. It had seemed fortunate that the media agitation had not interfered with or adversely influenced the process of choosing a replacement for Sullivan. And then the bombshell came. We get a thoughtful, statesmanly account of the development from the testimony of R. K. Ramazani, Edward R. Stettinius Professor and Chairman of the Woodrow Wilson Department of Government and Foreign Affairs at the University of Virginia, given before the Joint Economic Committee of the Congress of the United States in mid-November 1979.

Reviewing the "economic consequences of the revolution in Iran," Professor Ramazani had at one point emphasized the obvious eagerness of the new revolutionary government in Iran to maintain fully normalized relations with the United States. Government spokesmen in Tehran had gone out of their way to stress the acceptability of Cutler as Sullivan's successor. Then, abruptly, came word that the same Senate that approved Cutler's nomination had also "unanimously approved a resolution, sponsored by Senator Jacob K. Javits, condemning summary trials and executions in Iran of former supporters of the Shah and decrying Ayatollah Khalkhali's call for assassination of the Shah." Word of the Javits resolution caused much consternation in Tehran. And Ramazani continued his testimony on the matter in these terms:

> The Senate resolution had followed the execution on May 9 of Habib Elghanian, an industrialist who was a leader of the Jewish community in Iran and had been charged by the Revolutionary Court, among others, with fundraising for Israel. Deputy Information Minister Mehdi Monken, alluding to this fact, stated: "They have paid more attention and expressed more worry about this one than the sum of all other executions. The form and composition of the U.S. Senate is that they always support Israel and Zionists." Mr. Monken's view is not typical of everyone who serves in Prime Minister Bazargan's government; but it is interesting to note how the hardline Muslim fundamentalist view of international politics and those of lay radical nationalists sometimes coincide.

Ramazani notes that Foreign Minister Yazdi didn't pursue the Deputy Information Minister's line in the matter. He took a much more conciliatory line, hastening to say that Iran hoped to have "friendly relations between the peoples of the two countries." But, no sooner was that said than Iranian factions opposed to normalized relations started at once to make much of the fact that Yazdi had lived for many years in the United States and had even become, for a time, a naturalized citizen. Yazdi had, after all, led the rescue mission that restored control of the embassy to the Americans on February 14. To maintain his credibility in the face of that Javits resolution, says Razamani, Yazdi joined in protesting against it. He agreed that it presented a definition of terms for accepting the newly named ambassador that placed an impossible burden on the Iranian government. Cutler was deemed unacceptable, therefore, and President Carter was asked to delay naming someone else until something could be done to undo the harm done by the Javits resolution.

"The wisdom and timing of the Senate resolution," Professor Ramazani goes on to observe, "may be questioned on two grounds. First, it followed too closely the execution of Elghanian. . .who had been in trouble previously with the Shah's government as well. Second, the Senate resolution was passed only three days after Secretary Vance wrote the Iranian government that he 'wanted to broaden relations with our country and help Iran in the economic, social, cultural and other fields, including military aid,' and at a time when the Administration was attaching great significance to the assignment of a new Ambassador to Tehran as a means of clearing up past 'misunderstandings'."

It was perceived in Tehran that President Carter, after having eagerly pressed for quick Senate approval of Cutler's nomination, neglected to do anything to delay consideration and approval of the Javits resolution, at least until Cutler could have moved on to Tehran for formal acceptance by the Ayatollah's government. The White House must have understood — so officials in Tehran had to conclude — that genuinely normalized relations between the two countries could not hold up under the psychological pressure of such a unanimously approved resolution. Let Carter name another Ambassador to Iran; let the approval process take a fresh start. Starting fresh would serve to separate the appointment of a new ambassador from the Javits resolution. Unfortunately, the White House concurred with Senate critics in turning down that Iranian request; and the feeling in Tehran was that Carter agreed, in substance, to "put the relations of the two countries in a deep freeze for the time being" out of fear of otherwise alienating Jewish voters in the rapidly approaching presidential election of 1980. [85; *Economic Consequences of the Revolution in Iran,* US Print. Off., 1980]

We have, in the unanimous vote for the Javits resolution, the beginnings of the schizophrenia in our American government about how to deal, officially, with revolutionary Islamic Iran. Domestic politics, especially the electoral interests of Democratic office-holders, determined the course that was subsequently followed, down through the time of President Reagan's covert efforts to turn things around. Iran, at the time of the Javits resolution, was abruptly declared to be an "outlaw" state, despite the eagerness of the White House and the State Department to pursue fully normalized relations. It was suddenly recalled that the revolutionary government had "transferred" the old Israeli mission in Tehran to Yasser Arafat, immediately after the Shah's fall. And it was but a step from there to charging that the new government was otherwise "behaving" toward its Jews like another Nazi Germany.

Meanwhile, the State of Israel had, of course, already begun covertly to protect its large remnant of fellow Jews still living in Iran by making deals to supply Iranian "needs." The condition *sine qua non* for a successful Israeli operation in this regard was a total severance of all normalized U.S. relations with revolutionary Iran. If the Ayatollah's Iran was *ever* to get needed supplies from the United States it would have to be covertly, *through Israel!* Under sufficient pressure, in accordance with the normal conduct of American domestic politics, the Senate of the United States had moved, in the twinkling of an eye, from approval of an ambassador to Iran to a total condemnation of Iran for crimes on a par with those charged against the Nazi German leaders in World War II.

The Javits resolution had constrained the Iranian government to show its chagrin by refusing to accept the ambassador approved by the same Senate that had passed the resolution. So the State Department searched through its top diplomats for a man qualified to be an ambassador (and reportedly willing to work with the Iranian revolutionary government) to serve temporarily as a new charge d'affaires. The Department came up with L. Bruce Laingen. At the time of his appointment, Laingen told his family that he "would be away only briefly." His expectation, and that of the State Department and the White House, was that the controversy precipitated by the Javits Senate resolution would soon be settled and a regular ambassador quickly named and accepted. But that was not to be. As the news accounts would later put it, Laingen's "stay was extended day by day and week by week."

Laingen knew Iran. He had "previously served a diplomatic tour in Iran in the mid-1950s." And when he returned as chargé d'affaires in June, 1979, he reportedly "worked hard to establish some rapport with the Iranian revolution," attempting also, as a New York *Times* "Man in the News" profile would later put it [Jan. 28, 1981], "to reinvigorate an embassy staff, whose morale had been declining for some time." He made it clear, on his arrival, that he meant to turn things around; and all who were there to see the transformation acknowledged that he had succeeded in raising a "rock-bottom morale" to impressively elevated heights. Laingen made clear, too, by his conduct, that he was "particularly fond of the Marine contingent at the embassy."

Lowell Bruce Laingen was born in Minnesota on August 6, 1922, and raised on a farm, to which he regularly returned for vacations. He saw "action in the Philippines as a naval officer in World War II," and later resumed his education in Minnesota. Joining the Foreign Service in 1949, he was trained for posts in the Near East, South Asia, and the eastern Mediterranean, and took assignments in Afghanistan, Pakistan, and Malta (where he was Ambassador from 1976 through 1978), as well as Iran. He also held the post of Deputy Assistant Secretary of State for Near Eastern Affairs. His wife, who had been with him in Iran during the mid-1950s, told reporters that, in his first letters as chargé d'affaires, Laingen made clear that he liked the land and the people of Iran better than ever. "He told us how blue the sky there is, except, of course, when Tehran is covered with smog. . . . He really likes Iran. We all do. We still have many Iranian friends, over there and in this country, too." Mrs. Laingen was saying all of that in mid-November 1979, *after* the second seizure of the American Embassy, when Laingen and two other embassy officials were running their embassy mission from the offices assigned them in the Iranian Foreign Ministry.

Of what Laingen had hoped to do in Iran as chargé d'affaires, his wife said, on the basis of letters and phone conversations: "He was really trying to establish good relations with the revolutionary government." That was confirmed by fellow Foreign Service officers who did not hesitate to say: "Mr. Laingen understands what the Iranian revolution was all about and has a degree of sympathy for its aspirations." Laingen's first object, he himself said, was to try to repair the damage done by the Javits Senate resolution, and he appears to have had, for about a month, significant success at it. Certainly the Ayatollah's government tried to show Washington that charges about its revolutionary pacification "excesses" were largely unfounded, first of all, but also that "things were steadily improving." On July 10, 1979, for instance, the Ayatollah's government declared an amnesty for all "who committed offenses under past regimes," excepting cases in which the offense involved murder or torture. It was emphasized that such amnesty accorded with religious law in Islam. At the same time, statistics were presented to show that "less than 600 people were executed by special tribunals of the Islamic Republic as against nearly 20,000 killed by SAVAK under the Shah."

By way of contradicting charges that there were constant "minority uprisings" against the "oppressions" of the Shiite government, much publicity was given to the fact that Ayatollah Taleghani, a leader and spokesman for minority rights in the region of the Kurds, had arranged a cease-fire between the Kurds and government forces, on terms obviously acceptable to the Kurds — all the while that the U.S. press was continuing to report "minority uprisings." But it had to be noted, also, that within two weeks, on September 10, 1979, that same Taleghani, no doubt rejoicing in his accomplishment, had died quietly in his sleep to be mourned by the "entire nation."

But things changed for Laingen as the White House failed to resist the pressures first applied on it through the Javits Senate resolution. President Carter, a first-term "Southern" Democratic President, was anxious not to suffer the fate of Truman approaching his reelection challenge of 1952 or of Johnson approaching reelection in 1968. Carter's election of 1976 had occurred under very special circumstances. If he had not understood it then, it was no secret to him by the summer of 1979 that his party would not be particularly anxious to see him elected to a second term. All through his first term, and increasingly after its midpoint, he had to be mindful of the need to please a majority of the electorally most active Democrats, to secure his party's nomination. Otherwise, on the evidence of the 1952 and 1968 experiences of Truman and Johnson, he'd be apt to find himself so strongly challenged within the party that even if he squeaked through to renomination opposition would continue into the general election, with large percentages of Democratic dissenters making it clear that they'd prefer "any Republican," another Eisenhower, surely, but even a Nixon or a Ronald Reagan, to a second-term "Southern" Democrat plainly ready to abandon some of the voting blocs he had courted the first time around.

In Carter's case, the opposition of the American-Jewish voting bloc had long since begun to manifest itself; and the American efforts to normalize relations with the pro-Arafat anti-Israeli revolutionary government of Iran had given that opposition a powerful focal point. There had already been the Javits Senate resolution, as we have seen. But soon, plainly taking shape on the horizon, was the cause of the exiled Shah. The Shah's Iran, like the Egypt of Sadat, had loomed large in Israeli plans for "regional security." Not that Israel planned to tolerate an American preference for Iranian or Egyptian "leadership" in stabilizing conditions in the Middle East. Iran and Egypt were too large, and too populous, not to represent a threat to Israel's special claims as the only responsible American ally in the region. But, apart from that, it served Israeli interests to have the United States remain supportive of pro-Israeli regimes in the two countries and opposed to anti-Israeli regimes. Thus the Israelis greatly supported through the American Jewish community the efforts to disrupt normalized relations with the Ayatollah undertaken by Henry Kissinger and the Rockefellers mostly by pressuring the Carter government to provide a haven for the Shah in the United States.

6. Iranian Jews and Israel's "Realpolitik" for Winners

But before we take up the matter of Kissinger and the exiled Shah, we want to summarize and update, to this point, our account of the stakes of Iranian Jews in the troubled attempts of both Washington and Tehran to normalize U.S.-Iranian relations after the Shah's fall. We noted previously that official Israeli relations with Iran, which had been very close though not *de jure* under the Shah, had been at once reduced to zero under the Ayatollah's revolutionary government. Israeli Jews — diplomats, engineers, teachers, skilled technicians in various fields, industrialists, and financiers, as well as "intelligence" personnel and journalists — had been very numerous during the last years and months under the Shah. With the coming of the Ayatollah, they almost all left voluntarily or were, in effect, expelled. But the native Iranian Jews, whose basic language was Farsi, though written in Hebrew characters, were by no means forced to leave. On the contrary they were for the most part discouraged from leaving.

According to Dial Torgerson, the *Los Angeles Times*'s correspondent in Tehran, writing in early March 1979, on "the day after Khomeini took command in Iran, thousands of Jews marched from the Saadi Synagogue to the Ayatollah's headquarters to express support for his government and opposition to what they called Israeli propaganda and policies towards Iran which, they said, encouraged Jews to 'flee' to Israel." At the Ayatollah's headquarters, those thousands of assembled Iranian Jews were addressed by the Ayatollah's son, Haj Amed, who relayed his father's words: "We love you. We are against Zionism, but you are our brothers."

Reporter Dial Torgerson also acknowledged, however, that what a "successful carpet merchant," whom he identified only as "David," told him was typical. "Eighty per cent of the Jews here are like me," David had said: "They would leave if they could, but now it's too late. They only let women and children out of the country, but if they let men leave later, it would be without anything. We don't want to lose everything, so we stay. . . . We are not afraid of the new regime, if the Ayatollah runs it. We're afraid of the leftists and the Communists and the street mobs. They opened all the prisons and all the murderers are free, and everyone has a gun."

According to other Iranian Jews questioned by Torgerson, the leader of Tehran's largest Jewish congregation, Rabbi David Shofet, reportedly told some 1000 Jews crowded into his Central Synagogue for Sabbath services that "the Ayatollah is a good man and will take us under the protection of Islam." Asked if he "believed that," another Jew "expressed serious doubts about Jews putting themselves in the hands of a leader who urges a return to Muslim fundamentalism," and he then observed: "It's not true that half of us are anti-Zionists. We hear the Ayatollah say that Israel was cooperating with the Shah and Savak (the Shah's secret police) and we would be fools to say that we support Israel. So we just keep quiet about it."

That was the crisis atmosphere among Iranian Jews in early March 1979, start of the second month after the Ayatollah's return to Iran. From that moment on, a major concern of Jewish leaders in Israel and throughout the Jewish diaspora in Western Europe and the United States was to do whatever needed to be done to protect the Jews remaining in Iran. The contemporary generation of descendants of that most ancient Iranian Jewish community, dating back to the sixth century B.C., had thereafter to be looked upon as a community of hostages, numbering at least 40,000, for the protection of which sacrifices benefitting the Ayatollah's government in some way would have to be made.

With Israeli-Iranian relations totally severed, that moment marked the beginning of covert Jewish efforts, in Israel and throughout the Jewish diaspora, to somehow deal with the Ayatollah's people, to offer them benefits that met some of their most pressing needs which they could not otherwise supply. Before long such Jewish initiatives, started in 1979 and intensified in 1980, were to strain Israeli relations with the Carter administration, when some of them were prematurely revealed in Israeli-American intelligence exchanges. After that, they were sunk under the deepest cover, to surface once again and make large headlines in the United States in 1986-1987, with the apparently bungled efforts by special American White House agents to "tag along" with the Israelis in their covert dealings with Iran that had begun six years before.

The difference in the timing of the Israeli and U.S. initiatives to deal covertly with the revolutionary Iranian government is striking. The Israelis began their probes the instant relations were completely severed early in 1979. The first American probes were delayed at least four years, and when finally begun in 1985, they were indirect, as we indicated in an early chapter, with the Israelis leading them along. When the Reagan White House finally decided to make direct contacts, on its own, it found itself at once denounced at home and abroad for doing so. As Reagan's former National Security Adviser Robert McFarlane explained at an open congressional hearing at the time, it seemed obvious that the United States was not able to do the sort of things Israel so ably did on its own, and that it had been a mistake to try. "If there was a mistake," McFarlane said, attempting to be precise, "and I probably made it, it was this. . . . We are different; we are not Israel. Israel has a certain respect as being able to differentiate between terrorist states, to react violently or to negotiate. I erred."

The United States erred, in other words — McFarlane concluded — by trying to act as if it were Israel in dealing with the Iranian revolutionary leaders whom it had denounced as members of a terrorist-sponsoring regime. And he gave support to the idea that inexperience in such dealings, coupled with the self-righteous attitude of American critics toward covert dealings generally and especially with nations in the Islamic world, practically assured that the President — however "good" his intentions — would necessarily be ill-served in the process of trying to renew meaningful relations with a nation of such strategic geographic importance to the United States as Iran.

In a later chapter, we will return to the question of the difficulties the United States has recently encountered in trying to conduct covert dealings with manifestly hostile states whose leaders are daily pilloried in the American newsmedia. Here we want to say a word about Israel's "reasons of state" or "*Realpolitik* for winners," as we have called it, which we must later contrast with the "*Realpolitik* for losers,*" introduced in American statecraft largely by Henry Kissinger, during his service under Presidents Nixon and Ford. Although Israel qualifies, technically, as a Third World state, and even as an American dependent, if not quite a client, there is no doubt that, in its international dealings, it comports itself as absolutely independent, and indeed "sovereign" in the technical sense, ready to "stand against the world," if need be, where its real national interests are at stake.

One mustn't be misled by the State of Israel's "lobbying" to secure maximum support from elected American officials. That lobbying shows statesmanly prudence, not actual dependence. Many in America think that Israel would be "lost" without continuing American support, and the thought seems to be warranted by the fact that pledges of support are regularly exacted from almost all candidates of both major parties, as well as actual office-holders, year after year. Yet Israel has always made it clear that it cannot be effectively forced to "change its ways" as a state by threats of withdrawal of support. Often the response has been that the individual persons making such threats may find themselves driven from office, or never elected to office, if they persist in such threats. But more often the response is a pledge that Israeli will "go it alone," no matter what, counting on God as its helper, if other helpers fail.

There is also the important consideration that, although the United States is now Israel's chief foreign support, there was a time when *both* superpowers were its chief support; and, especially in the early years of Israel's existence, the Soviet Union actually proved to be a more reliable support. Israel makes it clear, periodically, to its American critics that, while U.S. support is more "pleasant," one must not imagine that the U.S.S.R. would not seize the opportunity to "pitch in" with full support if ever the United States were to turn its back on Israel. Very capable political analysts in the United States and Israel have shown that the Soviet turn against Israel and in favor of its Arab neighbors after the "Six-Day War" was largely rhetorical. Right after that war, there was indeed for the first time a tremendous outpouring of anti-Israel propaganda from the Moscow press. But as Leonard Shapiro explains in his scholarly introduction to *The Jews in the Soviet Union Since 1917* (Oxford, 1970), the aim of that anti-Zionist outburst, which has continued ever since, we may add, had been "no doubt partly to console the Arabs for the Soviet failure to give them any aid in the course of the war." [8]

Shapiro reminds us that while the U.S.S.R. has always objected to Zionist activity among Soviet Jews, it started quite openly to encourage such activities in the United States and its European allies toward the end of World War II, and, after that war, it took the lead in supporting the Zionist claims for sovereign Israeli statehood in what was then called Palestine. The United States, under Truman, hastened to accord Israel de facto recognition in 1948; but only when it learned that, within 48 hours, quite as previously programmed, Moscow would be according the new state full de jure recognition. And as for Israel's subsequent debt to the Soviets, as J. B. Schechtman, of the Jewish Agency, acknowledges in a paper titled "The U.S.S.R., Zionism, and Israel" (1970):

> During young Israel's struggle against the invading Arab armies, desperately needed arms came from Czechoslovakia with Moscow's tacit approval and in defiance of the United Nation's embargo on the introduction of arms and fighting men into the Middle East. Arms deliveries were paid for in a cash.... But at the time, arms — from whatever source and at any price — were a matter of life or death for Israel. In 1965, seventeen years later, when Katriel Katz, Israel's newly appointed ambassador to Moscow, presented his credentials to the Soviet head of state, he stressed that the Jewish people of Israel would never forget the deep understanding which the Soviet Union had revealed during the struggle for its establishment as a sovereign state; the Soviet Union, he said, occupied a special place in the history of Israel.

Rare is the American who grasps what the Soviet Union achieved by giving propaganda support, rather than effective arms and the know-how for using them, to the Arab-Muslim enemies of Israel. Yet Theodore Draper has said it with great candor in *Israel and World Politics,* where he discusses the geo-political strategy applied by the Soviets in the Middle East at the time of the Six-Day War — a strategy which they took the trouble to explain to Israeli statesmen before the event. As Draper tells it:

> While the Soviets were encouraging the Arab extremists, they also tried to reassure the Israelis. In 1964 and 1965, Soviet diplomats

sought out Israeli diplomats in order to get across the following message: The Soviets and the Arabs did not really have much in common. But the Arabs, as the Soviets had discovered a decade earlier, were determined to eliminate Western interests and influences from the Middle East. On this basis the Soviets and the Arabs could make common cause. But the Israelis did not have to worry and should not get exited. The Soviets intended to be a moderating influence in the Arab-Israeli conflict; Nasser was merely the best means of getting the West out of the region.

It is a fact that, just as the United States has, from time to time, sought to prevent Israel from striking "the first blow" in conflicts with its neighbors, so has Moscow tried to restrain Israel's local enemies. But, the U.S. has, of course, repeatedly failed to restrain Israel while continuing to supply it with the latest weaponry and technology. The Soviets, on the contrary, have always successfully restrained Israel's enemies, starting with Nasser himself. The irony of all that was not missed by the militant Arabs. In Egypt, after Nasser's death in 1970, the new regime prepared itself to expel the Soviet presence and rely rather on the pressure that the oil-rich Arab states could increasingly risk applying in the West — pressures which simply could not be applied effectively against the Soviet Union.

To this day, with its pro-Arab propaganda, the U.S.S.R. has made it virtually impossible for the United States to play an even-handed role in the Middle East. All the Muslim states, and especially the Shiite Muslim states like Iran, see the United States as inseparably tied to Israeli interests in the Middle East. That is why Khomeini's tirades are directed against "East and West," as also against international Zionism, which is perceived as manipulating both superpowers in its "anti-Islamic crusade" to take the Muslim lands away from the Muslims. On this point, in one of Ayatollah Khomeini's frequently consulted and cited "Legal Rulings" on the subject, we read:

> The establishment of commercial and political relations with states like Israel that are the tools of the tyrannical superpowers is not permissible and it is the duty of the Muslims to oppose such relations in any way possible. Merchants who establish commercial relations with Israel and its agents are traitors to Islam and the

Muslims, and they are aiding in the destruction of the ordinances of Islam. It is the duty of the Muslims to discontinue all dealings with those traitors, whether they are government or merchants, and compel them to repent and renounce their relations with such states.

Needless to say, when the Ayatollah's government, headed by Bazargan, first took office in February 1979, among the first things it did, as we saw, was to break off all relations with Israel, including trade relations — while retaining all such relations with the United States. The intention was, as we have indicated, to try to hammer in an effective wedge between Israel and U.S. interests in Iran. The United States, Khomeini repeatedly said, can deal with us; but its dealings must not be in the interest of Israel, and Israel must not be the chief instrument of its dealings. That attitude clearly persisted into the mid-1980s, when Khomeini's Iran rejected Israel's intermediary for the Iran arms transfer, even though he was, by birth and ethnically, an Iranian — namely, Manucher Ghorbanifar. That was because Ghorbanifar was reportedly functioning as an Israeli Mossad agent. Ghorbanifar, of course, never dared to accompany North and McFarlane to Tehran, for he would there have been immediately arrested. His replacement, Albert Hakim, on the contrary was acceptable in Tehran as a true Iranian; and the fact that he was an Iranian Jew — and a naturalized American citizen — didn't make him any less acceptable as an intermediary.

The State of Israel, we must say finally, was determined from the start to do all that it could for the many Jews remaining in Iran, who were not permitted to emigrate easily. But, a first priority was not to let Khomeini's Islamic republic of Iran get away with drawing a distinction between United States interests and Israeli interests. It proceeded to do all it could to prevent that, and to stop the process from advancing when it could not be prevented. In the end, it would seize the opportunity of the Iran-Iraq war to force Iran to turn to Israel for whatever it might ever hope to obtain, in the way of needed supplies, from the United States. In all of that, Israel's *"Realpolitik* for winners" proved successful, as we shall see.

CHAPTER ELEVEN

Who
"Lost" Iran?

The question "Who 'Lost' Iran?" began to be asked in the United States long before the second American Embassy seizure of November 4, 1979. Before that event, the Carter administration could insist that Iran had not been lost, since the Shah's fall hadn't brought on a formal break in diplomatic relations and the flow of Iranian oil to the West and to Japan had by no means ceased. Of course, the large sector of the American foreign policy establishment which had concurred in the Kissinger-Nixon policy of 1972 to "subordinate U.S. security decision-making in the Persian Gulf to the person of the Shah" — to recall Gary Sick's apt formulation [170] — had an altogether different perspective. The loss of Iran to the West had become "total" in its view with the Shah's departure in January 1979 and the adoption by the successor regime of an explicitly anti-Zionist foreign policy in the Middle East.

There were then, and there still are, many outspoken Americans who identify Israeli and American interests so completely that they find intolerable any suggestion — such as we have had since the 1986-1987 Iran arms transfer scandals — that U.S. and Israeli interests might conceivably be in conflict. Still, the question must be asked: Should the United States have maintained diplomatic relations with Iran after the Shah's fall? Hadn't the successor regime lived up to the highest standards of international diplomatic responsibility by responding effectively to calls for help from the U.S. Embassy in Tehran after it had been attacked on February 14, 1979?

Unlike South Vietnam, where the United States had maintained an American fighting presence of some 525,000 troops for years, Iran had never had any American military bases built and maintained on its soil. Iran had been supplied with (actually, sold) billions of dollars of American advanced weaponry and high-technology supports; but the United States Embassy compound and a few other embassy-related buildings in Tehran and elsewhere were all that ever really "belonged" to the United States in a strict diplomatic sense, and those were by no means "lost" immediately after the Shah's fall, except for a few hours on Febraury 14. It is true that the U.S. "presence" in Iran consisting of tens of thousands of military and civilian industrial-military experts had been greatly reduced, just before and after the Shah's departure; but it is surely arguable that, if the reduction added up to a loss, it was rather to the Iranian economy than to the American.

At any rate, during the nine months that separated the first embassy seizure in Tehran from the second, the Carter administration worked feverishly, as we have seen, to maintain and improve normal *de jure* diplomatic relations with the successor regime. And, all the while, its opponents in the Kissinger-Rockefeller foreign policy establishment labored feverishly to effect a total split, by demanding of the government an abiding "loyalty" to the fallen Shah, with whom a very personal deal had been concluded in 1972.

Since the American Embassy in Tehran had been, technically, all that the United States had had that it could possibly "lose" in Iran, that embassy's status immediately became the focus of concern for both parties in the dispute. That the Carter administration had "lost" Iran in February 1979 would have been amply proven had the successor regime failed to reestablish American control after the St. Valentine's Day attack. And, more to the point, if the embassy were ever seized again and the Iranian government failed to restore it to American control, that would be an ultimate proof of the "loss."

We noticed the steps Ambassador Sullivan had taken, after February 14, to secure the embassy compound against seizure. In "contravention of all normal diplomatic practice," he had asked that revolutionary Iranian guard units be stationed inside the compound, some of which he used to accompany him as bodyguards in his trips around the capital. After his departure, the Carter administration made strenuous afforts to end any and all contravention of normal diplomatic practice in Tehran, even while partisan efforts in the U.S. Congress succeeded in retarding the replacement of Sullivan by another fully-accredited Ambassador. What emerged in the course of 1979, as we saw, was a political tug-of-war between American proponents and opponents of fully normalized U.S.-Iranian diplomatic relations. All that was required for the opponents to declare themselves winners was a second seizure of the American Embassy that could not be brought, like the first, to a quick and happy conclusion. That became the great fear of the Carter administration, especially when Henry Kissinger began to intensify his "demands" that the Shah be admitted to the United States despite the expressed will of the Carter administration to the contrary.

Located in the heart of the city, surrounded by tall buildings from the roofs and windows of which left-wing militants had poured in a heavy barrage of pistol, rifle, and machine-gun fire on February 14, the American Embassy compound in Tehran looked for all the world like a Hollywood set built for the production of exactly the sort of TV drama that started to be filmed there, for world-wide nightly showing, on November 4, 1979. Nine months earlier, as already noted, several of the people involved in the first seizure had said that if they ever attacked the embassy again they would proceed differently. If one reads the embassy communications about provisions for the compound's protection during the intervening months, one detects a sense of expectation, a desire, one is tempted to say, for some sort of dress rehearsal, as it were, to test the latest security provisions. From the standpoint of avowed political partisans, there was anticipation of another embassy seizure, even if only as a staged "event" or "happening" to bring certain developments into focus. Attacks on American embassies in the Middle East and elsewhere, in the Third World especially, had become frequent occurrences. Protesting crowds were a familiar sight at the embassy gates in Tehran. What would it take to get at least a mini-series started for media-TV exploitation, especially as the debate over America's alleged responsibilities toward the deposed Shah intensified?

1. The Hostage-Crisis Before the Fact: William Bundy's Prescient Analysis

Typical of many anticipations of a second embassy seizure, or something of comparable "media" significance, was an article by William Bundy titled "Who Lost Patagonia? Foreign Policy in the 1980 Campaign," published in the Fall 1979 issue of *Foreign Affairs*. In retrospect, the very title seems to suggest that an ideal date for a "media-event" on the "loss" of Iran would be November 4, 1979, exactly one year to the day before the 1980 presidential election! The article's author was, of course, the brother of McGeorge Bundy, the Harvard professor and Dean of Faculty who paved the way for the careers of Walt Rostow, Henry Kissinger, and Zbigniew Brzezinski as nearly-omnipotent presidential advisers for national security affairs. But William Bundy had himself been a top-level decision maker in several administrations, and, as a longtime editor-in-chief of *Foreign Affairs* (official quarterly of the Council on Foreign Relations), he had continued to rank as one of the so-called Northeastern Foreign Policy Establishment's most authoritative insiders.

When Bundy's article appeared the Shah of Iran had not yet been admitted to a New York City hospital. In other words, the blitzkrieg propaganda assault mounted by Henry Kissinger and John McCloy, backed by the Rockefeller financial empire, had not yet battered the Carter White House and the State Department into submission: but it had already moved into high gear. Before long, Kissinger's equivalent of a lightening-swift commando raid would of itself virtually decide the outcome of the 1980 election against the incumbent President. But, during the brief relative calm before the storm — while U.S. relations with the successor regime in Iran were being steadily normalized — William Bundy could still reasonably ask: "What then of Iran? Is there a fair issue of policy raised by the Carter Administration's handling of the Iranian revolution?" Given the measure of U.S. military and industrial involvement in Iran's affairs since 1973, and, given the fact that the "revolution happened on Jimmy Carter's watch, with no serious indication prior to January 1977 that an early upheaval was likely," one could conclude on the face of it, says Bundy, that there "simply must be" a policy issue to be exploited in the coming election. "So it is not surprising," he adds,

> that, in private meeting places of Washington, and occasionally in print, one sees the testing and stirring of arguments that might be embellished in a campaign. Surely, it is argued, there must have been some crucial moment when the Shah could have used his armed forces to put down the revolt once and for all, or when the Iranian military might have launched a successful coup after the Shah had left.

What we get in Bundy's article after that is by no means a "brief" for the Carter administration's conduct. Bundy's intention, first of all, is to emphasize the obvious truth that U.S.-Iranian relations had altered radically from what they were in the days of Presidents Truman and Eisenhower. Despite all that Truman and Eisenhower had done for Iran, and for the Shah personally — the removal of Russians from Azerbaijan in 1946 and the restoration of the young Shah to his shaky throne by means of the "CIA coup" of 1953 — it could be said that, from 1946 through 1953, and on to 1969, the Shah had remained, as General Haig would later acknowledge, a ward of British and American protectors, and that his country ranked as an altogether dependent client.

Basically, the change that occurred in U.S.-Iranian relations after 1969 was a direct consequence of England's decision of 1968 to give up her role as chief peacekeeper "East of Suez," and especially in the Persian Gulf, completely by 1971. The "deal" of 1972, says Bundy, marked a turning point, breaking with all previous arrangements Washington had ever entered into with Imperial Iran. Bundy characterizes it as "the policy of all-out and unquestioning support for the Shah followed by the Nixon Administration from 1972 onward"; as a result of which "not even private advice, apparently, was ever offered to the Shah on such blatant issues as the corrupt practices of his family, and the policy was symbolized dramatically by President Nixon's blank check of May 1972 for the Shah to buy any U.S. military equipment he wanted regardless of its sophistication or the judgment of military experts as to Iran's needs and capacities."

All of that, says Bundy, had to be charged — if it was a mistake — entirely to the Republicans. A Democratic administration, he observes, could hardly have presumed to follow such a course during the same period, just as no Republican administration would have presumed to adopt anything like Carter's human rights policy of 1977, for application in dealings with Iran. The Kissinger-Nixon policy had made Iran an "independent ally," with tremendous financial resources. Encouraged by Kissinger, the Shah had, indeed, chastised Carter for presuming to treat him like a client — pressing inquires into the means employed by the Pahlavis to "ensure domestic tranquility" — instead of as a great power (a regional "superpower," no less!), charged with maintaining peace and stability throughout the Middle East. Carter had, of course, taken all past insults back, Bundy notes, with his "overcompensating toast in praise of the Shah in Tehran on New Year's Eve of 1977," But the political harm had been done; the Carter policy had given the Republicans a proper counter-issue on Iran for the 1980 presidential campaign.

Writing more than a year before the 1980 election, Bundy observed sharply that the Nixon-Kissinger blank check of 1972 and the Carter human rights policy of 1977 would be the focal points of contention. "It is natural," so Bundy puts it, "that Henry Kissinger has put his finger on human rights (as well as the Administration's alleged lack of general firmness), while George Ball, in reply, has attacked the 'blank check' Nixon military sales policy." But both points, Bundy charges, are basically irrelevant. It is true that the Kissinger-Nixon "blank check" corrupted the Shah by enabling him to "acquire sophisticated systems way beyond Iran's capacity." It is true that the "large numbers of American technicians" introduced in Iran as a consequence "were, on almost any analysis, a disturbing political factor. Vast resources and high-quality manpower went into a bloated defense effort and were thus conceivably denied to development programs, housing, and so on, and some American secrets were endangered."

But, asks Bundy, "suppose another American President had been more standoffish. Would the Shah have changed his priorities or would he simply have bought less sophisticated equipment elsewhere?" Bundy asks us to "leave aside the U.S. balance of payments, or the teasing question whether unlimited arms sales gave the United States any special influence on the Shah's oil price actions and votes in OPEC." Those questions remain of great interest in assessing Kissinger's motives, to be sure. But the essential point, Bundy stresses, is "whether the *internal* situation in Iran would have evolved any differently" without the Kissinger-Nixon blank check of 1972. Bundy doubts it. And the same can be said with regard to Carter's insistence, as far as it went, on human rights as a criterion for the measure of support his administration would give the Shah. Historians, said Bundy, will no doubt take an interest in such matters as "might have beens." But they could hardly be expected to count for much in the presidential election of 1980. It is too late, he insists, to make an issue that could get votes out of the Nixon-Kissinger blank check of 1972. And, as for Carter's human rights initiative, attacking it was surely "not the stuff of red-blooded politics." Bundy concludes that "any Republican campaigning in 1980 is far more likely to argue that the Administration was to blame for not pulling out all the stops, at all levels, in support of the Shah and above all for not encouraging him to act with maximum force, some time from September on. The fact that just this policy appears to have been urged within the Administration by Mr. Brzezinski, at least at intervals, lends the argument added weight."

2. Mastermind of the "Loss": Vance, Brzezinski, . . . or Kissinger?

Where can the Republicans place the blame for the failure of the Carter administration to "do right" by the Shah in his hour of peril? It can hardly be said, writes Bundy, that the Carter people actually "did" anything to prevent the Shah from acting with "maximum force" to secure his throne: "on the contrary, the repeated statements of support from the White House clearly implied that he would be backed whatever he decided to do." Still, there was, of course, *one* kind of American support that President Carter did not volunteer to give. And that was, in Bundy's words, "the direct support of American military forces if Iran forces sought to subdue the revolt and ran into trouble.'' Bundy points out that Carter was by no means alone in that attitude. Henry Kissinger, under President Nixon, first, and then under President Ford, had made clear that the so-called Nixon Doctrine had meant not any promise to *introduce* American combat troops to support ''allies'' but rather a promise to *withdraw* whatever troops might already have been introduced for the purpose. As we have stressed in an earlier chapter, when it was revealed that President Nixon had secretly promised to come to the forceful aid of Saigon if the North Vietnamese sought a military conquest, Kissinger, as we saw, never even half suggested that Nixon's successor should consider himself and the nation bound by the secret promises. That is a matter of fact, even though, as Bundy notes, Kissinger brazenly argued that it was the U.S. Congress that ultimately ''abandoned'' Saigon, and not his State Department and the Presidents that department was supposed to serve.

Bundy speaks with a measure of contempt for Kissinger's repeated allegations that the ''general perception of American geopolitical decline,'' after Watergate, ''had the consequence of demoralizing those whose stock in trade was cooperation with the United States, undermining their resolution towards potential revolutionaries.'' In the case of the Shah, says Bundy, it is absurd to speak of a ''general perception of American geopolitical decline'' as an ultimate determinant. The Shah could not conceivably have ''screwed up'' his courage ''to the sticking point,'' he writes, without some ''fairly direct assurances of contingent military support.''

What about the Shah's military leaders, with whom Ambassador Sullivan and General Huyser dealt directly? Bundy's words here are worth quoting at length. ''As for the idea of a coup by the Iranian military,'' he writes,

> the Administration sent a senior general, Robert Huyser, Deputy European Commander, to Tehran in January to maintain contact with the Iranian high command. Apparently his line was to ''cool it,'' or at any rate to plan with the utmost care any action taken. A contrary American position at that time — after the Shah left and before Prime Minister Bakhtiar fled and Khomeini arrived — might have led to what an advocate of such a course has

described privately as a "real throw of the dice." But what would
the chances have been? And, again, would the military have acted without some assurances of more than moral U.S. support?

We have already reviewed history's answer to that last question.
The Iranian military asked directly whether they would be supported by American military intervention if they attempted a military
coup and couldn't pull it off by themselves. Was Washington committed to preventing a triumph of the Islamic forces of the Ayatollah Khomeini? Was it viewed as an end worth fighting for? Or did
Washington fear that the Soviet Union might move in with troops
if the U.S. introduced combat forces? Bundy's discussion of the matter is quite frank. "The Soviet reaction to an attempted military
coup," he writes,

> without the presence of U.S. forces, might well have been res-
> trained; the Soviets played a cool hand throughout what actually
> happened, and probably would have calculated that even a suc-
> cessful military coup would be only temporary and that a failed
> or inconclusive one would only improve the eventual chances of
> a genuinely radical or even Soviet-oriented government. But if U.S.
> forces of any kind whatever had come in, the Soviets could, and
> almost certainly would, have invoked the 1921 treaty that expressly
> gave them the right to send in their own military forces in such
> a case. The least they might have done would have been to seize
> one or two northern provinces and hold them for bargaining or
> even retention.

But even if American troops went in and no Soviet intervention followed, Bundy continues, "any honest proponent of the hardline course must also acknowledge that, for good or ill, it would surely have involved the United States far more deeply and visibly in
the political future of Iran. The memory of what happened after the
overthrow of Diem in Vietnam in 1963 can hardly be confined to
Jimmy Carter and his advisers, who apparently gave this consideration great weight in their hands-off policy."

Bundy's conclusion, there, offers an important reminder. In
South Vietnam, where the United States was master of the local

government, the fall of Diem brought on by U.S. policy led to total Americanization of the war. To de-Americanize it after escalation to a troop level of 525,000 men, it became necessary to go through the cruel, not to say murderous procedures of total American troop withdrawals in the face of an increasingly triumphant and arrogant enemy. And we all recall what those withdrawals were like. To avoid a domestic backlash, they were carried forward in stages, punctuated by displays of force that did the enemy little damage, but served to appease the hurt feelings of the "silent majority" of Americans who did not like the idea of a deliberate U.S. retreat in the face of a determined enemy.

Kissinger worked hard, as we have indicated, to avoid the domestic backlash while completing the total withdrawal of American forces. That Kissinger's labors were not a daily matter of congressional inquires was entirely due to the fact that the old-time liberal opponents of Richard Nixon were fully aware of what Kissinger was doing under the cover of Nixon's indelible reputation as a hardline anti-Communist; and they liked it. Norman Podhoretz, the highly influential editor of *Commentary,* took the trouble to explain the phenomenon at length in the April 1976 issue of *Commentary,* doing so not without a large measure of admiration for Kissinger's daring performance. It is true, Podhoretz wrote, that Nixon aroused the ire of his liberal critics by sending "troops into Laos and bombers to Hanoi." All the while, however, he and Kissinger were plainly busy winding down the "main war" that was then going on in Southeast Asia. They also, Podhoretz reminds us,

> withdrew all American forces from that part of the world, inaugurated a policy of detente with the Soviet Union, and opened up relations with Communist China.... However one might choose to describe this policy, one could scarcely call it a species of anti-Communist interventionism. It is, rather, a policy of phased American withdrawal from anti-Communist interventionism. [In] withdrawing from Vietnam, Richard Nixon was executing in almost every detail the new foreign policy program of the liberals (in this way "dishing" the liberals, as the Tory Disraeli said he had "dished the Whigs" by executing their idea of democratizing the franchise).

But thanks to Nixon's decisions to withdraw gradually from Vietnam instead of all at once in 1969-70, the liberals were left free to go on attacking him; and thanks to the presence of Henry Kissinger in his administration, they had someone other than Nixon to whom they could assign credit...for a foreign policy which in every other respect was indistinguishable from their own: a policy, that is, of withdrawal from anti-Communist interventionism.

We have called it "defeatist interventionism" and "no-win belligerency"; but the policy was exactly what Norman Podhoretz said it was. It was a case, as he says, of Kissinger's "speaking loudly and carrying a small stick," of sounding "like Churchill" and acting "like Chamberlain."

Perhaps the most powerful critical account of the cruel and murderous procedures pursued in Vietnam to "cover up" what Podhoretz has correctly called a "withdrawal from anti-Communist interventionism" has been supplied with full documentation in Jonathan Shell's remarkably-impartial book *Time of Illusion* (New York 1976). Unlike Podhoretz, Shell (a journalist of impeccably liberal-intellectual credentials) thoroughly approves of Kissinger's ultimate goal in getting President Nixon to withdraw from the war; but the means offend him. To appease the sensibilities of the "silent majority" of American voters who he hoped would give him a landslide reelection victory in 1972, Nixon, encouraged by Kissinger, saw that his retreat from Vietnam "would have to be accompanied," in Shell's words, "by many awesome displays of unimpaired resolve."

Shell then proceeds to review the same evidence that Norman Podhoretz pointed to, referring us particularly to "displays such as the invasion of Cambodia" after half of the American forces had been pulled out of South Vietnam, "the mining of the ports of North Vietnam" when almost all the troops were out, and, later, "the carpet-bombing of North Vietnam" when the peace accords were about to be initialed by Kissinger and Hanoi's Le Duc Tho — an initialing that earned each of them half a Nobel Peace prize! As for the "goal" behind such cruel displays of "unimpaired resolve" to cover the retreat from Vietnam — the goal of Kissinger's defeatist interventionism or no-win belligerency — Shell defines it with precision as follows:

The war in Vietnam was, in a sense, a theorists' war *par excellence*. The strategists of the late nineteen-fifties were only slightly interested in the question of which country or countries might be the scene of a limited war. . . . Kissinger had warned in his 1957 book that the policy he was proposing would require "a public opinion which had been educated to the realities of the nuclear age." . . . One might say that the plan was to pay for nuclear peace with limited war. . . .and that it was in the very nature of the doctrine that it had to be presented misleadingly to the public and the world. For to explain the policy fully would be to undermine it.

In the light of that goal and the displays of "unimpaired resolve" required for progress toward it, the parallel drawn by William Bundy between the Vietnam and Iran situations becomes even more compelling. Bundy noted, as we saw, that, as a consequence of Kissinger's 1972-1973 "deal" with the Shah, the United States, by the end of 1978, "was enmeshed in the affairs of Iran to a greater extent than elsewhere in the Third World except wartime South Vietnam and perhaps South Korea in the 1950s." Bundy's choice of Vietnam and "perhaps" South Korea as comparable cases is significant. Korea had not been a defeat for the United States because of the way President Eisenhower had handled the last phases of the war there. America's conquering hero of World War II had stopped local communist aggression in Korea by threatening what came to be called massive retaliation. That Eisenhower threat had scandalized many leading members of the American liberal foreign-policy establishment. And it was in behalf of that scandalized leadership that Henry Kissinger, back in the mid-1950s, had been commissioned by the Council on Foreign Relations to write his heavily subsidized critique of the Eisenhower doctrine.

Bundy published his article before the start of the November 1979 hostages crisis. In April 1981, shortly after Ronald Reagan's inauguration, John Kenneth Galbraith spelled out the point of Bundy's parallel a bit more clearly. Stressing the importance of the Iran crisis in the post-World War II history of our international relations, Galbraith observed that "there have been only two incontrovertible cases of American reverses in the past 20 years. One of these is South

Vietnam (along with Cambodia), and the other is Iran. The lessons
are wonderfully clear. Vietnam and Iran were the two countries of
the Third World to which we accorded the closest military embrace."

The argument isn't difficult to follow. It is a fact that, long before the hostage crisis of late 1979 began, the U.S. had been
"present" in Iran on a scale we usually expect only when we have
involved ourselves in a Third World military conflict. In Vietnam,
Kissinger had indeed made us "pay for nuclear peace" by losing a
limited war, in accordance with the logic of his criticism of Eisenhower who refused to pay that price in Korea. In Iran, Kissinger's
plan had been from the beginning, as we saw, to pay for nuclear
peace without engaging American troops in a losing war. "Our side"
would lose "for the sake of peace" in Iran, but the price for "us"
would be far less bloody, though perhaps even more costly in terms
of arms and high technology.

The "trick" in Iran had been to prevent a bloody American military intervention no matter what the provocation. While Richard
Helms, former CIA director, was the U.S. Ambassador in Iran, the
expectation was that, if the Shah's rule were ever threatened, non-
military covert intervention would already be in place, on a scale
much grander than in the days of Kermit Roosevelt and General
Schwartzkopf. And given Sullivan's experience in secret negotiations
and covert bombings, it was assumed that non-military support of
the Shah had passed into even more capable hands. So — when the
Shah's rule was manifestly threatened toward the end of 1978: why
not a preemptive coup by the Iranian military without overt American support? Why not a repeat of the 1953 triumph of the CIA and
the old British and new Israeli covert intelligence forces?

3. *Kermit Roosevelt and General Huyser vs.* *Kissinger's Doctrine of "Defeatist Interventionism"*

Kermit Roosevelt back then had anticipated the question and
had supplied the obvious answer. He had said, "the people and the
army came, overwhelmingly, to the support of the Shah," as the
American intelligence analyses had at that time predicted they would.

But Kermit Roosevelt's concluding admonition, which we cited earlier, is worth repeating here: "If our analysis had been wrong, we'd have fallen flat on our, er, faces. But it was right. If we, the CIA, are ever going to try something like this again, we must be absolutely sure that people and army want what we want. If not, you better give the job to the Marines." [210]

The Shah, by January 1979, had lost the support of the people. The Iranian military were well enough informed on that account, and so was General Huyser. "Saving Iran" from a religious revolution had ceased to be a job for Iranian soldiers. If the Americans believed that the Shah's regime, under Bakhtiar had to be "saved" from Soviet domination, then it was a job not for the kind of duplicitous covert activity Ambassador Sullivan was planning and executing; it was a job, as Kermit Roosevelt had put it, for the U.S. Marines. That, at any rate, had been General Huyser's conclusion. Could a military coup have been mounted to "save" Iran? Huyser was confident that it could — provided the U.S. Government thought it a cause worth fighting for. Huyser said so at the time. He said so repeatedly after the Ayatollah Khomeini's government was established. And he has said so in his recent book, *Mission to Iran* (Harper & Row, 1987), with an introduction by Alexander M. Haig.

Reviewing "Dutch" Huyser's book for the New York *Times,* Robert Jervis gives an interesting account of the "split" in American governmental attitudes about the Iranian military, and particularly about the possibilities of using it to "support or supplant" the regime of the Shah's last Prime Minister, Shapour Bakhtiar. Huyser acknowledges that a serious obstacle in dealing with the Iranian military was their general "conspiratorial view" of the conduct of world affairs. They were constantly ascribing to American "strategy" what were often simply mistakes or total lack of planning. That would not, however, have handicapped Huyser very much, because he had dealt with the Iranian military for years. Jervis then adds:

> The second obstacle to using the military either to support or to supplant Mr. Bakhtiar was that the American Ambassador and the State Department thought it was wildly impratical. Instead, they favored a coalition between the religious and secular moder-

ates and segments of the military. Mr. Bakhtiar, they felt, was doomed. Thus, while the Secretary of Defense, Harold Brown, the national security adviser, Zbigniew Brzezinski, and General Huyser were urging full support of him and, if Bakhtiar faltered, the establishment of a military government, Ambassador Sullivan was trying to prepare for Mr. Bakhtiar's fall and a takeover by the moderates.

Jervis says all that as if he did not know that what Huyser had been seeking to do, backed by Brown and Brzezinski, was *official* American policy, declared to be such by the President, who, in so many words, declared Ambassador Sullivan's activity to be a case of traitorous, roguish recalcitrance, disobeying specific presidential orders. Jervis, a political science teacher at Columbia University, then benignly concludes: "Although General Huyser and Mr. Sullivan discussed their divergent evaluations of the military, the general did not know that while he was urging the top military to stay, the Ambassador was working on a plan that required them to leave. General Huyser obviously did not grasp the extent of the divisions in Washington." But the divisions at issue, in Washington and Tehran, involved conduct properly called treasonous — outright refusal to carry out a President's direct orders. There is no need to belabor the point. "Jimmy" Carter was up against an illegal establishment that had more real "power" than he had, and that he dared not, in the end, defy.

Huyser's book is valuable mostly because of its confirmation of Kermit Roosevelt's judgment of a generation earlier. When he returned to Washington in February 1979, Huyser was asked if he "would be willing to go back to Tehran and conduct a military takeover." Replying without ambiguities, he said that a military takeover would be impossible at that late date "without 10,000 American troops" and solid U.S. national support. With that, the Shah's Iran had joined South Vietnam as a sacrifice to the Kissinger-Nixon doctrine for avoiding nuclear war by declaring our clients to be allies and then abandoning them to their well-known incapacities to sustain themselves against determined enemies, whether religious or communist or both.

4. "Sticking with the Shah":
Kissinger's "Realpolitik" for Losers

The story of the exile of the deposed Shah of Iran was told at great length, in books, long magazine articles, and sometimes daily news reports that ran on for pages, while it was still going on. Briefly, it started with the Shah's Janaury 16, 1979 flight from Tehran to Egypt, and continued through stays in Morocco, the Bahamas, and Mexico, before his controversial flight of October 22, 1979, to New York City — which certainly was the immediate provocation of the second seizure of the American Embassy in Tehran on November 4, 1979. On December 15, 1979, the Shah moved from the U.S. to the Panamanian island of Contadora, where he stayed until late March 1980. There, the local government was on the verge of ordering his extradition back to Iran, when he took flight, with his wife, for Egypt. That was on March 23, 1980. Less than a week later, on March 28, he underwent surgery for removal of his spleen and a part of his liver. Then his health seemed to improve rapidly. Sadat's Egyptian government set him up royally in Kubbeh Palace — "an opulent 19th century building" with "200-acre palace gardens" that had formerly belonged to King Farouk, who had been for a time the Shah's father-in-law.

Death finally overtook the Shah in an Egyptian military hospital on July 27, 1980, in his eighteenth month of exile. He was 60 years old. His funeral drew Richard M. Nixon, of course, who, upon his arrival, spoke out emphatically in support of Kissinger's "*Realpolitik* for losers." He had done as much a year earlier, when he visited the exiled Shah in Cuernavaca, Mexico. At that time, he had made a point of explaining that he was trying to retrieve something of the "national honor" by breaking with President Carter over the treatment of the Shah in exile. "If the United States doesn't stand by our friends when they're in trouble," he had told reporters accompanying him, "we're going to end up without friends." On that occasion, Nixon personally assured the Shah that "millions of Americans in the United States are still his friends."

When he arrived in Cairo for the Shah's funeral — accompanied by "13 Secret Service agents" — Nixon made clear to reporters that he was not there representing the Carter administration. "I think that the treatment of the Shah by the Administration after he left was shameful"; and then he added: "It is one of the black pages of America's foreign policy history." Like Kissinger, Nixon is careful to speak of what we "owe" client-friends only *after* they have "left" office or fallen from it. What is required is loyalty to the loser *as loser*.

We took note earlier of William Bundy's impatience with Kissinger's repeated prophecies that America's failure to "stick" with our allies in defeat undermined the resolution of other client/allies towards potential adversaries. But, as we take up Kissinger's bold effort to force the Carter administration to "stick with the Shah" in defeat, it is important to get a clear sense of the distinction he has himself candidly drawn between what he says or writes as "an historian and a philosopher" and what he says as a practicing "statesman" or political "job applicant" seeking reappointment as Secretary of State by a new Republican President. We saw, for instance, that when he was addressing a Republican Governors Association meeting in Austin, Texas, on November 26, 1979, Kissinger did not hesitate to tell his audience what they wanted to hear about Carter and his handling of the revolutionary crisis in Iran. He said that he saw no virtue in using "impotence" as the "ruling principle of our foreign policy," and went on to say that, in his view, the public response to the second American embassy seizure in Tehran showed that our people "are sick and tired of getting pushed around and...of seeing America forever on the defensive."

Those of us who have troubled ourselves to read Kissinger's major writings know that he usually has much kinder words to say about "impotence" in international relations. In the book that presents a definitive version of his doctrine of fail-safe limited war, *The Necessity for Choice* (New York 1960/1961), for instance, Kissinger makes an interesting case *for* impotence in chiding academic colleagues who openly advocate American unilateral disarmament. He accuses them of a pathetic lack of realism in believing they could effectively influence American defense policy by such direct means. They seem to be arguing, he writes, "that America is bound to behave irresponsibly unless it is deprived of all alternatives to peace save suicide — and occasionally this proposition is made explicit. If this is true, no constructive policy of any kind is possible. A nation which cannot be trusted when strong will hardly be able to deal with the much more difficult task of living in dignity when impotent.''

In that book, as in his earlier *Nuclear Weapons and Foreign Policy* (New York 1957), Kissinger makes his theoretical case for an alternative to what he presents as the "unacceptable extremes" of the Dulles-Eisenhower defense strategy of "massive retaliation," on the one hand, and its opposite, the all-out peace strategy that called for unilateral disarmament and even surrender, if need be, to avoid a nuclear holocaust. Kissinger's proposed alternative to both those extremes, we must repeat, was a fail-safe form of limited war, with a built-in device to prevent escalation from limited to general warfare. The built-in device was to be very simple. The more powerful side — which is to say, the American side — in a limited war would stop fighting, and agree to lose, if the only alternative to losing was to risk escalation to the level of a general war.

That had been from the beginning the essence of Henry Kissinger's national security strategy for peace in the nuclear age. His much admired "Disraelian conservative" approach in its advocacy while working for Nelson Rockefeller and eventually for Richard Nixon involved the presentation of many purposive ambiguities. One needs to recall that John F. Kennedy repeatedly cited Kissinger's arguments in his campaign of 1960 against Richard M. Nixon, who, when he finally got his heart's desire in 1968, hired Kissinger for the Disraelian reasons so clearly grasped by Walter Lippmann.

No American President, let it be said, has every really accepted the idea. John F. Kennedy plainly never did, as the *Pentagon Papers* reveal. President Johnson never seems to have understood a word of it — which accounts for his total repudiation by the American liberal foreign policy establishment after 1965. Richard Nixon said that it reminded him of the Quaker philosophy of his mother and that it seemed worth pursuing, provided it didn't mean actually "losing" a war — provided it could mean that we'd win in the end anyway, by using clever dirty tricks, perhaps, instead of fighting. The idea had confused President Carter, though he flirted with it in his dealings with the Kissinger-loaded State Departement inherited from President Ford. And it proved from the beginning to be utterly alien, of course, to the feelings of Ronald Reagan.

In the case of Iran, as in that of South Vietnam and all other third-world countries with the possible exception of the State of Israel, that Kissinger theory of fail-safe limited war requires that the American government stick with its clients (called allies for the purpose) in defeat, so that there can be no mistaking the fact that it has lost with them. Each time it happens, each time our government allows or even constrains a client to be defeated, and yet "sticks with him," it helps to get Americans used to the "possibility of tragedy," as Kissinger has sometimes put it. It gets Americans used to the fact that their *status quo* world of nation states is not really up to the challenges of this age of "inevitable" revolutionary change.

On this point, Lewis S. Feuer, a master of the Marxist revolutionary legacy to the West, has provided some important clarifications. Writing in May 1976, Feuer took note of that fact that, by then, Kissinger had "become the most sophisticated spokesman of the philosophical defeatism that became fashionable among the American intellectual class in the latter sixties." Was that perception of Kissinger inconsistent with his periodic pleas for continued though *insufficient* support of doomed clients like Thieu and the Iranian Shah, and periodic displays of "military resolve," in the form of useless bombings, to punctuate an otherwise unilateral retreat from the fields of real battle? By no means.

In 1974, after five years in high office under Richard M. Nixon, Kissinger had thus clarified his position: "I think of myself as a historian more than a statesman. As a historian, you have to be conscious of the fact that every civilization that has ever existed has ultimately collapsed." To which Lewis Feuer later replied:

> The relationship between the Communist ideology and Mr. Kissinger's philosophy is worrisome. For there seems to be a practical complementarity between the Marxist "optimist" who says the triumph of the Communist system is inevitable and the American pessimist who says the decline of Western society is inevitable. . . . Mr. Kissinger's rationale of "crisis management". . . gives way to

the mood that concessions are inevitable, and that statesmanship consists in retarding the process but never reversing it. . . . This philosophy seems to many Americans to culminate in an art of graceful surrender.

Norman Podhoretz of *Commentary* deserves to be cited on this important matter because of his concern lest a similar attitude be taken regarding U.S. support of the State of Israel. Complaining of what William Bundy would later complain of with respect to Kissinger's attitude toward Iran, Podhoretz says: "Kissinger has been heard to say — and in public to suggest — that the Soviet Union is in an aggressive stage while the West has moved into the first stage of a Spenglerian decline." That is Kissinger talking, in his own terms, "as a historian more than a statesman." But Podhoretz is at pains to stress that the two roles interpenetrate one another, in Kissinger's case. "According to this reading of his," the *Commentary* editor explains,

> a responsible statesman presented with such conditions by the inexorable movement of history will do what he can to insure an orderly retreat. . . . Thus there will be moments when a show of force will have to be mounted or an impresson of resolution conveyed. . . . Thus the bombing of Hanoi, the mining of Haiphong, the invasion of Laos and Cambodia looked to many people like a widening of the Vietnam war when, as everyone now knows, all these actions were actually a tactic in an overall strategy of withdrawal. . . . Instead of retreating in order to advance, we advanced in order to retreat. . . . In Vietnam, Nixon and Kissinger put pressure on a reluctant Saigon government to accept the Paris Accords. . .

— and thereby to accept defeat. In the case of Iran, Kissinger, out of office, left the ugly task of maneuvering the Shah into acceptance of defeat to his skilled collaborator of past times, William H. Sullivan. His own public time he gave over completely to the more "pleasant" side of his "defeatist interventionism": the side that called for "sticking with the Shah" in defeat "unto death, and beyond." Naturally, in all of that, he could count on full Republican partisan collusion, for it seemed a certainty from the start that the issue of Carter's treatment of the Shah "after he left" would prove decisive, one way or another, in the 1980 presidential campaign.

5. Admitting the Shah

When the Shah was being pressed by Ambassador Sullivan, General Huyser, Zbigniew Brzezinski, and President Carter to make up his mind about the role he ought to play in the mounting crisis of late 1978, he had received assurances, as we saw, that, if he chose to go on an "extended vacation," he would certainly be welcome in the United States. For that he was grateful. When he seemed to have fully accepted the offer, Carter very prudently turned to the Shah's closest friends and supporters in the United States for assistance in providing accommodations that would be serviceable yet not altogether public in an official sense. The first person he called was Henry Kissinger, not alone for what Kissinger could do on his own but for his connections with the Rockefeller brothers, David and Nelson. Kissinger quickly agreed to help, for he saw at once that helping would put him in a position to "stick with the Shah" in a quasi-official capacity. From the standpoint of his *"Realpolitik* for losers,"* in other words, it was an opportunity not to be missed.

Long after the whole thing had soured for the President, when, indeed, the U.S. Embassy in Tehran had been seized for a second time, Henry Kissinger, who was being widely blamed for having precipitated the worst of it, asked the Carter administration for "permission" to publish his version of the role he had played in getting the exiled Shah admitted to the United States in late October 1979. According to Kissinger, it took a 70-minute discussion with Secretary of State Cyrus Vance to iron out objections to what he wanted to say in his own behalf; and, when all was settled, the result was a long article published in the *Washington Post.*

There, Kissinger explained that his official involvement in the matter began in January 1979, when the Carter administration asked him "to help find a residence in the U.S. for the Shah." As expected, Kissinger had quickly called for David Rockefeller's assistance, since David had for decades been chief international banker for the Shah's Iran. Shortly before the Shah's death in 1980, a *New York Times* news article (June 28, 1980) would put it this way:

> In exile, the Shah had one major consolation: his vast fortune.
> Bankers in New York said just before he left Tehran that much

of his personal fortune, which was estimated as well over $1 billion, was outside Iran. Much of the $2 billion or more that had been transferred from Iran to the United States since 1976, they said, belonged to him and his relatives. The Pahlavi family's riches stemmed in part from vast land holdings built up by the Shah's father, from shares in many Iranian industrial enterprises and, critics contend, from the proceeds of corruption.

But David Rockefeller declined to help in finding a U.S. home for the Shah, justifying his refusal on the grounds that, in his words, he didn't want "to jeopardize his bank's relations with any of the contending factions in Iran." Speaking for Chase Manhattan Bank, he later added, when pressed on the matter: "We never feel that we're dealing primarily with a ruler, though you can't overlook him. We try to make loans that are sound for the country, that the successor regime will find comfortable." [Anthony Sampson, *Daily News,* Nov. 5, 1980, p. 19]

With the tact of a courtier — such as he would never employ in dealing with a mere President of the United States — Kissinger raised no quarrel with David Rockefeller's refusal. He simply turned from David to his brother Nelson. According to the published account, "just two weeks before he died, Nelson Rockefeller — Kissinger's old friend and mentor — had helped to find a suitable residence: the Palm Springs estate of Walter H. Annenberg," multimillionaire publisher who had served during the Kissinger-Nixon-Ford years as U.S. Ambassador to Britain.

But, after all of that was settled, the Shah abruptly changed his mind and turned down President Carter's offer of asylum. As Kissinger says, the Shah "did not seek a U.S. visa; instead, he went to Egypt and then Morocco." And nothing more was made of the matter of the Shah's residence in exile, at least from Kissinger's vantage point, until mid-March 1979. We know, however, that once the Shah had made his decision not to come, Kissinger, like a true friend, became worried about his safety elsewhere; so, with considerable publicity, the ex-Harvard professor "dispatched" one of his own "bodyguards" to join the Shah's entourage in exile for the purpose of training the Shah's cadre of bodyguards in the latest techniques for preventing assassinations!

Why had the Shah turned down President Carter's early offer of U.S. asylum? In public statements on the matter, the Shah explained that he had decided to remain as close as possible to his country, within the Islamic world, so that he could return at once when the expected "summons" to do so came. The Shah was concerned, he said, to secure the succession for his son — for the dynasty. That is why, also, he opposed a military coup. He wanted to leave behind a legitimate government of his choosing. Then, if a revolution led by Marxists or religious fanatics overthrew that government, the Shah and his son in exile would still be legitimate. They would immediately constitute a government in exile, recognized by all the nations that had always maintained *de jure* relations with his regime. A military coup by his own armed forces, designed to take the reins of government in order to *prevent* a revolution, would very likely have precisely the opposite effect. The result then would almost certainly be the establishment of a republic on the model of that of Kemal Ataturk — such as the Shah's own father had contemplated establishing when he first made his revolutionary bid for power.

Military counter-revolutionaries acting in the Shah's absence, in other words, could hardly be expected not to want to wipe the slate clean! That is why the Shah asked his "friends" abroad to support Bakhtiar's government and restrain the military. Evidently the Shah expected that Bakhtiar's government would soon fall, and that all the Shah's friends abroad would look upon the successor regime, especially if it were headed by religious fanatics, as illegitimate. So that it would also, in turn, collapse. At which point the military would need a Pahlavi to justify their counter-revolutionary bid for power, calling it a restoration.

Needless to say, things didn't happen that way. When Bakhtiar's government fell, virtually all the foreign friends of the Shah, including the U.S., sought to do business with and recognize the successor regime. That had been foreseen by Walter Eytan, the Israeli diplomat and journalist, long before the fact. He had predicted that only the Israelis would be cut out of doing business with the new Islamic government. We have seen how eagerly the Bazargan government sought to retain the good will of the U.S. and other oil-consuming nations, while making the Bakhtiar government's new position on Israel its own.

Despite all that, President Carter had indeed offered the Shah asylum, and the Shah had turned it down. Had he accepted the offer at the time it was made, that fact would have registered itself as one of the givens of the revolutionary situation. It would no doubt have marked the low point in strained relations between the U.S. and the new regime in Iran. Yet, from that low point, it would have been possible to start to build on the strength of matched interests, with the question of the Shah left more or less out of account. What happened instead was that the U.S. and the new Iran moved quickly toward normalization, with the Shah completely on his own, outside the United States. The happy result of the intervention of the Ayatollah's commandos to "save" the American embassy on February 14, and restore its possession to the American Ambassador, had set the pace for normalizaton, as we have seen. And it was shortly after that happy event that the Carter administration made its gravest mistake with respect to Kissinger. It again asked him to intervene, this time to inform the Shah that he had better not think of coming to the United States until "feelings" in both the United States and Iran were brought under better control.

Only in retrospect, after the hostage crisis of November 1979 had begun, were the facts about that second Carter appeal to Kissinger for help made known, by others, first, and then by Kissinger himself. The December 10, 1979 issue of *Time*, for instance, summed up Kissinger's account as follows:

> In mid-March, said Kissinger, a State Department official asked him to advise the Shah not to seek admittance to the U.S. until emotions calmed in Tehran. Said Kissinger: "I refused with some indignation." Kissinger and David Rockefeller thereupon both asked the Government to help the Shah seek asylum in another country. Says Kissinger: "We were told that no official assistance of any kind was contemplated. This I considered deeply wrong and still do." [37]

By that time, the Carter administration had been grooming Lloyd Cutler to replace Sullivan as ambassador in Tehran. The Ayatollah's government had agreed to Cutler's appointment, as we saw, and the U.S. Senate had quickly confirmed it. That was when Senator Jacob

Javits launched his crusade for an official Senate condemnation of the Khomeini regime in terms previously reserved for the likes of Hitler. The Carter White House appealed to Kissinger to convey a request to the Shah. There was much talk that the Shah might suddenly announce his intention to "reunite" his family in the United States. That, said the Carter Spokesmen, could seriously upset an already delicate diplomatic balance. But "upset it" was exactly what Henry Kissinger had a mind to do, for he had by then actively joined the campaign to defeat President Carter in his 1980 bid for reelection.

For the events of April 1979 regarding the Shah, we have Gary Sick's apt appraisal. By the start of the month, he writes, "David Rockefeller, Henry Kissinger, and John McCloy" were maintaining

> a drum fire of appeals for the Shah to be admitted to the United States. Kissinger called Brzezinski on April 7, and at Brzezinski's suggestion, followed up with a phone call to President Carter. David Rockefeller saw President Carter two days later and raised the issue again. Carter was irritated by these approaches and rejected them. Kissinger responded with a speech on April 9 attacking the Carter administration for treating the Shah "like a Flying Dutchman looking for a port of call." [180]

By late April 1979, as the April 23 issue of *Time* reported, Kissinger was saying that he was utterly "appalled" by the Carter administration's decision to take back its original offer of asylum, and he was dismissing as spurious its suggestions that admitting the Shah would create "enormous security problems," as well as "difficulties. . .in improving relations with the new revoluionary government."

Despite his personal irritation, Carter responded to the pressure by sounding out the embassy in Tehran about the matter. The reply from the chargé d'affaires, Bruce Laingen, in early May — after arrangements had been made for the Shah's children to continue their education in the United States — was that there would be "serious problems" if the Shah himself or his wife were admitted. Then, in late July, Laingen was asked if it would make a difference if the Shah's entry were "accompanied by formal renunciation of his claim to the throne and his public agreement to forswear political activity while in the United States." The chargé's reply was that such renunciations and forswearing would be looked upon with much suspicion and would be "prejudicial to U.S. interests," at least for the present. Finally, in late September, during a brief stay in Washington, Laingen told Vance that the "very tenuous U.S.-Iranian relations could not weather the shock of the Shah's arrival in the United States," giving reasons that Vance later made public in a speech before the Council on Foreign Relations in New York.

The remarkable fact is that, despite the powerful forces at work to disrupt things, relations between the U.S. and Iran continued to improve on through the summer and into the fall of 1979. At the time of Vance's New York speech on why the Shah should not be admitted, some of the highest Iranian officials — persons closest to the Ayatollah Khomeini — were negotiating with American officials about the most essential matters in U.S.-Iranian relations. A news report of those days called attention to the fact that "Ibrahim Yazdi, who had been one of Khomeini's closest courtiers during the Ayatollah's last days of exile in France," and who had personally "secured the release of American diplomats during the earlier, and much briefer (two hours) embassy siege of last February 14," had talked with Secretary of State Vance "at the U.N. for four hours about military supplies for Iran and the future of U.S.-Iran relations." Certainly, at that time, "Vance came away from the meeting thinking that the Bazargan government was acquiring more authority over the rabble-rousing mullahs who surround Khomeini." [*Time,* Nov. 26, 1979, pp. 23-24]

It seemed for the moment that, despite tremendous extra-governmental pressures, the Carter administration might be able to muddle its way through to genuinely normalized relations. Still, there were the President's political advisers always on hand with polls showing how decisions about admitting the Shah might decide the outcome of the 1980 election. One "false move" might end his chances completely. But, which move would be "false"?

During the summer and fall of 1979, President Carter became increasingly aware that his partisan opponents, in his own Democratic Party as well as in the Republican Party, were waiting impatiently to take advantage of *whatever* he might be forced to do, or not do, by developing circumstances. The question became: what would hurt

Carter more, excluding a sick Shah, or admitting a symbol of autocratic tyranny, a darling of the Republicans, much hated by a most vocal faction of Democrats, with Senator Edward Kennedy in the lead? Woodrow Wilson had had a similar dilemma, when he was most eager to enter World War I on the side of England to fight the German Kaiser. Wilson had been asked: what about the Russian Czar? Doesn't Czar mean the same as Kaiser? Before he could "honorably" lead his country into war on the "right" side, Wilson had had to let forces be mounted to overthrow the Czar and establish a republic, however temporarily, in Czarist Russia!

Carter himself, it is now clear, was not in the least inclined, on his own, to admit the Shah — once the Shah had refused the initial presidential offer of asylum. But, with the extra-governmental champions of the Shah strenuously at work, the President, in the late summer and fall of 1979, began to visualize what might happen when a decision would finally have to be made. The danger was that the Shah might die, like a man without a country, after having been refused admission to the U.S.; or worse, that his admission even for humanitarian or medical reasons might cause that to happen at the American Embassy in Tehran which did in fact happen! After the event, classified documents found in the embassy by the hostage-takers of November 4 were made public; and among them was a memo from Bruce Laingen which said: "We should not take any steps in the direction of admitting the Shah until such time as we have been able to prepare an effective and essential force for the protection of the embassy." President Carter had often heard recommendations advising that the guard-unit at the embassy be strengthened — to which he had aptly and typically replied: "No embassy on earth is a fortress that can withstand constant attacks by a mob unless the host government comes to the rescue of the people within the embassy."

Was it true that the ailing Shah needed medical services — examinations and treatments by specialists — which were not available in other parts of the world? It had been well known that the Shah was dying of cancer. What was being claimed by Henry Kissinger and the Rockefeller people, at the time, was that some new complication had set in that required diagnosis. It was a claim difficult to contradict, since the Rockefeller people, at Henry Kissinger's request, had called upon the most prestigious doctors available to say that only New York City facilities were up to the task of making a thorough analysis and diagnosis. Moreover, there was the added Kissinger threat that, if the Shah were to die from his cancer ailment prematurely, after having been denied entry by the Carter administration, that fact might well have a human-interest impact on the American electorate decisive enough to defeat Carter's bid for re-election in 1980.

Although it appears that some of Carter's advisers had heard more optimistic reports about the Shah's condition, the President has insisted that the "choice presented to him" in those days was indeed, as the *New York Times* paraphrased, "to admit the Shah for medical treatment that was only available in this country or watch an ally of 37 years die in Mexico for lack of such treatment." [May 13, 1981]

Gary Sick and President Carter himself have left us accounts of the White House foreign policy breakfast meeting where Carter finally gave in to pressures to admit the Shah. It was October 19, 1979, a Friday. As Gary Sick represents it, Secretary of State Cyrus Vance brought in the "startling news" that the Shah might really be seriously ill — that he probably had obstructive jaundice, requiring immediate surgery, complicated by a cancerous spleen and a cancerous tumor in the neck that no longer responded to treatment, added to uncertainties about the extent of the Shah's lymphoma. On the strength of that "startling news," Secretary Vance had concluded, as Sick puts it, "that the United States could not in good conscience refuse the Shah access to medical treatment"; and he therefore "now recommended permitting the Shah to enter the country." [183]

In President Carter's account of the same breakfast meeting, we are told simply that Secretary Vance had there "made it obvious that he was prepared to admit the Shah for medical reasons." And Carter adds dolefully: "I was now the lone holdout." But he then reluctantly gave his approval "in principle," meaning by that that those present could "proceed on the assumption that the Shah would be admitted, subject to confirmation of Vance's preliminary infor-

mation 'about the state of the Shah's health'.'' Gary Sick adds at
this point: "But Carter had no illusion about the risks involved.
Looking at his assembled group of advisers, he wondered aloud what
advice they would give him when the Iranians took the embassy in
Tehran and held Americans hostage. Unfortunately, his sardonic
comment was to prove more prophetic than he had expected." [184]

Carter gives his account, here, a slightly different emphasis. "I
asked my advisers," he writes, "what course they would recommend
to me if the Americans in Iran were seized or killed." Secretary Vance
understood that the President was referring particularly to the embassy personnel, and therefore qualified his approval of admitting
the Shah with a suggestion, as President Carter explains, "that we
get another assessment of the question from Tehran." A call was
placed to the American Embassy in Tehran. It happened that Henry Precht, chief of the Iran desk in the State Department, had just
arrived in Tehran when the call from Washington was received. To
supply what was asked for, Laingen and Precht together called on
Prime Minister Bazargan and acting Foreign Minister Ibrahim Yazdi, top officials of the Iranian government. Laingen described the
situation in Washington for them, and he was at pains to indicate
that the decision to admit the Shah was being taken for purely humanitarian reasons, that there was no partisan or political motivation at work. He added that it was not a matter of offering the Shah
permanent asylum.

For Bazargan and Yazdi, there could hardly have been any less
welcome news. They were not persuaded that there was no political
motivation. But, on the other hand, as Laingen and Precht reported, the two officials were clearly surprised to learn of the advanced
state of the Shah's illness — revealing that the true story, in this case,
had indeed been kept secret, despite the widely held view that Iran
was supposed to be a "porous rumor mill." [185] Bazargan and Yazdi
then asked for confirmation, by Iranian doctors, of the reported state
of the Shah's health, and they supplied the names of Iranian doctors in America who could examine the Shah in their behalf. Laingen transmitted the names to Washington; but he, in turn, then asked
the Iranian officials to provide additional protection for the Embassy
and for Americans in Iran generally. Additional police, in fact, ap-

peared the next day, taking up positions around the Embassy, under the personal supervision of Tehran's chief of police. And, as Sick notes, those additional police "remained on duty in the days that followed." [185]

Laingen and Precht had met with the top Iranian officials on October 21, 1979. On the same day, upon receiving their report, President Carter gave the order to admit the Shah. Even then he made clear that he would admit the Shah only for medical need, that he wouldn't tolerate his posing for photographers on tennis courts, or shopping with his family, as he had posed in other "havens" of his exile. At any rate, the Shah arrived in New York by chartered jet on October 22, 1979.

The White House attitude, thereafter, was to wait and see. It was, after all, conceivable that the two "responsible" governments, in Washington and Tehran, might have a sufficient "authority," between them, to enable them to weather the expected storm, generated in both countries by the activities of extra-governmental factions. Carter waited to see, and the first developments he saw, coming on the heels of the Shah's admittance, were, from his vantage-point, very encouraging. Indeed, in some respects, the days immediately following the event were characterized by what seemed to be spectacular improvements in U.S.-Iranian relations on top governmental levels.

6. Reasons of State vs. the Claims of "Humanity"

In retrospect, it would seem obvious to many that admitting the Shah to the United States had been mistakenly viewed by the "secularist" powers in both countries as a matter devoid of religious significance. It is relatively easy to forget that, by adopting a pre-Islamic "dynastic" name and claiming to hold a throne with a continuous history dating back to c. 500 BC, the Pahlavis had boldly proclaimed their intention to play down the Islamic character of their country and its people, even as Egypt's Sadat had done the same by reveling in his country's King Tut inheritance. Playing down their Muslim identities helped both Egypt and Iran to have friendly relations with otherwise hated israel. But, people who know the power of religion in the Middle East saw the inevitable consequences. Israel had remained a Jewish state in seeking friendly, or shared-interest relations with the Shah's iran and Sadat's Egypt. But the Shah and Sadat had not remained very Islamic in reciprocating. Paying for the secular compromise should have been perceived everywhere as inevitable.

The head of the Iran desk in the State Department, Director for Iranian Affairs Henry Precht, would later say: "I think the one constant theme that obsessed the movement against the Shah, in both the leaders of the revolution and the followers, was a fear that the United States would repeat 1953 (when the Shah was restored to his throne with U.S. help) in destroying Iran's revolution. The secular people sometimes tried to woo us; the religious people tried to destroy all connections with us. When we brought the Shah to New York, it fueled those suspicions. . . . No government, no force in Iran, could support the United States when a question of the Shah was involved." [43]

Why, then, did President Carter who saw instinctively the religious difficulty, let himself be persuaded to admit the Shah? Gary Sick gives us an insider's view from a double perspective. Carter would not have let himself be persuaded by Republican partisan pressure. Moreover, everyone else in his administration appears to have been persuaded to admit the Shah before he was. Why did Secretary of State Vance persist in approving the Shah's admittance for health reasons, even after hearing the President ask what advice his "advisers" would give after Americans in Tehran were seized and perhaps killed? Was there possibly an element of political expediency? And what could political expediency mean under the circumstances? Was it certain how many in the U.S. foreign-policy entourage on Carter's presidential watch really wanted him to be reelected as president? Gary Sick, well aware that Vance felt more comfortable with a William H. Sullivan than with a "Jimmy" Carter, nevertheless raises the possibility of political expediency — but only to dismiss it in these terms: "No one who knows Cyrus Vance could seriously suggest that he would have exposed the personnel of the department to serious risks in the hopes that it might somehow improve the president's standings in the polls." [186] That is patently true. President Carter had repeatedly said that admitting the Shah to the United States just so that he could be seen "playing tennis several hours a day in California instead of in Acapulco" was not an idea that particularly recommended itself to him. [JC 453]

But, did the fact of the Shah's extremely bad state of health weigh heavily enough in the political balance, finally, to persuade Carter to give up his lonely stand? "It would be naive," writes Sick,

> to argue that President Carter and his advisers were oblivious to the political consequences of the decision.... President Carter could scarcely have hoped that this decision would suddenly improve his political fortunes. However, he could be certain that if he refused to allow the Shah access to medical treatment in the United States — possibly contributing to his death — he would be seriously criticized...by virtually all Americans, who would have seen his refusal as an abject rejection of humanitarian traditions. So far as I could tell, President Carter felt exactly the same way. Once the seriousness of the Shah's condition became known, there was simply no question of refusing him medical attention. [186]

There we have an example of a fateful decision taken on humanitarian grounds that could only too easily be perceived as politically motivated in a variety of seemingly contradictory ways. Could a purely humanitarian motivation have sufficed for Secretary of State Vance and President Carter to run the risk of exposing American personnel in Tehran to extreme danger? The mass of Iranian supporters of the revolution could not be persuaded that it was not part of an American plot to restore the Shah, as in 1953. What about the mass of Americans? Did they think it worth the potential risk to American personnel in Tehran? We have the word of an American Marine who lived through the 444-days of TV coverage of the hostage crisis as one of the hostages. In an interview of January 20, 1982, on the anniversary of his release as a hostage, former U.S. Marine Paul Lewis was asked whether he thought there were any lessons to be learned from his ordeal. He answered reluctantly with questions of his own — "transforming a public issue," as the journalist interviewing him put it, "into an intensely personal matter."

"Why," the ex-Marine asked, "did we have an Iran crisis in the first place? Why did Washington admit the Shah and ignore the warnings about an embassy take-over? Why was the government willing to endanger the lives of everyone in the embassy?" The former serviceman said he was proud to have served as a loyal Marine throughout the trying experience. He stressed the fact that he would forever treasure an American flag with his name on it that he had received from President Reagan in the White House welcome-home ceremony. Then, with great seriousness, he explained: "I did my part in the crisis. But until it provides some answers my country hasn't done its part in return. And that is going to bother me much longer than any problems I had as a hostage." [Source: "The Hostages One Year Later," by Arnold Abrams, *Newsday*, January 20, 1982, pp. 2-5]

One can easily share that ex-Marine's feeling that there can be no easy "humanitarian" or "political" explanation for the decision to admit the Shah taken in late October 1979. Much was said in those days about Henry Kissinger's motives in rallying the Rockefeller establishment behind his extra-governmental maneuvers to pressure President Carter to admit the Shah. Was Kissinger prompted in all of that by his yearning to earn a high place for himself in a victorious new Republican administration? It would be a mistake, one must conclude, to give such a "low reading" to Kissinger's motives — though ambition of that sort was certainly a factor. Kissinger did indeed make humanitarian appeals of the kind that ultimately persuaded Secretary of State Vance. But, in fact, at no time did he depart significantly, during his labors to get the Shah into the United States, from the main line of his so-called Nixon doctrine, which had guided him in closing out the Vietnam war.

That doctrine, as we have repeatedly noted, consisted essentially in forcing client states, wholly dependant on American support for their security, to pretend to function as "allies," as peers with sovereign responsibilities. As allies, they could be asked and required to be full "partners" in their own defense, so that, if they manifestly failed to do enough for themselves, we could abandon them to their own resources, requiring them to "stand on their own two legs" even when its was plain to all that they had no legs to stand on. To reward their "loyalty" as allies, the Nixon doctrine of American defeatist interventionism or no-win belligerency required of us that we remain their steadfast supporters in defeat. Thus we were repeatedly treated to the spectacle of Henry Kissinger begging the American Congress to vote "continued support" when the cause was absolutely lost — not to turn defeat into victory, but for old-time's sake. That's what Kissinger did to keep us locked with the Thieu government in defeat right down to April 30, 1975. That's what he did with respect to Angola, where he asked for continued support for "our" side — not to reverse the defeat in process, but as a gesture of abiding good will. And that's what he forced our country to do after the Shah's fall, even while our government in Washington was laboring, in accordance with the best Western/European diplomatic traditions, to normalize relations, in a civilized fashion, with the successor regime. The irony is, of course, that Kissinger's Disraelian strategy of "sticking with the loser," so that it will be clear that we have always meant to lose with him (to avoid the threat of a "nuclear holocaust"), has been passed off by many die-hard Republican partisans as a matter of *Realpolitik* for the nuclear age! In the case of the Shah, Kissinger proved that private citizens can indeed make American foreign policy on their own, and even bring down a President in the process.

7. Last False Hopes: The Brzezinski-Yazdi-Bazargan Meeting in Algiers

Had this not been the age of instant mass-media communications, one could have concluded, by the end of October 1979, that a triumph of quiet international diplomacy was somehow on the verge of being brought off, despite all the "fuss" about the Shah. Here are the facts: On November 1, Zbigniew Brzezinski, Carter's national security adviser, was scheduled to be in Algiers for an Islamic anniversary celebration. When Laingen in Tehran learned of Brzezinski's scheduled trip, he noted that the three top officials of the Iranian revolutionary government would also be there. The three were the Prime Minister, Bazargan, the acting Foreign Minister, Yazdi, and the Minister of Defense, Mustapha Ali Chamran. As Gary Sick reports, Laingen then "urged that Brzezinski, or others in the U.S. delegation, meet with the Iranians, in the belief that 'the more contact with this group the better'."

Laingen next called on Bazargan to suggest at least an informal meeting with members of the American delegation. Bazargan expressed interest. And when they arrived in Algiers, the Iranians got in touch with Brzezinski, who agreed to meet with them. Their meeting turned out to be, in appearance, at least, the high-point in post-revolutionary Iranian-U.S. diplomatic relations. As Sick stresses, until that moment, Brzezinski had qualified as "the harshest U.S. critic of the revolution." In his talks with the Iranian officials in Algiers, he took note of the fact that they were disturbed about the Shah's presence in the United States. They saw it as an added obstacle to normalized relations. But, in conversations like those between Robert McFarlane, Oliver North, General Richard Secord, and Albert Hachim and unnamed Iranian officials almost a decade later, Bazargan and his colleagues frankly discussed and came to share with Brzezinski, in November 1979, his evaluation of the "strategic interests that Iran and the United States had in common," and they expressly welcomed his words about the "possibility of cooperation, including the possibility of continued U.S. military aid." [189]

On the other hand, unlike the later meetings with members of Ronald Reagan's White House staff, the meeting of November 1, 1979 was public — with an international "photo session" at its close. There can be no doubt that Brzezinski, when he returned to Washington, was "quite positive," as Gary Sick says, "in his evaluation of the three Iranian leaders as intelligent and sensible men who impressed him with their seriousness of purpose and their realistic appraisal of the problems facing the new revolutionary regime." Harold H. Saunders, a leading State Department spokesman, would later observe that the brief meeting in Algiers that seemed to change the picture of developing relations had "not been part of any strategy plotted in Washington." [*Amer. Hostages in Iran*, p. 43] It no doubt served to relieve some fears in the White House as to what might have happened to Americans in Tehran because of the Shah's entry into the United States. But, as already noted, photographers had taken pictures in Algiers, and particularly pictures of Yazdi and Bazargan shaking hands with Brzezinski.

Imagine if pictures had been taken, years later, when McFarlane, North, and Hachim met with Iranian officials for talks in London, Frankfurt, or Tehran? One thinks of a picture of North and Manucher Ghorbanifar, "an Iranian arms dealer identified by U.S. intelligence as an Israeli agent," coming out of a hotel men's room, after the Iranian "Israeli agent" had offered North a milion dollar personal bribe, promised to arrange a meeting with high Iranian officials, and "proposed sending some proceeds to the Nicaraguan rebels, known as Contras," an idea which, as Ghorbanifar put it, had the "full knowledge and acquiescence and support" of Israel. [*Wall Street Journal*, Aug. 3, 1987]

The pictures taken of U.S. and Iranian officials shaking hands in Algiers on November 1, 1979, made the front pages in Iranian as well as American papers. The consequence was that opponents of normalized relations in both countries could quickly point accusing fingers. We know how reluctant the Reagan White House was to disclose the fact that Iranian officials had met with Americans secretly, to begin the process of reshaping responsible U.S.-Iranian relations in the late 1980s. Reagan said at that time that revelation of the transactions agreed to could jeopardize the lives of the Iranian officials involved as well as of the Americans held hostage in Beirut. That his fears were justified is amply shown by what happened in November 1979. In this respect, Gary Sick notes the double irony of the fact that, by "visibly swaying" the judgment of President Carter's National Security Adviser, Zbigniew Brzezinski, in favor of the Iranian leaders, that brief but much photographed meeting in Algiers "provided the excuse four days later for expelling Bazargan and Yazdi from the government." Such is the power of the press to topple Iranian "moderates" among other things, while serving the global public's right to know!

CHAPTER TWELVE

The Second
Embassy Seizure:
First Phase

Lecturing Geraldine Ferraro, the Democratic Party's candidate for Vice President in the 1984 presidential election, on the difference "between Iran and the embassy in Lebanon," Vice President George Bush said without qualification: "Iran — we were held by a foreign government. In Lebanon you had a wanton terrorist action where the goverment opposed it." There can be no doubt that George Bush was supported in that judgment by almost all official U.S. government statements on the matter — provided we limit ourselves to official statements made *after* March 1980.

Indeed, from November 4, 1979, when the U.S. Embassy in Tehran was attacked the second time, to early April 1980 — a period of five months — the government of the United States acted and spoke as if it fully believed that the November attack had been mounted in complete defiance of the will of the Ayatollah Khomeini, even though the attackers had from the outset claimed to be acting, not on the Ayatollah's orders — that was *never* claimed — but in his behalf. Through that five-month period, the head of the American Embassy in Tehran, Chargé d'Affaires L. Bruce Laingen, was in no sense a hostage. He had not been in the embassy when it was seized, and the Iranian government had quickly moved to provide him with full ambassadorial accommodations in ample quarters at the Iranian Foreign Ministry, its equivalent of the U.S. State Department. There, constantly operative phone lines were put at his disposal, enabling him to speak directly to the U.S. State Department and the White House and to communicate with the seized embassy.

During those five months, Laingen, who was always free to leave Iran, never represented himself as being held hostage. On the contrary, he repeatedly stressed his belief that the Iranian government was all the while attempting to do everything possible to restore control of the embassy to him; and also, that it had not ever presumed to take any action toward that end without consulting him. The intention at all times was not to put the lives of the American hostages at risk, as had occurred in Afghanistan earlier in the year. It was not forgotten that, on February 14, 1979, when Ambassador Sullivan had been seized in the Tehran embassy, the U.S. Ambassador to Afghanistan, Adolph "Spike" Dubs, had also been seized — "abducted on his way to work." Washington had asked the Soviet-backed government not to put the ambassador's life at risk. But the government ordered an attack to recover control anyway, in the course of which the American ambassador was killed. By contrast, back in February, the Ayatollah's government had effectively protected the entire Tehran embassy staff; and, on November 4, it assured Laingen that it would intervene forcefully only when, and if, authorized to do so by Washington.

What we have been briefly reviewing is, without a doubt, the most important fact about the second seizure of the Tehran embassy in 1979. For the serious historian, it is *the* critical fact, ignoring which makes an adequate understanding of the 444-day crisis impossible. By the end of March, the Carter administration gave up its belief that the Ayatollah's government could succeed in a peaceful recovery of the embassy; but even then it did not give authorization for a forceful counter-attack. Instead, in collusion with elements in the Iranian military establishment, it half-heartedly undertook the unfortunate rescue attempt of late April that so dismayed Secretary of State Cyrus Vance that he resigned over it.

Yet even after that failed rescue mission, the Ayatollah's government persisted in treating Laingen and the two other embassy diplomats who came with him to the Iranian Foreign Ministry with proper diplomatic courtesy — never in any sense as "captives," held against their will. In fact, as President Carter tells us in his presidential memoirs (1982), that remained so until all the Americans of the Embassy were finally brought together for their official release and flight out of Iran. Commenting on a diary entry for early January 1981, Carter notes: "The Iranians moved Bruce Laingen and his fellow diplomats from the foreign-ministry building to another location, presumably so that they could be with the other forty-nine. This move concerned me very much, because the three had never before been considered prisoners — merely diplomats in residence." [592]

But, we must review the matter in some detail. We mentioned in the preceding chapter that, by the time of the Shah's fall, the only "property" the United States still officially possessed in Iran that it could possibly "lose" was still just that same embassy that had been seized on St. Valentine's Day 1979, while Sullivan was in charge. Back then, the successor regime had acted quickly to restore American control. At the time, as we saw, the disappointed radicals who mounted that armed attack had vowed revenge. Never again, they said, would the Ayatollah's government have such an easy time of it in dealing with true militants. We noted the fact that, in those same days, the Israeli mission in Tehran had been similarly seized, and the response of the Ayatollah had been not merely to congratulate the attackers but to hand the whole mission over to Arafat's P.L.O. Why hadn't the response been the same in the case of the American Embassy? Instead, after being "congratulated" for their "revolutionary fervor," the St. Valentine's Day attackers were told to lay down their arms, free their hostages, and remove themselves from the premises instantly. Otherwise, the Deputy Prime Minister Ibrahim Yazdi had told them, they would be treated as persons engaged in a "conspiracy against Khomeini."

Interviewed immediately after the event, leaders of that first attack explained to American newsmen that they viewed with contempt the Ayatollah's first ministry, headed by the likes of Bazargan and Yazdi. They charged that Khomeini was being led astray by his appointees, and especially by Bazargan who, in their view, was as much a pro-American liberal as the Shah's last Prime Minister, Shahpour Bakhtiar. All the Ayatollah had done, they said, was replace a Tweedle-Dee with a Tweedle-Dum. And we cited the words of an American-educated militant girl known as "Mary," who said, "I'm not happy with the Bazargan government. It's like the Pahlavi regime, but with a different name"; and also: "We don't accept the

Cabinet, and if everyone listens to the Ayatollah, we won't have a revolutionary republic. Iran is not just for the mullahs.''

That first attack on the American Embassy clearly did not produce the results intended by its militant leaders, which had been to cause friction between the Ayatollah and his first appointees, and between the Ayatollah's government as a whole and the United States. On the contrary, the Ayatollah fully backed his appointees against the embassy attackers, and, as we have seen, relations with the United States rapidly improved. In fact, those relations did not begin to deteriorate until "partisans of the Shah" in America began to take much publicized steps to get the Shah admitted into the country. Also contributing to the deterioration, as we saw, was the successful pressure to get a censure resolution against the Ayatollah's government passed unanimously in the U.S. Senate. Even so, the American Embassy was still there, on the heights of Tehran, ever a temptation to local enemies of normalized relations — particulary after Ambassador Sullivan, who had enlisted revolutionary commandos for its protection, had gone home.

1. The Embassy After Sullivan

We need to remind ourselves that, under the Shah, the number of people working at the U.S. Embassy in Tehran had risen at one point as high as 1,500. The figure had plummeted to 73 when the Shah left. It is known that Sullivan had made plans to reduce the staff personnel to six — in effect, closing everything down, so that the chief occupants of the compound would have been the Ayatollah's elite commandos, many of them occupying what had formerly been the embassy quarters of the Marine guards. We earlier examined the "disposition" Sullivan had made of his three units of commando guards, some of which he positioned in the compound, to guard his residence, others to guard the embassy perimeter, and still others to accompany him, for safety, around the city.

After Sullivan left for Washington, or, at any rate, by the time L. Bruce Laingen assumed his duties as chargé d'affaires in mid-June, "reforms" were undertaken to bring things back to normal.

First among Laingen's changes was the removal of Col. Leland J. Holland from the special duties that Sullivan had assigned him when it first appeared that the embassy might be attacked. Holland not only stayed on after Sullivan left, but was among the hostages taken on November 4, 1979. When he was finally released with the rest of the Americans, he had a lot to say about "embassy security." And he was much interviewed on the subject primarily because he was highly critical of what Laingen had done and full of praise for Sullivan's "plans" for the embassy, which, because of Sullivan's abrupt departure in early April, were never carried out.

Holland and Sullivan have left us a rather full, though partisan, account of what became of "embassy security" during the nine months of nearly normalized relations "between embassy seizures." Both of them tell us that, in December 1978, after "an unsuccessful attempt" by a street mob to "breach the compound," Sullivan had abruptly relieved Holland of his regular duties as military attaché to assign him those of a security officer. By then, Sullivan had completed his 180 degree reversal regarding the Shah, which had so upset President Carter. He was then determined to clean out the embassy, to destroy all compromising documents, including, no doubt, the evidences of his dealings with the Iranian military to get them to abandon both the Shah and the Shah's last prime minister. Holland was evidently pleased with the assignment. In a February 1981 interview with Karen De Witt, after his release as a hostage, he explained how good a job he had done back in January and early February 1979. As De Witt reported it (2/8/81). Holland insisted that when Iranian militants entered the embassy on St. Valentine's Day, "there wasn't anything in the embassy that was worth American lives. . .not a piece of paper" that the attackers could exploit for propaganda purposes.

"Unfortunately," when Bruce Laingen took over, he undid all Sullivan had done. He removed Holland from his security post and restored him to his regular embassy duties. And the result, says Holland, was that when the embassy was again seized on November 4, 1979, the attackers had a field day with documents they found or were able to piece together from shredded remains that had not been effectively destroyed. The mistake that Laingen made, according to

Holland, had been to move too hastily in bringing "embassy opera-tions" back to "business as usual," even though it was not then "a business as usual situation." Thus, when the second attack occurred, the militants found ready at hand the "volume of documents that had accumulated since mid-June" — documents that soon became the basis of interrogations and accusations publicized around the world, and putting many lives at risk.

But there is more to be told about Holland. As Sullivan's chief of security, Holland was assigned the duties of embassy liaison with the revolutionary guards that Sullivan had asked.for from the Ayatol-lah's government. In that capacity, he put in much time among them, fraternizing with their leaders, who came to regard him as their American commander even as they looked upon Sullivan as "their" ambassador. Sullivan says in *Obligato* (1984) simply that all those Khomeini guards functioned "under the general supervision of our military attaché, who developed a close working relationship with them." Certainly the pair of them, Sullivan as well as Holland, came to be looked upon as the leading "pro-Khomeini Americans" in Iran — Americans who had indeed "joined the opposition to the Shah" even while the Carter administration was still seeking, with some desperation, to sustain the Shah, first, and after his decision to leave, the government of his prime minister. In fact, Holland himself tells us that, when the second attack occurred, its leaders immediately turned to him to enlist his collaboration. "They knew me," he ac-knowledges, "from my days at the gate [as Sullivan's chief of secu-rity] and they had my records, so they knew I was military intelligence." And he says further: "When they questioned me, they said they wanted to get the goods on Iranians who had dealt with Americans. They wanted to know who the Iranian officers were that I talked to and what they did. They had the telephone list."

In other words, the November 4 "militants" had the list of phone numbers of compromised generals and other officials kept by the embassy. Holland has insisted that he did not give his cap-tors "any additional information." His concern was to stress rather that, because of Laingen's reversal of Sullivan's practices, the cap-tors did in fact gain possession of papers, still intact, that "gave them insight into how the embassy works, information about economic ventures, visas, and the names of Iranian who had contacted the embassy for one reason or another."

Surely it would have been utterly naive of Holland, or Sullivan, to suppose that commandos sent in by Bazargan and Yazdi to rescue the embassy on February 14 and then to serve as its interior as well as exterior guards would limit themselves to ordinary guard duties while enjoying the run of the place, so to speak. In *Iran Under the Ayatollahs* (1985), Dilip Hiro, in fact, suggest one very important thing those revolutionary guards probably achieved during their extended tour of duty at the American embassy. Soon after Bakhtiar's ouster, Hiro points out, the new revolutionary government seized and put on trial Nematollah Nassery, who had been head of SAVAK from April 1965 to June 1978. His interrogators drew out of him, says Hiro, the fact SAVAK had had an "undercover agent, codenamed Hafiz, inside the US embassy in Tehran." Once identified, that agent was contacted by the Central Revolutionary Komiteh of the Ayatollah Khomeini's government.

"Since Hafiz was neither Iranian nor American," Hiro explains, "he felt vulnerable," and therefore hastened to cooperate. He was offered "immunity if he would continue the past activity. . . . Before he was allowed to leave the country in early September, he passed on two sets of documents to Hojtalislam Hashemi-Rafsanjani, then deputy minister of the interior. These documents contained secret cables exchanged between Cyrus Vance and Sullivan and later Bruce Laingen." They showed, among other things, that efforts were being made to admit the Shah to the U.S. [137]

Hiro says that a desire to get more such information, after Laingen's reforms removed "Sullivan's commandos," brought on a high-level decision to mount another "invasion" of the embassy. Hiro would have us believe that Khomeini's 35-year-old son, Hojatalislam Ahmed Khomeini, had been "put in over-all charge" of the attack, the planning of which had allegedly been facilitated by the fact that its organizers had been supplied with "the detailed layout and plans of the American embassy complex in central Tehran" before they started their recruitment of the "forty to fifty of their hardcore supporters on the project." [137] Whether or not the Ayatollah's son was actually involved (Hiro is hardly a Khomeini admirer), there can be little doubt that, in those days, the leaders of the militants might well have had the impression that Sullivan and Holland, who had worked so hard to make a peaceful transfer of the allegiance of most of the Iranian military over to the Ayatollah, would sympathize with and support their efforts to keep the revolutionary process on a radical course.

It should be recalled that Sullivan, in his memoirs, underscores the fact that, in bringing the revolutionary commandos into the embassy compound as guards, he had made an "unorthodox decision. . .in contravention of all diplomatic practice." [275] We cited earlier Sullivan's account of the uses to which be put those guards, including the very unit, "headed by a huge, hairy butcher named Marshallah," which had liberated the embassy on February 14. But Sullivan also mentions in his memoirs that, after he left the embassy in April 1979, those guard units began to get themselves in trouble, by pushing to excess some of the assignments they had taken on while serving Sullivan. Of the smaller unit of guards protecting the ambassadorial residence, Sullivan says that they had taken over the task of supervising the embassy's "outgoing air freight." And more specifically, as he says:

> This function developed as we sought some way to ship out the household possessions of our departing staff without subjecting them to pilferage. For some informal considerations, we engaged the group to "ride shotgun" on our shipments from the embassy to the airport and through the mujahidin guards that controlled the airport departures. This soon led to a share in airport departure controls, and, in due course, to a shakedown racket in which they "rescued" a number of expensive carpets from departing baggage and reclaimed them as "national treasures." When some of their rivals in the business denounced them, after my departure, most of them were arrested. [276]

One must not miss the point that Sullivan makes about "informal considerations" to get those guards to ride shotgun on shipments of personal possessions from the embassy to the airport, etc. Sullivan may have viewed it as a centurion's initiative; but, had he had as unfavorable a media environment to work in as, say, General

Richard Secord, Albert Hachim, and Colonel Oliver North had in the early days of the Iran-Contra congressional hearings, his offense might have come to be very differently described. He himself saw the shakedown business as a virtually inevitable extension of the tasks for which he and the rest of his embassy people had supplied "informal considerations."

As for the group of guards who "adopted" Sullivan as "their" ambassador and accompanied him in "chase cars" around the city: "This group," writes Sullivan, "also came to a bad end." The embassy maintained a warehouse on the compound , we learn, the wares of which served to "stock our commissary and convenience store," as Sullivan puts it, adding: "This warehouse contained a large supply of liquor, as well as luxury items such as watches, television sets, and cameras. It was a temptation our protectors could not resist." That was the set-up resulting from Sullivan's "unorthodox decision" to use such guards in the embassy compound "in contravention of all normal diplomatic practice." About what happened to that second group of guards after he left the embassy, Sullivan writes:

> Their pilferage from our warehouse engaged them in black marketeering and conflicts with local *komitehs* of the revolution. Their identification with Americans led them to sharp anti-Soviet positions, which eventually resulted in a raid conducted personally by Marshallah in which he arrested a Soviet KGB representative meeting with a senior member of the revolutionary leadership. Although the Soviet was expelled and the leader arrested, this action sowed the seeds for Marshallah's own arrest and his incarceration in the infamous Evin prison.

Sullivan acknowledges that such behavior led to a Washington decision, "long after my departure, to have the guards withdrawn from the embassy compound." And after all he had himself said about the "inevitability" of their corruption under the circumstances, Sullivan can yet bring himself to conclude: "I was, by that time, out of our government and cannot assess the wisdom of that move. I have, however, often wondered whether our people would have been taken hostage had some tolerable Iranian presence still been there on November 4, 1979." [278]

Gary Sick tells us, in *All Fall Down* , what the prevailing view in Washington had been of Sullivan's final "security arrangements." Henry Precht at the State Department "believed," as Sick put it, that the embassy in Tehran "would require a more effective local guard force than the ragtag group of revolutionaries who had installed themselves in the embassy compound after the February attack, and he also proposed sending additional U.S. security guards to reinforce the embassy" when the Shah's admittance to the United States was being contemplated. As for the steps actually taken for the physical security of the embassy during the summer and early fall of 1979, "nothing," writes Sick, "was left undone"; and then he specifies:

> The entrances to the chancery building — certain to be the principal target of any attack — were equipped with heavy steel doors, backed by automatic alarm system, electronic surveillance cameras and remote-controlled tear-gas devices. Windows were fitted with bullet-proof glass, steel boxes filled with sand for ballistic protection, and steel grills. The embassy was stocked for self-defense, and contingency plans were designed to permit the embassy to hold out unassisted for two to three hours until help could arrive. In fact, it worked out exactly as planned with only one crucial exception — help never came.

As to why "help never came," Gary Sick adopts the answer we discussed at the beginning of this chapter, arguing that it was a case — without "modern precedent" — of a nation "renouncing its international obligations and throwing its support to the mob." Sick is ready to concede that, for at least five months, the Ayatollah's government seemed to be striving hard not to do what is charged against it; but he argues that, in the end, it let itself be bent to the purposes of the hostage-takers. Yet that remains to be seen.

Sick did not conceal from himself the fact that, in order not to risk the lives of the hostages, Khomeini had, in effect, let himself be blackmailed by domestic terrorism into dismissing one administration after another. Writing of the events of March and April 1980, which caused "Washington's patience to run out," Sick takes note of the pathos of the spectacle of one Iranian administration already sacrificed and another on the verge of being sacrificed to the black-mail of the hostage-takers. "Bazargan's government," he writes, "was swept away in the first few days of the crisis, and Bani-Sadr's authority was permanently blunted during the course of secret negoti-ations." There seemed no end in sight — unless the Unites States were to give its consent to a military storming of the compound that would certainly result in the deaths of many American hostages!

One thing is certain. In the end, Khomeini's government was pleased to have been able to gain the release of the hostages without a fatality. At the close of his book, Sick gives the final word to the most pro-American of the Iranian statesmen who fell victim to the blackmail of the hostage-takers. Having summed up the results up to the final negotiations for release of the Americans — and bear-ing in mind that the Carter administration had never authorized its "friends" in Iran to retake the embassy by force — Sick writes: "The U.S. negatiors could not improve on the words of former Iranian Foreign Minister Yazdi: 'Generally speaking, the hostage issue has not been handled well and politically we have lost in the world'." With that, Sick recognizes that Iran's government, attempting to spare the lives of the American hostages at all costs, proved in the end to be the primary blackmail target of the second seizure of the American embassy, led by radicals who had vowed to take revenge on the Ayatollah's government for its having restored control to the Americans after the St. Valentine's Day attack.

2. First Hours of the November 1979 Attack: State Department Perspectives

In the earliest newsmedia accounts of the second seizure of the U.S. Embassy in Tehran, we find a mass of details that mixes iden-tities, motives, and plans — which is no doubt how such matters first surface in the immediate impression made by revolutionary events. Later on, in retrospective accounts, the three tend to be sepa-rated, with the plans and motives, especially, treated in the abstract. For instance, in the generally authoritative volume *American Hostages in Iran: The Conduct of a Crisis,* previously cited, which provides definitive accounts of all major aspects of the crisis by the leading State Department participants, the hostage-takers are no-where identified and their alleged plans and motives are mentioned only in passing. And even then, we find them defined for the most part in terms that appear to have proved useful to State Department officials in their daily efforts to deal with Iranian leaders, either directly or through foreign intermediaries.

But first, we must give credit where it is due: to the American diplomat whose name heads the list of contributors to the volume. He is Deputy Secretary of State Warren Christopher — "whom I have described openly," President Carter has written, "(without dissenting comments) as the best public servant I ever knew" [521] — and who says in his introduction:

> A great deal still is to be learned, and much probably never will be learned, about the identity of the captors and their relationship with various elements in the government. Howewer, it seems plausible to me that they were not initially controlled by the government but were in fact seen by it too as a dangerous element that had to be treated gingerly and then co-opted. Those struggling for power in Iran probably feared that they would lose the support of the revolutionaries holding the embassy and their followers if they moved to resolve the crisis. If that is the case, then the hostage crisis was as much Iran's quagmire as it was ours. For other host governments, the costs to Iran teach a powerful lesson. It is to move promptly to take control of such situations and to accept whatever immediate political cost that might entail in order to avoid vast losses of every other kind further down the road.

We cited much of that passage earlier in this book, but not its concluding judgment, where Christopher acknowledges that the Iranian government was clearly the chief victim of the embassy seizure of November 4, and then hastens to blame it directly for having failed to respond at once, as the State of Israel would surely have responded in a parallel situation, and as the Soviet-supported government of Afghanistan in fact responded when the American Ambassador in Kabul was seized. Christopher's is a statesmanly judgment, though it passes much too lightly over the fact that, had the Ayatollah's government plunged with full force into the "quagmire" created by the second attack on the U.S. Embassy, not only would the hostages have died, but the United States, with Kissinger and Jacob Javits in the lead, would certainly have blamed the Ayatollah for the whole thing — with God knows what ultimate consequences.

But, within a matter of pages, Christopher proceeds to simplify. He acknowledges that the embassy seizure probably occurred without planning, indeed "almost by accident"; and even that the captors perhaps "fully expected that the government security forces would soon arrive and drive them out." And then he speculates hurriedly about why the security forces didn't make an appearance. In his words:

> Various government factions may have feared a violent reaction against them if they attempted to remove the captors, and so the government decided to co-opt the action rather than oppose it. As the days wore on, the captors may have been caught up in their own rhetoric and so enamored of the new prominence that they could not let go. We can only speculate. But it is at least conceivable that the crisis grew out of an impulse rather than strategic planning and that the crisis continued out of inertia. In those few hours at the beginning, however, the die was cast for a long-running ordeal that would cost Iran dearly.

Careful reading of all else that Warren Christopher has written makes it clear that he believes it is Iran that paid dearly for what happened during "those few hours at the beginning," not the United States. Iran was the victim, not the perpetrator of the seemingly anti-American attack. Her government was confronted with a choice laid before her by blackmailers. The blackmailers said, to paraphrase Christopher: co-opt our action, don't oppose it: for, if you send security forces against us to drive us out of the embassy, we'll kill the American hostages. Take heed!

Second in importance to the long introduction by Warren Christopher, for our purposes, are the three chapters contributed to *American Hostages in Iran* by Assistant Secretary Harold H. Saunders, who is identified in the book's Foreword as having been the "senior working-level official responsible to the Secretary of State for coordinating recommendations on the crisis." Within the department, Saunders headed a bureau consisting, as he says, "of 110 people in Washington and 1,000 in thirty-seven diplomatic and consular posts in twenty-four countries from Marocco to Bangladesh." Throughout the crisis, he was the recipient of all reports on its development from every possible quarter. And all of that is reviewed in his contributions to the book, starting with a chapter titled "The Crisis Begins," which supplies an account of the first "on-the-scene reports by telephone from the embassy's political officer, Ann Swift, as the embassy was being overrun," and continuing through detailed chapters titled "Diplomacy and Pressure: November 1979-May 1980" and "Beginning of the End."

In our review of the important first few hours when, as Christopher says, the "die was cast" for the entire crisis, we want to be guided by Saunders' outline of details, which sums up the official State Department perspectives, even as we draw on other eyewitness accounts from several of the principal participants. Such witnesses tell as that, just before the attack, a group of some 500 or more student-marchers, with girls in the lead, had walked past the embassy reportedly on their way to a university campus to stage "another" American-style sit-in protest. But, having passed the gate, with no armed Marines on guard, the group seemed to have turned about spontaneously. It was around 10:00 a.m. Tehran time and, in a matter of minutes, they were in the compound.

In her call to the State Department, received at 3:00 a.m. November 4, Sunday, Ann Swift had reported that "a large mob of young Iranians had poured into the embassy compound, was then surrounding the chancery building, and was breaking into other buildings on the compound." Swift stressed the fact that, "unlike the armed guerrillas who had overrun the embassy the previous February 14, shooting as they came, this mob appeared unarmed," although it was later revealed that many carried concealed weapons as well as visible sticks. Swift also informed Washington that the embassy chief, Bruce Laingen, was absent at the time, having gone to the Iran Foreign Ministry with two colleagues on routine business. She was particularly asked for any evidence of what the mob "wanted," and, after two security officers had gone out to talk to the apparent leaders, a glance out a window revealed that the "whole image they were trying to convey to us was conveyed by a long streamer held up below the big plate glass windows in the ambassador's office by a bunch of women students who would not be fired on." As later reported, their large banner read: "We do not wish to inconvenience you. All we want is a sit-in."

But as the two security officers who had gone out into the yard (and were therafter detained and bound) soon made clear, the crowd was adamant in its demand that the entire embassy be peaceably surrendered at once for the purposes of their demonstration. As evidence of their determination, they "used a truck to pull a grill off one of the windows on the ground floor and entered the building." Before that, "most of the 70 to 80 persons" on the ground or first floor of the building, including many Iranians as well as American staff, had "moved for safety to the second floor behind a steel door." The Marines held the first floor and the stairs for some 45 minutes, without using their firearms, but then they too joined the others, with their weapons, behind the steel door. On her open line to Washington, Ann Swift was heard exclaiming to the Marines: "For God's sake, put that down. Put away the guns. No weapons here."

Before long, the two security officers held by the mob were "urging that the group on the second floor come out, that further resistance would be useless," and that the captors had arms and were threatening "to kill" staff members "taken in other parts of the embassy compound," unless all doors were promptly opened. By then, Bruce Laingen at the Iranian Foreign Ministry had assumed charge by phone, and, supporting the two security officers, he gave orders for a peaceful surrender while files of sensitive papers were being destroyed. Looking back at that moment after her release and return to the United States in January 1981, Ann Swift said: "Our whole thought was to give up peacefully so we could be released peacefully." Saunders adds that everyone in Washington concurred in that judgment, and then he writes:

> Each of the parties on the phone remembered the attack earlier in the year on February 14, when the staff surrendered to a heavi-

ly armed mob in an effort to prevent bloodshed. On that occasion, the embassy was taken over for a few hours but turned back to then Ambassador William Sullivan by senior officials of the revolutionary government, who came to the compound and dispersed the attackers. A key figure in the February 14 rescue was the man who was now the Foreign Minister, Ibrahim Yazdi. The expectation that any captivity would again last only a few hours conditioned the judgment that surrender was preferable to confrontation.

At 4:50 a.m. — 12:20 p.m. in Tehran — Swift reported, "We have just opened the door.". . . Then Swift said simply, "We're going down." They started down the stairs into what no one at that stage could know would eventually add up to 444 days as hostages. Swift had not hung up. She had put the phone down, leaving the line open. [41]

Saunders' chapter then sums up what the American staff learned of the purposes of the captors during their first conversations with them. In Saunders' words, the captors early told their hostages that they "wanted to bring people into the streets in support of the religious element's efforts to purge the government of secular leaders who, they feared, might be too quick to rebuild a relationship with the United States." The November 4 attackers made it clear from the start that everything else demanded was subordinate to that first named purpose. "Holding the embassy hostage," a spokesman emphasized, "while demanding the Shah's return from the United States for trial, seemed a way of rallying" street support for the true goal, which was simply to force a complete break in U.S.-Iranian relations.

In other words, ever since the Ayatollah's government had rescued the U.S. Embassy from the attackers of February 14, 1979, and restored it to the American ambassador, that government had labored to normalize its relations with the United States. The opponents of normalization in the United States had been headed by Henry Kissinger outside of government and by Senator Jacob Javits inside. In the rest of the world, it was the State of Israel that pressed, as we saw, the strongest objections. In Iran, it was not the Ayatollah who objected to normalization — quite the contrary. It was his government that pursued the policy, that went to Algiers and met cordially with Zbigniew Brzezinski. No Iranian could seriously accept the view that Bazargan and Yazdi, leaders of the Khomeini revolutionary government, were somehow in a "conspiracy to restore the Shah."

That ought to have been the one hard fact of the crisis for our State Department decision-makers. They should have been insisting, night and day, that the attack on the U.S. Embassy had for its purpose simply to force a break between the United States and the Islamic Republic of Iran — nothing more, nothing less. Instead, as Saunders makes clear in his detailed account, at a certain moment there occurred some careless phrasing on the part of American diplomats that permitted the American newsmedia to misrepresent the attack, to treat it as if it had been inspired by the Ayatollah Khomeini himself, for the purpose of preventing a CIA coup of some kind to restore the Shah! Thus, at this key moment in his account, Saunders correctly notes that the "photos in the Tehran newspapers the day before showing Bazargan and Yazdi shaking hands with U.S. National Security Adviser Brzezinski in Algiers" had "dramatized to the Islamic purists in the revolution the realization of their worst fears — renewal by government leaders of a closer relationship with the United States." He ought then to have pointed out that that was a far cry from assuming that Bazargan and Yazdi had entered into a conspiracy to restore the Shah — that the photos indicated quite the opposite: the start of a process of international legitimization of the Islamic revolution that *overthrew* the Shah.

Instead, Saunders proceeds at once to cite the words of a State Department colleague, suggesting that, because it had been forced by the Kissinger-Rockefeller group to admit the Shah to the United States for medical-humanitarian reasons — with Carter avowedly the last official holdout in Washington in mid-October — the Carter administration might reasonably be attacked by "Shiite diehards" as a champion of efforts to restore the Pahlavis. Saunders writes:

> As State Department Director of Iranian Affairs Henry Precht wrote in retrospect, "I think the one constant theme that obsessed the movement against the Shah, both the leaders of the revolu-

tion and the followers, was a fear that the United States would repeat 1953 (when the Shah was restored to his throne with U.S. help) in destroying Iran's revolution. The secular people sometimes tried to woo us; the religious people tried to destroy all connections with us. When we brought the Shah to New York, it fueled those suspicions, which were further sparked by the Brzezinski-Yazdi-Bazargan meeting in Algiers. No government, no force in Iran, could support the United States when a question of the Shah was involved.

After quoting Henry Precht's statement, Saunders never again takes up the matter of the motives of the hostage captors without suggesting that he agrees with its premise, which is that the purpose of the November 4 attack was somehow to prevent the Ayatollah's government from conspiring to restore the Shah or his Pahlavi dynasty. We may here note in passing that elsewhere in *American Hostages in Iran,* as its index shows, there are only two other passing references to the motives and plans of the embassy captors, in both of which the assumed premise is obviously the same. One reference repeats an intermediary's statement to the effect that it was necessary "for us and our government to understand that the taking of hostages was an act of self-defense in a revolutionary process," and that "Iran wanted only to protect itself against a recurrence of the sort of counterrevolution that had occurred with the help of the C.I.A. in 1953." The second reference further simplifies matters, again citing an intermediary who is manifestly seeking to gain adherents to his view. The intermediary is the Paris lawyer Hector Villalon, who, in attempting to enlist American support for the efforts of Sadegh Ghotbzadeh to get hold of the reins of government in Iran, relates "Ghotbzadeh's reasons for believing that getting rid of the hostages would wrench from the radical religious groups one of the weapons they were using against secular revolutionaries." With that weapon, Villalon explained, the "radical religious groups. . .had already felled Bazargan and Yazdi. . . . and Ghotbzadeh saw himself the next target."

    There we have a typical pattern of simplification, brushing aside, in effect, Warren Christopher's cautious reminder that we still have much to learn about the identity of the captors and their relations to various elements of the government. Clearly, if the aim of the November 4 attack had been to prevent a "recurrence" of what had happened in 1953, the Ayatollah's government ought to have supported it 100%, and neither Bazargan and Yazdi nor Bani-Sadr and Ghotbzadeh would have been threatened by it. By assuming that such was indeed the purpose, the U.S. State Department was constraining the Ayatollah's government, which thoroughly opposed the attack, to pretend to support it. Let us review the facts. The government headed by Bazargan and Yazdi — the Ayatollah's first government — had quickly declared the attack to be criminal and indeed traitorous. Both Yazdi and Bazargan had assumed that Khomeini would support them, as he had on February 14. That was their assumption when they assured Laingen that the February 14 scenario would be repeated. In Saunders' words, "Yazdi told Laingen that our colleagues were safe in the compound and that security forces were outside the compound", and also "that one of the religious leaders of the revolution was going to the compound — perhaps Khomeini's son."

But here, we must shift from the perspective of Saunders in Washington to that of Bruce Laingen and his two embassy colleagues in the Iranian Foreign Ministry, for we are focusing, now, on a crucial moment of the first hours of the hostage crisis — the moment when the State Department made its critical mistake, forcing the new heads of the Ayatollah's government, after Bazargan and Yazdi resigned, to feign that they were on the side of the hostage takers, in order not to put the lives of the hostages at risk.

As we shall see, after Bazargan and Yazdi, one pro-American leader after another in the Ayatollah's governments had to feign support of the attackers in order to gain their confidence. And there can be no doubt at all that a State Department decision taken in the early hours of the crisis forced the Iranian leaders to engage in such a pretense, for which one of them, Sadegh Ghotbzadeh, eventually paid with his life.

3. Bruce Laingen and the Trials of the Bani-Sadr/Ghotbzadeh Leadership

As we noted in passing earlier, at the time of the November 4 attack, Bruce Laingen and his two staff colleagues, Michael Howland and Victor Tomseth, had been on their way from the Iranian Foreign Ministry back to the embassy when they got news of the event by car radio. The news came with a warning that great crowds had gathered at the embassy gate, and that an embassy car would probably be instantly attacked. So Laingen and his colleagues headed back to the Foreign Ministry to seek governmental help.

At that very time, the heads of the Ayatollah's government, Prime Minister Bazargan and Foreign Minister Yazdi, were just getting back from their November 1 meeting with Brzezinski in Algiers and were on their way into Tehran when they got the news, informing them not only of the attack but also of the fact that Laingen was at the Foreign Ministry, with the facilities of Yazdi's office placed at his disposal. Or, to be precise, in Gary Sick's words:

> Bruce Laingen was offerd the use of Yazdi's office upstairs, and from there he set up a direct telephone connection with the State Department Operations Center in Washington. His two colleagues remained on the first floor, where they could watch what was happening outside the building. They also established a direct line to Washington. Other direct lines were established with approximately sixty embassy staff people trapped on the second floor of the chancery and the U.S. Cultural Center some three miles from the compound.

Gary Sick was, of course, himself at one of the receiving ends of the lines to Washington, and therefore had first-hand knowledge of the kind of communications Laingen and his American colleagues in the Iranian Foreign Ministry were able to maintain. In his account, he stresses that the open telephone lines linking four locations in Tehran directly with Washington provided Washington with "more rapid and accurate information than was available to anyone in Tehran" about the developing situation there during those first hours of crisis. He notes, for instance, that when radical students assembled in front of the Foreign Ministry, "seeking the three missing Americans to add to their collection of hostages" held at the embassy, Howland, who observed them from the Foreign Ministry's first floor, reported the fact directly to Washington; and it was Washington, in turn, that called to inform Laingen on the second floor, who, in turn, informed Yazdi. And Yazdi, in turn, writes Sick, was simply "dumbfounded to be informed by Washington of what was happening only a few floors below him in his own country."

Needless to say, the "dumbfounded" pro-American Yazdi did not surrender Laingen and his colleagues to the chanting radicals outside the Foreign Ministry. Like their militant colleagues in the embassy compound, the students assembled in front of the Foreign Ministry to demand the head of the American Mission, so that he might be carted off to confinement, were perceived not as supporters of Yazdi's government, but as its foes. Yet, what needs to be stressed at this point is Sick's account, repeatedly confirmed by Laingen, of the Iranian government's initial response to the second embassy seizure. Sick writes: "The Iranian foreign ministry was obviously taken entirely by surprise by the attack, and they did everything in their power those first hours to attempt to resolve it."

After his return to the United States, at the end of the long hostage crisis, Bruce Laingen supplied the *New York Times* with his own account of those first hours and days of the crisis. "Mr. Laingen," we read in the February 2, 1981 issue of the *Times,* "continued to direct his besieged staff from the ministry, ordering people to destroy documents, to avoid using their guns, and, finally, to surrender. The three diplomats stayed that night in the old diplomatic reception area on the third floor of the ministry, and that remained their living quarters for most of their captivity."

Foreign Minister Yazdi, who had successfully liberated the embassy after the first seizure back in February, initially compared the November seizure to an American sit-in, and he was confident that it would be resolved "within 48 hours." He said that a call had been placed to the Ayatollah Khomeini in Qom, and that the Ayatollah would no doubt call the militants to order or perhaps even send his son. Laingen had, however, pressed Yazdi to go personally to the embassy as he had in February. Yazdi is quoted as having replied:

"Then the lives of the people in the embassy were in danger but that is not true now." In retrospect, Saunders has taken that statement as an indication of Yazdi's recognition, that he "did not have the clout to do what he had done earlier." At any rate, Bruce Laingen apparently concluded that he ought to keep the pressure up on Yazdi and Bazargan. Citing Laingen's words in its retrospective account of early February 1981, the *New York Times* put it this way:

> Though the Iranian officials at the Foreign Ministry assured the three early on that they could leave, . . . Mr. Laingen would not relieve them of the burden of the American presence. "Our position throughout," said Mr. Laingen, "was that we shouldn't do anything to reduce the responsibility of the Government of Iran." He said that he and his two colleagues reached decisions by consensus, though Laingen continued throughout the crisis to act as leader. "I thought it was important that I maintain it for the benefit of the Iranians with whom we dealt," he said, "that they know that the chief of the mission was still there and that he was available as a mechanism to deal with the Government of Iran. Technically, I was still the President's representative in Iran until we broke relations in April, and I wanted them to see that in my conduct."

The same *Times* retrospective article noted that the open overseas telephone lines provided for Laingen and his colleagues in their Foreign Ministry office, together with "a telex machine," enabled them to "communicate regularly with their families and their superiors in Washington and to learn the broad outlines of negotiations for their release. More news came from visits with other foreign ambassadors, which Mr. Laingen said seemed not to have been monitored." That remained so from November 4, 1979 until early January 1981, when the three were brought together with their colleagues who had literally been held hostage, in preparation for their flight home.

The point here is that Laingen had indeed done his duty by constantly reminding the Ayatollah's government of its accountability for the safety of the hostages. But it would have been a grave error on his part had he even for a moment permitted himself to believe that the Iranian government could at that time have restored the embassy to American control without putting the lives of the hostages at total risk. Laingen had asked Yazdi to go to the embassy, and Yazdi had replied that an Iranian security force was standing just outside the compound, awaiting a repeat of the orders of February 14, and also that, in an effort to avoid bloodshed, the Ayatollah's thirty-five year old son Ahmed would make an appearance in person. Gary Sick tells us of the rejoicing in Washington when it was learned that Ahmed was on his way. In fact, Ahmed quickly arrived at the gate. And we have eye-witness accounts of what occurred. The captors inside the embassy compound refused to open the gate. To get in, Ahmed had literally to "storm" the place. In Sick's words: "What Yazdi (and we in Washington) had not expected was that Ahmed Khomeini would clamber excitedly over the embassy wall, losing his turban in the process."

There is a suggestion in Sick's words that the Ayatollah's son had *preferred* to clamber over the wall instead of entering by the gate, perhaps as a gesture of solidarity with the captors! Is that conceivable? Hardly. Once inside, Ahmed was by no means cheered by the militants. To be heard at all, he started at once to praise the daring of the captors as "Followers of the Imam's Line," which is what they had called themselves from the beginning. He eventually left the compound, and there was no offer on the part of the captors to "surrender" the embassy, as in February. Outside, the security forces were still standing guard — the Ayatollah's security forces. Why didn't they storm the embassy to effect by force what Yazdi and Bazargan and the Ayatollah's son had tried but failed to effect peacefully?

For serious scholars, that question takes us to the crux of the matter. All the evidence shows that, while urging Bazargan and Yazdi to "do their duty under international law" and wrest control of the embassy from its captors, Laingen and his superiors never said that, if peaceful means failed, the Ayatollah's government had Washington's consent to resort to force. That was why Bazargan and Yazdi, who were prepared to take the course retrospectively recommended by Warren Christopher — to take control of the situation whatever the "immediate political cost might be" — resigned. And that is why their successors, first Bani-Sadr and then Ghotbzadeh, attempted to gain release of the hostages by feigning to be on "their side," and not, like Bazargan and Yazdi, against them.

On the day of the attack, Washington agreed on what Saunders has called a "Two-Track Strategy: Pressure and Providing a Way Out" for the Iranian government. The essence of that strategy is reviewed for us from a military standpoint in Gary Sick's contribution to the *American Hostages in Iran* volume. Sick, who had been a Navy captain, fittingly titles his chapter "Military Options and Constraints," and he notes at the outset that both the options and the restraints were clearly defined by President Carter by the "second day of the crisis." The conclusions drawn on that day, he says, "established the framework for consideration of military options throughout the entire course of the 444-day drama." [147] As Sick paraphrases President Carter's official guidelines, the overall object was to increase the costs to Iran of holding the hostages until those costs clearly "outweighed" the benefits. More particularly, Sick itemizes the military considerations:

> * Peaceful means would be explored and exhausted before resort to violence.
> * The United States would retaliate militarily if the hostages were put on trial or physically harmed.
> * The U.S. government would make no threats it was unable or unwilling to carry out.
> * No military action would be taken that was not reversible. Specifically, President Carter was determined to avoid a situation when a limited military action would trap the United States in an open-ended escalatory cycle leading to land combat in Iran.

In other words, the most serious military option contemplated, from the beginning, was something like the failed rescue mission of late April 1980, designed to permit complete withdrawal of the entire force employed, so that, except for an accident, there would be no trace of American force having been used, if the mission failed.

Needless to say, there was never an "option" for pressuring the embassy captors directly, as the Israeli government might have done in a parallel situation. We know that when three "Palestinian terrorists" seized an Israel rural school with some forty children in it, and demanded the release of jailed Palestinians, the response of the Israeli government was unambiguous: Give up, or die. The three Palestinians refused to give up. Israeli security forces attacked. The three Palestinians were indeed killed — but so were all the Israeli children, for whom all of Israel immediately went into mourning. In the American Embassy compound, the ratio of captors to hostages was very different — 60 American captors to over 500 Iranian militants — and none of the Americans were children. But, as we all know, it was the decision of the Carter administration from the beginning that nothing was to be done to put American lives at risk; and that decision had been immediately conveyed to the Ayatollah's government, with a warning that if, for any reason, American hostages were killed, it would be held fully accountable. Indeed, President Carter — Saunders tells us — explicitly "rejected the idea of a statement that went beyond repeating that we expected the Iranian authorities to make good on their assurances that our people would be safely released. There was some tentative discussion of possible punitive military action that might be taken if Iran harmed any of the hostages." That meant, of course, that, if Iran's government ventured to do what the Soviet-controlled government of Afghanistan had done, "Iran" would be punished .

Iran had thus been backed into a corner. It had to be on guard against doing or even saying anything that would make the hostage-takers appear to be under official attack or censure. The result was to force "the Ayatollah and others" — like Bani-Sadr, as we have seen — "to envelop any profession of moderation," as Sick puts it, "in the most inflammatory language," intended to placate the hostage captors, lest "any of the hostages were harmed." We know that, by November 12, 1979, less than a week after the attack, the new Foreign Minister, Abolhassan Bani-Sadr was plainly taking President Carter's "guidelines" to heart in communicating his government's "demands" to Washington — demands that turned out to be exactly what the hostage captors had demanded of the Ayatollah from the first hours.

Everyone in Washington who knew the facts was aware that those demands had been co-opted by the Bani-Sadr government so as not to put the lives of the hostages at risk. Bani-Sadr had then gone directly to the embassy compound to tell the captors that his government was wholly on "their side." Unlike the Ayatollah's son Ahmed, who hadn't gone that far, Bani-Sadr was allowed to "slip in," as it were, through a slightly opened gate. Once inside, he followed Ahmed Khomeini's example, praising the "Followers of the Imam's Line" for their boldness and loyalty. They had made their point impressively, he said, with all the world taking notice, especially in the United States. But then, in cautiously measured words, he went on to say, or rather to hint, that it might be wrong to continue the seizure of the embassy much longer, since there was much else to be done. The government had adopted their demands. The time was at hand, therefore, to transfer control of the hostages to the government. Otherwise, he hinted, the Ayatollah himself might begin to view them as perhaps acting like "a state within a state."

The hostage takers rose in fury against that suggestion, demanding that Bani-Sadr be instantly dismissed as the government's spokesman. After that, no one again threatened the embassy captors, except to say that, if Ronald Reagan were elected President, the price to pay for their recalcitrance would be too great. Bani-Sadr managed to survive in the government after his rejection by the embassy captors, but only by feigning to be more militant, more anti-American than they. On this point there is an important diary entry for February 4, 1980, in Carter's presidential memoirs. It reads:

> Apparently Bani-Sadr is sending word to us directly that he wants to proceed with a resolution of the hostage question. His inclination is to wait until after the 26th of February, when he can put his government together. . . . He does not want us to identify him as a friend of the United States or as a moderate. He wants to be known as a revolutionary, protecting the interests of Iran against both superpowers. [485]

President Carter called that news — of Bani-Sadr's request to be treated as hostile to the United States, and as a fanatic rather than a moderate — the "most encouraging development since our embassy had been seized." By that, Carter could only have meant that he believed Bani-Sadr was on the right track, doing what the "American government" believed would have to be done to keep the hostages alive at all costs. What Bani-Sadr could not know at the time was that President Carter, his campaign advisers, and a few trusted members of the State Department and his White House staff were the only Americans who would ever know he was only "pretending" to be an anti-American Islamic fanatic. Indeed, it could never have occurred to him, at the time, that, if his ruse failed, and harm came to the hostages, the American President and all those in on the secret would nevertheless fully blame Bani-Sadr and the Iran government as a whole for the failure.

What did the top diplomats of our State Department think of an approach to the hostage crisis that required Bani-Sadr and the other pro-American leaders of the Ayatollah's government to feign to be fanatical anti-Americans? Saunders tells us matter-of-factly that, in all State Department dealings with Bani-Sadr and Ghotbzadeh, first through French lawyers, then through U.N. General Secretary Waldheim, and then through some seventeen other channels, his object was always to develop a scenario for release of the hostages which would "work" in Tehran as well as in Washington. Each step of any practical scenario would have to be "described," as he says, "in ways and revolutionary language to have maximum appeal in Tehran." In practice, as he explains, it took hours to work up statements of each step, in French and English versions, designed to preserve the "revolutionary" and "fanatical" identities of the chief Iranian contacts, while laying out clearly the matters to be agreed upon by all parties. In passing, Saunders tells us how he learned to handle the challenge of so elaborate a deception: "As a veteran of the Kissinger shuttles, Camp David, and the Egyptian-Israeli peace treaty negotiations, I had learned infinite patience with endless hours of straining over details." [121]

Here we should not fail to note, however, that, when Saunders and his top State Department colleagues sought the advice of leading American academicians specializing in Middle East/Islamic studies, they found themselves advised to do exactly what Bani-Sadr had been induced to do. In Saunders' words, almost all of them "described the risk of the United States identifying too much with governments and inadequately with peoples," and offered a "conceptual framework for American foreign policy reaching well beyond security issues," presenting the United States "ideally as a partner in a global interdependence with other nations," and stressing how the "American public needed every opportunity for a better understanding of Islam and the diversity of the Islamic nations." Later in this book we mean to look back to a time when our American statesmen confronted hostage crises very differently and when the advice of scholars was a bit more to the point.

4. The Hostage Captors: Religious or Secular Student-Militants?

One of the earliest reports on the identities of the embassy attackers was a *New York Times* news story dated November 11, 1979, headed "Iran Student Tells of Plan for Attack," and subheaded "A Leader of U.S. Embassy Raiders Thought That Many Would Die." The "leader" interviewed was reportedly "one of the handful of students allowed to leave the compound"; but, as he acknowledged, he was carefully searched on leaving and would be searched again "on his way back." Interviewed just outside the embassy gate, he told reporters that "none of the hostages, including the seven or so women, would be released unless the United States returned the deposed Shah." The hostages, he added, were mostly Americans, but included some Japanese, Koreans, Filipinos, and "at least one Bangladeshi." Asked if the attack had been planned,

> he said the idea for the takeover came at a meeting of four to five Islamic students at a Tehran university on Oct. 26. He declined to name the university. . . . The young man said the students picked four leaders and organized a demonstration for the morning of Nov. 4. Before then only about 10 students knew of the plan.

By November 4, the four original leaders had managed to assemble large groups of students at each of four universities, adding up to over a hundred in each group. The assembled students were told of the plan and given instructions on where to go and what to do once inside the embassy compound. They were to expect to be fired upon and expected to fight back. But, as the interviewee stressed, "really we had a maximum of ten pistols between us." Leaving the four universities, the 500 students assembled on Roosevelt Avenue as 10:30 a.m. and proceeded down Taleghani Avenue to the embassy. "The girls marched first," we are told,

> and we all sang and chanted. We let the girls march past the gates, then turned and faced the embassy. A few handpicked men ran at the gates and clambered over. The gates were not padlocked and they were able to open them easily to let us all in. There were three or four Iranian policemen, armed with pistols, inside the gate, but they were dumbfounded. Anyway, we knew policemen were under strict orders not to shoot anyone. . . . We all went to our arranged positions, occupying the chancery, the visa section, and the bungalows first. Most of the Americans calmly put their hands on their heads when they saw us.

The *New York Times* interview ended on that calm note, ignoring the fact that the "dumbfounded" Iranian policemen on guard were the Ayatollah's policemen, so that, from the very beginning, it was the Ayatollah's "authority" that was being abused as well as the sovereign integrity of the U.S. Embassy.

A much fuller introduction to the early interviews with the hostage captors is the long account by Don A. Schanche that appeared in the *Los Angeles Times* (December 9, 1979). It was headed "Captor Relates Early Siege Plot," though a subhead hastened to add that "Student says plans set before Shah arrived in U.S. didn't include taking hostages." Schanche's focus is, of course, on the identities and personalities of the students interviewed. One of their apparent leaders explained at some length, while insisting on anonymity, that "only four student leaders, from the National University, Tehran University, Sharif Technical University, and Tehran Polytechnic Institute, were initially involved." The four had reportedly met on Oct. 1, when a decision was first taken to "organize an assault on the embassy." The schools named, it should be noted, are not Islamic theological seminaries, but rather Iran's equivalents of American schools like Yale, MIT, the City College of New York, and the University of Chicago. As reporter Schanche further explains:

After their first session, each of the original four returned
to their respective schools to enlist about half a dozen trustwor-
thy fellow conspirators. From that group of about 25, a central
committee of eight emerged: the original four and one additional
student from each of the four universities. Those eight are now
[as of December 8, 1979] said to constitute the ruling central council
of the tightly organized group still holding the embassy. The leader
who was interviewed was apparently one of the 25 but would not
confirm whether he was included in the original four or in the central group of eight . . . privy to all plans and preparations.

It was that "central group of eight," according to the interviewed leader, that proceeded to recruit the more than "500 young
men and women involved," most of whom "did not know one
another before the attack on the embassy began." As for the motives of the original four who allegedly met on October 1 to plan
the attack, *The Los Angeles Times* reporter got them to distinguish
two related goals, which he thus summed up:

Their first objective was to embarrass the United States, in
concert with the expressed anti-Americanism of their idol, the
Ayatollah Ruhollah Khomeini. There was no thought then of turning the embassy seizure into a long-term act of terrorism. The second goal was to create sufficient political turmoil to force the
resignation of Prime Minister Mehdi Bazargan and his goverment,
including the American-educated foreign minister, Ibrahim Yazdi, who, in the students' view had become an "unwholesome"
influence on Khomeini: too soft on the United States and other
Western nations that were then trying to patch together some semblance of normal commercial relations with Iran.

In other words, the second attack on the U.S. embassy in Tehran
had been made with exactly the same goals as the earlier February
attack — but with two important differences. One difference was
that the militants had now identified themselves as strict adherents
of Khomeini's policy line. They were pure and simply "with the
Ayatollah!" The second difference was that, by October 1979, things
in the United States had changed radically, for the reasons already

indicated. Henry Kissinger had been pulling all strings imaginable to get the Shah admitted into the United States, despite strenuous warnings against it from the American Embassy in Iran; and Senator Jacob Javits of New York had succeeded in getting unanimous Senate approval of his resolution condemning the new Islamic Republic's prosecution of person's accused of wrong-doing as members of the Shah's government. The labors and intentions of Kissinger and Javits in America and of a cadre of some eight students from four elite Iranian universities coincided and reinforced one another in October 1979. The effect was like that of a planetary syzygy compounding the gravitiational pull of the moon on the earth; one must, in either case, expect destructively high tides.

But we must return to the record of what the embassy captors initially told American reporters. And here Gary Sick supplies a useful reference in *All Fall Down* (1985), where he informs us that the "most authoritative account" of which he is aware as to the identity of the embassy captors and the chronology and changing scope of their plans "was the series of articles in the Iranian publication *Mojahed* (issue Nos. 101-6, some undated) in December 1980 by one of the students who became disillusioned with the political in-fighting associated with the hostage taking." Sick notes that those articles, "together with some original interviews and investigative reporting, formed the basis of several reports in the U.S. media." And he refers us, for example, to "Bill Baker, 'Iran Militants Planned to Hold U.S. Embassy Only Days, Student Claims,' *Christian Science Monitor* , December 31, 1980; and John Kifner, 'How a Sit-in Turned into a Siege,' the *New York Times Magazine,* May 26, 1981." [352]

We recommend adding to Sick's list an article by Christos P. Ioannides, titled "The Hostages in Iran: A Discussion with the Militants," which appeared in the Summer 1980 issue of *The Washington Quarterly* (III, 3, pp.12-36), published by the Center for Strategic and International Studies, Georgetown University. The published discussion consists, as Ioannides explains, of "an exact transcript of the interview. . . recorded on March 1, 1980, inside the U.S. Embassy in Tehran." The two students interviewed are identified as *"Mary (real name, Nilofar Ebtekar), 21 years old. . .* a second-year chemistry student" who speaks "excellent English, with a slight American accent"; and *"Shapoor (code name), 23 years old* . . . a third-year medical student" who, although he was recognizably a leader among the students, "must have been in an inferior position to Mary" who "on three occasions . . . interrupted and corrected him," while he "never interrupted her while she was talking, an indication of deference."

The Ioannides interview is valuable because of its relatively early date — earlier than the interviews listed by Sick — and even more because the pair interviewed were zealous militants, not dissidents. "Mary" was probably a member of the eight-member central council, though she declined to say so when pressed. But she and her companion appear to have confirmed the identities of the five allegedly "known" members of the central council of eight, listed by Ioannides as Hajatolla Mohammed Moussawi Khoeni, 41 years old, said to be "the Imam's representative to the students"; Mohsen Mirtamadi, 22, "considered a Muslim socialist"; Naimi (code name), 22, considered a "Muslim fundamentalist"; Hussein (code name), 23, also allegedly a Muslim fundamentalist; and Hassan Habaibi (code name), early 20s, probably a Marxist.

We mentioned Dilip Hiro's suggestion that "the seizure of the American embassy on 4 November by militant students was a well-planned affair," and that Khomeini's son Ahmed might have been among the early planners. The Ioannides interviews do not support that in the least. But neither do they support Gary Sick's suggestion that "the students first began planning their attack shortly after the Shah was admitted to the United States," alleging further that they then "met with Khoeni, who later became the spiritual advisor to the students in the embassy and their primary liaison with the Islamic leadership." With regard to the last point, Sick cautiously stresses that Khoeni only "later became" a liaison between the militants and the Islamic leadership, thereby making it clear that he does not think Khoeni was a leader in the actual assault of November 4, as many reporters and some scholars have repeatedly suggested. Sick also notes, in 1985, that Khoeni "remained silent about his role," and that "the exact truth of what happened must remain speculative." [197-198]

Christos Ioannides has also challenged the widely held assumption that most of the November attackers were Islamic zealots "studying religion and theology or were not students at all." They were indeed students, he concludes, but, as their leaders identified them, "the majority were students of sciences, including mathematics, chemistry, engineering, and medicine." And Ioannides's conclusion in this regard was to be fully confirmed by the released American hostages themselves, during long interviews at West Point, after their return to the United States in early 1981.

At West Point, Bruce Laingen was particularly asked whether he or the other Americans who spent most of the 444 days at the Iranian Foreign Ministry — the embassy's political counselor Victor Tomseth, and Michael Howland (who had replaced Col. Holland as its security officer) — had a sense, from their special position, of what outside forces might have operated on the captors: "Were they responsive to some outside force? Or were they simply an anarchic entity in and of themselves? And I wonder if I could get both your perspective and that of someone who was on the other side [with the hostages in the embassy]?"

Bruce Laingen asked Vic Tomseth to answer for those at the Foreign Ministry, and Tomseth said: "Well, in dealing with Iran all throughout this period there was always the question of who's in charge and frequently among ourselves we made the comment that nobody's in charge and everybody's in charge. And it was clear to us that the students did have at least one mentor in the person of a mullah by the name of Mousavi Khoeini who certainly subsequent to the seizure of the embassy played a fairly important role within the government." As for whether he thought Khoeini might have participated in long-range prior planning, Tomseth said he thought it "not very likely that there was prior knowledge — at least not to any extensive degree within the formal government of that time that was headed by Prime Minister Bazargan — regarding the plans to seize the embassy, although several of the students and this mullah, Mousavi Khoeini, did indicate subsequent to the seizure that it had been in accordance with a previous plan."

Tomseth was saying, in other words, that, while it was absurd to call the seizure a *government* plan, it might well have been planned by enemies of the government, seeking to embarrass it and prevent normalization of relations with the United States. When the questioner asked more particularly whether someone in government apart from Bazargan might have been influencing things, Tomseth said: "I think that very unlikely, quite frankly." As he viewed it, therefore, the November embassy seizure was in no sense an Iranian *government* act. That is, of course, a very important point.

John Graves answered the same question from the vantage point of the hostages in daily contact with their captors. "I was taken in the compound," Graves said, "so I can perhaps talk a little bit about the people who captured us and guarded us during our long stay in Iran." He then scolded the American newsmedia for their treatment of the subject, saying:

> I'm uncomfortable with the fact that much of what I see in the press seems to be a kind of almost willful distortion or diluting of the sort of wishful thinking. I think there's enormous evidence, completely cogent evidence for the proposition that the people who took us, that captured us, were students. I don't think there's any doubt of that at all. As to their goals, it would take me a great deal of time to explain what they were up to. What I can tell you or maybe intrigue you with is the fact that in my opinion at least, and I'm very sure of this, they were not interested at the outset in getting the Shah back. That was a pretext or a way of getting these masses to respond. So that much of what's been said about the people who captured us is pretty wide of the mark. They were students.

The intriguing side of the response is clear enough. The students didn't attack the embassy because they wanted the get the Shah back. Their object was, indeed, better served by not getting the Shah back. One can argue that their object was quite compatible with that of Kissinger in bringing the Shah to the United States in the first place — namely: to effect a complete severance of U. S.-Iranian relations! Once it is established, as it easily can be, that the captors were not religious fanatics, it behooves us to seek out what other interests — besides those of religious fanaticism — could have been served by deliberate seizure of the embassy. Clearly the attack on the embassy in Tehran was not a governmental undertaking any more than the initial movement to get the Shah admitted to the United States was a governmental undertaking. Kissinger in America and the hostage takers in Iran were alike acting contrary to the intentions and interests of their governments. Strange bedfellows, perhaps, but nevertheless bedfellows.

What did Khomeini think of such students, pursuing Western-style studies in the more prestigious Westernized Iranian universities? We have many remarkably frank statements of the Ayatollah on the character of such schools — indeed, many full-length lectures and sermons. In his "New Year's Message" of March 21, 1980 — at the height of the hostage crisis — Khomeini said very typically: "A fundamental revolution must take place in all the universities across the country, so that professors with links to the East or the West may be purged. . . . All of our backwardness has been due to the failure of most university-educated intellectuals to acquire correct knowledge of the Iranian Islamic society, and unfortunately, this is still the case. Most of the blows our society has sustained have been inflicted on it precisely by these university-educated intellectuals." [291-2, AK, *Islam and Revolution: Writings and Declarations of Imam Khomeini,* Mizan Press, Berkeley, 1981] And in an address of April 30, 1980, he added:

> We have had universities in our country fifty years now [since 1935]. . . . But show us the achievements of our universities. . .! Our universities have served to impede the progress of the sons and daughters of this land; they have become propaganda arenas. . .; if this were not so, our universities would not have been transformed into a battlefield for ideologies harmful to the nation. If Islamic morality existed in the universities, these shameful clashes would not occur. . . . Those who are creating disturbances on the streets. . .and creating problems for the government and the nation are followers of the West or the East. . . . My beloved listeners! We fear neither economic boycott nor military intervention. What we fear is cultural dependence and imperialist universities that propel our young people into the service of communism. We do not wish our universities to produce more people of the same type. . . . I beseech God Almighty to grant hap-

piness to our nation and to its young people, and I hope that our universities will be cleared of all elements of dependency. [295-9]

It was a cadre of "elite" students from just such universities that led the November 4 attack on the U.S. Embassy. The four original organizers of the attack came from elitist schools, as we saw; and each of them had been charged to recruit six additional "activists" from the same schools. Then, out of those first twenty-eight, the central council of eight was chosen to be in absolute charge. Next, some 400 to 500 additional students were recruited, most of whom hadn't previously known one another.

It should be noted, moreover, that not all of the 400 to 500 students making up the total of so-called militants holding the embassy were eager participants. The inner core of leaders had intimidating control over the rest. Indeed, what Bani-Sadr repeatedly tried to do was to show that, as President of the emergent constitutional government, his proposals were consistent with what those militants professed to believe as loyal "Followers of the Imam's Line." On February 10 1980, a spokesman for that inner core had told the Tehran newsmedia — and a London reporter had filed the story for the Associated Press — that militants in the embassy had been angered by a radio interview the day before in which "Iranian Foreign Minister Sadegh Ghotbzadeh said. . .that Iranian authorities would use force 'if necessary' to free the U.S. hostages held in Tehran." The spokesman's reply was that the hostage captors had all along had "contingency plans for any U.S.-oriented commando raid on the embassy"; and he warned all parties concerned to accept it as a "political given that all the hostages would die in any attack on the embassy, whether instigated by Americans or Iranians." [Wm. Worthy, 138-139]

After that, Bani-Sadr had hastened to make it clear that the object was now to put together a functioning parliament, able to carry out the will of the Ayatollah which was that the fate of the hostages should finally be decided by "representatives of the people." But that would take time; meanwhile, as a gesture of good will, the militants, said Bani-Sadr, ought to turn control of the hostages over to the Islamic Revolutionary Council, which included several members who identified themselves with the aims of the student militants. But, on March 6, 1980, the students rejected Bani-Sadr's request, declaring that they would wait for the convening of the parliament (Majlis) before handing over the hostages; and they also rejected his request to "allow the special five-member United Nations Commission, visiting Tehran, to meet the hostages." That was a defeat for Bani-Sadr. But there was a strong indication that he was on the right track when, "as a result, those students who agreed with Bani-Sadr's stance left the embassy, bringing down the number of Iranian occupiers . . . to about 300." [Hiro, 149]

We have just reviewed what have remained to this day the most widely held opinions about the motives of the hard-core militants who led the November 4 attack on the U.S. Embassy. The so-called "Khomeini line" adopted by those militants proved effective, as we have seen, to shield them from open attack, even though it manifestly served only as a cover for terrorist blackmail of the governments authorized by Khomeini. Writing of the fall of the Bazargan government in his richly documented book *The United States and Iran: The Pattern of Influence* (New York, 1982), R. K. Ramazani observes that the "extremist elements" managed to bring down "both the provisional minister and his Foreign Minister Yazdi" for having tried to "normalize the relations of revolutionary Iran with the United States." The same sort of blackmail, backed by threats to kill the American hostages if the extremist demands were not heeded, was used, in Ramazani's words, "to discredit Ghotbzadeh, who worked for any early settlement of the hostage dispute," and also Bani-Sadr, in his "last-minute attempt to exploit the settlement of the hostage dispute in favor of his struggle with the Beheshti-Rajai-Rafsanjani triumvirate" — though that triumvirate managed in the end, with a boost from President-elect Ronald Reagan, to beat the hostage-takers at their own game, as we shall see.

CHAPTER THIRTEEN

Ending the Crisis:
Victory for the Foes
of Normalized Relations

In the October 29, 1980 issue of *Time,* Hugh Sidey's editorial essay on the presidential election stressed the fact that the Carter-Reagan race that year was very close indeed, with the "pollsters almost to a man" believing that "one good puff of wind from the Persian Gulf or Moscow," or Israel, "could turn the tide one way or another." For Moscow and Israel in that statement, one could correctly substitute the names of Leonid Brezhnev and Menachem Begin as the foreign "parties" most apt to cast decisive votes in an American election. For the Persian Gulf, the name would of course be that of the Ayatollah Khomeini, whom *Time* had just distinguished, with a touch of apology, as its "Man of the Year."

And yet, with respect to events in U.S.-Iranian relations, Khomeini's importance could be said to have been eclipsed temporarily by what the captors of the U.S. Embassy might choose to do. They had seized the embassy on November 4, 1979, and, as the days, weeks, and months slipped passed, the coincidence of dates with the next year's national elections seemed fateful indeed. By consistently refusing to release control of their American hostages to any "higher authority" — Iranian or international — the hostage captors had apparently matched the boast of Archimedes about his newly-formulated principle of the lever: "Give me but one firm spot on which to stand and I will move the earth." The embassy attackers of November 4, 1979, in total defiance of the Ayatollah, had found that one firm spot in the midst of the revolutionary turmoil of Iran, and they were indeed using it as an Archimedean point of leverage to move and topple governments near and far.

In Tehran, they had set themselves up in the American Embassy. Touch us if you dare, they had said to the Ayatollah's government of Bazargan and Yazdi, warning all parties that the American hostages — blindfolded and lined up occasionally for display — were their lever and the embassy compound their fulcrum. Go ahead! Move against us, or even just speak against us, and see what happens! The Ayatollah's first government had proclaimed itself to be Islamic, to be sure, and also anti-Zionist; but, from the very beginning, as we have seen, it had refused to be anti-American, seeking instead to normalize U.S.-Iranian relations as quickly as possible. No, said the hostage captors, you must be Islamic, anti-Zionist, *and* anti-American too. That was the gauntlet thrown down. And the ministries appointed by the Ayatollah that presumed to pick it up all fell. One after another, they each tried to be revolutionary and anti-Zionist but not anti-American. So long as they did that, whether overtly or covertly, they were doomed. Many of them, throughout the crisis, met first openly and then secretly with American emissaries to make their dilemma clear. They explained that there seemed to be no way of wresting control of the hostages from the November 4 captors without using fatal force or taking up their anti-American demands — co-opting them, as Christopher put it — starting with the demand for the return of the Shah and all the wealth he and his family had sent abroad.

We have repeatedly asked, *cui bono?* To whose advantage were the American hostages held for 444 days? Certainly not to the advantage of the governments of the pro-American ministers of the Ayatollah in Iran or of the Carter administration in the United States, which had been so obviously determined to try to normalize relations with revolutionary Iran as soon as possible. The gainers in the United States were all the political partisans, including Democrats as well as Republicans, who were eager to see President Carter defeated in his bid for a second term. Outside the United States, the chief gainers were the statesmen of Israel who were determined not to permit normalization of U.S.-Iranian relations at Israel's expense. As the Israeli scholar Eytan Gilboa, author of *American Public Opinion Toward Israel and the Arab-Israeli Conflict* (1986), acknowledges, the November 4 seizure of the American embassy and related events greatly improved the favorable ratings for Israel in "the Yankelovich and Gallop polls" of American public opinion, contributing, as he says "to Israel's enhanced image in the United States as a stable and strong democracy." [61]

Eventually, politico-religious factions in Iran would also find ways of "profiting" from the hostage crisis. But, even those factions, in the end, lost more than they could have hoped to gain. After their apparent victory over rival contenders for power, those factions had to turn humbly to Israel to try to get — for the safety of their nation — what, except for the hostage crisis, they might much more easily have obtained directly from the United States through normalized relations.

1. The "Evil of Factions" in Iranian and American Domestic Affairs

An indispensable book on the link between the 1979-1981 hostage crisis and the Reagan administration's efforts of 1985-86 to make direct contact with the Ayatollah's government is *The Eagle and the Lion: The Tragedy of American-Iranian Relations* (New Haven, 1988), by James A. Bill. Even the severest critics of Professor Bill's conclusions acknowledge that he must be ranked as one of the two or three best informed scholars on recent Iranian affairs; and anyone who takes the trouble to read his book must conclude that what he has to say about the principal American and Iranian factional leaders in the "Iranian crises" of the Carter and Reagan administrations is most carefully and thoroughly documented.

James Bill stresses late in his book that the origins of the November 4, 1979, embassy seizure in Tehran must really be traced back to the impression made on the Ayatollah's government, and on all Iranians supporting it, by the actions and statements of three leading pro-Shah Americans between May and October 1979, while the Carter administration's efforts to normalize U.S.-Iranian relations, after the Shah's fall, were in high gear. Carter had appointed a new ambassador to Iran — after receiving assurances from Tehran that the man named was fully acceptable — and the U.S. Senate had quickly voted favorably on the appointment. But, as we noted earlier, right on the heels of the Senate's approval came the drive, led by Senators Jacob Javits, Henry Jackson, and Abraham Ribicoff, to bring the normalization process to a dead halt. Javits, Jackson, and Ribicoff did not merely condemn the Ayatollah's government for executing Shah supporters in Iran "without due process"; they also joined their voices with Henry Kissinger's in affirming that the United States should indeed "stick with the Shah" in defeat and try perhaps to turn that defeat into victory. In the words of Senator Ribicoff, during the Senate debate on the May 17 Javits resolution: "the Shah was a proven and true friend of the United States. The entire world should condemn the excesses now taking place in Iran."

The head of the American Embassy in Iran at the time, chargé d'affaires Charles Naas, thus summed up the Iranian response to the Javits Senate resolution: "The place went wild." And Professor Bill reminds us that American diplomats in Tehran received news of the resolution "with consternation," for they had been "anxiously awaiting the arrival of the new U.S. ambassador, Walter Cutler, who was ready to leave for Iran as part of the process of normalization." Naas had at that very time been in the midst of arranging what was to be a first meeting of American officials with the Ayatollah Khomeini himself. As James Bill tells it:

> Naas's plans for a meeting with Khomeini were laid to rest forever, and Naas, who had been working on Iranian affairs since 1974, left Iran in June in a gloomy and despondent frame of mind. Many believe that this Senate action, promoted by American Pahlavites with especially close ties to the state of Israel, was the first major event leading to the U.S. Embassy takeover five months later. Charles Naas stated that the Javits resolution "really hurt us" and that from then on the Iranians "refused to play ball." [284-5]

Professor Bill, who has read with care the 58 published volumes of documents left intact or pieced together from shreds found in the Tehran embassy, calls attention to a pieced-together communication addressed to Secretary of State Cyrus Vance by Bruce Laingen, dated October 28, 1979. Laingen reports on the Iranian response to

Henry Jackson's interview with "Meet the Press" in which the pro-Israeli Senator said that "the Iranian revolution was doomed to failure and that the country was about to break up into small pieces." That anti-Ayatollah statement, writes Bill, was "greeted with some concern in Iran, where officials assumed that this public pronouncement by an influential American senator was not only proof of American hostility but also an indication that the United States had plans to help break Iran into little pieces." Citing the words of Laingen's report, Bill concludes: "According to one high-ranking Iranian official who was then in touch with U.S. Embassy officials, Senator Jackson's words 'had hit the upper levels of the foreign ministry like a bombshell.' Again, in Tehran, American diplomats were horrified. Senator Jackson's statement represented one more milestone along the way to American-Iranian estrangment." [285]

By the end of the Carter term on January 20, 1981, it was clear that the American foes of normalized U.S.-Iranian relations, led by Henry Kissinger and the Rockefeller group as a whole, had completely triumphed. The Israeli statesmen were pleased, and so were the militants who had seized the American Embassy in Tehran on November 4, 1979. The Ayatollah's government was almost as much a loser as the Carter administration, though not quite, for, in the end, it succeeded, at least, in preventing the militant hostage-captors from killing any of the Americans.

Professor Bill supplies an instructive assessment of what he calls the "three major power struggles within Iran" brought on by the second embassy seizure. The most widely publicized "confrontation" that resulted was that "between the extremists and the moderates" in the government as a whole. But Bill assigns far more importance to the struggle that developed between the "formal government apparatus represented by the Islamic Republican party [IRP]. . .and the student militants within the embassy compound." It is true that, "like Khomeini himself, IRP leaders such as Muhammad Hussein Beheshti" initially opposed the embassy takeover, only to feel constrained to co-opt the captors' position as their own when they saw no other way of saving the lives of the captive Americans. "Nevertheless," writes Bill, "tension persisted between the government and the students," with government leaders "privately warning the militants that if any of the hostages were to die, the student captors would themselves pay with their lives.'' [296-7]

That ultimatum laid down by the religious leaders in the government must not be ignored in assessing how the Ayatollah's government acted in trying to meet its international obligations. It is impossible to avoid the conclusion that it acted in a more civilized fashion than the Carter administration, which persisted in holding the pro-American governments of Bazargan and Yazdi, Bani-Sadr and Ghotbzadeh fully responsible if any harm came to the Americans. The Javitses, Jacksons, and Ribicoffs had been permitted, without official censure, to advance the most barbaric sorts of factional and racial-religious accusations against the Bazargan-Yazdi government while that government was plainly seeking normalized relations with the United States. In this regard, Bill points to the least publicized of struggles precipitated in Iran by the November 4 embassy seizure. Bill refers to it as the ''third and more specific power struggle'' which ''occurred on the embassy grounds itself, where the students formed various factions that included an important left-right division.'' We have taken notice of the fact that, at a certain moment, about 150 of the students occupying the embassy surprised their colleagues by abruptly moving out, declaring that they agreed with Bani-Sadr's assertion that continued occupation of the embassy would hurt the revolution. But Professor Bill stresses another level of the internal struggle — one which went on after the supporters of Bani-Sadr had left the embassy. Bill writes:

> Although the religious extremists outnumbered the students of Marxist inclination, the latter were in many ways more desperate and therefore more likely to take some dramatic retributive act against an American prisoner. There was a serious danger, especially during the beginning months, that such an act might occur, thereby forcing military confrontation between Iran and the United States. Such an act would introduce a new level of conflict — war — and would benefit both the radical left within Iran and quite possibly the Soviet Union.... Partly because of this danger, the left was gradually purged within the student ranks, and the Islamic extremists took control. [297]

Thus, while the IRP gradually made itself the voice of student militancy in the government, it sought also to create among the militants holding the vast American Embassy compound — spread out over the equivalent of about 25 "city blocks" in the heart of Tehran — a new leadership that would have no intention of killing the hostages. It wasn't an easy thing to do; but, in the end, it was done. In the end, the "students of Marxist inclination" among the embassy captors lost their leverage; but for a whole year, at any rate, they had enjoyed a tremendous press in the United States, all to the delight of the American factional foes of normalized U.S.-Iranian relations.

Professor Bill dwells on the gross misrepresentation of the significance of the final release of the 52 American hostages in the American news media — a misrepresentation encouraged, unfortunately, by the campaign directors of both major political parties. In Bill's words:

> Although many Americans proclaimed the release. . . a victory, the hostage episode was, if anything, a serious defeat for American foreign policy. After calling attention to a sign in one of the celebration parades that read "U.S. 52, Iran 0," former hostage Barry Rosen writes that this mentality "expressed the wishful thinking of hundreds of people I talked to, most of whom resented my opinion that we hadn't *won,* and that I myself was proof of this." He concludes that "the entire episode was closer to defeat for both sides, which no amount of celebrating could tranform into its opposite." [302]

Bill adds that, "in the longer run, Rosen's analysis is quite correct." The governments of Carter and Khomeini were indeed both losers. But, it is hardly true that there were no winners. The winners, we must repeat, were the domestic factional opponents of those two governments. In the United States, those opponents were led by Kissinger as spokesman for the Rockefeller group; in Iran they were led by the still-unidentified mentors of the left-oriented students who used the second embassy seizure to destroy the Ayatollah's pro-American goverment headed by Bazargan and Yazdi.

Ironically, both Barry Rosen and James Bill unhesitatingly acknowledge that, "within the short-term context of Iranian revolutionary politics," the "militants and extremists" who seized the American embassy "gained a great deal from the hostage episode," with the United States becoming what Bill calls "their unwitting ally by publicizing the event far out of proportion to its significance in the world of politics." "Unwitting" is the correct word to use about President Carter's "services" as an "ally" of those militants; but surely there was nothing "unwitting" about what the Kissingers, Javitses, Jacksons, and Ribicoffs did. On the contrary, their purposes as opponents of normalized U.S.-Iranian relations were better served in the end than the ultimate purposes aimed at by the militant captors of the U.S. embassy, who were made to pay dearly for their stunt once control of the hostages was finally wrested from them by the Ayatollah's government — though, as we shall see, after the Islamic Republican Party leaders finally wrested control of the hostages from the original captors, and after the Americans were safely returned to the United States, many of the IRP leaders were themselves assassinated by disgruntled left-wing factional leaders.

Compounding the irony is the fact that, as Bill observes, the "widely discussed congressional hearings" on the hostage crisis "held in March 1981 proved to be nothing but brief, perfunctory exercises involving limited, shallow questions." He points out that several of the better informed American hostages — particularly those fluent in Farsi, who could understand what their captors were saying among themselves — were "embarrassed and disturbed" to learn that, not only the congressional committee, but the Department of State itself "chose to ignore" what had really happened. Bill writes:

> In the words of John Limbert, an extremely talented Iran specialist and former hostage: *"No one* spoke to any of the Persian speaking political officers among the hostages to find out what happened and who the captors were. . . . My overall impression is that most officials, with a few exceptions, just didn't care." A serious examination of what happend and why would certainly have uncovered many unpalatable truths. It would have also done America an enormous favor by providing a badly needed explanation so that errors, oversights, and misunderstandings made in the past may not necessarily have to be repeated in the future. [303-304]

Fortunately, what the congressional inquiries and the State Department failed to do back then has since been done more or less effectively by scholars like Tim Wells who; for his book titled *444 Days: The Hostages Remember* (New York 1985), spent two and a half years "talking with the former hostages" and recording their responses to questions and other statements. Wells traveled "over twenty thousand miles and gathered in excess of five thousand pages of interview transcript"; and his declared object was to "redress the grievance" expressed by most of the released hostages which was that "much of what had been written about them in the popular press" was "neither accurate nor truthful." Wells adds that, "in spite of the steady stream of publicity, precious little was known about the actual circumstances of the hostages' captivity. Most of the information received by the American public was based on speculation, rumor, and the militants' own propaganda. Hard facts simply did not exist." Wells's book runs to some 500 pages; but he notes that all the taped interviews, "along with verbatim transcripts" that run to 5,000 pages "are being housed at Perkins Library on the campus of Duke University, where they will be made available to scholars, historians, and interested persons." [ix-x]

On the State of Israel's gain from the effort of the November 4 embassy attackers to bring the process of normalizing U.S-Iranian relations to a halt, the Wells interviews with the released hostages throw little light. The chief political officers among them, it is clear, had all been fully persuaded that the Javits Senate resolution condemming the Ayatollah's government for its executions of Shah supporters, including a very prominent Iranian Jew, had rendered the embassy most vulnerable, since it was generally viewed in Iran as an effort to force the Carter administration to identify itself more completely with Israeli interests. It is clear, also, that the Iranian Jews employed by the embassy were fearful of being singled out for special punishment by the attackers because they were Jews.

That had been the case also on February 14, 1979. It is Colonel Leland Holland, the army attaché under Ambassador Sullivan, who tells Wells that, when Sullivan "put me outside in the main corridor to surrender the building when these guys [the heavily armed attackers of February 14] made their way up to the second floor of the build-

ing,'' he had brought out with him, to act as interpreter, "an old
Iranian. . . who spoke Farsi with the same kind of accent" as the attackers. Holland says "I thought we were going to be killed. There
wasn't any other thought in my mind.'' Needless to say, his interpreter was even more fearful. In Holland's words:

> He was going to pieces. He had tears running down his face.
> I said, "Damn, man, don't break down on me now. I need you."
> He said, "I'm a Jew. When they figure that out, they're go-
> ing to kill me."
> "Hey, we're both in this together," I said. Then I opened
> the door.
> These guys came bursting in and fanned out immediately. We
> were slapped around and put up against the wall.

On February 14, the fears of the Iranian Jew "who spoke Farsi with
the same kind of accent" as the attackers proved to be unfounded.
And that proved to be the case also in the second embassy seizure.
There were no attacks of an anti-Semitic character either on Iranian
Jewish employees of the embassy or on American-Jewish members
of the embassy staff. What the attackers of November 4 did,
however, that had a strong bearing on American-Israeli relations was
to include in the materials for the 58 volumes of embassy documents
subsequently published several official reports on Israeli intelligence
activities in Iran under the Shah. The object of publicizing those
reports was to show that the United States and Israel were inseparably linked in such activities and that, therefore, if they justified severing Iranian/Israel relations completely, the same ought to apply to
relations with Israel's chief supporter in all the world, the United
States.

James Bill reviews this matter of the "Mossad-SAVAK connection," as discussed in embassy-CIA reports pieced together by the
November 4 attackers, in some detail. According to one such report,
"the main purpose of the Israeli relationship with Iran was the development of a pro-Israeli anti-Arab policy on the part of Iranian
officials. Mossad has engaged in joint operations with SAVAK over
the years since the late 1950s. Mossad aided SAVAK activities. . . .
The Israelis also regularly transmitted to the Iranians intelligence

reports on Egypt's activities in the Arab countries, trends and developments in Iraq, and Communist activities affecting Iran." Another embassy report spoke of the "fruitful private relationship" maintained between Iran and Israel which permitted "senior representatives" to reside "in each other's country even though diplomatic relations do not formally exist. Intelligence information is exchanged regularly, and several Israeli technical assistance projects in agriculture and other fields are underway in Iran. Despite the Arab oil embargo, Iran has never cut its flow of oil to Israel and today [1977] provides 50 percent of Israel's oil requirements." [430-1]

Looking ahead, James Bill notes that, "due to the persistence of Israeli leaders and the wartime needs of the Islamic Republic of Iran after the Shah's overthrow, this Israeli-Iran connection continued to exist, albeit in a much modified form. The heavy Israeli involvement in arms supplies to Iran became a matter of public record with the 1986 exposure of the Reagan administration's secret Iran policy." [431] But, at the point we have reached in our review of Carter's handling of the hostage crisis, the factional fight on the embassy grounds had not yet resulted in defeat for the students of the radical-left. Determined, as they were, to make a normalization of U.S.-Iranian relations impossible, they had still in their grasp the power to assist their American counterparts in their aim of frustrating Carter's bid for reelection. By November 4, 1980, those Marxist militants who were anything but "religious fanatics," had undeniably been able to exercise, in the name of religion, an influence in American politics almost on a par with the laboriously-acquired influence that Jewish leaders in America have frequently claimed.

2. Tipping the Scales in the 1980 Presidential Election

Early in 1980, President Carter, an avowed "born-again Christian," saw himself unmistakably faced with what his chief campaign advisers identified as a serious "Jewish problem." He learned, first of all, that there was a publicly professed reluctance on the part of organized Jewish political-action groups in the United States to favor second-term Presidents almost as a matter of principle. Thus, on the eve of the election, the *Jewish Week-American Examiner* (October 26, 1980) ran an editorial focused on the question: "Is Israel better off in the second administration of any President?" The editorial made the point that second-term Presidents are apt to ignore the electoral power of their Jewish constituencies, which they couldn't afford to do during their first terms. That, it was feared, might prove particularly true, and unfortunate, in the case of Carter.

At about the same time, Emanuel Rackman, a highly respected Jewish-American leader, clarified the argument by way of explaining why he would not vote for the "incumbent"in 1980. "No one can convince me," he wrote, "that Carter's record is one for which I can be grateful and this is his record during a term when he hoped to be elected for a second term. What he will do when he has no eye on another term and no concern for the Jewish vote I dare not visualize. Are his opponents any better? I do not known. . . . But I am displeased with what I now have." In the same Jewish weekly cited above, Robert Weintraub spelled out the argument in these terms:

> Let us understand that we have the power to deny the Presidency to Mr. Carter. No Democrat in recent years, with the exception of Lyndon Johnson in 1964, could have won the Presidency without overwhelming Jewish support. In 1976, Carter won and our support was crucial to his victory. If he appreciated Jewish support, it never showed. On the contrary, no President has been so abusive of Israel as Carter. . . . We must do everything we can to deny Carter another term. . . . Why should Carter merit our trust now?. . . It remains to be seen whether Jews can overcome old fears and prejudices and vote for either [John] Anderson or Reagan on November 4.

We get a more considered, scholarly account of the phenomenon in Nimrod Novik's *The United States and Israel: Domestic Determinants of a Changing U.S. Commitment* (1986). The author reminds us that Carter had received "70% of the Jewish vote when first seeking office" as President in 1976; and then, to give us a fair measure of the fall from favor in 1980, he points out that Carter in fact broke "a 56-year record in receiving less than 50% of that vote in his race for a second term." The last time a Democratic presidential candidate received less than 50% of the Jewish vote had been in 1924, when Republican Calvin Coolidge won, while the Progressive and Democratic Party candidates split the opposition vote between them. Then came the 1928 election of Herbert Hoover over Alfred E. Smith, in which the loser got well over 50% of the Jewish vote, after which Jewish majorities were to be consistently counted as favoring Democrats, win or lose, until 1980.

Franklin D. Roosevelt, building on Al Smith's appeal, won four times in a row, from 1932 through 1944, always with over 50% Jewish support. Similar majorities went to a victorious Harry Truman in 1948, to a twice defeated Adlai Stevenson in 1952 and 1956, to victorious John Kennedy in 1960 and Lyndon Johnson in 1964, next to the defeated Democrats Hubert Humphrey in 1968 and George McGovern in 1972, and to victorious Jimmy Carter in 1976. Thus it was indeed a 56-year record that was broken in 1980, when Jewish voters divided well over 50% of their vote between Ronald Reagan and John Anderson, in what was plainly "an anti-Carter demonstration," as Novik puts it. Explaining the reversal, Novik observes that Carter's "Middle East policies were found less popular among Jews than those of any President since Eisenhower." [It is significant that, in 1984, the principled distrust of second-term Presidents among Jewish-American voters took its toll. As Dick Zander of *Newsday* observed (Nov. 18, '84), "Nationally, Jews voted 2-1 for [Walter] Mondale over Reagan. They were the only ethnic group to show less support for Reagan this year than in 1980."]

But in 1980, when polls began to show that the defection of Jewish votes would of itself cost him the election, President Carter quite humbly made the rounds of the states, particularly New York, Florida, New Jersey, Pennsylvania, and California, where the "Jewish vote" is "disproportionately influential," and in which a shift of relatively few votes would tip the electoral scales in his favor. Many Democratic leaders, including Mario Cuomo of New York, urged Carter to "do a Houston" with Jewish voters — appealing to them the way John F. Kennedy had appealed to Protestant voters who had been apprehensive about Kennedy's Catholicism in 1960. As

Albert H. Hunt wrote in *The American Elections of 1980* (A. Ranney, ed. Washington, 1980):

> In 1980, Jewish antipathy to Carter, mainly over what was perceived to be insufficient support for Israel, was extraordinary, if somewhat irrational. Many Jews gave the president little credit for what was probably the most impressive achievement of his term: the Camp David summit. . . . Carter did stage a miniconfrontation at a Jewish community center in New York in mid-October, but there never was a dramatic encounter. Still the president made other moves with an eye on the Jewish vote: he announced, with great fanfare, that the United States would not sell parts to Saudi Arabia for the war planes the United States had sold the Arabs earlier, and in late October former Israeli defense minister Ezer Weizman was conspicuously present on the president's campaign plane. [159]

Still, some of the keenest political commentators described it as rather obvious that Carter was then more concerned with "swinging" a far more distant "constituency" in his favor by election day. It evidently seemed to him that he wouldn't need a return of his 1976 Jewish support to win — if only he could get Iran to release the American hostages by November 4, 1980, the first anniversary of the start of the crisis.

Whether it was true or not, many Americans apparently became persuaded with the start of the presidential primaries in 1980 that President Carter was, on a daily basis, "playing politics" with the lives of the American hostages in Iran, first to win Democratic primaries against Senator Edward Kennedy, and then to prevail over Ronald Reagan in the national election. In his book, *The Other Side of the Story* (1984), Carter's chief White House spokesman, Jody Powell, has extensively documented his charge that first the *New York Times* and then the *Washington Post* laid the groundwork for subsequent reporting of news of the Iran hostage crisis on a daily basis as evidence of "crisis diplomacy" contaminated to the core by political ambition. Powell cites front-page stories of late March and early April 1980 that were headlined: "Iran's Shadow on the Primary" and "Carter Victories Abetted by Oval Office Television."

Those early headline stories, says Powell, were "incredibly damaging because they set the tone for the treatment of the President that
was to continue throughout the campaign and beyond." [219]

Other news stories in those days reflected the extent of opposition to Carter in his own party. As in the case of Lyndon Johnson
and Harry Truman before him, a large percentage of Democratic
activists — perhaps a majority — would have preferred to see a
Republican elected rather than suffer "four more years" of Carter
in the White House, with his "Georgia mafia" attempting to do irreparable damage to the hated northeastern Democratic establishment. But, after Carter managed to win enough of the primaries to
assure his nomination, Republican partisans took over the attack,
with abundant support, however, from disgruntled Democrats. A
central focus of the Reagan presidential campaign of 1980 became,
of course, the charge that President Carter was working on what
came to be called an "October surprise" — to gain the release of
the hostages by hook or crook before November 4, or even to plunge
the nation into war in a politically-motivated attempt to gain sufficient instinctive public support to assure his relection.

In retrospect, it has become clearer and clearer that the kind
of covert connections with Iranain revolutionary leaders that surfaced during the Iran-Contra public inquires in 1986-1987 had their
beginnings in the extralegal efforts of the Republican campaign operatives, back in 1980, to prevent Carter's profiting from any "October surprise." That became the central issue of the campaign and
led at once to magnification of the hostage crisis into a spectacular
media event comparable to the "living-room" TV coverage of the
Vietnam war that earlier forced President Johnson to give up his
bid for reelection in 1968.

It is true, as we have already noted, that political leaders in
Iran also "played politics" with the crisis, once it was clear that
the American hostages would not be surrendered to the Ayatollah's government until that government had convincingly
"legitimized" the patently criminal embassy seizure. Yet it was political factionalism in the United States, not its counterpart in Iran,
that effectively prevented the United States from pursuing a truly
statesmanly response to the crisis, once the initial decision was taken

by the White House to make the physical safety of the hostages its absolute priority.

3. The Fail-Safe Rescue Mission that "Safely Failed": April 1980

Between November 4, 1979, and early March 1980, the United States, as Gary Sick summarizes, "worked through the United Nations, with the international community, with intermediaries, and with a negotiating scenario consciously designed to give Iran a dignified way out of the impasse without sacrificing fundamental U.S. honor and interests." The negotiating effort referred to, making use of "French and Argentine intermediaries," had really collapsed by March 10, although "President Bani-Sadr and his Foreign Minister, Sadegh Ghotbzadeh, continued to improvise desperately" for over a month, to salvage the negotiating process; and, in Sick's words, "no one in the U.S. government wanted to see the negotiating effort collapse, especially since the two Iranian principals had staked their political lives on the issue." [151] Still, Sick permits himself to add that, "in each instance," the U.S. efforts to "give Iran a dignified way out" had been "rejected contemptuously by Iran's revolutionary leadership." That is a strong statement. The fact is that, through all the period of such "rejections," both governments, Carter's and the Ayatollah's, were being much abused in the American newsmedia. And so a civilized recognition or acknowledgement of the sort of dilemma each of them was facing became impossible.

A parallel situation would later be faced by the Reagan administration when it decided, in the mid-1980s, to trade arms to the Iranians directly, instead of through the "more experienced" Israelis. The Reagan White House had then to face charges, from Arthur Schlesinger, for instance, that it had been *duplicitous* in its *covert* activities because it had *overtly* said it would *not* trade with Islamic Iran. Needless to say, as Schlesinger knows only too well, *covert* means *duplicitous,* and cannot be anything but duplicitous, having to be done while, on the surface, it is said that nothing of the sort is being done. The Reagan administration has found itself in the same "fix" the Ayatollah Khoemini found himself while encouraging his brain-trust — consisting of Bazargan, Yazdi, Bani-Sadr, and Ghotb-zadeh — to try to prevent a total severance of diplomatic relations on the part of the United States. It is important to stress that *at no time* did the Ayatollah take any initiative to break off diplomatic relations with the United States. And that is nothing to marvel at, for it was manifestly not in the interest of his Islamic Republic of Iran to do so. It was rather in the interest of its enemies.

Why then does Gary Sick, who knows better, speak of the Ayatollah's having been "contemptuous" in rejecting U.S. efforts to give his government a "dignified way out?" The answer is that Sick, in the line of duty, is "covering" for President Carter's political impatience, for as he puts it, by that time, Carter had "made it very clear to his advisers that he was unwilling to sit passively for another three or four months in the vague hope that the revolutionary chaos in Iran would eventually resolve itself." [153]

But what were the feasible alternatives to passively waiting? Would Carter be willing to intervene militarily to "teach the Iranians" and other leaders in the Third World a lesson? Was he ready, in Sick's words, to order "punitive military action. . . against selected Iranian targets," like "refineries, rail facilities, power stations, docks," etc? Was he willing to ask Congress to "declare war" for the sake of the national honor? The answer was obviously an emphatic No! Punitive action against selected targets — to say nothing of declaring war! — was ruled out, writes Sick, "because it was believed" that it would "put the hostages' lives in danger and would risk pushing the new Iranian government into the arms of the USSR." [153]

There we see the vicious circle drawn all the way around. The White House had effectively prevented the Iranian government from using force to "free the U.S. Embassy" from its criminal captors: it had admonished that if any Iranian initiative brought harm to the hostages, the U.S. would promptly take punitive military action against that government, confident of overwhelming domestic American support for the action. At the same time, prior coercive use of military force by the U.S. was ruled out for the reason given above. That was Carter's impossible dilemma. Doing nothing was ruled out, but so was recourse to the only means that could have sufficed to force the issue. That meant the Carter handling of the crisis was doomed to fail.

And yet, despite the consequent collapse of the Carter Presidency, and the collapse also of its fully reciprocated efforts to normalize relations with the Ayatollah's government, we have the paradoxical conclusion drawn by Harold Saunders, on behalf of the U.S. State Department, that the "entire experience" had, indeed, by late January 1981, "provided the world with a singular example of the art of diplomacy." [296] Such a judgment would be patently absurd, unless Saunders meant the term "singular example" to be taken in an utterly negative sense — which is hardly the case.

Having ruled out the alternatives of doing nothing and applying exemplary, punitive force, the Carter White House fell back on a number of intermediate positions and tried them all. "The strategy adopted during the first two weeks of April 1980," writes Sick, was a combination of (1) "efforts to locate alternative channels of communication to Khomeini," (2) "additional unilateral sanctions," (3) efforts to "persuade other nations to impose sanctions," (4) semi-military sanctions like blockading ports or mining selected harbors, and (5) an "independent effort. . .to extract the hostages by a rescue mission." The first four means were pursued publicly, with much publicity, partly in the hope that they might succeed, but mainly as a cover for implementing the fifth means, a covert rescue mission.

Here we must remind ourselves that, like Kissinger's war in Vietnam, for which Kissinger had written the blueprint in 1957, as criticism of Eisenhower's use of a threat of massive retaliation to contain local enemy aggression in Korea, President Carter's effort to extract the hostages by means of a desert rescue mission in early 1980 was a "fail-safe" military operation, "designed to be conducted," as Sick writes,

> in a series of related steps, each of which would be reversible without escalation and with minimum casualties should something go wrong. The need to be able to terminate and withdraw at any point, together with the need for absolute secrecy, added to the complexity and difficulty of both planning and execution. The first

stage of the plan involved the positioning of men, material, and
support equipment at key locations in the Middle East and Indi-
an Ocean. . . . The insertion of the force into Iran was a grueling
and technically difficult operation. Under cover of darkness, eight
RH-53D helicopters and six C-130 aircraft were to depart from
different locations, fly into Iran, and rendezvous at an airstrip
some 500 miles inland. [154-155]

Those were the phases of the mission actually carried out. On the
rendezvous airstrip, the aircraft would discharge their loads, the
helicopters would be refueled, and, with their combat crews on board,
they would fly to a "remote site in the mountains above Tehran,"
where they would be camouflaged until the assigned time for entering Tehran under the cover of darkness. The combat team would
then be transported to Tehran in local trucks supplied by local agents.
Its members would penetrate the embassy in darkness, taking the
guards by surprise, quite in the manner that the hostage takers had
originally taken the Ayatollah's embassy guards by surprise — "with
the helicopters making the briefest possible appearance to pick up
the team and the hostages." [156] In the end, the helicopters would
take the team and hostages to an abandoned airfield near Tehran,
to board transport aircraft, which would fly out "under heavy U.S.
air cover," leaving the helicopters behind. Of course, as Sick reminds
us, the "actual rescue mission failed long before it arrived at the embassy walls." There were several mishaps and miscalculations. In
the end, a helicopter collided with a transport aircraft, resulting in
the death of eight crew members and the wounding of five others,
the dead being left behind with the abandoned helicopters.

When one considers carefully the fact that the rescue attempt
was intended to be "fail-safe," which is to say, "reversible without
escalation" at every stage, it can be deemed to have been a success
— except for the accidental loss of American lives! Even the announcement that the attempt had been made (issued at 1:00 a.m.
on April 25) and President Carter's subsequent TV address assuming "personal responsibility" for its failure, had "fail-safe" com-
ponents built into them. As Gary Sick explains: "The purpose of
the announcement and its timing were intended to insure that Iran

would not mistake the events at Desert I for an invasion attempt and retaliate against the hostages. From all accounts, Iran became aware of the raid only when officially informed of it by President Carter." [159]

Of course, although the failed rescue mission of April 1980 had never been intended as such, it quickly came to be treated by some Iranian factions as "an assault to overthrow the Iranian government," rather than simply to assist it, under a display of force, in gaining control of the American hostages. Following immediately upon the failure came Secretary of State Cyrus Vance's resignation. Vance had flatly opposed the mission, or any other use of force, to rescue the hostages or recover the embassy — and he had in effect handed in his resignation before the event. His resignation, coupled with the mission's failure, encouraged the most hostile Iranian factions to "dramatize" the moment, in the words of Harold Saunders, as "an example of the United States' depravity and impotence." And that Iranian charge found much support in the ranks of American Carter-foes, eager to make use of the failure to gain an electoral victory.

4. Alternatives and Pseudo-Alternatives

After the aborted desert rescue mission was disclosed, many military, or semi-military alternatives were publicly discussed. In his chapter on military options and restraints, Gary Sick himself very soberly discussed the option of a U.S. declaration of war against Iran, which surfaced at least three times in White House National Security Council meetings: first, right after the November 4 embassy seizure, then again in January 1980, after the Soviet veto of the United Nations Security Council resolutions on sanctions against Iran, and finally in early April, after the secret negotiations through French lawyers, Bani-Sadr, and Ghotbzadeh collapsed. In each case, it appears that the damage to be expected by the Carter administration from a serious effort to get Congress to "declare war" far outweighed any conceivable advantages. Though the Democratic Party controlled both houses of Congress, it was certain that Carter would have found himself as much opposed there as Lyndon Johnsón had been during the last two years of his elective term, when the pro-Kennedy factions of his party joined the Republicans in condemning his conduct of the war in Vietnam.

The Carter/Lyndon Johnson parallel needs some clarification. Some commentators on Johnson's conduct of the Vietnam war have identified what has come to be called a *"Pueblo* syndrome," which surfaced in the Johnson White House when, just before the North Vietnamese "Tet Offensive" of early 1968, the North Koreans seized the American military-intelligence ship *Pueblo* with all its officers and men, who were then held hostage by the North Korean government. North Korean combat vessels had made the attack — so that there was no question about its being an official government operation. Even so, President Johnson had given his national security establishment, including his new Secretary of Defense, Clark Clifford, a direct order of priorities, indicating without qualification that his primary concern was to assure the personal safety of the officers and men taken hostage.

It is ironic that the seizure of the *Pueblo* did not, at the time, "come to dominate American politics and foreign policy" to anything like the extent to which the Iran hostage crisis did, even though the number of hostages taken with the *Pueblo* was 80 as compared to 52 in Tehran, and the length of captivity was about the same. As to the consequences of President Johnson's stand in the 1968 hostage crisis, there can be no doubt that they were very serious from a national security standpoint. His insistence on the safety of the hostages as an absolute priority sent a signal to Hanoi that, if they escalated their attacks on American personnel in South Vietnam (as they did in the "Tet Offensive"), the Johnson White House would respond as it had to the seizure of the *Pueblo*. They knew that there would be no "massive retalitiation," or even a threat of massive retaliation, such as President Eisenhower had made to end local aggression in Korea. A way had thus been prepared for the Kissinger-Nixon unilateral withdrawal of all American combat forces in Vietnam, as a fail-safe means of reducing American casualties.

But here is Gary Sick's apt paraphrase of President Carter's version of the *Pueblo* syndrome, which we have earlier identified also as Kissinger's fail-safe strategy of no-win belligerency and defeatist interventionism:

> By openly proclaiming the hostages' physical safety as the central concern of U.S. policy and by focusing almost exclusively on diplomatic rather than military instrumentalities during the first critical months, the United States may have unnecessarily relinquished a useful psychological weapon. Khomeini and others were able to conclude rather early in the crisis that, as long as the hostages remained physically safe, the United States would limit its response primarily to the realm of economic sanctions and international public opinion. [170]

But, as for Carter's insistence that the physical safety of the hostages had to be the first priority, Sick correctly concludes:

> To lead is to chose. The President of the United States largely chose to forego the use of the violent means at his command. Iran remained intact, but the hostages spent an agonizing 444 days in captivity. Partly as a consequence, the President was defeated at the polls. . . . The Iranian hostage crisis touched directly on American national values and raised questions of profound, even philosophical, importance. How does a nation or its leadership reconcile the contradictions between the protection of innocent human lives and the preservation of national honor? . . . As participants and observers, we are entitled to our opinions, but final judgments are the province of history. [171-2]

Very different from Gary Sick's assessment of the alternative of resorting to war, or comparable military force, in meeting the challenge of the Tehran embassy seizure was the approach urged by William Safire in one of his widely read "neo-conservative" columns for the *New York Times,* published a few weeks after the seizure (Nov. 26, '79). A chief speechwriter for President Nixon and proud companion of Henry Kissinger in several of the latter's major diplomatic exploits, Safire suggested some very bold initiatives, to be taken either by Carter or, preferably, by a Republican successor. With his usual candor for much-favored causes, he hailed the second embassy seizure as an opportunity almost too good to be true — indeed, as something beyond any partisan good fortune the enemies of Jimmy Carter had a right to expect. Offering Carter his unsolicited advice, Safire wrote: "The Ayatollah's provocation is heaven-sent. The President's job is neither to turn the other cheek nor to retaliate in fury, but to use the incident with audacity to assert American power in the mid-East and to reverse the strategic decline over which he has presided."

Given his close links with Kissinger, one might have expected Safire to note the obvious parallel, and contrast, between the November 4, 1979 embassy attack in Tehran and the storming of the U.S. Embassy in Saigon in April 1975, after the last Americans had been effectively driven out of the Vietnam peninsula. It was in Saigon that U.S. "honor" suffered its worst humiliation on record, whereas in Tehran, from beginning to end, the hostage crisis did far more damage to Iran's short and long term interests than to those of the United States. But, with his partisanly-sharp pen, Safire proceeds to argue as if it were a fact that the Iranian govermnent had officially launched the attack and therefore merited the sort of "lesson" he was proposing. The attack was a heaven-sent provocation because of what it obviously "authorized" the United States to do in response. The "best part of it," he adds, "is that the aggressor is neither Arab nor Soviet." Then, without bothering to explain why that is the "best part," he hastens to add:

> Rather than merely react, . . . we could thoughtfully respond — in a way that projects our forces into the area on a long-term basis. We could recoup the losses of a decade and re-establish our strategic preeminence. First, we should lease the two airfields being returned to the Egyptians by the Israelis in the Sinai. These are among the most sophisticated airbases in the world, built with our equipment, capable of handling our B-52s. . . . Long-term leases of these desert outposts — no population nearby, no security problem — would position us legally as firmly as at Guantanamo. A substantial rental would help ease Egypt's economic woes. To protect the bases, a permanent U.S. ground force would be needed — which could double as an Egypt-Israel peace-keeping force — and could be strengthened by air quickly if Saudi Arabia or the oil emirates were threatened.

Safire says all of that as if he had never heard of the "Nixon doctrine," which Henry Kissinger had concocted and Safire himself had helped to formulate in words. He says all of that as if he didn't know that the Kissinger-Nixon decision to "Vietnamize" the fighting in Vietnam had been inextricably linked from the beginning with the Kissinger-Nixon plan to build up Iran as a mid-East semi-superpower *without* an active presence of U.S. military forces. It had taken over four years to withdraw all U.S. forces from Vietnam, in preparation for a diplomatic surrender to Hanoi that would not humiliate President Nixon before the 1972 election campaign. The strategy for Iran had been, as we have seen, to pour in arms and technology (paid for by 400% increases in Iranian oil revenues) without any intrusion of American fighting forces. In fact, when the Shah fell, the United States had no bases of any kind in Iran, not even for gathering "electronic intelligence." The Iranians had used equipment purchased from American companies to gather intelligence, with tens of thousands of American civilian military experts employed to help operate it; but the results were always under Iranian control — information handouts being regularly sent to the U.S. Embassy for further distribution — except in the measure that Israel's Mossad might have succeeded in maintaining independent intelligence resources.

Safire's proposal to use American-Israeli built airfields in the Sinai region as a U.S. power base, with permanent U.S. ground forces on the scene, was about as farfetched a proposal as even the *New York Times* could risk imposing on its otherwise wholly sympathetic readers. Safire's vision had, of course, nothing to do with the hard facts of U.S.-Iranian relations in the fall of 1979. But it made excellent partisan use of the second embassy seizure; and it had no doubt lain in the back of Safire's brilliantly neo-conservative mind for some time, simply waiting for an appropriate occasion.

Shortly after the American hostages were released and returned to the United States, with none having been killed in captivity, Israeli General Moshe Dayan drew from the much-publicized experience what he called three principles for America's guidance in the future. But, before spelling out those principles, he was at pains to stress the "unique" character of the crisis. What made it unique,

he said, was that "the Iranian regime gave state backing to the seizure of the Americans." That, he observed, has rarely happened in
history.

In all "previous cases of terrorism that have affected the United States at home and abroad," Dayan argued, "not one nation supported the terrorists, and the governments upon whose soil the acts
of sabotage or assault took place did their best to safeguard the victims and strike the attackers. This was not the situation when the
Americans were taken hostage in Tehran." George Bush's version
of it in lecturing Geraldine Ferraro applies here. Iran, it is charged,
has done something uniquely barbarous. That is Dayan's presuppo-
sition, on which he bases the "three principles" he recommends for
America's guidance in future hostage crises. The first principle takes
the form of a response to the question: should the United States have
"stormed the embassy" on its own? Dayan says no. The United
States, he says, should not have attempted even the modest thing
that it actually attempted, and was forced to abort. In reproof, Dayan
says that the United States ought not to have engaged "its prestige
in such an important affair as though it were an Israel liberating its
people at Entebbe."

What then was the alternative? The question of authorizing the
Iranian government of Bazargan to act like "Israel liberating its people at Entebbe" doesn't come up for Dayan, because he assumes
that government supported the terrorists. That is patently false. There
were many Iranians taken hostage in the compound. The Bazargan
goverment could have "pulled an Entebbe" rescue, except for the
fact that the chances of freeing the Americans alive were slim, and
the American partisans of Israel and the Shah would take it to have
been a deliberate slaughter. So what specifically are the principles
offered by Dayan? They are that the U.S. should be better informed
about the possibilities of terror by frenzied masses in backward places
like Islamic Iran under the Ayatollah; that it must not try to effect
rescues of its people as if it were Israel going it alone; and finally,
in Dayan's last words, that it "should not act weakly, stealthily, or
apologetically."

That was indeed the kind of advice to be expected under the
circumstances from an Israeli statesman serving his nation's true in-

terests. It amounted to saying that the United States shouldn't attempt to have any direct dealings with a state like the Ayatollah's
Islamic Republic of Iran, unless it got a prior clearance to do so by
statesmen of long experience in the region, like himself. Unfortunately, Robert McFarlane would take such advice to heart during his congressional questioning on the Iran-Contra affair.

5. Hardline Precedents: From Republican Rome to the American Founding Fathers

Throughout the Iran hostage crisis, but especially after the aborted rescue mission of April 1980, many articles appeared in
newspapers and magazines reminding us that there have been precedents, to be sure, dating back to the beginnings of recorded history,
and in our own case, to the first years of our national existence. A
large part of the history of hostage taking — that having to do with
the detention of conquered subjects to assure compliance with the
terms of an imposed peace — has no bearing on the circumstances
of the American experience in Iran. In the strictest military sense,
the entire populations of the nations of Europe, Africa, and Asia
occupied by the Axis Powers during World War II were held hostage
as a means of keeping the peace imposed upon them. Later, when
Germany, Italy, and Japan were conquered and occupied, the ta-
bles were turned. Such hostage-taking as an instrument of war has
lost some of its traditional legitimacy in theory as a consequence of
the contemporary efforts to de-legitimize war altogether. But, despite
their silence on the subject — a silence procured by setting up what
have amounted to puppet-regimes in the lands of unconditional surrender — the conquered nations of World War II are fully aware
that they have been held hostage all these years.

Interestingly enough, one of the greatest historians of the
Western world, the Greek statesman and political theorist Polybius,
was just such a hostage at the time that he wrote his incomparable
history of Rome. As the great dictionaries of Greek and Roman antiquities typically summarize the matter: after Rome had imposed
its peace on Greece, Polybius, following in the footsteps of his father

Lycortas, general of the Achaean League, rose to high political and military rank in that league, becoming finally a leader among the Achaean elite that sought to maintain the independence of the league. When local opponents denounced that elite for allegedly plotting against the authority of Rome, Polybius particularly "attracted the suspicion of the Romans and was one of the 1000 noble Achaeans who in 166 were transported to Rome as hostages, and detained there for seventeen years." As Evelyn S. Shuckburgh tells us in the introduction to his classic translation of *The Histories,* those hostages were supposed to have been put on trial in Rome on charges of conspiracy. But the court to try them was never impanelled. In fact, writes Shuckburgh, the hostages were not

> allowed even to stay in Rome, but were quartered in various cities of Italy, which were made responsible for their safe custody: and there they remained until 151 B.C., when such of them as were still alive were contemptuously allowed to return. [Some few, it appears, had managed to escape, though at the risk of certain execution if caught.] . . . More fortunate than the rest, Polybius was allowed to remain in Rome. [xxvi]

The Republican Romans took and held those hostages, as already suggested, to discourage future Achaean conspiracies against their peace. Polybius became a tutor in the family of Scipio Africanus, who had defeated Carthage's Hannibal in the Second Punic War, and the child he taught was destined to become Scipio Africanus the Younger who conquered and destroyed Carthage in the Third Punic War, with Polybius by his side as constant adviser. But, earlier, in 151, it had been Polybius himself who pleaded for and secured the liberty of his fellow hostages. As Shuckburgh tells it: "There was now, it was thought, no reason for retaining these unfortunate men. The original thousand had shrunk to less than three hundred; middle-aged men had become in sixteen years old and decrepit, and were no longer likely to venture on organizing any opposition. . . . Still the debate in the Senate was long and doubtful. . . ." Or, as Polybius himself writes, in words that may now remind Iranians of the debates in their own Majlis in late 1980:

Cato was consulted by Scipio, at the request of Polybius, on behalf of the Achaeans; and when the debate in the Senate, between
the party who wished to grant it and the party that opposed it,
was protracted to a considerable length, Cato stood up and said:
"As though we had nothing else to do, we sit here the whole day
debating whether some old Greek dotards should be buried by
Italian or Achaean undertakers." Their restoration voted, Polybius and his friends, after a few days' interval, were for appearing before the Senate again, with a petition that the exiles should
enjoy the same honors in Achaia as they had before. Cato,
however, remarked with a smile that Polybius, like another Odys-
seus, wanted to go a second time into the cave of the Cyclops,
because he had forgotten his cap and belt. . . . [35.6]

That is all pleasantly told by Polybius, who understood that Cato
had used high diplomacy to have his way with the hardliners in the
Roman Senate — which had indeed been a Cyclops's den for sixteen years. As we shall see, some of the crypto-friends of our American hostages in the Iranian leadership would in the end speak, if not
smile, quite like Cato.

Before the Romans became masters of the Mediterranean world,
they themselves had suffered humiliating experiences as hostages in
the hands of less gracious hosts. A famous instance is that resulting
from the unconditional surrender of an entire Roman army to Samnites in 321 B.C. after it had let itself be trapped in the pass at Cau-
dium. Historians have noted that, while most peoples delight in
celebrating their victories, the Romans of republican times rather
perversely preferred, as Wilhelm Ihne aptly observes, to show their
greatness by "keeping continually before their eyes the evil days when
the god of battles was unfavorable to them, and by celebrating the
anniversaries of their defeats, in a certain degree, as days of national humiliation." Of all Roman defeats, that of the so-called Caudine Forks was by far the most humiliating, for there, as Ihne sums
it up, "four legions agreed to purchase life and freedom by the
sacrifice of military honor."

The relation of the Samnites to the Romans in those days was
not unlike that of the Ayatollah's Iran to the United States in 1979.

Sheer luck had delivered the Romans into the hands of the Samnites; and, like the Ayatollah's government, the Samnite chiefs didn't know how to handle their captives. The Roman historian Livy speaks of their "unheard of good fortune," and of the advice given them by an old soldier who admonished them either to let the Romans all go free and unhurt, "and so appeal to their best and warmest feelings," or kill them all. But the Samnite commanders decided instead to follow a middle course. The Romans were "forced to swear a treaty of peace" and to "give 600 equites as hostages." All the rest of the prisoners were made to lay down their arms and pass under a humiliating yoke before being sent back to Rome wearing simple cloaks. They had their lives but no honor. Back in Rome, one of the surrendered army's commanders, the Consul Postumius, immediately denounced the peace he had sworn, urging the Senate to reject it and to send him and the other commanders back to the Samnites, escorted by a Roman ambassador — which the Senate promptly did.

Standing once again before his Samnite captor Pontius, Postumius struck the Roman ambassador with his knee so as to cast him aside or drive him off; and then he cried out: "I am now a Samnite, you an ambassador: I thus violate the law of nations; you may justly now resume the war." The Samnite leaders realized at once what a mistake they had made by pursuing a middle course. Pontius correctly complained that Postumius ought to have come back with all his soldiers, so that they might all be captives once more. So Postumius's surrender was refused, and he was sent back to Rome, though the 600 equites continued to be detained as hostages — about whose fate Livy tells us nothing further. Machiavelli, centuries later, will comment on this passage of Livy, observing that

> when he returned to Rome, Postumius was received by the Romans more gloriously for having lost than Pontius was by the Samnites for having won. Here two things are to be noted: the one, that glory can be acquired by any action; for, while it is ordinarily acquired in victory, in defeat it can be acquired either by showing that this defeat was not due to your fault, or by quickly doing some act of virtue which counteracts it: the other, that it is not a disgrace not to observe those promises which were made by force:

and always forced promises regarding public affairs will be disregarded when that force is removed, and he who disregards them is without shame. [Dis. 3.42]

Turning to American precedents, professional experts on modern terrorism and on hostage-taking in particular, as an instrument of terrorism, like to emphasize the allegedly unprecedented aspects of the contemporary varieties. So, for instance, an article by Brian Jenkins and Robin Wright on the subject (July 23. 1987) was titled "The Fearsome New Forms of Hostage-Taking"; and it started by noting that the "Reagan administration's arms-for-hostages swap with Iran" of 1986 "was not the first time the United States made staggering concessions in exchange for human life." The example supplied was one of 1795, when "Congress voted to pay the dey of Algiers almost $1 million to free 115 American sailors seized over the previous decade by Barbary pirates." The authors point out that the ransom indicated represented "one-sixth of the federal budget" in those days, and that it "included a 36-gun frigate and ammunition."

But it is important to stress, as Jenkins and Wright do not, that soon after 1795, the United States developed the means for handling hostage crises — means that were manifestly much more honorable and more conducive to the *salus populi*. The point was well made by Richard C. Clark in a paper on "The Lost Political Realism of Thomas Jefferson," read at the annual meeting of the American Political Science Associaton in Washington in early September 1988. Professor Clark, who also qualifies as an expert on modern terrorist-revolutionary doctrine (see his *Technological Terrorism,* 1980), singled out for special praise Glen Tucker's *Dawn Like Thunder: The Barbary Wars and the Birth of the U.S. Navy* (1963), which he describes as "one of the (strangely) few major works" on that "early crisis" in American national security affairs. Tucker's book reminds us that in the early years of the Republic our Presidents rather persistently made the mistake of paying ransom to secure the safety of merchant vessels off the coast of North Africa and that, indeed, between 1786 and 1799 they signed four treaties of tribute with the so-called Barbary powers — Morocco, Algiers, Tripoli, and Tunis —

only to find that the tribute paid did not in the least "diminish the insolence of the recipients" who persisted in seizing American vessels and holding the crews and passengers hostage for the payment of ransom.

Thomas Jefferson was an early advocate of the proper remedy, which was to build a navy capable of protecting American trade and of inflicting exemplary punishment when seizures occured. In a letter of August 23, 1785, to John Jay, Secretary of Foreign Affairs, Jefferson had said:

> Our commerce on the ocean and in other countries must be paid for by frequent war. The justest dispositions possible in ourselves will not secure us against it. It would be necessary that all other nations were just also. Justice indeed on our part will save us from those wars which would have been produced by a contrary disposition. But how to prevent those produced by the wrongs of other nations? By putting ourselves in a condition to punish them. Weakness provokes insult and injury, while condition to punish it often prevents it. This reasoning leads to the necessity of some naval force, that being the only weapon with which we can reach an enemy. I think it is to our interest to punish the first insult: because an unpunished is the parent of many others. We are not at this moment in a condition to do it, but we should put ourselves into it as soon as possible.

By 1800, after the last tribute-treaty had been signed, the American commander of the frigate *George Washington* uttered the famous words: "I hope I shall never again be sent to Algiers with tribute, unless I am authorized to deliver it out of the mouths of our cannon." That was to be Jefferson's approach when he became President; and, at the height of President Carter's Iran Hostage crisis, the distinguished academician Forest McDonald fittingly pointed to the contrast with Jefferson, observing:

> Jimmy Carter is not the first American President to be faced with a hostage crisis in the Islamic world. George Washington, John Adams, Thomas Jefferson and James Madison were repeatedly plagued with just that problem. It was Jefferson and his secre-

tary of state and successor Madison who came up with a solution. . . . Jefferson would have no part of it [ransom]. He threw the entire Navy, such as it was, against Tripoli — not to free the hostages, but to teach the Tripolitans never to trifle with the U.S. again.

In other words, Jefferson did not make it his first priority, as Lyndon Johson and Carter did in the *Pueblo* and Iran crises, to secure the physical safety of the hostages at all costs. Jefferson applied exemplary punishment. There was some "spectacular fighting," but soon enough the "pashi of Tripoli" was made to agree to "cease plundering American ships and to waive the American tribute in the future." The moral, says McDonald, is "too obvious to mention"; but, pointing to Carter's misgivings, he concludes: "Would that we had a President today with the wit and guts to heed it." [RCC, pp. 17-18]

Commenting on McDonald's account, Professor Clark notes that Jefferson did all that he had to do to end the Barbary ship seizures and hostage detentions without any congressional declaration of war or other approval. As to the price he was ready to ask us to pay to prevent such abuse of our "separate and equal station" among the powers of this earth, Jefferson appealed without hesitation to his moral attitude toward the conduct of the Revolutionary War by means of which that separate and equal station was gained. In a letter of January 3, 1793, he had drawn the balance sheet for that war, setting precious life beside a precious national cause, and he had concluded: "My own affections have been deeply wounded by some of the martyrs to this cause, but rather than it should have failed, I would have seen half the earth desolated. Were there but an Adam and an Eve left in every country, and left free, it would be better than as it now is."

Moshe Dayan and other modern Israeli militants who take such a view of the cause of Israel as a sovereign nation might, of course, argue that, in Jefferson's time, the U.S. was not a superpower and had therefore to secure its ultimate safety in its separate and independent "station" by more militant, not to say desperate means, than would be appropriate today. Yet, what is at issue here is the fundamental attitude required to teach would-be terrorists and hostage-takers a lesson. Jefferson was of course well aware that the same hardline attitude permits us to effectively normalize relations with the very same nations — after they have "learned to behave properly" in their international dealings.

6. Bargaining With Blackmailers: In and Out of the Media's Glare

The unpleasant truth is that, in the Iran hostage crisis, not only did our government fail to act in accordance with the best precedents in our national history but it also constrained the government of Iran to pursue an utterly wrong course. Because of the restraints imposed on the Iranian government to end the crisis without putting the lives of the hostages at risk, the Carter administration was able to reenforce the threat against that government posed by the hostage-captors. Thus, with Washington's support, the militants holding the embassy had found a way of putting the Iranian government itself on trial. It was a way that, by late 1979, had certainly become quite familiar to Americans at home. Surely in the United States, the newsmedia, the university faculties and students, the major publishing houses, make it a regular practice to put all American administrations on constant trial, even such as have been elected by landslide majorities of the sovereign people. It had been done to Lyndon Johnson during his elective term; it had been done to Richard Nixon during his second term; and it was even then being done to Jimmy Carter during his bid for reelection.

The American examples, or models, are important, because, like the American groups capable of putting governments on trial, the Iranian hostage-takers were not in any strict sense armed revolutionaries. The weapons of our Marine guards had fallen into their hands, but they had brought in no more than ten weapons — pistols — of their own. They functioned, indeed, like students and faculty conducting a sit-in on a thoroughly radicalized American campus. Their one true weapon was, of course, the safety of the Americans they had taken hostage, which they were prepared from the beginning to "play" like a bargaining chip. No one in the Iranian government could say "no" to them, seriously, without risking the lives of the Americans. That was all there was to the second embassy seizure. But that proved to be a lot, because no government official, in Tehran or Washington, was prepared to acknowledged the fact, fearing that, if the fact were acknowledged on one side, it would probably be flatly repudiated on the other.

Let us ask once more: Who, on the Iranian side, could have dared to order a storming of the embassy without prior authorization from Washington? And who in President Carter's Washington could have dared to so much as suggest such a thing, at a time when powerful domestic factions were condemning the Ayatollah and his government in terms once reserved only for Hitler, though now applied also to the P.L.O.? Exactly such a dilemma would confront the Reagan administration in 1986, when it was secretly attempting to deal directly with the Iranian government, to gain its cooperation, instead of dealing with it secretly only through Israeli intermediaries. It is hardly deniable that the Ayatollah Khomeini had approved of the efforts of his top brain-trust of 1979 — consisting first of Bazargan and Yazdi and then also of Abolhassan Bani-Sadr and Sadegh Ghotbzadeh — to try to prevent a total severance of diplomatic relations on the part of the United States. What he did not approve of was any decision taken in haste that might force the hostage-takers to make good their threats to "kill hostages" if force of any serious kind was used against them.

In other words, the conditions initially imposed by the White House on "Khomeini and others" in the Iranian government for their handling of the hostage crisis laid upon them a virtually impossible task. Again and again in their reviews of the crisis, President Carter, Warren Christopher and Harold Saunders as well as Gary Sick have stressed the fact that, during the 444-day ordeal, the Khomeini government repeatedly failed in its efforts to gain actual control of the hostages. In *All Fall Down*, Sick had noted with candor that there were serious doubts from the beginning "about Khomeini's actual control over the students in the embassy." (224) In support of that, he wrote of reports "being received almost daily in Washington" indicating that "in a showdown with the students, Khomeini could not be certain that he would prevail,'' and that he was therefore "avoiding any steps that might undermine his authority or bring him into conflict" with those students. [245]

To stress how little control the Ayatollah's people had over the hostage captors, Sick recalls their response when reports began to circulate that, "almost from the day of the takeover," nothing had been heard about six of the hostages, giving rise during the first two months to a fear that the "missing six. . . had been killed or seriously injured." As Sick tells it:

> Despite the international outcry that greeted this new revelation, embarrassed public officials in Tehran were forced to admit their total ignorance of what was going on inside the embassy walls. Foreign Minister Ghotbzadeh confessed in a news conference that he did not know even how many hostages were being held and had been unable to find out, despite his best efforts. Curiously, Washington's best information on the subject was provided by the students themselves. The telephone lines inside the embassy still functioned, and. . . on occasion it was possible to glean some information about the inner workings of the embassy prison. One talkative student let slip the fact that they were holding fifty prisoners. . . and seemed to confirm that all the hostages were alive and physically present in the compound. It was only one more peculiarity of the circumstances that the U.S. Department of State should have had more success eliciting information from the student captors than the foreign minister and the Revolutionary Council of their own government. [246]

That incapacity of the Iranian government to deal directly with the captors continued through all the months of the crisis — and could not but continue so long as that government felt bound to avoid doing anything that would provoke those captors to kill the hostages. We must not permit ourselves to forget what sort of threat hung over that government's head, like a sword of Damocles, throughout the crisis. As Sick explains, when President Carter was told by Admiral Stansfield Turner of the hostage-captors' public threat that "any action aimed at freeing the hostages would result in their being killed," Carter's response was — then as always later — that "if the hostages were killed. . . we should be able to conduct an operation that would 'blast the hell out of Iran'.'' [214-215]

All the hostage-captors cared to communicate to the Ayatollah and the heads of the governments appointed by him was that the Americans would be killed unless the Ayatollah took their side against whatever government leader they singled out for political attack. What chance could there be that they would, under the circumstances, ever contemplate giving up the hostages until they themselves, or their most trusted outside advocates, took full control of the entire government? In fact, the strategy proved to be altogether successful, so long as that sword of Damocles hung over the Ayatollah's head. In the end, the Ayatollah's government had to go all the way in that direction, presenting itself to the hostage-captors and to the entire world as insanely pursuing the ends proclaimed originally by the those captors at the very time when the Ayatollah's first government was busy normalizing relations with the United States.

James Reston of the *New York Times,* it deserves to be noted, wrote several columns of advice for President Carter on the hostage crisis, based on his perception that the Ayatollah Khomeini might not have direct governmental control over the hostage captors. One column, written while the exiled Shah was still "isolated at an Air Force base in Texas," urged the President, as a born-again Christian, to make a religious appeal to the Ayatollah Khomeini, who was perceived even then as obviously "not responding to the politics of power." Carter, said Reston, should make it clear to the Ayatollah that, in admitting the Shah to the United States, he was "not trying to save the Shah's throne, but merely, as part of his religion, to save his life."

That was Reston's perception of what Carter's religion might contribute to resolution of the hostage crisis. The assumption was that the Ayatollah, acting consistently with his Islamic faith, might respect Carter's acting consistently with his Christian faith. But Reston apparently ignored the difference between religions whose "kingdoms" are indeed "of this world" — like those of Khomeini's Iran and Zionist Israel — and religions like President Carter's, the "kingdom" of which is generally held not to be of this world, and most certainly not of the United States, with its wall of separation between church and state. But behind Reston's suggestion that

President Carter make a religious appeal to the Ayatollah was a growing conviction that, as we have indicated, the Ayatollah probably had only religious, not political control, over the militants holding the American hostages. Reston in fact wrote: "I have reason for believing, on the testimony of responsible Iranians in this country who have been in personal touch with the most intimate advisors of the Ayatollah in the last few days, that he is not wholly in command of the 'students' surrounding the American Embassy, and. . . is looking for a compromise and a way out."

Interestingly enough, soon after the aborted desert rescue mission, President Carter began to trust in more practical means than prayer to try to strike a bargain with the heads of Islamic Iran. In fact, major American efforts to secure release of the hostages moved at that time into a sphere which had already been operative but which now became central. It was the sphere of completely unpublicized dealings between international bankers and their agents around the world. In retrospect, it is clear that the essentially private banking arrangements that had been built up between Iran and the U.S. since 1976 — Kissinger's last year as Secretary of State — were on a scale and of a complexity without parallel in previous American experience. Although international litigation regarding those arrangements had started early in 1979, at the time of the Shah's flight, it was not until "shortly after the failure of the rescue mission in April 1980" — as John E. Hoffman, Jr., one of the leading bank representatives involved, informs us — that truly intense "confidential contacts and negotiations between U.S. bank lawyers and Iranian representatives began."

And those contacts and negotiations were to continue without interruption, Hoffman stresses, through the rest of 1980, to "culminate in the structuring and execution of a multi-billion-dollar financial transaction in January 1981 which was essential in freeing the hostages." [235] According to Hoffman, the great fear of all the bank people involved through all that period was that negotiations might fail, as comparable negotiations on a much smaller scale had indeed previously failed "in the case of the post-revolutionary Cuban lawsuits, which after twenty years [as of 1984] are still being litigated in U.S. courts." [242]

The U.S.-Iranian financial negotiations came to involve, as Hoffman expresses it, "battalions of lawyers" on both sides, as well as bankers and public officials numbering in the hundreds. Meetings took place while, on the surface, official relations between the two governments seemed irreparably severed. Thus it may be said that, at a time of deep crisis, the international banking community supplied, in Hoffman's words, a "useful channel of communication out of the glare of publicity," virtually unaffected by the kinds of public confrontation and conflict that "loomed constantly during the hostage crisis and always jeopardized a prompt solution."

Still, it was in the "glare of publicity" and in the heat of public confrontations and conflicts that the physical transfer of control of the hostages out of the hands of their original captors had actually to be effected. All that the financial arrangements — involving billions upon billions of dollars — could actually contribute to the final release was a convincing public assurance to the Iranian people that their government had exacted a sufficient ransom for the American hostages to "illegitimize" their continued detention by the hostage-takers. But the inside drama of the Iranian government's efforts to wrest control of the hostages from their captors has yet to be fully and correctly told. As we have been indicating, American help and understanding of a kind hard to come by was necessary for the thing to finally happen; and such help was largely supplied under a cover of deep secrecy almost as impenetrable as bankers' negotiations.

All through the months of secret bankers' deals, American diplomats were busy in Europe trying to "open channels to the religious leaders of Iran" who, it was finally recognized, could alone have the kind of muscle needed to end the public blackmail of the hostage-takers. Harold Saunders and several colleagues in the State Department had in those days traveled to Paris, Bohn, Vienna, London, and Bern, carrying a "list of seventeen key figures in Tehran" and asking "each government to examine its own channels to each of those leaders." Their purpose, after the failed rescue mission, was to set the stage for a "new longer-term diplomatic approach."

Among the people they were introduced to by European governments as possible channels was "Archbishop Hillarion Capucci, who had a relationship with a number of the leaders in Tehran." The fact that he had previously been "jailed by the Israelis, allegedly for facilitating arms shipments to the Palestinians," had endeared him to many. Capucci made clear to the American diplomats his view of the situation in Tehran. For him, it was the Iranian government that was being directly blackmailed by the threats of the hostage-takers to kill the hostages if that government did not accomodate itself to their will. He spoke of his ongoing efforts, through "Arab diplomats," to "help Iran release the hostages," and asked for American support. What he told them was greatly appreciated by the Americans who met with him, though they had to acknowledge that, given Capucci's Palestinian connections and his consequent bad press in America, "chances of pulling" his plan "together seemed remote." But, eventually, they got to the people in Iran who had the authority and power to get the thing done.

We have already reviewed James Bill's account of how the clerical leaders of the Islamic Republican party (IRP), who eventually gained control of Iran's new parliamentary government, finally inherited the task of freeing the American hostages from the their original essentially-Marxist captors. The effective head of the IRP had not been a member of the secular brain-trust of the Ayatollah that had produced Bazargan, Yazdi, Bani-Sadr, and Ghotbzadeh. He was Mohammad-Ali Rajai, a man of humble origins but of high religious and moral authority. After long struggles with Bani-Sadr and Ghotbzadeh, Rajai was raised to the post of prime minister. And it was then that he began to make himself the government's "official representative" of the claims of the militant students holding the American Embassy.

But that took time. Four months before Rajai become prime minister, Khomeini had announced that he wanted the decision about the hostages to be made not by individual leaders, like Bazargan or Bani-Sadr, but by a duly elected Cabinet government. In retrospect, it is clear that Khomeini's strategy was to make it impossible for the embassy captors to single out individual scapegoats to justify their refusal to release control of the hostages to the government. Bani-Sadr and Ghotbzadeh had no doubt seen the necessity for that and may also have advised Khomeini to move in that direction. Their hope had been to head the parliamentary government themselves. But that was not to be; the embassy captors rejected them as official spokesmen, even after Bani-Sadr had managed to get himself popularly elected as President of the Republic. As President, Bani-Sadr had tried to control the naming of the prime minister and cabinet; but again and again he was frustrated by a clerical minority in the Majlis. Finally, on September 10, 1980, the Majlis voted to accept the fourteen-man cabinet headed by Rajai as prime minister.

Yet, even as ministerial head of the cabinet government authorized to settle the crisis, Rajai could not immediately force the militants to surrender control of the hostages. It was still necessary, as James Bill has pointed out, to purge the "students of Marxist inclination. . . within the student ranks" to make sure that actual control had passed really into the hands of the genuinely religious students who could be trusted not to kill the hostages. That was a task that took much maneuvering, and it was Mohammed Ali Rajai who finally accomplished it. It must be said that what he personally achieved, by way of compelling the hostage-takers to submit to a decision of the Iranian government without jeopardizing the religious-moral authority of the Ayatollah Khomeini was a feat of high diplomacy and statecraft that must not be underestimated. It was a maneuver of some delicacy for which the stage was set only as late as October 18, 1980, just a few weeks before the American presidential election, when Rajai came to New York to present Iran's case against Iraq's military aggression at the United Nations.

It was then that Rajai made bold to announce that the United States had "in effect" already "substantially met" the militants' demand for an apology, which the government had made a demand of its own; and that, since the United States had "in effect" apologized, no further form of formal apology would be asked for. Rajai said, indeed, with a sovereign demeanor that neither Bani-Sadr nor Ghotbzadeh ever dared to adopt, that he was "refusing" to meet with the Americans on the hostages, reserving for the Majlis final specification of the "conditions for their release."

Rajai in fact said at a press conference: "I could tell you with assurance that the moment the parliament, or Majlis, makes its decision, which I think that moment is not far away, for my government the question will be final and solved." On the matter of a Carter apology, he explained: "The passage of time and what we have heard from responsible people in the government and other officials close to the government, for us it seems that this condition in practice already has been answered. All it needs is probably to put something on paper." Then, mindful that at issue from the beginning of the crisis had been the threatened lives of the American hostages — the single trump card of the militants — Rajai expressed sympathy for the families, saying: "I know how they feel. I know how they suffer, because I, myself, have been a prisoner, but not a simple prisoner. And several of my colleagues in the government have been prisoners and have been tortured."

Rajai intended his remarks as much for the militants still holding the hostages at the embassy as for an American audience. The militants had exploited the American mania for giving them constant TV and newsprint coverage. "They have us," an astute White House aide had observed. "by the networks." To match the militants in the embassy and the American TV networks that never missed a counted day, Rajai looked straight into the cameras to say that his family had never known where he was as a prisoner, and also that he had been tortured every day. He said "his nails were pulled out and the soles of his feet were beaten. . . . At that point Rajai pulled the shoe and sock off his right foot and exhibited the bare foot to reporters to show what he said were marks left by the beatings." It was not the sort of thing the militants at the embassy could match or repudiate.

Washington, to be sure, waited impatiently for word of a positive Majlis vote on the matter of final conditions for the release of the hostages. In a kind of prelude to what would dominate the media six and seven years later, during efforts to free American hostages held in Beirut through covert contacts with Iran, journalist and ardent Ronald Reagan supporter George Will had charged, on November 1, that Carter's White House had been cutting legal-ethical corners to try to get the hostages back on the eve of the November 4 election. On that same day, the columnists Rowland Evans and Robert Novak took up the story. As Gary Sick recalls, Evans and Novak distributed a special "bonus" column to their subscribers, citing "multiple U.S. and foreign sources," to the effect that a "deal exchanging American hostages for military equipment" had been completed two weeks earlier. They also asserted that critical parts for Phoenix air-to-air missiles had recently been moved from storage in preparation for delivery to Iran. The similarity between the Evans and Novak column and George Will's report was striking, as was the timing of this news — just three days prior to the election.

Washington did not get word of the Majlis vote, specifying conditions for release of the hostages, until November 2. The White House and State Department groups concerned met with the President to review the conditions, and President Carter finally said, "There are several things in the list of conditions that we cannot do," and he added that the "best we can do for the next few days is to indicate our willingness to pursue negotiations" with the committee the Iranians themselves had proposed for the purpose. Eventually the objectionable conditions were to be withdrawn: but they had by then sufficed to cost President Carter the election.

7. Wresting Control: Iran's Compliance in a Thankless Task

From Iran's point of view, the drama of the 444 days consisted, as we have already indicated, in a long drawn out duel to get the hostages out of the original captors' control, in the course of which some factions in the goverment took greater risks than others in either siding with the captors or opposing them.

Why, it has been asked, couldn't the Ayatollah have faced the militants down, if he didn't really accept their claim to be the "conscience of the Islamic revolution"? The answer, as we have shown, is that, had he risked standing up to the original Marxist-oriented captors while they ran the compound on their terms, those captors could have charged that they had been betrayed; then they might have killed the hostages, thereby bringing the long contained wrath of a born-again Christian President down upon the entire Iranian people. The Ayatollah was no doubt warned by all his advisers, after the fall of Bazargan and Yazdi, not to provoke the embassy captors into killing the hostages.

Ultimate responsibility fell to the Ayatollah Khomeini himself, to be sure; and he had to exercise his sovereign prerogatives again and again with a will of steel to prevent the captors from bringing ruin down upon the Islamic Republic by killing the hostages. Khomeini, as we have previously suggested, could have been relieved of that awesome responsibility only by an American decision demanding of his government that it storm the embassy come what may. If the Iranians had decided to storm the embassy on their own, without explicit U.S. authorization, they would have been charged with doing so with the intention of getting the hostages killed. The truth of that is undeniable. So long as Washington could not bring itself to *ask* the Ayatollah's goverment to storm the embassy, all efforts to try to get the hostages out alive had necessarily to be efforts accommodated to the demands of the captors, demands more destructively pressed against the government established by the Ayatollah than against the United States.

When exactly did the militants surrender control of the hostages to the Iranian goverment? We can start with President Carter's account of how things stood two days before the 1980 elections. At that time, certainly, the hostages were still all in the hands of their original militant captors, though encouraging word had been received of the Ayatollah Khomeini's having "told the militants that he wanted the hostages turned over to the government so that all the students holding them could help on the war front." Carter tells us further that "two large buses, which had not been there before, were now being kept parked just outside the compound" of the U.S. Embassy in Tehran, evidently waiting for the captors to release the Americans, in keeping with the government's announcement that "the Algerians," acting as intermediaries, would thereafter be "responsible" for the hostages.

As we all know, the hostages were not freed at that time. Over two months more of cajoling and veiled threats, and the specter of Ronald Reagan's accession to the Presidency, would be needed to break the hold of the militant blackmailers on their American prisoners. From the standpoint of Sick, Christopher, and Saunders, there had been many times before election day when it seemed that, by co-opting the rhetoric of the student militants, goverment officials anxious to end the crisis might have succeeded, with a little luck, in wresting physical control. On March 1, 1980, for instance, according to Harold Saunders, Sadegh Ghotbzadeh had told French intermediaries that "members of the Revolutionary Council and the militants holding the embassy had met" and that "the transfer of the hostages. . . should take place the following day." But by separate communication, Bani-Sadr had informed those same intermediaries that he "remained concerned about the actual step of taking the hostages into governmental control."

Saunders writes of "Carter and his senior White House staff" having been "involved almost hour by hour for several weeks," by that time, "in the effort to push Iranians over the line in taking custody of the hostages," and also of Ghotbzadeh and Bani-Sadr having come "very close to gaining control over the hostages at two moments." But even Saunders seems to want us to conclude that the Iranian government officials under Khomeini, and Khomeini himself, didn't try hard enough. We earlier noted that, after the aborted rescue attempt of late April 1980, the hostages had been widely scattered, but their actual captors were still the militants who had seized the embassy. "Throughout the summer," as Saunders writes, "we had received fragmentary reports from sources all over Iran about groups of hostages here and there — seen on an airplane, visited by a doctor, seen in the garden of one of the closed U.S. consulates." By mid-December 1980, they had all been returned to Tehran, while negotiations for their release moved into their final stages. Still, the government had by no means gained control. A diary entry for December 28, 1980, in Carter's presidential memoirs tells us that the Algerian delegation to Tehran had finally been permitted to visit "all 52" of the hostages, 49 of whom were apparently "located within 10 or 20 minutes of the American Embassy in two separate locations — in a hotel or apartment building type of place." [590] Yet in a diary entry for January 2, 1981, Carter tells of having instructed "my people" to "prepare for a breakdown in negotiations and possible hostage trial," and also of his intention to "declare a state of belligerency or ask Congress to declare war against Iran." [591]

Indeed, on Monday, January 19, when "the Americans had been moved out to the vicinity of the airport" and Algerian planes were standing ready in Tehran, the militant captors remained in control. Some of them, the truly religious supporters of the Ayatollah, were fully ready to cooperate with the government headed by Rajai. But there were others who still posed a threat to the hostages, who feared what might happen to them when they lost their "trump card." They were aware that things would abruptly change for them on the next day, when President-elect Ronald Reagan would take the constitutionally prescribed oath and officially assume the prerogatives and duties of the nation's highest office. And they seemed to want to cling to their advantage — control of the hostages — to the very last minute. The release was stalled; and Carter writes: "The planes were returned to standby condition. The Americans. . . were back in their prison. Again I began to fear that the hostages would not be freed." And at that moment, Carter writes with pathos, but a single day remained "before my team and I left office." [8]

Gary Sick acknowledges that "Iranian apprehension about the appearance of a new administration in Washington" — with the swearing in of Ronald Reagan as President on January 20, 1981 — "was valuable in establishing a credible deadline and enforcing it." Of the value of all that for the negotiators, Warren Christopher has said: "The deadline. . . probably made the Iranians somewhat more pliable at the end, for they knew that at a minimum, the new administration would require time to inform itself on the issues and might well take an even harder line on the settlement terms. President-elect Ronald Reagan had used some blunt language in referring to the crisis, which we [the Carter negotiators] did not hesitate to highlight as an added incentive for the Iranians to come to terms." [6]

As for the very final days and hours, they are as important for an understanding of the crisis as the early hours and days. *New York Times* reporter John Kifner, cited by Gary Sick as one of the better authorities on the identities of the hostage-takers, happened to be, in the end, the "only American newspaper correspondent in Tehran when the hostages were freed" on January 20, 1981. In his contribution to the special May 1981 issue of the *New York Times Magazine* on "America in Captivity: Points of Decision in the Hostage Crisis," Kifner gives a day-by-day account of "How A Sit-In Turned Into A Seige" at the U.S. Embassy. While he lapses from objectivity often enough in repeating the State Department line that the Ayatollah's government was itself ultimately responsible for the detention of the Americans, he is honest enough to stress throughout that at least some of the captors "regarded the Iranian Government as the opponent from the start," and that their tactic throughout was to threaten to kill the hostages if Khomeini ever took a decision against them. As to when those original captors finally surrendered actual control to the government, Kifner, as an eyewitness, writes without equivocation:

> The young militants held on to the hostages to the end. Algeria was so fearful the students might not give them up that it sent along a planeload of tough commandos. "Death to America," the students shouted one last time as they hustled the dazed-looking Americans up the ramp of the red-tailed Algerian 707 that would take them to freedom. As the plane took off, minutes after Jimmy Carter turned over the Presidency to Ronald Reagan, the former hostages could see from the windows, most of them probably for the last time, the full moon outlining the sharp white peaks of the Alborz Mountains where it all began.

That reference to the Alborz Mountains links the end of Kifner's article with its beginning, where he tells us that, on "October 26, 1979, four days after the Shah had been admitted to New York Hospital Cornell Medical Center," the student organizers of the November 4 attack met and reached a decision that a sit-in protest would be "staged at the American embassy," scheduled to last, "at most, three to five days." Read at this late date, the pathos of Kifner's account — so explicit in its details — is that our entire government and newsmedia has so absurdly turned its back on the obvious truth about exactly why the Iran hostage crisis lasted 444 days, until the inauguration of President Reagan. It was because the Ayatollah's government had been threatened with perhaps total annihilation of Iran, by the Carter administration, if it did anything that might bring death to the hostages. As the hostages themselves have made clear, in the interviews published by Tim Wells (cited earlier), the hostage-captors toward the end were obviously persuaded that Reagan, once inaugurated, would very likely reverse things. As Warrant Officer Joe Hall put it: "Personally, I didn't anticipate being released before the inauguration. . . . I knew they were afraid of him, so that worked in our favor. I was hoping that as soon as he became president he would say, 'Release the hostages or suffer the consequences'. " [471]

Release came shortly after Reagan took the 35-word constitutionally prescribed oath. But, in fact, the Iranian government of the Ayatollah Khomeini *never* took physical control of the hostages. Their armed original captors had tried for several days to persuade the Americans to speak well of them after being released, but they kept them under their own control to the very end. The embassy's communications officer Bill Belk thus describes how he was finally delivered over into the hands of the Algerians by his captors:

> I was seated up near the front of the bus, so I was one of the first people to go. A couple of militants grabbed me and jerked me toward the door. They ripped my blindfold off, and there were bright lights shining right in my face. I could see the television cameras and a howling mob of idiots down there. About fifty or sixty of these guys had formed a gauntlet from the door of the bus to the base of the airplane ramp. It was sort of like being forced to run through an Indian paddle wheel. . . and they were all yelling and chanting *"Marg bar Amrika! Marg bar Ree-gan"! . . .* I started chanting right along with them, *"Marg bar Khomeini. . . ."* Two students behind me pushed me forward and ran me through the crowd. . . all the way to the plane." [429]

The students that pushed the American through the crowd were undoubtedly members of the faction cooperating with the IRP to restrain their Marxist colleagues. Most of the other hostages interviewed reported the same thing. Not for a single moment were any of them surrendered to the control of Iranian officials. How each was "escorted" through the crowd to the plane recalls how the defeated Roman soldiers were forced to march humbly "under the yoke" at the Caudine Forks. In the words of Sgt. Paul Lewis (a Marine security guard whom we quoted earlier): "When I got to the plane, I saw the guys with machine guns, and I wasn't sure if they were Algerians or Iranians. Then an older gentleman patted me on the arm and said, 'You don't have anything to worry about. They won't get on this plane'." [430]

The May 1981 special issue of the *Times* Magazine cited above also included an article by Terence Smith on a related "point of decision," titled "Putting the Hostages' Lives First." Smith reviews the official American responses to the November 4, 1979 attack, and it is clear that there was "nothing Roman" or "Jeffersonian" about any of them. President Carter was at Camp David when word first reached him. Recalling the moment shortly after leaving office in January 1981, Carter told Smith that he had "experienced almost immediately, a nightmare vision that would haunt him for months to come." In the former President's words:

> I could picture the revolutionaries keeping the 72 hostages, or whatever the number was at the time, in the compound, and assassinating them one every morning at sunrise until the Shah was returned to Iran or until we agreed to some other act in response to their blackmail. It's still a very vivid memory to me.

We know that, in Carter's view, the Ayatollah himself had been prepared to give up the hostages at least as early as late March 1980, and that his "moderate" advisers, like Bani-Sadr, cautioned him against saying so publicly, for fear that the hostage-captors might respond by killing their prisoners. But what Carter never brings up is the question as to whether he ought to have assured Bani-Sadr that, if the Ayatollah's commandos stormed the embassy with Israeli-like dispatch, he would have given official American support to the move. What if all or most of the Americans held in the embassy had died as a result? Ironically, it is now fairly obvious that an American-authorized attack on the embassy would have saved Carter's Presidency, and that his unwillingness to take that course assured his defeat — though he had hoped all along that it would have the opposite effect. When he decided to undertake the late-April 1980 desert rescue mission, he was grieved to find himself strongly opposed by Cyrus Vance who argued that any such military venture would certainly "kill more hostages than it would save." Before offering his resignation, Vance had told the President, among other things, that he thought the "Joint Chiefs' estimate of 15 casualties among the hostages was likely to be short by half."

Carter would later express publicly his strong resentment of Vance's resignation and, even more, of Vance's refusal to obey a direct order — a refusal to which Carter refers in a diary entry for April 21, 1980, several days before the desert rescue mission was launched. Carter had asked Vance to defend in public a possible presidential decision to take military action. Vance had replied that he "would not do it." And Carter comments: "Not another word was said. Although simply stated in my diary, this was a very serious moment — the first time I, as President, had ever had anyone directly refuse to obey an official order of mine. . . . Cy came back to me late in the afternoon and submitted his letter of resignation, since he could no longer support my policy toward Iran."

The irony of that resignation is, of course, that Carter had authorized only a fail-safe rescue attempt. As Terence Smith correctly concludes, at no time did President Carter contemplate any military action of an irreversibile kind. Toward the close of his article Smith notes that the only trace of a hardline position ever to surface in Carter's handling of the crisis was the use his spokesmen made of Reagan's "sharp public condemnations of the student militants in Iran as 'barbarians' and 'kidnappers'," warning the captors that they had better not let the Carter term end without surrendering control of the hostages. Carter acknowledged, in retrospect, that "Iran suffered horribly" from the second embassy seizure, that the hostage-taking had made the country militarily vulnerable, and that it had, he thought, "precipitated the Iraqi invasion." Generalizing on his experience, he told Smith that, for the United States, the long crisis was "vivid proof" that "there are limits even on our nation's great strength" — limits which he compared to the "kind of impotence that a powerful person feels when his child is kidnapped."

8. Khomeini's Last Word on the Crisis

Some four months into the crisis, on February 11, 1980, the Ayatollah Khomeini had taken the trouble to announce that he still intended to seek normalized relations with the United States, despite some factional opposition to it in his own country and even stronger opposition to it in the United States and Israel. After the hostages were finally released on January 20, 1981, Khomeini addressed himself to the task of reuniting the factions that had been polarized in opposition to one another over the seemingly impossible task that had been laid on the Iranian government by President Carter. None of the hostages had died — and that result had been attained only by performance of what amounted to an elaborate charade by means of which Mohammad Ali Rajai and his partisan leaders successfully represented themselves as uncompromising advocates of the student militants holding the American hostages.

As John Kifner reported in a *New York Times* article of February 9, 1981, Khomeini told the rival Iranian factions: "You want to destroy the country. The nation must not listen to those who are arguing against each other and must condemn those who are weakening each other." And he contrasted their behavior with that of the American partisan factions after the victory of Ronald Reagan over Jimmy Carter in November 1980 and after Reagan's inauguration in January 1981. "I cannot speak in detail because my health is not good enough," Khomeini said, addressing a crowd in a Tehran mosque in a speech broadcast by Tehran Radio. But he quickly went on to speak, as Kifner reported, of the factions then rallied around "Abolhassan Bani-Sadr, the leader of Iran's secular and more Westernized elements, and his longtime rival, Prime Minister Mohammad Ali Rajai, who is supported by the Islamic clergy that controls Parliament"; and he admonished:

> God help them if they are unwittingly weakening this country. God forbid that there should come a time when I feel obliged to do my duty. I advise them to keep calm, not to claw one another's faces, but to join together to help the country prosper. Solve our differences of opinion in a brotherly fashion. . . . You saw recently

the opposition betwen two parties in the United States that wanted to choose a President. When one won and became President, the other party did not attack it and impose work stoppages. They congratulated him and are busy serving their country, and with the unity of words are promoting their country.

Those are perhaps the most statesmanly comments by any foreign leader on the transition from the Carter Presidency to the Reagan Presidency. They are words worthy, indeed, of being laid beside Tocqueville's comments in *Democracy in America* on the extraordinary capacity of Americans to carry on their government by discussion in times of extreme crisis and sharply polarized partisan opposition.

It is false to say that Iran's Islamic leaders were even remotely as ignorant of the realities of American politics as their counterparts in Carter's government appeared to be of Iranian political realities. After those words of early February 1981 expressing profound appreciation of the American electoral system the Ayatollah's people found that they still had a considerable price to pay for the charade they put on to assure the safety of the hostages. Bani-Sadr was soon under such strong attack that he chose to leave the country, despite Khomeini's pleas that he start anew with a chastened heart. But worse was in store for the leaders of the Islamic Republican Party who had secured the safe release of the American hostages. By mid-year they were targeted for assassination by the Marxist-oriented factions which had opposed release of the hostages. Chief among those factions, as Professor James Bill observes, was the "Sazman-i Mujahidin-i Khalq (the Organization of the Crusaders of the People)," a "radical left-wing Islamic socialist group," members of which, "on June 28, 1981," set off "a sixty-pound bomb. . . in the headquarters of the Islamic Republican Party, killing over one hundred people, including dozens of members of the Iranian political elite," among them the "founder of the IRP, Muhammad Hussein Beheshti." Professor Bill thus sums up what he calls the "ensuing cycle of violence":

> On August 30, 1981, the violent opposition carried out an unprecedented assassination in which both the head of government

(Prime Minister Muhammad Javad Bahonar) and the head of state (President Muhammad Ali Rajai) died in a bombing. . . . In response, the Revolutionary Guards (Pasdaran-i Inqilab) went on a rampage and, using every means at their disposal, destroyed the armed opposition to the regime. Ayatollah Khomeini gave his full support to this campaign of repression. . . . By mid-1982, the Mujahidin were finally broken within Iran. . . . In the process of mopping up the Mujahidin, the new ruling clerical elite also effectively and relatively easily destroyed the liberal intelligentsia, who suffocated in an atmosphere of extremism and who maintined a visceral aversion to violence. [272-3]

Thus, even as the Carter administration, which also "maintained a visceral aversion to violence," was wiped out in the United States, its counterpart in the Islamic Republic of Iran — the administrations of Bazargan, Yazdi, Bani-Sadr, and Ghotbzadeh — met the same fate. Hardliners took over in both countries. But the American opponents of normalized U.S.-Iranian relations were by no means defeated. In fact, when Reagan's White House tried to deal directly with the Ayatollah's government, even only covertly at first, the hue and cry of those opponents nearly brought the administration down. Indeed, even in the presidential election of 1988, the opposition party tried very hard to make its way by attacking the heads of the Iranian government in the same terms that the Kissingers, Javitses, Jacksons, and Ribicoffs had used to attack it almost a decade before.

CHAPTER FOURTEEN

Seeds of Irangate:
Retrospectives of a
Professor and a General

For several months in 1987, Murray Kempton, one of the ablest of contemporary American journalists, persisted in referring to the congressional hearings on the recently revealed covert U.S. arms transfers to Iran as the "Contrayatollah hearings." That was by way of stressing what he believed they were *really* all about. Most Americans at the time viewed the televised hearings as so many episodes of a day-time soap-opera, about fumbling spies and greedy arms merchants, tripping over one another for comic relief. The central episode, however, was one that viewers had to picture mentally for themselves — though the temptation must have been great for TV newsmakers to want to offer colorful dramatizations of the much-described details.

1. Gifts, But No "Blank Check," for the Magi: Up Close With James Bill and Gary Sick

As all commentators agree, the event that turned the U.S.-Iran arms transfers of 1986 into a purportedly scandalous "Iran *Contra* Affair" was the flight of a "black Boeing 707 aircraft" from Tel Aviv, Israel, to Tehran on Sunday, May 25, 1986. Six passengers had boarded the plane in Tel Aviv. As James Bill sums it up in *The Eagle and the Lion*, the six passengers — all carrying Irish passports — "included former National Security Council head Robert "Bud' McFarlane, Lt. Col. Oliver North, NSC official Howard Teicher,

Central Intelligence Agency Iran specialist George Cave, a CIA communications expert, and Amiram Nir, an Israeli counterterrorist expert and a confidant of Prime Minister Shimon Peres of Israel," who, as Bill stresses, "made the trip disguised as an American named Miller."

On that May 1986 mission, which "had been approved by President Reagan himself," according to Bill, the team of six men carried with them "a chocolate cake prepared in a kosher bakery in Tel Aviv, six Blackhawk .357 Magnum pistols in presentation boxes, and one pallet of spare parts for Iran's Hawk missiles." The mission's purpose was evidently, in Bill's words, to "exchange the badly needed spare parts for four Americans being held hostage in Lebanon." But, things quickly began to go bad. For some unexplained reason, the plane from Tel Aviv landed in Tehran almost two hours ahead of schedule; and the American-Israeli team, with their Kosher-baked cake, found themselves, still in Bill's words, "immediately embroiled in controversy and tense diplomatic conflict." After three days, Bud McFarlane, as head of the mission, decided to abort it. Later he would tell the staff of the Reagan-appointed Tower Commission that he hadn't ever really believed it would work. His hope, he then said, had really been all along that the mission's failure would teach the White House not to try ever again to deal directly with the Ayatollah's people. As for the link with an otherwise unrelated White House-directed national security operation that apparently grew out of that failed Tel Aviv/Tehran mission, Bill writes:

> When the six flew away three days later, the pallet of arms remained in Tehran. The four American hostages remained in Lebanon. United States-Iranian tensions had deepened, not relaxed. A secret risky mission that Colonel North had expected to go "peachy keen" had failed ignominiously. Yet it was on the return trip to the United States that North had confided to Robert McFarlane that the escapade had not been a "total lost cause," since funds received from the Iranians for arms had been applied to Central America. [2]

Upon their return, the three team members with National Security Council connections reported directly to the President, in the presence of Vice President Bush, White House chief of staff Donald Regan, and national security adviser John Poindexter. It is clear that Oliver North, on that occasion, didn't defend the mission in the terms he had used with McFarlane on the return flight. Bill cannot resist saying, at this point, that the "bizarre incident" he has described occurred at a time when the President was "publicly proclaiming Iran a terrorist state and when his secretaries of State and Defense were pursuing a decidedly anti-Iranian foreign policy." One has to read much beyond the first two pages of his book to become aware that Professor Bill would have preferred a more openly pro-Iranian declaration of policy by the President, so that "professionals" like himself might have been able to support it and implement it more effectively.

In Professor Bill's view, "Bud" McFarlane, who had called for a "new approach" to Iran a few years before, seemed hardly the sort of "diplomat" to be charged with undertaking an official rapprochement. Evidently aiming to please his interrogators on the Tower Commission, McFarlane had thus characterized the Iranians with whom he had dealt during his three-day Tehran visit of May 1986: "It would be best for us try to picture what it would be like if after a nuclear attack a surviving Tartar became Vice President; a recent grad student became Secretary of State; and a bookie became the interlocutor for all discourse with foreign countries." Although Bill has been a severe critic of Gary Sick, as also of Sick's boss, Zbigniew Brzezinski, it is significant that the Iran academic expert and his counterpart on the Carter national security council staff (who, according to Bill, gained his expertise "on the job") have taken virtually identical stands on the impropriety of entrusting any kind of Iran-rapprochement effort to a team like McFarlane's on the Tel Aviv/Tehran flight. In "Iran's Quest For Superpower Status" *(Foreign Affairs,* Spring 1987), an article updating his conclusions in *All Fall Down,* Sick has said:

> Regrettably, there is no evidence that the U.S. officials who planned the daredevil McFarlane mission had given any serious thought to the foreign policy signal it might convey. On the contrary, their decision to bring with them a chocolate cake inscribed

with a small key suggests that the mission was regarded as an adventure, even a lark, and it betrays an embarrassing lack of understanding about the nature of the individuals with whom they were dealing. [704]

Bill and Sick are, of course, aware that the American critics of any kind of U.S.-Iranian rapprochement had long since won their battle in the public sphere, that virtually the entire Democratic majorities in the two houses of Congress and perhaps majorities also of the Republicans were rather eager to make known their full agreement with Alabama Senator Howell Heflin who, on the first day of the May 1987 congressional hearings, described the affair under investigation as one dominated by "rogue elephants, rug merchants, loose cannons, soldiers of fortune, privateers, hostages, and contras."

Although Professor Bill starts his *Eagle and the Lion* with a contemporary reference, his purpose in the book is, as we have seen, to review the history of U.S.-Iranian relations as far back as is necessary to develop basic patterns. Among the questions he raises and tries to answer are these: "As a case study in U.S. foreign policy, what might this history indicate about the strengths and weaknesses of such policy-making? How might it affect relations with other Middle Eastern and Third World countries? What does it indicate about the future of the United States in a world caught up in the midst of revolutionary change? Can we avoid similar imbroglios elsewhere as we navigate ourselves through stormy international waters toward the year 2000?" [6]

In other words, Professor Bill's purpose parallels our purpose in the present study, with the difference that he minimizes consideration of the role of U.S. relations with Israel as a determinant of U.S.-Iranian relations. Certainly, what he has to say about Israeli influence on U.S.-Iranian relations since 1969 — the start of Kissinger's official White-House tenure as national security adviser — is said with commendable frankness. But he resists going into detail on the strengths of what we have called Israel's *Realpolitik,* preferring to leave us with the impression that, even from the Israeli standpoint, the Iran arms-transfer affair amounted to no more than a "diplomatic imbroglio."

Yet, it can hardly have been an "imbroglio" in view of Israel's long range foreign-policy concerns. As we have shown, the so-called imbroglios that have characterized U.S.-Iranian relations since the Shah's fall leave us with one impression when viewed in the light of Henry Kissinger's "strategy for peace" in the nuclear age, and quite another when we consider Israel's stakes in that fall. Kissinger's nuclear-age peace strategy found its first implementation in Vietnam, during the Kennedy-Johnson years. As applied by Walt Rostow and Robert McNamara, it led immediately to the fall of President Diem in 1963 and total "Americanization" of the war by 1967-1968. When Kissinger himself took charge of the Vietnam fighting in 1969, the result was "Vietnamization" of a war which had obviously been, by then, irreversibly Americanized. "Vietnamization" was accomplished, as we saw, by unilateral withdrawal of American fighting forces, in the course of which U.S. fatalities rose from 25,000 to over 55,000, while the American troop level fell from 525,000 in January 1969 to zero in January 1973.

That left our Saigon client, now called an "ally," with but a brief "decent interval" of sham self-reliance before the armies of Hanoi — lodged in South Vietnam since the Spring of 1972 — crushed abandoned Saigon. Thus, in accordance with Kissinger's "strategy," the United States had indeed "learned" to lose in a limited war, when the only alternative to losing is to do what Eisenhower threatened to do to avoid losing in Korea.

That same policy, minus U.S. combat military involvement, had begun to be pursued in Iran after the Kissinger "deal" of 1972-1973 with the Pahlavi Shah. Except for the absence of combat troops, American military-industrial involvement in the Shah's Iran soon proved to be as extensive as it had been in Korea and Vietnam, and the outcome, after six years, had been exactly the same as in Vietnam: our client was declared an ally and left to fend for himself on the grounds that to sustain him by American means might involve us in a general war with the Soviet Union — something to be avoided, according to Kissinger, at all costs.

2. The Kissinger-Sullivan Legacy in Iran: General Huyser Looks Back

The closest the United States came to military involvement in the defense of the Shah's Iran was the so-called Huyser mission, undertaken in the last days of the Shah, when his government was headed by Shapour Bahktiar. But that mission proved to have been utterly vain, as General Huyser has himself acknowledged in retrospect, because the Carter administration had by then lost control of the conduct of its foreign relations in the Middle East. Henry Kissinger's scenario for Iran had yet to be played out: the Shah had first to fall, like President Thieu in Saigon, before Kissinger's *"Realpolitik* for losers"* could be effectively applied. In Thieu's case, when his cause was lost, Kissinger, with Disraelian guile, began to press Congress for a "few more weeks" worth of supplies, not to gain a victory for Saigon, but to show the world that we "don't turn our backs on an ally" when he is defeated. In the Shah's case Kissinger did exactly the same, and worse; he called on the intimidated Carter administration to (1) stick with the Shah, (2) condemn the successor government as a terrorist state, (3) admit the Shah to the United States, and (4) take the consequences as the "only honorable thing to do."

General Huyser, it should be noted, clearly understood how the Kissinger "strategy for peace" in the nuclear age could get itself implemented in Iran despite American presidential opposition. In his book *Mission to Tehran* (New York, 1986), Huyser tells us that, when he reported to President Carter on February 5, 1979, on the details of his just-completed mission, the President asked him directly: "What do you think I should do about Ambassador Sullivan? Should I relieve him and bring him home?" General Huyser's reply was that the President ought to reassert his prerogatives as Sullivan's boss by giving the Ambassador some direct instructions. Carter, startled by the reply, said that Sullivan had received the same instructions that Huyser had received, but had apprently refused to follow them. Huyser's frank answer had been that, in passing through the State Department, the instructions actually received by Sullivan had evidently sufferred a sea-change. "I knew," writes Huyser, that "for some reason," many of Sullivan's conversations with Washington at the time "had been with lower-level State Department people, and they may very well have added their own gloss to the President's directive." [273]

Although Huyser was then still Alexander Haig's deputy in the NATO-American command, he seemed not to know of the close ties Haig and Sullivan had had as Kissinger collaborators in winding down the war in Vietnam. Huyser had been sent to Tehran to do everything possible to keep the military intact in the face of mounting popular Islamic protests. Yet, he was never informed about what Sullivan had been doing in that regard because nobody in the Carter White House had been informed by the Ambassador, who was operating either as a "loose cannon" or as "Kissinger's Man" in Iran, rather than Carter's. Early in his book, Huyser gives us this parenthetical observation:

> (Had I known what I learned some five years later, in Gary Sick's book, about Ambassador Sullivan's plan to work with the opposition; the progress he had made in that direction, unknown to any of the leadership in Washington; and about his plan to compel about one hundred senior Iranian military officers to leave the country — a plan directly opposed to my mission, which was to keep them and assist them — then my conclusion [about prospects of the mission's success] would certainly have been different.) [17]

Those words point to a foreign policy scandal back in 1979 that dwarfs to insignificance the Iran*Contra* scandal of 1986-7. Perhaps our nation would have been much better prepared for rapprochement with Iran during Reagan's second term had our Congress been under Republican control when Sullivan's blatantly-recalcitrant acts became known. At any rate, in drawing up the lessons of his relatively brief but important experience at the heart of U.S.-Iranian relations during the Carter Presidency, Huyser chides himself, with soldierly candor, for having been perhaps too naive, too trustful of his political superiors in Washington. It should be remembered that Huyser was not a typical military-establishment general, ready to roll with the punches. As a recent biographical profile stresses, he was at that time "the first draftee to have attained the rank of four-star general in the U.S. Air Force — the highest rank possible in peacetime." [308] And it is certainly not as an establishment figure that he writes:

> Looking back on my mission. . . I believe that my trust and faith in the upper strata of our government was a real weakness on my part. My naivete in assuming that if I carried out the tasks assigned to me with the Iranian military, then the political wing of my government would march smartly along in lock-step, was a gross mistake. I should have asked many hard questions that might have revealed the true positions in Washington and how the other half of the equation was being implemented by the State Department through the Ambassador. [292]

The witness of General Huyser on this important matter is worth a great deal, for it is central and unimpeachable. He is aware that at issue is the burden of our constitutional system of checks and balances on the conduct of foreign relations. Huyser knows that a case can be made for the "realist" claim that the restraints imposed by the Constitution on our President are not suitable "for the formulation of a coherent long-term foreign policy." He is not, however, prepared to challenge the wisdom of our founding fathers on that score, being aware that the President's prescribed oath of office obliges him to take the necessary initiatives despite those restraints. But, "what must surely be wrong." Huyser concludes,

> is to compound the scope of confusion by fragmenting the Executive Branch. There have been any number of instances when our friends have accused us of running three foreign policies at any one time — and they have been saying this for the last half-dozen Presidencies. Because the Secretary of Defense is habitually at odds with the State Department, it was thought necessary to create a National Security Council, whose head would be the Chief Adviser to the President, distilling the options presented from all sides. Is this the best system available? It certainly did not work in my case. The National Security Adviser seemed to be just another voice in a discordant chorus that did not always harmonize with the President. [293]

Huyser underscores the fact that, with respect to Iran, Washington was obviously implementing "conflicting policies simultaneously." But, Sullivan's recalcitrance and secrecy was something far worse. "Little did I realize," Huyser writes, "until I read his book, how Ambassador Sullivan felt about smoothing the way for the Ayatollah Khomeini, while his own government was striving to keep him out, and some of its members even contemplating a preemptive military coup with varying degrees of zeal." Huyser then generalizes on the lesson learned. A nation like ours, he says, should not repeatedly let itself incur defeat by constraining ourselves to operate, and even to "fight, with one hand tied behind our backs." A unified foreign policy may sometimes be wrong, to be sure; but a "disjointed foreign policy" *has* to be wrong, since it can "only confuse our friends and give comfort to our enemies." As for the events of 1978 and 1979 in Iran, Huyser writes, "we are still counting the cost"; and he adds: "I guess the bottom line is that a country must get its own act together before it can hope to put another's house in order with any success." [293-4]

Like James Bill in *The Eagle and the Lion,* Huyser identifies the circles of influence — groups working at cross purposes in the United States — that have brought on a series of national defeats. In his terms, we have repeatedly failed ignominiously, since the early 1960s, in our efforts apparently aimed at putting "another's house in order," first in Vietnam, then in Iran, and, most recently, in Central America. But what neither Bill nor Huyser seems prepared to accept is the fact that at least one major group operating to frustrate White House policies in such places is one that has a carefully elaborated policy and agenda of its own, which calls for "failures" of precisely the kind we have been witnessing — failures designed to teach us, as we have previously stressed, how to accept defeat graciously for the sake of avoiding the risk of superpower confrontations in the nuclear age.

Plainly the events in Iran from November 4, 1979 through January 20, 1981, represented defeats for the governments of the United States and Islamic Iran; but they all added up quite clearly to victory for the foes of normalized relations between the two countries. The victory was so complete that, in Washington as in Tehran, all subsequent efforts to get the normalization process started once again had to be pursued underground, while, on the surface, leaders of the two governments could speak of one another only in the terms of hatred that the foes of normalization on both sides had originally introduced. Here, Professor Bill deserves to be cited once more for what he says in support of President Reagan's basic attitude toward Iran, as contrasted with the attitudes of Secretary of State George Shultz and Secretary of Defense Caspar Weinberger. Speaking of White House Chief of Staff Donald Regan, Vice President George Bush, and CIA Director William Casey, Bill observes that "this group, which included President Reagan himself, had a number of very good tactical and strategic reasons" for supporting the Iran rapprochement initiatives (including the McFarlane mission of May 1986), for which it offered arguments to which "Shultz and Weinberger had difficulty responding." He finds it ironical that,

> in the strategic sense, the NSC, CIA, and White House itself seemed to have a better grasp of the realities of American long-term interests regarding Iran than did the secretaries of State and Defense. Unfortunately, they implemented that policy against a background of ignorance compounded by misinformation and distorted interpretation provided by biased, uninformed, and self-centered consultants like Manuchehr Ghorbanifar. Even Casey's CIA distrusted the consultant-intermediaries relied on so heavily by North, McFarlane, and Poindexter. George Cave, the CIA Iran specialist who was again called into action in postrevolutionary Iran, consistently warned the NSC planners about the unreliability of these consultants. [413]

In comparing how U.S.-Iranian relations were handled first by Carter and then by Ronald Reagan, Professor Bill stresses that an important difference lay in the fact that, "finally, an external force played a major role in the deliberations of the Reagan administration." That force, he says, was, of course, the State of Israel and its powerful, multifaceted American lobby. Israel, Bill explains, "exerted a direct influence on Reagan's NSC and was deeply involved in the Iran-Contra episode," whereas its "influence was considerably less in the offices of the NSC and the White House during the days of the Carter administration.''

Professor Bill is careful in those words to minimize the influence of Israel and its American lobby only in ''the offices of the NSC and the White House'' during the Carter Presidency. For he knows it would be false to suggest that Israel's long-range interests were not being well served in those days by Henry Kissinger and Jacob Javits in the United States and by the militants who seized the American Embassy in Tehran on November 4, 1979. We have shown that the Shah himself, through his last Prime Minister, Shapour Bakhtiar, had authorized a reversal of policy toward Israel to placate the Iranian Shiite masses. And we argued, on strong evidence, that the labors of Kissinger's ''Man in Iran,'' Ambassador Sullivan, were central to a strategy designed to topple the Shah, even as Diem and Thieu had earlier been toppled in South Vietnam. All of that contributed, from the vantage point of our study, to a situation that served Israeli interests in the same measure that it damaged the interests of the Carter Administration, at a time when both the State of Israel and its most ardent American supporters greatly feared what Carter might do with respect to the Middle East if reelected.

We must stress once more that legitimate reasons of state dictated Israel's conduct during those trying times. Israel was anxious for the well-being of the nearly 40,000 Iranian Jews effectively held hostage by Shiite Islam under the Ayatollah, even as millions of Jews have been held hostage in the Soviet Union since the end of World War II. Caring for threatened Jews throughout the world must be a top priority of the Israeli government if it wishes to be taken seriously as a genuinely religious commonwealth. Normalization of U.S.-Iranian relations pursued at Israel's expense was accordingly viewed as an intolerable prospect, to be prevented at all costs, even while covert dealings were being pursued to eventually assure a hostile Shiite Iran that ''all things would be possible'' so long as Israel could serve as the exclusive international broker in satisfying Iranian needs. Israel and its American supporters have sought to play a similar role, though on an altogether different level, as brokers between the superpowers all through their cold-war confrontations.

But that takes us to the theme of another kind of book. We

must limit ourselves here to American involvement in Israeli-Iranian relations as a piece of unfinished business — business not interrupted but merely brought into sharper focus by the events of the so-called Irancontra arms-transfer scandal. As publicized in the United States since 1986, that scandal has effectively ended all American efforts to deal directly with Islamic Iran rather than through Israel-approved intermediaries. The scandal must therefore be registered in the annals of contemporary history as an Israeli diplomatic triumph. Already a suitable scapegoat has been tried, convicted, and sentenced, in the person of Lt. Col. Oliver North, who assisted the national security advisers of the Reagan presidential terms in a capacity paralleling that of William Sullivan during Richard Nixon's first term, while Henry Kissinger was chief national security adviser. Earlier, we suggested a contrast between the fates of Sullivan and North as public servants engaged in covert activities, the former contemptuously defying a President's expressed will, the latter loyally and perhaps too eagerly carrying out a President's expressed will. To round off our study we can fittingly return, briefly, to that contrast to stress its aesthetic dimension as a failure in poetic justice.

We had noted in its proper place that Kissinger's first public reference to Sullivan's collaboration in toppling Thieu occurred during the notorious peace-is-at-hand news conference of October 26, 1972. Kissinger's introductory statement on that occasion had been prepared with the help of Sullivan and Alexander Haig (who now seems eager to identify himself, finally, as the "Deep Throat" of Watergate fame!). During the questioning period following his statement, Kissinger was pressed by reporters for details about eventual supervision of the cease-fire he had just negotiated with Hanoi. Reporters wanted to know how in the world a jubilant Hanoi could be restrained from attempting a military conquest after all U.S. forces were withdrawn from South Vietnam. The ex-Harvard professor tried hard to deflect the questions; but then, in his deepest professorial voice, and with a knowing wink, he said that the details of supervision were of a complexity and length which "will no doubt occupy graduate students for many years to come, and which as far as I know, only my colleague, Ambassador Sullivan understands completely."

Surely it is worth noting that Oliver North was credited with comparable omniscience in his narrower area of expertise when his name was first made very public by his Reagan Administration superiors. The occasion was the notorious "secret-within-a-secret" White House press conference of November 25, 1986. But it was not the President's national security advisor who pointed to a collaborator's omniscience on this occasion. Admiral John Poindexter, in Kissinger's old post, had already handed in his resignation; and so it was left to President Reagan himself to inform reporters of that fact, and then to add that "Lieut. Col. Oliver North has been relieved of his duties on the National Security Council staff."

After that brief citation of North's name, the President turned the podium over to his Attorney General, Edwin Meese 3rd. Meese avoided names in his prepared statement. But as soon as questions were invited, members of the press asked: "Who in the NSC was aware that this extra amount of money was being transferred to the so-called contras, or under their control?" And again: "Did Admiral Poindexter specifically know? Who else knew? And did the CIA know? Was CIA Director Casey aware of this?"

Responding to such pointed questions, Mr. Meese said: "The only persons in the United States Government that know precisely about this -- the only person -- was Lieutenant Colonel North. Admiral Poindexter did know that something of this nature was occurring but he did not look into it further." Pressed about CIA Director Casey, Meese then supplied a string of names of high administration officials who, like Casey (and Meese himself, of course), knew nothing. That served to sharpen the initial indication that, indeed, the "only person" with precise knowledge of the Irancontra arms-transfers and profits-diversions was Oliver North. When North, two and a half years later, finally took the witness stand in his own defense at his trial in early 1989, he told his jurors of his feelings when he sat looking at the fateful televised news conference. "It was very clear," he quietly said, that those words "were part of the political finger-pointing at Ollie North: he was the only one who knew what was going on."

North testified further that he had long before that moment understood that he might have to "take the blame" for the covert operation when the chips were down. Churchill, as we saw, and even his Sovereign King, had acknowledged that they would undoubtedly have to pay dearly if the facts of their "secret war" against Neville Chamberlain's appeasement policies were disclosed prematurely. But what shocked North as totally unexpected, he explained, was a realization that he might be charged as some kind of common criminal in the course of what was plainly a political controversy that ought not to have led investigators to uncover non-political details.

Utterly shameless, with respect to North's long ordeal as a scapegoat, was the statement of his chief federal prosecutor who, at the trial's close, presumed to say that, in North's conviction, "the principle that no man is above the law has been vindicated." For a federal prosecutor to make such a patently false statement ought to be deemed, hereafter, a crime of lese majesty. Nothing could have been further from the truth, not only in general, but especially in the particular instance. More than a dozen charges originally brought against North that might have put that principle on trial — charges having to do with a so-called conspiracy to divert U.S.-Israeli-Iranian-arms-transfer profits to the Contras — had been dropped prior to the trial because the government "refused to disclose classified information necessary for a fair trial."

Thus no question of the "sanctity of the written law" was seriously at issue. On the contrary, North's trial fully vindicated the adamantly sustained view of Presidents Washington, Jefferson, Jackson, Lincoln, Wilson, and Franklin D. Roosevelt (as well as Fawn Hall) that the written law is *not* the highest law of the land, that an undefinable *salus populi* is still *suprema lex* when brave statesmen invoke it. When North's trial started, no substantive charges of constitutional merit remained against him. Even so, throughout the trial, the federal prosecutor had persistently argued that the jurors ought to apply the "lofty principle of justice" laid down by Germany's conquerors at the end of World War II — that obedience to the laws of a defeated country can never justify personal conduct deemed criminal by that country's conquerors.

The judge in North's trial dutifully supported that "American-Soviet" contribution to jurisprudence in his final instructions to the jury. But North's peers sitting in judgment showed how right old

Protagoras was, back in the days of Socrates, when he said that e-
very human being has a true sense of justice written in his heart,
which he cannot violate without a blush of shame. Supporting the
prosecutor's view, the judge had instructed the jurors that a claim
of "obeying orders," even presidential orders, could not exonerate
North of anything that might otherwise be deemed criminal. The
jurors, however, impatiently brushed the judge's instructions aside
— and in the end, the judge himself expressed relief that they had
done so. North's peers (not one of whom was officially identified
as ethnically or racially white) declared him to have been guiltless
in all that he did in loyal service to his Commander in Chief, who
is uniquely sworn to preserve, protect, and defend the national Union of which the Constitution is the ordained and established law.

Oliver North was in fact convicted only of the relatively petty
transgressions of the law to which he had himself confessed in court,
thereby binding the jurors to respect his personal dignity as a man
of honor, ready to take full responsibility not only for what he does
but also for what he suffers to be done to him. President George
Bush and former President Ronald Reagan have persisted in declaring that they all along expected and hoped, and still hope, that North
would and will be fully exonerated. North has grasped that he is a
victim of the American constitutional separation of powers that, for
the sake of personal freedom, periodically puts our unity of government under a seemingly impossible strain, when different parties control its legislative and executive branches. Had the Republicans
retained control of the Senate in 1986, there would never have been
an Irancontra scandal. And had the Republicans controlled both
houses of the Congress at the time, the covertly pursued effort to
reverse the course of U.S.-Iranian relations would soon enough have
become successful, overt, national policy.

We noted in passing that, in the days of Ambassador Sullivan's
recalcitrance (described by President Carter as conduct either
traitorous or insane), the Democratic Party, in control of the entire
federal government, simply swept the whole business under the carpet. Walter Bagehot and his American disciple Woodrow Wilson
have both written at great length about the advantages and the disadvantages of that aspect of what they called Presidential "govern-

ment by discussion" to distinguish it from parliamentary or congressional government by discussion. It is a system that has so far served us well. Twice in recent decades divided control of the legislative and executive branches has led to great scandals: Watergate in the days of the Disraelian manipulations of Kissinger and Nixon; and, despite the callous prosecution of Poindexter, Irancontra in the more patriotic, flag-waving days of Reagan and Bush. Watergate had the salutary effect of stripping first Tricky Nixon and then the Inscrutable Henry of inordinate power for ill; and Irancontra may yet have the salutary effect of making clearer than ever before the dangers of permanent enmities and permanent alliances in dealings with countries whose leaders believe, like the Muslims of Iran and the Jews of Israel, that God is literally and forcefully on their side in all their international transactions.

3. Conclusion

A peaceful year and a half has passed since the death of the Ayatollah Khomeini on June 3, 1989, at the age of 88, despite a widespread belief that the Imam's death would precipitate a crisis. Israel's attention has meanwhile become sharply focused much closer to home because of its *intifada* — which its American friends have identifed as the "third modern strategy" of its ancient Arabic foes, against whom it has been defending itself for thousands of years, before and since the rise of Islam. Originally, the modern Arab leaders had hoped to combat expansive Zionism by uniting all Arab peoples in their crusade; then, say their pro-Israeli accusers, they were reduced to the desperate means of international terrorism; and now finally they are resorting to strictly *national* means, attempting to do to the established Israeli government in the occupied territories what the Israelis themselves had originally done to drive out the British before 1948. It remains to be seen whether the rock-throwers of the occupied territories can be as effective against the Israelis as the Israelis were against the British. Time will tell, in other words, since time is ultimately the wisest and will not be rushed into pronouncing its oracles prematurely.

Leaving important things to time, we must now ask ourselves: What can the government of the United States say, finally, to the Israelis and the Islamic Iranians that will be consistent with what it must say to all the other powers of this earth among which it still claims for itself no more than a separate and juridically equal station? It must, first of all, heed Spinoza's advice, cited earlier. It must say to "God's people" that we do not, and cannot recognize them as God's favorites in anything but a metaphoric sense. It must say to them what it has already plainly (and effectively) said to the governments of the Union of Soviet Socialist Republics and the People's Republic of China — which is that we are prepared to deal with them in relationships of mutual recognition and respect for the separate and juridically equal stations that make us peers, regardless of our diverse sizes, shapes, and histories.

We must not conceal from them the fact that we *prefer* to deal with states that share our view of the world's diversity, even as we seek always to accommodate the new with the old when we encounter it. We are committed to an ideal of "government by discussion" for ourselves, rendered secure by means of internal checks and external balances of power. We consider internal checks of separated governing powers as necessary to secure individual or personal freedom. And we consider external balances of power as necessary to prevent totalitarian foreign states, which lack internal checks, from gaining hegemonic power over governments like our own which have such checks. Yet we can get along with states of all kinds, whatever their stage of development, provided only that they recognize and respect our sovereign independence, as we are prepared to recognize and respect theirs, when it is responsibly assumed.

But, as the Preamble to our 200-year-old Constitution specifies, we the people of the United States of America value six ends (and only six) *above* peace. The six are: "to form a more perfect union, establish justice, insure domestic tranquility, provide for the common defense, promote the general welfare, and secure the blessings of liberty to ourselves and our posterity." Of our citizens of whatever ethnic, racial, or religious background, our government still asks only what George Washington presumed to ask in his Farewell Address of 1796. "Citizens by birth or choice of a common country," he said with precision, "that country has a right to concentrate your affections." George Washington was aware that other countries generally asked for much more of their citizens by birth or choice. And he was reminding his fellow Americans not to tempt themselves to place a heavier requirement on citizenship because of inherited religious, racial, or ethnic attachments of an older, more stringent kind.

INDEX